www.wadsworth.com

wadsworth.com is the World Wide Web site for Wadsworth and is your direct source to dozens of online resources.

At *wadsworth.com* you can find out about supplements, demonstration software, and student resources. You can also send email to many of our authors and preview new publications and exciting new technologies.

wadsworth.com
Changing the way the world learns®

American Government
Readings and Responses

Monica Bauer
Metropolitan State College
of Denver

Wadsworth
Thomson Learning..

Australia • Canada • Mexico • Singapore • Spain • United Kingdom • United States

Publisher: Clark Baxter
Assistant Editor: Cherie Hackelberg
Editorial Assistant: Jennifer Ellis
Marketing Manager: Diane McOscar
Marketing Assistant: Kristin Anderson
Signing Representative: Jane Pohlenz
Print Buyer: Barbra Britton

Permissions Editor: Joohee Lee
Production and Composition: Summerlight Creative
Text and Cover Designer: Jennifer Dunn
Copy Editor: Minda Corners
Cover Photograph: Ernie Leyba
Printer: Von Hoffmann Press / Custom

For permission to use material from this text, contact us:
Web: http://www.thomsonrights.com
Fax: 1-800-730-2215
Phone: 1-800-730-2214

Wadsworth/Thomson Learning
10 Davis Drive
Belmont, CA 94002-3098
USA

For information about our products, contact us:
Thomson Learning Academic Resource Center
1-800-423-0563
http://www.wadsworth.com

International Headquarters
Thomson Learning
International Division
290 Harbor Drive, 2nd Floor
Stamford, CT 06902-7477
USA

UK/Europe/Middle East/South Africa
Thomson Learning
Berkshire House
168-173 High Holborn
London WC1V 7AA
United Kingdom

Asia
Thomson Learning
60 Albert Street, #15-01
Albert Complex
Singapore 189969

Canada
Nelson Thomson Learning
1120 Birchmount Road
Toronto, Ontario M1K 5G4
Canada

Library of Congress Cataloging-in-Publication Data
Bauer, Monica.
   American government: readings and responses /
    Monica Bauer.
    p. cm.
Includes bibliographical references.
ISBN 0-534-45280-4
   1. United States—Politics and government. I. Title.

JK21 .B28 2000
320.973—dc21   00-033029

For Neil and Joanna

Contents

4 four

Civil Rights   51

7

Political Parties   **123**

8 eight

Public Opinion 163

9 nine

Voting and Elections 181

A PERSONAL PERSPECTIVE ON ELECTIONS 181
MONICA BAUER

10 ten

The Media   197

13 *The Judicial Branch* *283*

appendix

Meet the Students   **A.1**

Introduction to Students and Teachers

THIS IS A DIFFERENT KIND OF "READINGS." IF THE OBJECT OF EDUCATION IS TO GO BEYOND inchoate thoughts and feelings, to learn more, to try on each other's shoes, and learn to think in a coherent, synthetic, logical way—then this book of readings and other features may lead you there.

The Chat Room

Our subtitle—"Readings and Responses"—reflects this book's main difference: the presence in each chapter of what we've called the "Chat Room," or edited versions of the conversations I've had with my students on the issues highlighted in the readings. Here concepts and ideas from your main American Government text will come alive for you. In the Chat Room, I hope you will recognize not only your own ideas but also ideas so different from your own that they make you think twice. The students in the Chat Room come from a variety of backgrounds. I tried hard to balance every group with liberals and conservatives, Republicans and Democrats and Libertarians, and men and women of varied ages and experiences. You will find their autobiographies in the Appendix.

Students might try reading a given chapter's selections first, then turn to the Chat Room, then go back into the selections a second time. Decide which students you agree or disagree with and why. Who has the best evidence to support their arguments? Who is just blowing smoke? Am I leading the students to my own opinion, playing devil's advocate, or throwing out new evidence? Answering those questions will help you learn the important skill of critical thinking.

The Readings

These are the center of each chapter. You will find liberal, moderate, conservative, and even extreme positions in the readings. I chose each set with an eye to balance, sometimes controversy, but always with the intention of spurring you to think about, analyze, and decide your own position on an issue. The readings number fewer than in most other American Government books of readings for two reasons.

First, we wanted to allot space to the interviews and the Chat Room and still keep the book a manageable size. We were able to do that because of the second reason: InfoTrac.

InfoTrac

This book comes bundled with a password for InfoTrac, an electronic library of more than five thousand articles dating back five years. Because politics changes so rapidly, especially in election years, we decided to give you access to the most current readings available and reserve our print selections to classic concepts. You will find "For Additional Reading" and InfoTrac Key Terms at the end of each chapter.

Face to Face Student Interviews

Several chapters also contain interviews conducted by the students with people in leadership positions in politics and areas that affect politics—a U.S. representative, a cabinet secretary, the chair of a state party organization, a civil rights activist. These will give you insight into how government and politics really work. The interviews add flesh to the concepts in your main American Government text—they make real the political concepts as they are lived by a diverse group of people. For example, the concept of racial unrest and racial harmony can seem abstract or limited to our own experience. But reading the interview with Vincent Harding may reveal the civil rights movement in a whole new light.

Personal Perspectives

These introductory writings open most of the chapters and provide me the opportunity to discuss an issue from my personal experience. Some political scientists are uncomfortable sharing their own political views with students, and I respect that. But I have always felt that studying American politics should involve not only evidence and analysis, but also human passion, pain, and joy—the "words and music" of American political life. In my training as a student at Brown University, Yale Divinity School, and the University of Nebraska, and in my years of teaching everywhere from Williams College to the American University in Cairo and now at my beloved Metro—home to mostly part-time students with jobs and families—that sense of teaching both the words and the music has only grown over time.

If we fail to teach the music, then our students leave us with perhaps a greater understanding of the mechanics of politics but perhaps still feeling distant from politics, as though they do not need to care. I would argue that such a learning experience does not serve the discipline of political science. Most political scientists I have met, and certainly most politicians, have spent their lives in this discipline because it engages not only their heads, but also their hearts. Furthermore, of course, I believe the American Government class can and should play a role in creating not just good students, but also good citizens.

A Note on Methodology

The student essays and remarks in the Chat Room have been edited for space and clarity. On occasion, as the editor I have reshaped students' comments to make them clearer to the reader. But the students' remarks reflect their own political ideas and ideologies. Comments made by those interviewed were also edited to fit the space allotted.

Acknowledgments

Many people made this book possible, and they deserve a big round of applause. First in line would be Peter Adams, formerly a political science editor at Wadsworth, who first suggested I write a textbook after hearing me mouth off at an American Political Science Association conference. Wadsworth Sales Representative Jane Pohlenz suggested that I write an innovative reader. Last, but definitely not least on the Wadsworth list, my editor, Clark Baxter, gave me the encouragement I needed to do something new. His hard work and unwavering support kept me going.

I must thank my department chair, Norman Provizer, for his support and help, as well as our administrative assistant Diane Schwindt. I received a President's Professional Development Grant from the Metropolitan State College of Denver for spring 1999 that allowed me to work on this project. I also thank Kelley Daniel, a fine adjunct instructor, for many hours of research assistance and advice—between his own campaigns to become a member of the Colorado state legislature. With dedication and professionalism, Metro student Gareth Bevan assisted my friend Betty Deverieux with transcribing most of my tapes of student conversations.

Most important, I must thank the students and interviewees who make this book unique. I had the pleasure to work with eighteen remarkable individuals who accepted my invitation to be the backbone of this project as student discussants. I hope you will get to know them all as you read their comments in the Chat Rooms and their biographical essays at the end of the book.

The Students

Laura Barfield
Krystal Bigley
Suzanne Bowen
Robert Cohen
Turi Gustafson
Clint Hess
Steve Hites
Shane Jackson
John Mahaney

Sonya Marquez
Andrew Nicholas
Mike Nuñez
Asaliyeh Rabih
Will Schneider
Gino Stone
Sarah Echohawk Vermillion
Jesse Wilkins
Tony Young

Interview Subjects
The Hon. Diana DeGette, Member of Congress
Former Secretary Federico Peña
Vincent Harding, Ph.D.
Jene Nelson
Former Governor Richard D. Lamm
Colorado State Republican Party Chair Robert Beauprez

I hope you will enjoy reading this book as much as I enjoyed working with the many talented students who I consider in a way my co-creators. Let me know what you think. You can write to me at monicaeb@aol.com.

Monica Bauer
Denver, Colorado
June 2000

1 one

The Constitution

MONICA BAUER

A PERSONAL PERSPECTIVE ON
Why Constitutions
Matter

AMERICANS TEND TO TAKE THEIR GOVERNMENT FOR GRANTED. They don't study its history, they don't examine the way it works. Students are bored by the study of politics and see no connection between politics and their everyday lives. I wish I could take all of my students on a field trip to another country. Then they might see how important politics can be.

I speak from experience. I spent the school year of 1993-94 teaching political science at the American University in Cairo. Most of my students were born and raised in Egypt. Often they were fluent in three or more languages, and, in their search to make their own government work better, they were hungry to understand different governments. They understood how the politics of their own government directly affected every part of their lives, from their ability to get and keep a job to the conditions they worked under, the pay they received, and whether or not they would get retirement benefits in their old age.

My Egyptian students knew more about American government and its history than most Americans do. But few understood it—particularly the presence and effect of a strong, written constitution. Along with most of the 178 nations in the world, Egypt has a constitution, but because it is weak, the population generally understands that the government can ignore the constitution when it chooses. Let me give an example.

In 1979, the president of Egypt, Anwar Sadat, was assassinated. Following the rules in the Egyptian constitution, Sadat's vice president, Hosni Mubarak, became the president. So far, the story resembles that of the United States when President John Kennedy was killed and Lyndon Johnson, the vice president, succeeded him. But then, the story takes a different turn.

Even though the Egyptian constitution lays down rules for regular elections, Mubarak became a kind of president-for-life. According to the Egyptian constitution, the government in power has the right to determine which parties may run candidates for which offices and what kinds of elections may be held. In the late summer of 1993, I arrived in Cairo in the midst of an election. Banners flew, posters hung, but on every one a single name appeared: Mubarak. I asked my students about this, and they just laughed. "What election?" they said. "The choice is either Mubarak or Mubarak!"

My students pointed out other peculiarities of the Egyptian constitutional government. Mubarak has no vice president because he has decided that the presence of a vice president is an invitation to his own assassination. Of course, that also ensures that no one close to Mubarak rivals his power. And Mubarak does worry about rivals; he and his political party have controlled government power since the first years of his presidency. The Egyptians cannot impeach and remove Mubarak. Although every cab driver in Cairo can tell you how Mubarak has abused his power as president to enrich his friends and punish his enemies, the Egyptians will be governed by him until he dies. The only way to remove Mubarak from office is by assassination, so the president of Egypt never travels by car in his own capital city; he prefers to fly everywhere in a helicopter.

But without Mubarak, the Egyptians would face a chaotic struggle for power. Mubarak's political party dominates the Egyptian parliament and has made it illegal to belong to any strong opposition party. Small, token, opposition parties are tolerated, but should any of them attempt to grow into a major opposition party, they run the risk of being declared illegal.

Although the press is nominally free, the government owns the television stations and, for the most part, the major newspaper, which has the effect of making the press only as free as Mubarak wants it to be. Sometimes an opposition newspaper is shut down for a week or two until they learn their lesson. Sometimes an opposition political leader ends up in jail a bit longer. I taught several students whose parents had been put in prison by a previous Egyptian president (Nasser), then freed by Mubarak, then kicked out of the country by Mubarak. The crime in each case? Speaking out in political opposition to the government.

The wonderful, gifted, and challenging students in Egypt were proud of their country, but many wanted a genuine, enforceable constitution. The odds of that happening were, and still are, remote. I had dinner with the leader of one of the courageous opposition parties. Mr. Salim (not his real name), whom I met through one of my politically active students, had spent time in prison and time in exile. Since then, he has spent his energies trying to give parliamentary representation to outlawed political parties and skirting the law by allowing their candidates to run under his party's label. He gave me a great lesson about government that evening.

"In my country," he said, "we can only go as far as Mubarak lets us go. The constitution has no meaning if it is not enforced, and who is supposed to enforce it? Mubarak! Did you know he declared martial law as soon as he took power, and every four years since then, he makes a great show of going to Parliament and asking for permission to extend martial law four more years? By asking Parliament, he follows the provision in the constitution! But by ruling under martial law, the constitution has no power to protect anybody, because when we have martial law, Mubarak's word is the law. Martial law was designed for temporary emergencies such as war time. According to Mubarak, we have been in continuous emergency since 1979!"

Not only does Egypt ignore its constitution, but also it has no effective Bill of Rights. In the United States, the Bill of Rights contains the first ten amendments to the Constitution and is intended to protect citizens from the brute force of government power. For example, the First Amendment precludes the establishment of a national religion and protects the individual's freedom to exercise his or her own faith. Many scholars contend that the two religion clauses in the First Amendment must be read together, that the first part (no official religion, the "establishment clause") is the key to the second part (freedom of religion, the "free exercise clause").

In Egypt, Islam is the established religion. Although the government claims it is secular, the Egyptian constitution proclaims the Holy Koran as the source of all laws, and the government pays the salaries of many of the most important Imams, or religious leaders. Technically, other groups are granted "free exercise" of their religions, but it is a precarious rather than ironclad protection.

For example, the Christian church I belonged to in Cairo could not get a government permit to repair its building. Some Christian churches are literally falling apart, but the unofficial government policy is to refuse to give building permits to Christian churches lest they try to make their churches larger. Christianity is allowed, in the sense that you can't be arrested for attending church, but it is officially discouraged. Although the great religion of Islam teaches that the Christian and Jewish scriptures are also revealed by God's prophets, it is a crime to hand out Bibles in Egypt.

Every once in awhile, some villagers in the countryside go on an anti-Christian rampage, looting Christian stores and beating up Christians. When I was in Egypt, some Muslim teachers preached that stealing from Christians was not stealing at all because Christians were infidels (non-Muslims), and infidels had no rights. The government routinely looked the other way as Christian businesses were destroyed, particularly in the countryside.

Although some of my students envied the freedom of religion and the separation of church and state in the United States, others could not understand why our Constitution reportedly guarantees that public schools may not teach "the truth about God." One of these students, Sherine, a brilliant young teenager who always came to class covered from head to toe, as she believed was correct for a proper Muslim woman, would laugh and say, "But Dr. Bauer! Isn't it true that in America, there is much drug use and many crimes, including rapes of young girls? I think this is because you do not teach respect for God to all your children. Here in Egypt, we are all taught the Holy Koran and the teachings of the Prophet, blessed be He. And you see how safe it is to live here! In your country, the government gives you too much freedom. You are even free to say bad things about religion! Maybe you should learn from us!"

Sherine had an interesting point. It is true that Cairo, one of the largest cities in the world, is also one of the safest. I was able to enjoy in Cairo things that I would never attempt in an American city, such as taking long walks alone after dark. As in other Muslim countries, the rate of rape, murder, and just about any other crime is much lower than in the United States. And this is true even though, by American standards, the majority in Egypt are desperately poor, and most never receive education past the sixth grade. Uneducated and hungry in a city where they watch stretch limousines take the ultrarich to luxury hotels, the poor of Cairo still do not engage in much crime. If this is because of an established, common religion, then perhaps it is indeed a blessing.

As a teaching political scientist, however, I responded to Sherine by raising the question of trade-offs—compromises that a free democracy makes. The trade-off in this case is the government's right to protect its citizens versus the individual's right to freedom of religion. Is a government-established religion a good trade for a lower crime rate? And what does it mean that crimes against Christians, who make up ten percent of the Egyptian population, go unpunished? What would my students think if Egypt followed the direction of some Arab nations where the Islamic fundamentalist influence is so deep in the law that women are prohibited from driving (as in Saudi Arabia), or where women are prohibited from attending school (as in Afghanistan)? Without a strong written constitution separating church and state, what is to prevent a government from restricting freedoms in favor of enforcing a religion?

There are trade-offs in the American system, too, of course; we don't often think about them, but they are there. For example, the very existence of our Constitution requires a trade. Instead of an ongoing freedom to write whatever laws please the current majority, we obey a document written more than two hundred years ago. We try to interpret what those words, written in 1787, should mean today. If we stray too far from the Constitution, by interpreting it in bizarre ways, we are no different from Mubarak playing games with the Egyptian constitution.

Our Constitution is meant to be our fundamental law, the law against which all other laws are measured. It holds supremacy over decisions made by local majorities in states, cities, and towns. If we want to amend or change it, we have to make a big effort. When our Constitution and Bill of Rights were written in the last part of the 18th century, women and slaves knew their places, and people lived their whole lives in the context of one community. Yet the Constitution has been amended only seventeen times since the first ten amendments, the Bill of Rights, were added in one fell swoop in 1789. Although some amendments were designed to give newly freed slaves their rights (the Thirteenth, Fourteenth, and Fifteenth), and another amendment gave women the right to vote (the Nineteenth), most amendments concern issues that rarely arise. These include the issues of who assumes the duties of the president if he (or she) is alive but incapacitated while in office (the 25th Amendment), or representation to the Electoral College for the population of the District of Columbia (the 23rd Amendment). The Constitution lays out the methods for its own amendment, and those methods require so much agreement among members of Congress, members of state legislatures, and ordinary voters, that the document is resistant to change. In other words, most of what we know about American government was settled a long time ago.

Each new generation must struggle to interpret and apply the Constitution and Bill of Rights to a new set of problems while continuing to respect the limits that the framers placed on government. These tasks are difficult if each generation perceives the need to address its social problems by change so drastic that the fundamental nature and intent of the Constitution is lost.

Recently, the difficulty of interpreting the Constitution took center stage when the House of Representatives, for the second time in our history, impeached a president. Those attacking and defending President Clinton tried to explain the meaning of the words in Article II, Section Four of the Constitution: "The President . . . shall be removed from Office on Impeachment for, and Conviction of, Treason, Bribery, or other high Crimes and Misdemeanors."

This is why we begin the study of American government with a look at our past. The decisions made in 1787, when the founders wrote the Constitution, and in 1789, when the First Congress adopted the Bill of Rights, shape our arguments today. Throughout our study, we should keep in mind the trade-offs we live with, and the compromises we make, for our particular reliance on a written constitution and Bill of Rights. The American Constitution means more to me because of my experience living and working in Egypt. Here is a question to keep in mind as you read the selection for Chapter 1: What does the Constitution mean to you?

Patriot Games
Paul Glastris

One June day two years ago, James Douglas Nichols was pushing 70 miles per hour down a country road not far from his Decker, Michigan, farm when he was caught in the crosshairs of a sheriff deputy's radar gun. The deputy pulled Nichols over and issued him tickets for speeding and for driving without a valid license.

Soon after, before a courthouse hearing in Sanilac County in eastern Michigan's "thumb," Nichols offered a bizarre defense of his actions. The government, Nichols insisted, does not have the constitutional power to regulate private citizens in their cars. "I have put everyone concerned here on notice of what is going on here," declared Nichols with paranoid melodrama, "to violate my rights to free travel as cited in the Constitution of the United States and the Constitution of Michigan."

Presiding District Court Judge James A. Marcus patiently explained to Nichols the long-accepted legal distinction between a private citizen's constitutional right to travel freely and the government's legitimate right to regulate the operation of a motor vehicle. But Nichols was not about to buy the judge's fine distinction; he had done plenty of his own research. Nichols continued his losing protests, citing Supreme Court case after Supreme Court case. "He'd lift a sentence or phrase that he thought was applicable, but he'd do so out of context so that the meaning was completely incorrect or nonsensical," recalls Judge Marcus.

The Sanilac County courthouse, a gracious brick edifice with a hideous concrete-block addition stuck on the back, is no stranger to twisted logic. Earlier that year, James's brother Terry Nichols had tried his own hand at finding his

salvation in do-it-yourself legal reasoning. He didn't really owe that $31,000 in bank credit card debt, he announced to the court, because the banks had lent him "credit," not "legal tender." He offered to pay with what he called a "certified fractional reserve check"—a worthless piece of paper. "You can't follow their arguments," explains Judge Marcus, "because they're listening to a different music no one else hears."

But now, after the Oklahoma City bombing, plenty of people are straining to hear the melody. James and Terry Nichols were both picked up after the bombing, though only Terry, and their friend Timothy McVeigh, have been charge with being directly involved. The search for possible motives behind the worst terrorist attack in the nation's history has turned the nation's attention to the so-called "patriot movement," the subculture of shadowy para-military groups and screwball ideas to which all three men were drawn.

The media has portrayed the movement as full of gun-loving right-wing extremists, and Timothy McVeigh, given his obsession with weapons and Waco, certainly fits that description. But that portrayal obscures a key fact: Most members of the patriot movement are less obsessed with guns than with laws. (James Nichols, for one, never joined a militia.) For every camouflage-wearing amateur soldier drilling on weekends there are several amateur lawyers sitting at home reading federal statutes.

The patriot movement is a loose, motley affair. It includes plenty of racists and anti-Semites, but also a good number of people who are not. Much of their ideology can be safely classified as extreme versions of contemporary conservative, anti-government dogma. Yet their absolutist notions about personal liberties put them closer to the ACLU and the New Left than to William Bennett and the Heritage Foundation.

What all "patriots" do seem to share beyond the well-publicized fear that the federal government is stealing their rights, is a passionate devo-

Reprinted with permission from *The Washington Monthly*, June 1995, 23–26. © 1995 by *The Washington Monthly*. Copyright by The Washington Monthly Company, 1611 Connecticut Ave., N.W., Washington, D.C. 20009. (202) 462-0128.

tion to the precise language of the nation's founding documents. Imagine Robert Bork and Nat Hentoff dropping acid in the woods and you begin to get the picture.

Better yet, imagine a fundamentalist revival meeting where the Bible is replaced by *The Federalist Papers.* As I chased the Nichols story around the prairie-flat eastern Michigan farm country on the wind-swept shores of Lake Huron, time and again friends and neighbors of James Nichols would bring up the Constitution, the Declaration of Independence, or *The Federalist Papers,* chide me for not having studied them, and quote from them as if from scripture. The religious parallels were unmistakable, even down to the millenarian belief, almost universally shared, that Washington's attack on individual liberty is a prelude to the imposition of a "New World Order": a totalitarian, one-world government controlled by the United Nations.

Suspicious, even dismissive, of the interpretations of scholarly priests (i.e. judges), patriots prefer an extreme version of Martin Luther's "priesthood of all believers" in which each individual can clearly grasp the framers' intent by reading the sacred texts for themselves. But like Christian fundamentalists, these patriots are guided by an idiosyncratic political agenda. They tend to quote selectively and read literally, "isolating the part from the whole and pretending that there can be only one reading," notes University of Chicago theologian Martin Marty. They are Constitutional fundamentalists.

One of the movement's gentler, more thoughtful members is James Nichols's neighbor and friend Phil Morawski, a bearded, pudgy, vaguely hippyish-looking farmer who sports a cowboy hat with a large silver crucifix and the words "To Live in Christ" scrawled on it. Morawski became a familiar figure on network television in the days after the raid on the Nichols home, speaking to reporters in a Foster Brooks-like hiccupy slur ("He doesn't drink," swears another neighbor, "he just talks that way.") Morawski lives with his mother and brother only a mile south of the Nichols place, on a farm complete with braying goats and a red, American Gothic-style barn. On the barn, in large, faded-white letters, are the words "Happy Birthday America." Though not a militia member, Morawski says he has attended some of their meetings where he "swore an oath to the Constitution."

Like most "patriots," Morawski's frustration with the federal government arose from a personal trauma. Along with millions of other farmers, he took out large expansion loans at the urging of the U.S. Department of Agriculture in the seventies, then found himself buried in debt in the eighties, when land and commodity prices plummeted. He spent years in and out of court fighting the farm credit system, and managed to hold onto his land only by learning the intricacies of agricultural law with the help of various grassroots farm groups, many of which eventually evolved into patriot organizations.

In the process he picked up some odd ideas. Nailed to the front of his farmhouse is a copy of the farm's title, or "patent," which the land's first settlers received from the federal government in the nineteenth century. Morawski and many other patriot farmers firmly believe that the language of these patents exempt them from local zoning ordinances. (Only the courts disagree.)

James Nichols, too, was drawn into the orbit of the patriot movement after a bitter personal legal battle. During a nasty divorce settlement in the late eighties, his ex-wife Kelly accused him of child abuse. Nichols passed a lie detector test and the charges were dropped. But the episode, which included a police search of his house, left him feeling both furious and humiliated.

After that, Nichols plunged into the literature of the newly emerging patriot movement.

He read the Constitution and *The Federalist Papers,* along with "Spotlight," a *National Enquirer*-like patriot paper, which runs pieces such as an exposé about concentration camps being constructed to hold domestic political prisoners. During the winters, with little farm work to do, Nichols curled up with *Black's Law Dictionary* and the Uniform Commercial Code—an encyclopedia-length volume of rules that regulate commercial transactions. He was looking, he told friends, for legal means to take himself "completely out of the system." He attended meetings of We the People: a tax-protest group whose members believe the Federal Reserve system is unconstitutional. Soon, he, too, was marking all his money with a red stamp that said he is not responsible for its value. He even tried to get the county clerk to expunge his marriage license from the public record, and claimed to be "no longer one of your citizens of your *de facto* government."

Nichols' notions were not exactly original. Virtually all of them had roots in the Posse Comitatus, a radical anti-federal-government movement founded in Oregon in 1969 and popular in the rural Midwest during the eighties farm crisis. Posse members believed, among other things, that the Federal Reserve is in the pockets of a cabal of Jewish international bankers and that all constitutional amendments other than the first 10—the ones written by and for white Christians—are suspect. The Posse died out in the mid-eighties after some of its leaders were jailed or killed in shoot-outs with federal authorities. But the movement's legalist protests, such as refusing to carry drivers licenses and paying debts with "fractional reserve checks," made their way into the patriot movement and into the minds of the Nichols brothers.

Although he never joined the militia, James Nichols attended several of their meetings, usually to give informational speeches on how to "drop out of the system." He won few converts. "He's a little bit farther than we are," admits Art Bean, commander of the Michigan Militia of Tuscola County (just west of Sanilac County).

Not that the militia members are middle-of-the-roaders. Bean, among others, is "very disturbed" by the Federal Emergency Management Agency's statutory language, which he says gives the president the power to declare martial law: "Read the law and make up your own mind." He fully expects Clinton to use that power before the 1996 elections, in part to stop the militias.

In his search for ways to drop out of the system, Nichols came upon the teachings of a radical constitutionalist named Karl Granse. A self-professed legal expert, Granse runs an outfit called Citizens for a Constitutional Republic, headquartered in Apple Valley, an upscale Minneapolis suburb. In the fall of 1994, Nichols and several friends traveled to Minneapolis for one of Granse's seminars on how to shuffle off the legal coils of taxes and licenses. Nichols returned to Michigan $600 poorer, the price of the weekend lecture plus various books and videotapes.

Eager to watch one of the videotapes, I went to visit a Nichols friend, Jim LeValley, who had borrowed one. A member of the Michigan Militia, LeValley raises flowers and herbs in a commercial greenhouse next to his home on the banks of the Cass River. He greeted me in a camouflage cap, his boots caked with dirt. We settled into the Ethan Allen furniture in his living room and flipped on the videotape.

On the tape, Granse points to the wall behind him, where an overhead projector displays fragments of statutory language defining those people subject to the federal income tax as "residents of the United States." He then posits that no one in the room meets the criteria because they live in the individual states. "The 'United States' implies more than one," he proclaims with great flourish, teasing an audience member from Illinois to illustrate his point: "You can either live in the United States or in Illinois. Which is it going to be? . . . You see, we have to stop and analyze the words," Granse instructs. "Law is a precise language."

As the tape played on, LeValley told me why he finds Granse's ideas so appealing. "If you are not part of the corporate entity of the United States you don't have to worry about the laws set forth by the United States to govern its people," LeValley explained. "It makes life a whole lot easier." I though of W.C. Fields, who once insisted that he had studied the Bible scrupulously for 18 years, looking for loopholes.

When the tape was over, LeValley pulled a dollar bill from his pocket, flipped it over, and pointed to the Latin words beneath the Masonic eyed-pyramid: *novus ordo seclorum*. "You know what that means?" he asked me. "That means, 'New World Order.' It means eventually they want us to be in a one-world government. That's why they want to take away our guns."

As I drove off, I wondered whether LeValley and his self-taught colleagues would someday see through the patriot movement's paranoid misreadings of history and the world. It might help if they knew that the words on the dollar bill, a quotation from the Latin poet Virgil meaning "New Order of the Ages," were chosen not by international conspirators, but by a committee of this country's first patriots, the revolutionaries who wrote the Constitution.

Andy
a moderate

Sarah
a Native American,
liberal Democrat

Laura
a conservative
Republican

Steve
a Libertarian

Playing with the Constitution
★ ★ ★

Dr. Bauer: I have two questions for you. Who do we trust to interpret the Constitution for us? And what happens when we try to interpret it for ourselves? For example, in "Patriot Games," how does the patriot movement interpret the Constitution?

Steve: What I found interesting about that article is the condescending view of the patriot movement trying to interpret the Constitution for themselves. But lots of other groups do the same thing, like the Christian Coalition. The Supreme Court has interpreted the Constitution one way, but the Christian Coalition disagrees. They want to go back to the original intention of the framers and interpret things for themselves.

Dr. Bauer: What happens when the militia interprets the Constitution? Is there anything different about the message they get from the Constitution?

Laura: In terms of the radical way they view things, their interpretation is very different. I thought *this* was interesting in "Patriot Games": the media portrays the patriot movement as "full of gun-loving right-wing extremists," but they are more obsessed with laws than with guns. It's almost as if they could do more damage with their interpretation of the Constitution than they could with guns. They may be going back to the literal words of the Constitution, but a lot has happened since those words were written.

Dr. Bauer: The article calls the patriots "Constitutional fundamentalists." What does that mean?

Andy: I think it means that they follow, literally, the words of the Constitution. Like, the literal words of the First Amendment to the Constitution say, "Congress shall make no law . . . abridging freedom of speech." But you can't yell fire in

	a crowded theater if you're not serious, because that *abuses* freedom of speech and puts other people in danger.
Dr. Bauer:	So when the literal words of the Constitution create a conflict with public safety, we take the side of public safety.
Sarah:	That's why we have the Supreme Court to decide a conflict for us. They interpret the intentions of the Founding Fathers and framers of the Constitution.
Dr. Bauer:	But what happens when we don't trust the Supreme Court to tells us what the Constitution means? In "Patriot Games," a man is stopped for speeding, and he says the Constitution does not give the government the right to regulate people in their cars. Now, that's literally true. Steve, you've got a copy of the Constitution sitting in front of you. Does it say anything at all in there about transportation?
Steve:	No. And it doesn't say anything about cell phones or the Internet or abortions, either.
Dr. Bauer:	Or a ton of other stuff that we have to deal with. What about the patriot movement's attempt to use the Constitution to avoid paying debts?
Laura:	They say they were issued credit by the credit card company, instead of real money . . . so they don't have to repay real money, which in the literal sense is true, but the courts have interpreted it differently.
Dr. Bauer:	They've never bought the argument that credit can't be enforced by debt collection. What would happen to the whole credit card industry if it weren't legal for them to collect their money? The patriot movement also rejects income taxes. Did you hear about the case in New York where a number of police officers got from the militia movement a kit they used to show them how to get away with paying zero federal taxes?
Sarah:	I remember that. They tried a loophole, and a lot of them got charged with federal tax evasion. They lost their jobs.
Dr. Bauer:	And these were police officers. If they don't understand that the courts have the final power to interpret the Constitution, and not some militia members, then heaven help the rest of us! What is it that makes the Constitution so difficult to work with?
Sarah:	For the ordinary person, say with a high school education, the language in the Constitution, and the phrasing, is too difficult, formal, and old-fashioned.
Dr. Bauer:	Should we try to reword it so it's easier to understand?
Steve:	I think we should leave it exactly the way it is. There was some Supreme Court justice who coined a phrase, "brilliant omissions," to describe how the Constitution could allow interpretations to change with the times. He meant that it is simple and open-ended enough to provide us with a framework that we can interpret as society changes. So I think it's a document that's just fine

as it is. There will always be different interpretations, but they change with the times, too.

Andy: I see some problems with that framework argument. Like you're building the framework to a big office building that years down the line you can furnish however you want. But what if two hundred years later that framework doesn't allow us to put in our Internet cables? The framework may not be *able* to help us with today's society. The Constitution's framework doesn't say anything about some of the biggest controversies we have today.

Steve: I don't think I agree with your framework objection, Andy. Although the Constitution may not deal directly with technology or modern problems, it still has these big, important *principles* in it. The First Amendment, the Fourth Amendment—we can apply these things today to any circumstance. The principles are there, and that's what a Constitution is supposed to do, set out these big principles.

Sarah: But those principles can be so vague that groups like the militia can interpret the Constitution the way they see fit.

Laura: I don't think the Constitution allows the militias to do bombings or get out of paying taxes. They misuse it. You don't give up on something just because it can be misused. I go back to that term "brilliant omissions" because I think there's a lot of truth in that idea. It's meant for us to interpret the Constitution in different ways in different times, and as society changes, and as technology changes.

Dr. Bauer: But somebody has to fill in the blanks for all those brilliant omissions, right? And—

Andy: And that's the Supreme Court. Their constitutional responsibility is to interpret the law, and our fundamental law is the Constitution. Now the politics of the Supreme Court become part of the deal. If we can't tell what the Constitution means from the plain words, which sure seems the case when you look at what the patriot and militia movements come up with when *they* look at the words, then we are depending on a court, and if that court is too conservative, or too liberal, then those blanks get filled in very differently. I still say, going back to my framework argument, that some of the language in the Constitution is *so old* that the framework is brittle now. Interpretation depends on your politics. Here's where I see the patriot movement's frustration. Why shouldn't their opinion be heard?

Steve: If you think there are politics on the Supreme Court, watch out for the politics of people who want to live only by their interpretation of the Constitution! As a criminal justice major, I am grateful that there is a Constitution. There would be chaos if everyone, militia and other groups, were allowed to interpret the Constitution for their own benefit. The patriot movement is a tiny, unrepresentative group. If they want to change things, they should do what the

Libertarians do: form a political party and work through the system. If our Constitution doesn't fit the times, like you said, Andy, we can fix it, but only through *democratic* means, with the consent of the governed.

Andy:

But the Supreme Court can change the meaning through interpretation, and it isn't an elected, representative body!

Sarah:

True, but the president appoints, and the Senate confirms, so the people have some indirect influence. Look, there's nothing wrong with militias or the patriot movement people having opinions. But if they can't get their opinions accepted in a democracy, maybe it's because they are seen by the majority of voters as being *way too extreme*.

Steve:

That's the other thing about our Constitution—you can't change it to represent some extreme view. The framers set it up to be changed only when an overwhelming majority wanted to—our Constitution is *extremist-proof*.

★ ★ ★

For Additional Reading

Go to InfoTrac College Edition, your online research library at

http://web1.infotrac-college.com

Enter the following search terms using the Subject Guide or Key Terms.

American democracy   the Constitution   U.S. constitutional amendments

Articles of Confederation

2 two Federalism

United States v. Lopez (1995)

Edited by Monica Bauer

Chief Justice Rehnquist delivered the opinion of the Court.

In the Gun-Free School Zones Act of 1990, Congress made it a federal offense "for any individual knowingly to possess a firearm at a place that the individual knows, or has reasonable cause to believe, is a school zone." The Act neither regulates a commercial activity nor contains a requirement that the possession be connected in any way to interstate commerce. We hold that the Act exceeds the authority of Congress "To regulate Commerce . . . among the several States. . . ." U.S. Constitution, Article I, Section 8, Clause 3. . . .

We start with first principles. The Constitution creates a Federal Government of enumerated powers. As James Madison wrote, "[t]he powers delegated by the proposed Constitution to the federal government are few and defined. Those which are to remain in the State governments are numerous and indefinite." *The Federalist* No. 45. This constitutionally mandated division of authority "was adopted by the Framers to ensure protection of our fundamental liberties." "Just as the separation and independence of the coordinate branches of the Federal Government serves to prevent the accumulation of excessive power in any one branch, a healthy balance of power between the States and the Federal Government will reduce the risk of tyranny and abuse from either front."

The Constitution delegates to Congress the power "[t]o regulate Commerce with foreign Nations, and among the several States, and with the Indian Tribes."

. . . First, we have upheld a wide variety of congressional Acts regulating intrastate economic activity where we have concluded that the activity substantially affected interstate commerce. Examples include the regulation of intrastate coal mining; *Hodel,* supra, intrastate extortionate credit transactions, *Perez,* supra, restaurants utilizing substantial interstate supplies, *McClung,* supra, inns and hotels catering to interstate guests, *Heart of Atlanta Motel,* supra, and production and consumption of home-grown wheat, *Wickard v. Filburn* (1942). These examples are by no means exhaustive, but the pattern is clear. Where economic activity substantially affects interstate commerce, legislation regulating that activity will be sustained.

Section 922(q) (The Gun-Free School Zone Act) is a criminal statute that by its terms has nothing to do with "commerce" or any sort of economic enterprise, however broadly one might define those terms. Section 922(q) is not an essential part of a larger regulation of economic activity, in which the regulatory scheme could be undercut unless the intrastate activity were regulated. It cannot, therefore, be sustained under our cases upholding regulations of activities that arise out of or are connected with a commercial transaction, which viewed in the aggregate, substantially affects interstate commerce.

The Government's essential contention . . . is that we may determine here that 922(q) is valid because possession of a firearm in a local school zone does indeed substantially affect interstate commerce. The Government argues that possession of a firearm in a school zone may result in violent crime and that violent crime can be expected to affect the functioning of the national economy in two ways. First, the costs of violent crime are substantial, and, through the mechanism of insurance, those costs are spread throughout the population. Second, violent crime reduces the willingness of individuals to travel to areas within the country that are perceived to be unsafe. Cf. *Heart of Atlanta Motel.* The Government also argues that the presence of guns in schools poses a substantial threat to the educational process by threatening the learning environment. A handicapped educational process, in turn, will result in a less productive citizenry. That, in turn, would have an adverse effect on the Nation's economic well-being. As a result, the Government argues that Congress could rationally have concluded that 922(q) substantially affects interstate commerce.

We pause to consider the implications of the Government's arguments. The Government admits, under its "costs of crime" reasoning, that Congress could regulate not only all violent crime, but all activities that might lead to violent crime, regardless of how tenuously they relate to interstate commerce. Similarly, under the Government's "national productivity" reasoning, Congress could regulate any activity that it found was related to the economic productivity of individual citizens: family law (including marriage, divorce, and child custody), for example. Under the theories that the Government presents in support of 922(q), it is difficult to perceive any limitation on federal power, even in areas such as criminal law enforcement or education where States historically have been sovereign. Thus, if we were to accept the Government's arguments, we are hard-pressed to posit any activity by an individual that Congress is without power to regulate.

. . . The possession of a gun in a local school zone is in no sense an economic activity that might, through repetition elsewhere, substantially affect any sort of interstate commerce. Respondent was a local student at a local school; there is no indication that he had recently moved in interstate commerce, and there is no requirement that his possession of the firearm have any concrete tie to interstate commerce.

To uphold the Government's contentions here, we would have to pile inference upon inference in a manner that would bid fair to convert congressional authority under the Commerce Clause to a general police power of the sort retained by the States. Admittedly, some of our prior cases have taken long steps down that road, giving great deference to congressional action. The broad language in these opinions has

suggested the possibility of additional expansion, but we decline here to proceed any further. . . .

For the foregoing reasons the judgment of the Court of Appeals is
Affirmed.

Justice Breyer, with whom Justice Stevens, Justice Souter, and Justice Ginsburg Join, Dissenting.

The issue in this case is whether the Commerce Clause authorizes Congress to enact a statute that makes it a crime to possess a gun in, or near, a school. In my view, the statute falls well within the scope of the commerce power as this Court has understood that power over the last half-century.

Applying these principles to the case at hand, we must ask whether Congress could have had a rational basis for finding a significant (or substantial) connection between gun-related school violence and interstate commerce. Or, to put the question in the language of the explicit finding that Congress made when it amended this law in 1994: Could Congress rationally have found that "violent crime in school zones," through its effect on the "quality of education," significantly (or substantially) affects "interstate" or "foreign commerce"? As long as one views the commerce connection, not as a "technical legal conception," but as "a practical one," the answer to this question must be yes. Numerous reports and studies—generated both inside and outside government—make clear that Congress could reasonably have found the empirical connection that its law, implicitly or explicitly, asserts.

For one thing, reports, hearings, and other readily available literature make clear that the problem of guns in and around schools is widespread and extremely serious. . . . And, Congress could therefore have found a substantial educational problem—teachers unable to teach, students unable to learn—and concluded that guns near schools contribute substantially to the size and scope of that problem.

Having found that guns in schools significantly undermine the quality of education in our Nation's classrooms, Congress could also have found, given the effect of education upon interstate and foreign commerce, that gun-related violence in and around schools is a commercial, as well as a human, problem. Education, although far more than a matter of economics, has long been inextricably intertwined with the Nation's economy.

... Scholars estimate that nearly a quarter of America's economic growth in the early years of this century is traceable directly to increased schooling; that investment in "human capital" (through spending on education) exceeded investment in "physical capital" by a ratio of almost two to one; and that the economic returns to this investment in education exceeded the returns to conventional capital investment.

... The economic links I have just sketched seem fairly obvious. Why then is it not equally obvious, in light of those links, that a widespread, serious, and substantial physical threat to teaching and learning also substantially threatens the commerce to which that teaching and learning is inextricably tied? That is to say, guns in the hands of six percent of inner-city high school students and gun-related violence throughout a city's schools must threaten the trade and commerce that those schools support. The only question, then, is whether the latter threat is (to use the majority's terminology) "substantial." ... At the very least, Congress could rationally have concluded that the links are "substantial."

... To hold this statute constitutional is not to "obliterate" the "distinction of what is national and what is local," nor is it to hold that the Commerce Clause permits the Federal Government to "regulate any activity that it found was related to the economic productivity of individual citizens," to regulate "marriage, divorce, and child custody," or to regulate any and all aspects of education. For one thing, this statute is aimed at curbing a particularly acute threat to the educational process—the possession (and use) of life-threatening firearms in, or near, the classroom. The empirical evidence that I have discussed above unmistakably documents the special way in which guns and education are incompatible.

... In sum, a holding that the particular statute before us falls within the commerce power would not expand the scope of that Clause. Rather, it simply would apply pre-existing law to changing economic circumstances. See *Heart of Atlanta Motel, Inc.* v. *United States* (1964). It would recognize that, in today's economic world, gun-related violence near the classroom makes a significant difference to our economic, as well as our social, well-being.

... The majority's holding ... creates ... serious legal problems. First, the majority's holding runs contrary to modern Supreme Court cases that have upheld congressional actions despite connections to interstate or foreign commerce that are less significant than the effect of school violence. ...

In *Katzenbach* v. *McClung* (1964), this Court upheld, as within the commerce power, a statute prohibiting racial discrimination at local restaurants, in part because that discrimination discouraged travel by African Americans and in part because that discrimination affected purchases of food and restaurant supplies from other States. In *Daniel* v. *Paul* (1969), this Court found an effect on commerce caused by an amusement park located several miles down a country road in the middle of Alabama—because some customers (the Court assumed), some food, 15 paddleboats, and a juke box had come from out of State. In both of these cases, the Court understood that the specific instance of discrimination (at a local place of accommodation) was part of a general practice that, considered as a whole, caused not only the most serious human and social harm, but had nationally significant economic dimensions as well.

... It is difficult to distinguish the case before us, for the same critical elements are present. ...

The second legal problem the Court creates comes from its apparent belief that it can reconcile its holding with earlier cases. . . .

. . . [I]t threatens legal uncertainty in an area of law that, until this case, seemed reasonably well settled. Congress has enacted many statutes (more than 100 sections of the United States Code), including criminal statutes (at least 25 sections), that use the words "affecting commerce" to define their scope. . . .

. . . For these reasons, I would reverse the judgment of the Court of Appeals.

Respectfully,

I dissent.

Clinton: Overturn School Gun Rule
Associated Press

Washington. President Bill Clinton complained yesterday that the Supreme Court had thrown out a "common-sense" ban on guns around schools. He gave the attorney general one week to find a legal way around the ruling.

"I want the action to be constitutional, but I am determined to keep guns away from schools," Clinton said in his weekly radio address. "We must reverse the practical impact of the court's decision."

Clinton was reacting to a ruling Thursday in which the high court threw out a federal law that banned possession of a gun within 1,000 feet of a school. The court said Congress lacked authority to enact the law.

Clinton said he was "terribly disappointed" by the ruling, saying the 1990 Gun-Free School Zones Act had represented "a bipartisan approach to school safety based on common sense."

"This Supreme Court decision could condemn more of our children to going to schools where there are guns," Clinton said. "Our job is to help our children learn . . . in safety, not to send them to school and put them in harm's way."

The president said he had ordered Attorney General Janet Reno to present him with ideas in one week on how to get around the ruling.

He offered one possible solution, saying Congress could encourage states to ban guns from school zones by linking federal aid to school-zone weapons bans.

The president said the court's ruling was particularly disappointing in light of the recent Oklahoma City bombing. "If anything good can come out of something as horrible as the Oklahoma City tragedy, it is that the American people have reaffirmed our commitment to putting our children, their well-being and their future first in our lives," he said.

The Supreme Court overturned the gun ban based on a finding that the law did not fall within Congress' authority to regulate interstate commerce.

School Gun Law Ironic Throwback

Anthony Lewis

In 1933, with farmers bankrupt and desperate in the Great Depression, Congress passed the Agricultural Adjustment Act to regulate farm production. Three years later the Supreme Court held it unconstitutional: beyond the power of the federal government.

The AAA decision and others of the time paralyzed government efforts to bring the country out of the Depression. And they brought on a crisis for the Court itself: a crisis of public confidence.

In 1937 the Supreme Court abandoned its pinched view of federal power and began sustaining new economic and social legislation. That was the end of the crisis. But was it really the end?

The question has to be asked after the Court's astonishing decision last week that the 1990 federal Gun-Free School Zones Act, written by Sen. Herb Kohl, D-Wis., was unconstitutional. The law made it a crime to have a gun within 1,000 feet of a school.

A 5–4 majority held that the law was not within Congress' power to regulate interstate commerce: the first such decision by the Supreme Court since 1936.

The way Chief Justice William Rehnquist wrote the opinion of the Court opened the possibility that all kinds of modern legislation could now be upset: laws on machine-gun sales, attacks on abortion clinics, and many other subjects. That is because the opinion relied on abstract categories to decide whether something is within or outside the commerce power.

Rehnquist said, for example, that education was not "commercial." But the Court in 1971 upheld a law against loansharking in purely local circumstances because it might affect commerce. And it upheld a law against racial discrimination in motels that might serve interstate travelers.

Again, the majority opinion said that something could be regulated by Congress only if it had a "substantial" effect on commerce. That sounded like a throwback to the opinions of the early 1930s that tried to draw a line between "direct" and "indirect" effects on commerce: a distinction that foundered on its own confusion.

Justice Stephen Breyer, in a dissent for himself and Justices John Paul Stevens, David Souter and Ruth Bader Ginsburg, noted that schools cost the country $230 billion in 1990 and that education was crucial to American prosperity in a world economy.

It was rational for Congress to decide, he said, that the menace of guns in schools did the country economic harm.

Rational is the key word. For decades now the Supreme Court has given Congress leeway to legislate under its commerce power so long as it had a rational basis for its action.

Souter, in a separate dissent, reminded the majority of what happened in the 1930s when willful judges decided that mining and manufacturing were not "commerce."

In the AAA case in 1936 Justice Harlan Stone, dissenting, said the decision reflected the notion "that it is the business of courts to sit in judgment on the wisdom of legislative action." Souter, echoing that theme, said it was not for the Supreme Court to say "whether Congress was correct" in passing the school gun law. "The only question is whether the legislative judgment is within the realm of reason."

When it comes to individual rights such as freedom of speech, the courts have a special duty to scrutinize what legislators do. For minorities by definition are not likely to be protected in legislatures. But the claims of states' rights have ample influence in Congress.

There is a wonderful irony in the Supreme Court stepping forward—or more accurately stepping backward—to limit the legislative power of the federal government. States' rights used to be a rallying cry for conservatives, but today they are demanding federal action in all kinds of areas traditionally left to the states.

Federalization of tort law is an example. Conservatives are even demanding a federal medical malpractice law. *The Wall Street Journal* editorial page, voice of the right, is all for federal tort reform—but it cheered the Supreme Court decision on the school gun law. It depends whose ox is gored.

Jesse
a conservative
Libertarian

Shane
an African
American, liberal
Democrat

Aussie
a Jewish
Palestinian, liberal

Gino
a moderate
Democrat

John
a liberal
Democrat

This Means More than Just Guns in Schools
★ ★ ★

Dr. Bauer: We'll begin with *U.S.* v. *Lopez.* And where does the Court say that the power of the federal government stops? What is decided in this case?

Aussie: Any power that is not vested in the federal government lies in the states, solely in the states. Congress passed a law making it a federal crime to have a gun in a school zone, but the Court said that Congress didn't have the power to do that because they were stepping on the power of the states. I don't understand the logic of that. In Israel, whatever the Knesset says is the law, that's it. Tel Aviv, Jerusalem, the law's the same.

Gino: Yeah, but Israel doesn't have the same problem that we have; they don't have states making state law and a federal government making federal law.

Jesse: Israel is a unitary state. One government, one set of laws. But Israel is also about half the size of a small American state, so it makes sense for them. America is gigantic. Four times zones. Different subcultures. What do Minnesotans have in common with Texans? Sometimes, not much! Federalism makes sense for us.

John: You just asked what Texans have in common with Minnesotans, and the important thing is that they are both part of the United States. The federal government, a national body of laws, makes it impossible for people down in Texas to pay their people a lower minimum wage or to have a different standard for freedoms and liberties. I like knowing that if my job takes me from Texas to Minnesota, all the important parts of American government will be in both places.

Dr. Bauer: The political scientist Thomas Dye calls this *competitive federalism* and describes it as an improvement. If you don't like the conservative laws in Texas, move back to more liberal Minnesota. If the laws in one state are truly awful, people will "vote with their feet," and truly awful laws will disappear anyway as states compete to keep educated workers.

Gino:	No, they won't! If Texas has laws that make it easier for business to pay me less, chances are the businesses will also "vote with their feet." And all the jobs will go to the states with the worst laws for workers. My only choices will be to stay unemployed in Minnesota or move to Texas!
Aussie:	I can't imagine what would happen if this idea that the Court is pushing in the *Lopez* case, if that idea really took off. I suppose it could become, in an extreme case, like moving from one nation to another, going from Minnesota to Texas. How bizarre!
John:	I agree with Aussie, it would be bizarre. The scary thing about the *Lopez* decision, for me—when it says the Interstate Commerce Clause doesn't allow the Congress to make a national law about guns in schools—is that it sets the stage for that kind of drastic outcome. The whole constitutional basis behind nearly everything Congress does has been the Interstate Commerce Clause that gave the federal government, the Congress, the right to tell states how to regulate all sorts of things.
Dr. Bauer:	What's the big deal about interstate commerce?
Jesse:	Article I, Section Eight of the Constitution gives Congress the right to make laws that regulate interstate commerce, and that's called the Commerce Clause. For the last seventy years or so Congress has used that as a lever to expand the scope of the federal government in terms of being able to legislate on civil rights, education, labor laws, and now school gun law.
Dr. Bauer:	Jesse just said this has been going on for about seventy years. What's some of the history of this federal-state relationship? Why did things change?
Gino:	Didn't they start to change during the Depression era when Roosevelt needed to get his programs started, and he was being blocked by the Supreme Court's interpretation of the Constitution? There's a good history of this in the Anthony Lewis article, "School Gun Law Ironic Throwback." For a long time, the Supreme Court kept ruling that the Constitution gave very little power to the federal government.
Dr. Bauer:	There is a lot of history on this issue of the Court and federal power that Lewis did not have space for in his column. For example, in the early 1930s the Court struck down federal regulations that would have created, for the first time in American history, a national minimum wage. Now this was a big blow to the New Deal. One of the things the New Deal was trying to do was standardize wage and hour laws all over the country. Why is it important for there to be some federal standards that apply everywhere in this country over certain issues?
Gino:	Because if you don't, the states will take care of their own, and there will be different regulations and unfair labor practices in different states.
John:	Just like I said earlier, what if the minimum wage were lower in Texas? Or if they decided in their state legislature to have no minimum wage? Businesses will go to those states where the regulations are the weakest, and instead of

wages rising or remaining stable, there might be a race to see who could pay their workers the least.

Aussie: Each state's going to be working independently. That's all right until you have a national problem that demands a national solution.

Shane: The Depression was so bad in the 1930s that any business could hire workers for pennies a day, but the problem was, at the end of the week, those employees didn't have any money to purchase the things they made in the factories. Without the federal minimum wage, owners would continue to do what was in their short-term interest, which is to pay the lowest salary possible, without looking to the long-term interest of the whole community.

Dr. Bauer: Here's some more history that Lewis didn't have space to put in his article. The New Deal proposed all sorts of new federal laws, one of them to eliminate child labor in factories. Until 1937, when the Court changed its mind, the Supreme Court kept saying that the Constitution wouldn't allow the Congress to outlaw child labor or regulate the working conditions of pregnant women. This was all left up to the states, and a few states with progressive state legislatures had good laws, but in states where the legislature was a wholly owned subsidiary of the business community, like New York, there was almost no regulation at all. And how did that change?

Gino: In 1937, the Supreme Court caved in to the pressure from Roosevelt and ruled that the Commerce Clause in the Constitution allowed the Congress the power to regulate anything that could possibly be tied to business that moves between states.

Jesse: See, before 1937, we had a generally libertarian-type government, in the sense that the federal government left almost everything up to the states, and the states didn't do much regulating, either. Then the Supreme Court discovers the Commerce Clause, and that starts us down a long road to the present day, when I think the federal government has too much power for our own good. And Rehnquist just wants to make things a little more balanced, go back to some of the ways we used to look at the balance between federal and state power. Toward the end of the opinion, he says that you can make anything be a part of "interstate commerce" if you really work hard enough, and that sloppy interpretation has given too much power to Congress.

Dr. Bauer: Okay, Jesse. Here comes that libertarian in you. You want the states to have more power.

Jesse: Well, insofar as I want government to have any power, I would rather it be at the state level. To me, this case is about freedom. It's about liberty. It's about how much the government in Washington can push us around out here in Colorado. I think Rehnquist describes the states as laboratories of democracy. We can have the freedom to experiment with different ways we want to do things. And that liberty should be important to everyone.

Dr. Bauer: Justice Breyer's dissent makes the argument that the federal government ought to have the power to regulate guns in schools, so he has to interpret the Commerce Clause in a broad way. Chief Justice Rehnquist agrees with Jesse and wants a narrower interpretation that gives more power to states. This is a great example of two important legal minds looking at exactly the same thing and interpreting it in different ways. What does Breyer say?

Aussie: Doesn't he say that people who carry guns affect people, are a threat to society, and therefore that threat could carry across state borders?

Gino: Well, he follows three points of logic actually when he's talking about it. First, gun violence is a serious problem, the problem has an adverse effect on classroom learning, and that adverse effect on classroom learning affects interstate commerce, because if you have students who aren't learning, your state cannot effectively use interstate commerce because you won't have educated people in your state.

Dr. Bauer: Thanks, Gino. So basically, what do you think of that argument, Shane?

Shane: I think it's a bit of a reach. But I support what Breyer's trying to do. Leaving matters up to the states is not something I'm comfortable with.

Dr. Bauer: But is it the job of the federal government to fix everything that's going wrong in the states? That's the issue.

Jesse: And under our principles of federalism, I argue that it is not. I think the federal government makes these laws in fits of bravado and pre-election hype so politicians can say to their constituents: "This is the law that I passed. Look, I made our schools safer because you can't take guns within a thousand feet of a school." They're taking liberty away from me, and there's not a thing I can do about it, other than change one vote in a congressional district, which doesn't do much to change the law. I'm a Denver citizen, and I live 475 feet away from a school. Yes, I measured it! That means that I can't have a gun in my house, and I certainly can't transport it from my house to a firing range or go hunting, because as soon as I take it out of my front door, I am violating that federal law. That law probably couldn't pass in Colorado. But the federal government has no idea what the differences are between a highly urbanized New York City area and less-urbanized Colorado where we do things in the outdoors. We hunt, we shoot, we do things like that.

Gino: "We" meaning . . .

Jesse: People, citizens in general.

Shane: Don't include me in that. I don't want to see guns anywhere, especially not in my neighborhood. Here's the problem as I see it. Guns, absolutely, should be outlawed around schools. And I'm afraid you're right Jesse, that law would not get passed in Colorado. But it should be illegal everywhere to have guns around children. The issue should be the safety of children, and if it takes a federal law to do it, then God bless the federal government.

Jesse:	What happens when the federal government takes away a right that you think is important? Won't you be singing my tune then? You don't think gun rights are important, fine. But I do. And if the government can tell me what to do about guns, then some day they might tell you what to do about something where your own freedom is at stake.
Shane:	The history of the whole civil rights movement is that my freedom can only be guaranteed by the federal government. When you left it up to the good people of Mississippi to decide how they treated their people of color in 1965, then you were leaving things up to the wrong people. State government is not known for giving rights to people of color.
Jesse:	Well, as a Libertarian, I think that the state government isn't necessarily all that much better than the federal government, but of the two, the state governments have been more responsive to the desires of local citizens. Now, that can be bad if the local citizens are racists, but that's not what we're talking about here. The federal government shouldn't have much power, because I can go to Colorado Governor Bill Owens's house. I can't go to Bill Clinton's. At least not to drop off a flyer on his doorstep.
Gino:	You can go to Bill Owens's house? You don't have to have a million dollars to do that now?
Jesse:	No, that's my point.
Gino:	You don't have to be a corporate lobbyist?
Shane:	Jesse, I have a hard time seeing your point of view, especially when you're dealing with kids here. I mean, we're not talking about adults who are responsible, we're talking about kids. And if guns are around kids, regardless, I don't care if it's you or anybody else that carries a gun around kids—that's wrong. Government needs to deal with that. And you said earlier, in Colorado we probably wouldn't deal with it, because we have a lot of people who like their guns. Fine. Then let the federal government do it, because somebody has to.
Gino:	In Colorado, they wouldn't pass it. What do you think they are going to do in Texas?
Dr. Bauer:	Well let's look at that because *U.S.* v. *Lopez* is a Texas case. A young man, a high school senior, was caught with a gun at Edison High School in San Antonio, Texas, where it was against the law. He was arrested and charged under a Texas law. I'm reading from the first page of the opinion: "The next day state charges were dismissed after federal agents charged respondent with violating the Gun-Free School Zone Act of 1990." Now, why do you think they dismissed the charges under the Texas law and charged him under the federal statute?
Jesse:	That's fairly simple. He can't be charged under both; that's double jeopardy.
Dr. Bauer:	How about this for a reason: The federal penalty is probably tougher; that's usually why a prosecutor drops state charges and goes for a federal indictment. And why is the federal law probably tougher? Because when the Texas

Jesse:	Sure.
Aussie:	Yes.
Dr. Bauer:	OK, so if we allow the states to vote on laws based on their differences, we're going to have wimpier gun laws in Texas than we are in New York, and that's what happened here. When Lopez was charged under the Texas statute, I will bet you dollars to doughnuts that Lopez would have gotten off easier under Texas law than federal law.
Jesse:	I think it still sets a pretty scary precedent because . . . look at it from the other side. I mean, pick a hot-button issue to conservatives, maybe abortion. Say, in 2000, the presidency goes over to the Republicans or a conservative Republican. The House and the Senate are still in Republican hands, much like the executive and the legislative are in the same political party in Colorado. Federal law then criminalizes abortion except to protect the life of the mother, no exceptions, not even for cases of rape or incest, and that becomes federal law. All fifty states have to follow it even if some states have liberal majorities. How would that feel to you all?
Dr. Bauer:	But, the Supreme Court would have to agree. The Supreme Court struck down the Gun-Free School Zone Act because a majority decided that this was not constitutional. That same Court would not allow states to make abortion criminal.
Jesse:	All right, but can't you imagine some scenario where a conservative federal government would do something that a liberal state wouldn't like?
Aussie:	What I can imagine is the example that Shane gave, earlier. The federal government had to force some states to do the right thing about racial discrimination in the 1950s and '60s. Can you imagine what would have happened if Kennedy and Johnson had said, "Let's leave everything up to the states"?
Dr. Bauer:	That's the second time in history the Supreme Court stepped in and said the federal government had power over the states through the Commerce Clause. The first time was to enforce the New Deal, the second was to enforce federal civil rights laws on all the states. Jesse, you've just had Constitutional Law with Dr. Provizer. Do you remember the case?
Jesse:	I think it was the *Heart of Atlanta Motel* case. In *Heart of Atlanta Motel,* what you had was a motel in Atlanta where white owners did not want to have African American guests at their hotel. The owners had a segregated hotel and an African American wanted to stay there. The owners turned him down saying, "We do not serve African Americans at the Heart of Atlanta Motel." And this gentleman sued.
Aussie:	I remember that case. The federal government's role in regulating discrimination came down to the fact that this motel, although it was in the middle of

	Atlanta, occasionally had guests from out-of-state. And because they occasionally had guests from out-of-state, the motel was involved in interstate commerce. And because of interstate commerce, the United States Congress could invoke the Commerce Clause and enforce civil rights laws against discrimination on the basis of race at the hotel.
Dr. Bauer:	Good. This is the case that Lewis referred to when he wrote that the Court had previously "upheld a law against racial discrimination in motels that might serve interstate travelers." Lewis is upset in this reading because he thinks those rulings are all put into question by the *Lopez* ruling. Now, Rehnquist says in the *Lopez* case, "We conclude, consistent with the great weight of our case law, that the proper test requires an analysis of whether the regulated activity 'substantially affects interstate commerce.'" This interpretation of federalism is called *New Federalism,* because it is such a break from what the Court had ruled from 1937 to 1995. Now, clearly the Gun-Free School Zone Act can't be stretched so far that guns in schools "substantially effect interstate commerce," even though Breyer and others try very hard to make that work in the dissent. Here is where I agree with Anthony Lewis that this New Federalism is disturbing. Even though, if you read the full opinion in *Lopez,* Chief Justice Rehnquist went out of his way to say that *Heart of Atlanta* was not overturned by this decision, I can't figure out why not! My question to you is, if the *Lopez* standard had been used in *Heart of Atlanta Motel,* would the federal government have been able to force the Heart of Atlanta Motel to rent rooms to African Americans?
Shane:	No, and that's what scares me about the *Lopez* case. Imagine the likelihood that the state of Georgia's lily-white legislature in 1964-1965 would have passed state laws to force businesses to desegregate!
John:	Shane, I agree that is scary. But the *Lopez* case doesn't bother me that much. There are still ways for the federal government to get what it wants. Like you know what, if the Gun-Free School Zone Act is unconstitutional, we can still get the federal government to help us keep guns out of schools. Congress can always tie compliance to a reward; you keep guns out of your school, you get more federal education funding. That would just about force state legislatures to pass local laws about guns in schools. This is, I think, what Clinton meant in the reading, "Clinton: Overturn School Gun Rule."
Dr. Bauer:	That's constitutional. The term for that is *fiscal federalism,* using the carrot of money to get the states to do what the federal government wants.
Shane:	That's what the federal government will have to do to protect our children, because the states will not do it.
Jesse:	Right now in Colorado our highway funds from the federal government are tied to mandatory seatbelt laws, speed limits, and the drinking age. Eventually the state can say, fine, we're going to remove all these restrictions because they cost more to enforce than the fed gives us in revenue. That's the risk the federal government runs in tying strings to all of these grant programs. Some

states are already fighting back when the federal government tells them what to do but won't give them the money to pay for it. That's got to be the ultimate in federal tyranny.

Dr. Bauer: You just described the problem with unfunded federal mandates. But, when the State of California sued over an unfunded federal mandate, they lost. States are certainly free to turn down federal incentives, but they are not free to refuse to do something just because it costs money. A prime example is special education. The law that forces states to supply special education programs is a federal law, but it is the states that have to cough up the money. Unfair, but legal.

Jesse: I repeat, I still think that's tyranny. Unfunded mandates are tyranny, and the Gun-Free School Zone Act is tyranny. And I'm glad the Supreme Court is giving less power to the federal government.

★ ★ ★

The War Between the States . . . and Washington
Garry Wills

Some people play favorites with the Bill of Rights. The favorite amendment of gangsters is the fifth (no self-incrimination), of liberals the first (free speech), of drug dealers the fourth (no unauthorized search), of gun fondlers the second (to bear arms). Now, many people have a new favorite, the long-neglected 10th (powers not specifically assigned to Washington are reserved to the states). As recently as 1985, when the Supreme Court reversed one of its rare decisions based on the amendment (*Garcia* canceling *Usery*), the 10th was being called a dead letter. Certainly few people tried to "take the 10th" the way gangsters and fellow travelers "took the fifth."

But now the amendment has many takers. The Supreme Court used it in 1992, 1995 and 1997 and shows an eagerness to extend that run. Bob Dole, in his last year in the Senate, began carrying the words of the amendment around

with him for instant recitation. Newt Gingrich's insurgents relied on it in 1994 to preach devolution of power from the Federal to the state level. Even President Clinton gives states the title Louis Brandeis thought up for them, "laboratories of democracy." Gov. Tommy Thompson of Wisconsin thinks it is high time for the amendment to be resurrected. He claims he has been a voice for the 10th crying in the wilderness for many years.

The change is not just a matter of theory. States and localities are manifesting a new energy, almost a frenzy, in starting, altering, or killing programs. In education alone, they have pioneered charter schools, vouchers for private schools, the canceling of affirmative action in colleges, the retrenchment of bilingualism, new rules for immigrant children, different approaches to truancy and various approaches to teaching religion in public schools or allowing religious groups to gather on public grounds.

In crime, states have reintroduced capital punishment and passed "three strikes" laws.

Excerpt from *The New York Times Magazine*, July 5, 1998, 26. © 1998 by The New York Times Company. Reprinted by permission.

They have experimented with "truth in sentencing" (no parole), mandatory sentencing, alternative sentencing and victims' compensation.

In politics, they have promoted term limits, tax caps, mandatory spending percentages, public campaign financing, the control of union dues and extensions of the ballot initiative.

On sexual morality, the states have enacted or reversed bills on gay rights, repealed sodomy laws, supported unmarried partners' benefits and proposed or opposed marriage between homosexuals.

On welfare, the states have tried different forms of job training and placement, compulsory work, public employment or compensated private employment and various forms of benefits for mothers on welfare (including child care and health insurance).

On the environment, they have regulated business, formed new protected areas and successfully defied Federal regulations (for example, on the disposal of nuclear waste in *New York* v. *United States* in 1992).

On health, they have considered regulations on assisted suicide, H.M.O.s, late-term abortions, and insurance affecting AIDS patients.

On guns, they have passed bills to protect concealed weapons or to impose local restrictions. They have defeated Federal restrictions on guns near schools (*Lopez*, 1995) and the attempt to use local sheriffs to implement the Brady Bill (*Printz*, 1997).

On a whole range of such issues, the states have been out ahead of Federal programs, reversing a long-term trend. In the Progressive era, regulation of corporations was sought at the national level. In the Bull Moose movement, and during Woodrow Wilson's first term, intellectuals aspired to policy roles in Washington. With the New Deal, their drift toward the center became a stampede. From that point on, an overlapping series of crises (Depression, world war, cold war) led to central mobilization and control of resources. But now, with the end of this half-century of crisis, people with new ideas and a passion for public policy are turning away from Washington and attacking social issues at the state and local levels. This shift raises deep questions about the virtues of direct democracy, the merits of federalism and the possibility of isolating states from the national society. . . .

The foremost champion of local control among the governors is Tommy Thompson, a short, chunky man from Elroy, Wis. (population 1,500), who has a Cagney strut and very modest amounts of modesty. "We started it," he says. "I was the front-runner because I started looking at the Federal laws and figuring how I'd go to Washington and get waivers." Such waivers are special dispensations from Federal regulations. "I'm the only governor who still has waivers in existence, in the area of welfare, from Presidents Reagan, Bush, and Clinton. I think I've got 75 outstanding waivers, which changed Federal law in over 200 instances in the area of welfare."

Welfare is not the only policy on which Thompson has been an innovator. In education, he fought truancy with "Learnfare" and set up choice schools, charter schools, "prep tech" and apprenticing and high-school courses for college credit. He talks of a "broad menu" of options for students. He clearly does not think that local government has to mean minimal government.

In fact, his administration (begun in 1986) has been a kind of mini-New Deal for proliferating programs, acronyms, and slogans—P.F.R. (Parental and Family Responsibility), S.S.F. (Self-Sufficiency First), W.E.J.T. (Work Experience and Job Training Program), Work First, Work Not Welfare, Children First. Many of these have been folded into his master plan, implemented this year as W2 (shorthand for W.W., or Wisconsin Works). His critics say that some of those plans have come and gone so fast they are impossible to evaluate. But he says they should be judged as steps toward his overall plan, whose parts are still being assembled.

He has a health plan for the poor (Badger Care) that awaits more waivers. ("President Clinton is setting on it now.") His job-training program is similarly stymied by Washington: "There are 163 different kinds of rules and regulations dealing with school-to-work and job-ready money from the Federal Government. It's just plain idiotic."

Thompson has moved further and faster than other governors in taking control of his state's activities on many levels, but he says he cannot be judged until his whole plan is in operation and that will not happen until Washington unties his hands. Naturally, since he thinks he is just beginning to get his schemes in place after 12 years in the Governor's Mansion, he is adamantly opposed to term limits: "If you have people dumb enough to keep running for office, like me, you should let the people decide." . . .

Governor Thompson is certainly not a champion of localism if that means cities or counties or the State Legislature can defy his general strategy. He boasts of the 290 items he vetoed in the first budget submitted by the Legislature. He has used the line-item veto more than 1,500 times.

Advocates of direct democracy, like Robert Wiebe, the political historian and theorist, oppose "government by experts," and Thompson sometimes makes fun of Washington "know-it-alls" who could not pass his "Elroy test" (what his little hometown knows is good for it). But Thompson also boasts of his reliance on experts, called in from all quarters to help him with planning. One of those experts, Lawrence Mead, wants to make welfare "the new paternalism," frankly telling people what is good for them. Temperamentally, Thompson is inclined to such hectoring certitude, despite his populist campaign rhetoric. . . .

Governor Thompson claims that the states are sure to do things better than the Federal Government, since they are closer to the peoples' needs and wants. "The new ideas are coming from the governors, and when you have that clash of ideas, you're going to bring out the best in education or in government."

When I suggest that not all the ideas coming from the states are great ones, he is quick, as ever, to the challenge: "Tell me some that aren't." I name term limits, three-strikes, anti-immigration measures, anti-gay measures. "You're right," he says. "I'll grant you there are some examples. But tell me some things in Wisconsin you don't like."

Thompson believes that the government closest to the people is the best government, which many people take to be a truism of democracy. Alexis de Tocqueville, during his 1831 visit to America, noted that "the Federal Government scarcely ever interferes in any but foreign affairs; and the governments of the states in reality direct society in America." The result, according to Tocqueville, was a "tyranny of the majority," by which local prejudice and conformity received no outside challenge.

It is the same complaint Madison had against the states' autonomy under the Articles of Confederation. The people were, in effect, the judges in their own cause—which always leads to skewed judgments. John Jay, arguing in "The Federalist" for a larger union, said that the people least likely to make wise policy about Native Americans were those in the friction of greatest proximity to them. It is the same lesson we learned, in this century, from the assertions of Southern leaders that they best understood blacks.

Though popular sentiment must be expressed in popular government, it is clear that some kinds of dispute need impartial arbiters. The effort of some states to deny education to the children of illegal immigrants, or legal rights to homosexuals, or organization to unions, shows that popular sentiment can be harsh with unpopular people.

CHAT
ROOM

Jesse
a conservative
Libertarian

Shane
an African
American, liberal
Democrat

Aussie
a Jewish
Palestinian, liberal

Gino
a moderate
Democrat

John
a liberal
Democrat

We Are in a New Era, and Nobody Knows How It Will Turn Out
★ ★ ★

Dr. Bauer: Let's look at the Garry Wills article because it sums up a great deal of material about federalism and how it works or doesn't work in the real world. Wills talks about unfunded mandates, welfare, about the *Lopez* case. A good portion of the article is taken up in a kind of discussion between Garry Wills, who is a liberal, and Tommy Thompson, the conservative Governor of Wisconsin. What's the author's main point? Does he think Thompson is right?

John: Garry Wills is critical of Thompson, and Thompson stands for states' rights. He thinks Thompson is a Tenth Amendment fundamentalist.

Jesse: Well, the Tenth Amendment does exist. I know you liberals like to forget certain amendments, but there they are. The Second Amendment exists, and the Tenth Amendment exists, too.

Dr. Bauer: And there are many arguments about what these amendments meant when the framers first put them into the Constitution, and what they ought to mean today. What's the controversy over the Tenth Amendment?

Aussie: Nobody is exactly sure what it means because the language is so vague.

Jesse: I don't think it's vague at all. Let me read it from my pocket copy of the Constitution: "The powers not delegated to the United States by the Constitution, nor prohibited by it to the States, are reserved to the States respectively, or to the people." Clear as a bell to me.

Gino: And what does this clear statement mean to you?

Jesse: That the framers were as scared of too much federal power as I am. They wanted it made clear that states should have most of the power, so any powers *not* given directly to the federal government were kept for the states, and anything the states did would be perfectly fine as long as it didn't conflict with

	the powers given to the federal government by the Constitution. So, short of Colorado declaring war or trying to take away freedom of speech, Colorado should be left alone to do what its citizens want.
Dr. Bauer:	A "Tenth Amendment fundamentalist" could be described as a person who sees state governments as the good guys and the federal government as the bad guys. According to Wills, does Thompson see himself as a kind of enemy of the federal government?
Jesse:	Thompson thinks the states have a better knowledge of public policy than the federal government does, because states have to be more responsive. Somebody who is voting in Congress may come from Georgia, but he's telling people in Montana or California how to administer programs. Somebody, by contrast, who is in the Colorado state legislature is more in touch with the realities of Colorado when deciding what is the best public policy for Colorado.
Dr. Bauer:	So the states are supposed to know best. What's the political science term for taking power that used to be exercised by the federal government and giving it to states?
Aussie:	Isn't that *devolution?* The power devolves down to the states.
Dr. Bauer:	Yes. Governor Thompson is a big fan of devolution. This is all based on Jesse's argument: the closer you are to the people, the better public policy you will make. Therefore, the state governments should be better than the federal government. But by that logic, Wills points out that town government should be even better than state government. But what does Governor Thompson think about local town and city governments?
Gino:	He thinks that the local government is too close and does the wrong things and that they try and countermand his executive fiat as head of the state of Wisconsin. So the exact same thing he criticizes in the federal government, he is guilty of on the state level.
Aussie:	Yes, Governor Thompson looks a bit hypocritical. Wills says, "He boasts of the 290 items he vetoed in the first budget submitted by the legislature. He has used the line item veto more than 1,500 times." He certainly thinks the state legislature ought to shut up and do as he says.
John:	And he doesn't rely on local people for advice; he goes to big-name experts. All of this runs against the original argument for more local control; national experts aren't likely to be closer to the problems of the people than the state legislature is. And Thompson hates his state legislators!
Shane:	I thought it was pretty interesting, because this is all a part of his logical inconsistency. If these local yokels down in the small towns of Wisconsin aren't as smart as Tommy Thompson, he's going to walk all over them. Also, Wills makes the argument that some state governments are smarter than other state governments. Just being local doesn't make you better. That was certainly true about civil rights. Sometimes local people are just operating out of their bias-

es. In the federal government, there are so many more voices from so many more places and communities, I think there's a better shot at getting good laws.

John: I think that Wills would agree with Shane's argument. For example, Wills described John Jay arguing against too much local power in the *Federalist Papers*. Jay said the people least likely to make wise policy about Native Americans were those "in the friction of greatest proximity to" Native Americans. Jay knew that locals could make policy based on their prejudices.

Jesse: But, the federal government has biases, too. And when they make laws, they don't just screw up one state with their biases, they screw up all fifty states. With fifty state governments, you have fifty different things going on. Some of them may be great, some of them may be inexcusable. If you have one national government, and it's wrong, we're all affected. That's the thing that concerns me about a stronger federal government in charge. Unless you want to argue that the Congress somehow has no biases whatsoever, I would think you'd be on my side in this.

Shane: No way. The Congressional Black Caucus certainly has more power in Congress than the only black man in the Colorado State Legislature does! And I know for a fact there are many state legislatures with little or no minority representation. The national Congress is still a better deal for minorities.

Aussie: Wills quotes Alexis de Tocqueville, who knew how majorities can ignore the needs of minorities. He said our local governments led to a "tyranny of the majority" because the federal government back in the 1830s didn't interfere except in foreign affairs. There was no strong federal government to check and balance the prejudices of the state and local governments. In Israel, this is a struggle every day. The Arab minority has to live with the laws passed by the Knesset, where they have some representation, but very little real power. Democracy isn't much help when you're outnumbered, so I understand what Shane is saying about minorities in state legislatures being virtually powerless.

Shane: Jesse and his fellow libertarians would like to go back to those good old days before the federal government had much power over the states. But Wills says that those "good old days" weren't that good, and I have to say amen to that.

Dr. Bauer: To be fair, Governor Thompson does have some good arguments for devolution. Thompson says, "There are 163 different kinds of rules and regulations dealing with school-to-work and job-ready money from the federal government. It's just plain idiotic." We have to give these devolution advocates some credit: the federal government makes incredibly complicated rules and, as a result, the state governments are drowning in paperwork. When I dealt with welfare-to-work programs in the early 1980s, the number of federal regulations was astounding. It's not always the case that the federal government is helping minorities, Shane. Sometimes they end up hurting minorities by the sheer number of rules and regulations the federal government requires.

Shane: I would say that's more the norm, and I agree with you. Regulations can be a waste of time and effort. In the programs I work with that help kids, there's a ton of things we can and cannot do. But at least Congress is trying to address these problems, and I don't see the State of Colorado ready to deal with it. There's a great quote in this article that I agree with one hundred percent: "The effort of some states to deny education to the children of illegal immigrants, or legal rights to homosexuals, or organization to unions, shows that popular sentiment can be harsh with unpopular people."

Dr. Bauer: Governor Thompson also has some choice words to say about fiscal federalism. Did you get that?

Jesse: Yes, the federal government has programs that give the states matching money only if they follow what the Feds tell them to do. And here you have to sympathize with Thompson, because he is going above and beyond what the federal government is trying to do with reforming welfare. Shane, I know you think that local government can't be friendly to minorities, but look at Thompson. He's trying a very ambitious program to help people not only get off welfare, but find real, decent jobs. He's giving out free child care, health insurance. He wants to give incentives to parents on welfare to make sure their kids stay in school. This has got to be a big help to poor communities. And what does Bill Clinton, the supposed champion of the poor, do to help Thompson out? He can't get matching funds from the federal government, because he won't deal with their picky regulations.

Gino: He won't get federal matching funds because his own ideas are so screwy. Here is a Republican governor pushing a program that spent $14 million dollars to save $3 million in welfare costs! I don't blame the federal government for looking twice at Governor Thompson's big ideas.

Dr. Bauer: How has the Clinton administration handled devolution?

Jesse: There's been more devolution under Clinton than there was under any Republican president that I know about. Clinton was, for most of his political life, the governor of a small state. Clinton knows what it's like to want to try and experiment and get stuck on some federal regulation. Clinton has done a lot for devolution; he just hasn't moved fast enough to please people like Thompson.

Dr. Bauer: So if you had to predict what the trend is going to be in the coming years, where do you see the idea of devolution?

Shane: I know it's the wave of the future. I just want the federal government to retain some ability to make the states conform to some national standards of justice and equality.

John: There's no doubt that after the Clinton years, it's going to be impossible to run all, or even most, public policy from Washington. And there are good things about that. Washington isn't perfect. And, as a future teacher, I sure don't want federal mandates forcing me to teach certain subjects and not others, or teach them a particular way. Local control is the bedrock of the American education system, and that's a good thing. The experiments that states are doing with charter schools, for example, are good things. We can all learn from these experiments.

Jesse: Why not go all the way and allow states to experiment with voucher programs, make the public schools compete with the private schools?

Aussie: That's what Thompson wants, but the Constitution may stand in his way. No matter what the Tenth Amendment says, the First Amendment says there will be no establishment of religion, and giving money to religious schools may be over the line. It's perfectly legal in Israel, but not here!

Gino: Bottom line: We have a system of government that contains both the Tenth and the First Amendments. We have to try to balance the needs of the states to run their own programs against the federal government's need to hold us all together.

Aussie: If you work it right, you can get the best of both worlds. But that also means that neither side will be completely satisfied.

★ ★ ★

For Additional Reading

Go to InfoTrac College Edition, your online research library at

http://web1.infotrac-college.com

Enter the following search terms using the **Subject Guide** or **Key Terms.**

federalism	separation of powers	*United States* v. *Lopez*
Federalist Papers		

3 Civil Liberties

MONICA BAUER

A PERSONAL PERSPECTIVE ON The Christian Coalition and Separation of Church and State*

RANDY TATE, THEN EXECUTIVE DIRECTOR OF THE CHRISTIAN COALITION, released to the media a press release that also was published on the World Wide Web on June 2, 1998. In this release, Tate offered his own interpretation of Thomas Jefferson's thoughts. The press release was headlined "Library of Congress Skewers 'Wall of Separation' Myth."

Randy Tate was referring to a new Library of Congress exhibit, "Religion and the Founding of the American Republic." The exhibit, he claimed, contained a "stunning discovery" concerning the meaning of Jefferson's phrase a "wall of separation between church and state." Here is some of what Mr. Tate had to say:

> It's a liberal myth that Jefferson intended his words to be used as justification for expelling religious expression from the public square. It was the Supreme Court in 1947, in *Everson* v. *Board of Education,* that took his words out of context, created new legal language that does not appear in the Constitution and used the new language as their basis for striking down the Constitutionality of school prayer in *Engel* v. *Vitale* in 1962.

*Editor's Footnote: One of the original readings used by the Chat Room for the discussion of this topic was a June 2, 1998, press release I found at the Christian Coalition's Web site (http://www.cc.org). The Coalition, however, denied permission to reprint the release because its author, Randy Tate, the coalition's former executive director, is no longer with the organization. Because the release remains part of a useful discussion of the First Amendment, I have paraphrased it here. Students who want to read the original article in full or learn the current position of the Christian Coalition on the separation of church and state can refer to the coalition's Web site.

I can agree with part of Mr. Tate's thinking. In researching my doctoral thesis on the separation of church and state, I found numerous discussions about religion by the founders of the Constitution, even including statements by Jefferson on the importance of prayer. So, the Library of Congress exhibit contained no news that startled me! It is a plain fact that the founders lived in an era when public religious expression was common and that they linked the teaching of religion to the development of good citizens. But they were also in disagreement with each other about which religious teachings were true and which were false. No one would advocate teaching false religious doctrines to create good citizens, would they? And there lies a problem.

What all the founders did seem to agree on was the proposition that there should be no official federal establishment of religion. An establishment of religion occurs when the government favors an expression of religion with support in the form of tax dollars or the favorable government treatment of some religions over others. The founders knew all too well that struggles to establish an official State religion had drained the blood of several generations of British, French, and German citizens in religious wars of the seventeenth and eighteenth centuries. The Supreme Court has had some disagreements within its own ranks about how to interpret the Establishment Clause of the First Amendment, but a majority has held firm since 1962 that official prayer time in public schools is unconstitutional. That majority includes justices appointed to the Court by both Republicans and Democrats. One task for students is to understand how that came to be so. In the following Chat Room, students discuss that history.

The Christian Coalition supports prayer in schools. On its Web site, as of mid-February 2000, it asserts that it "believes that it is the right of students to have a moment of voluntary prayer at the beginning of a school day, or for a school team to pray with their coach before a game. . . . The First Amendment was designed to protect freedom of religion, not freedom from religion."

As students, your critical thinking exercise is to decide for yourselves if you think that Jefferson would be in favor of prayer in the schools, as Randy Tate suggests in his 1998 press release and as his former organization states. Compare Tate's view of Jefferson with the reading you have from Jefferson's own hand. Then debate the ideas found in the reading "A Wing and a Prayer" and see what you think about a "freedom from religion." Does the First Amendment religion clause offer public school students "freedom from religion," or does it step on the rights of students to "freedom of religion"?

On Religion
Thomas Jefferson

The legitimate powers of government extend to such acts only as are injurious to others. But it does me no injury for my neighbor to say there are twenty gods, or no God. It neither picks my pocket nor breaks my leg. If it be said, his testimony in a court of justice cannot be relied on, reject it then, and be the stigma on him. Constraint may make him worse by making him a hypocrite, but it will never make him a truer man. It may fix him obstinately in his errors, but will not cure them. Reason and free inquiry are the only effectual agents against error. Give a loose to them, they will support the true religion by bringing every false one to their tribunal, to the test of their investigation. They are the natural enemies of error and of error only. Had not the Roman government permitted free inquiry, Christianity could never have been introduced. Had not free inquiry been indulged at the era of the Reformation, the corruptions of Christianity could not have been purged away. If it be restrained now, the present corruptions will be protected, and new ones encouraged.

Was the government to prescribe to us our medicine and diet, our bodies would be in such keeping as our souls are now. Thus in France the emetic was once forbidden as a medicine, and the potato as an article of food. Government is just as infallible, too, when it fixed systems in physics. Galileo was sent to the Inquisition for affirming that the earth was a sphere; the government had declared it to be as flat as a trencher, and Galileo was obliged to abjure his error. This error, however, at length prevailed, the earth became a globe, and Descartes declared it was whirled round its axis by a vortex. The government in which he lived was wise enough to see that this was no question of civil jurisdiction, or we should all have been involved by authority in vortices. In fact, the vortices have been exploded, and the Newtonian principle of gravitation is now more firmly established, on the basis of reason, than it would be were the government to step in, and to make it an article of necessary faith.

Reason and experiment have been indulged, and error has fled before them. It is error alone which needs the support of government. Truth can stand by itself. Subject opinion to coercion: whom will you make your inquisitors? Fallible men; men governed by bad passions, by private as well as public reasons. And why subject it to coercion? To produce uniformity. But is uniformity of opinion desirable? No more than of face and stature. Introduce the bed of Procrustes then, and as there is danger that the large men may beat the small, make us all of a size, by lopping the former and stretching the latter. Difference of opinion is advantageous in religion. The several sects perform the office of a *censor morum* over such other. Is uniformity attainable? Millions of innocent men, women, and children, since the introduction of Christianity, have been burnt, tortured, fined, imprisoned; yet we have not advanced one inch toward uniformity. What has been the effect of coercion? To make one-half the world fools, and the other half hypocrites, to support roguery and error all over the earth. Let us reflect that it is inhabited by a thousand millions of people. That these profess probably a thousand different systems of religion. That ours is but one of that thousand. That if there be but one right, and ours that one, we should wish to see the 999 wandering sects gathered into the fold of truth. But against such a majority we cannot effect this by force. Reason and persuasion are the only practicable instruments. To make way for these, free inquiry must be indulged; and how can we wish others to indulge it while we refuse it ourselves. But every state, says an inquisitor, has established some religion. No two, say I, have

Reprinted from *Notes on Virginia*, by Thomas Jefferson, 1784. © 1996 by Portland House, a division of Random House Value Publishing.

established the same. Is this a proof of the infallibility of establishments? Our sister states of Pennsylvania and New York, however, have long subsisted without any establishment at all. The experiment was new and doubtful when they made it. It has answered beyond conception. They flourish infinitely. Religion is well supported; of various kinds, indeed, but all good enough; all sufficient to preserve peace and order; or if a sect arises, whose tenets should subvert morals, good sense has fair play, and rea-sons and laughs it out of doors, without suffering the state to be troubled with it. They do not hang more malefactors than we do. They are not more disturbed with religious dissensions. On the contrary, their harmony is unparalleled, and can be ascribed to nothing but their unbounded tolerance, because there is no other circumstance in which they differ from every nation on earth. They have made the happy discovery that the way to silence religious disputes is to take no notice of them.

A Wing and a Prayer: Religion Goes Back to School
Wendy Kaminer

Governor Fob James Jr. of Alabama has promised to resist a recent federal court order prohibiting organized, officially sponsored religious activities in DeKalb County public schools. The court order, issued in *Chandler* v. *James* on October 29, includes an injunction against an Alabama law permitting organized, student-led "voluntary" prayers at school events.

It's unclear what form the Governor's resistance might take, but James was last heard threatening to call out the National Guard to protect the prerogative of state court Judge Roy Moore to hang a copy of the Ten Commandments in the courtroom, in defiance of the First Amendment and the federal courts. Meanwhile, Judge Moore has declared the recent federal court order on prayer in school an "unconstitutional abuse of power," refusing to recognize it as the law in his county. High school students, no doubt emboldened by these pronouncements, are protesting the court order, marching on city hall, walking out of class and leaving the stands at football games to pray. "Having Jesus in our school is something

Reprinted from *The Nation*, December 15, 1997, 18–20. Copyright © 1997 by Wendy Kaminer. Used by permission.

that we need. It gives us strength," one student explained.

Advocates of organized school prayer will laud this uprising as a demand for religious freedom, defending the "right" of students to pray. But what is at stake in Alabama is the right not to pray to Jesus or be subjected to religious indoctrination. The facts of the case that led to the most recent federal injunction on organized prayer in school tell a very different story from that of the posturing of Alabama officials.

Chandler v. *James* involved a challenge to the virtual establishment of Christianity in DeKalb County schools. The case was brought by parents of public school students (including the assistant principal at one school) who protested sectarian prayer and Bible readings organized by school administrators and clergy, conducted in classrooms, at athletic events and during commencement exercises. Prayer was not voluntary. One teacher required students to pray out loud in class. Students who chose not to pray were encouraged to appoint surrogate worshipers, whose prayers they were required to attend. Christian devotionals were routinely delivered at school, assemblies, and other activities during which students were a captive audience. Gideon Bibles were distributed in school, even in the classroom.

All these practices were clearly unconstitutional and violated numerous federal court decisions, but Alabama has a history of defying federal law protecting civil rights and liberties. Pamela Sumners, attorney for the plaintiffs in *Chandler v. James,* has observed that Governor James is "whipping up" religious bigotry the way George Wallace once whipped people into a frenzy over race.

So the *Chandler* decision is unlikely to end religious persecution in Alabama public schools. It clarified no constitutional principles that were not already clear and had not already been rejected by public officials. In fact, after an earlier decision in the *Chandler* case struck down the state's student-led prayer statute, a similar lawsuit, *Herring v. Key,* was brought against Pike County, Alabama, public schools.

The *Herring* case, now pending before the same federal district court that issued the injunction in *Chandler v. James,* involves four Jewish children who have the misfortune to attend public school in Pike County. They report being tormented by school officials and classmates because they are Jews, denied the right to practice their faith and forced to participate in Christian religious observances. Three of the children, Sarah, David, and Paul Herring, are in the sixth, seventh, and ninth grades, respectively; they are also represented by Pamela Sumners.

The complaint in the *Herring* case makes you wonder if Pike County is part of America or Iran. It alleges that: Christian prayers and devotionals are aired over the school's public address system; the elementary school principal has led prayers at assemblies and introduced preachers to captive student audiences; children are required to bow their heads in prayer during assemblies; sixth-grader Sarah was expressly ordered by a teacher to bow her head for a "student-initiated" prayer; and seventh-grader David was physically forced by a student teacher to bow his head in devotion to Jesus. The children have been required to

attend Christian sermons; Sarah was once led crying and shaking from an assembly after being told by the preacher that all students who did not embrace Jesus as their savior would burn in Hell. Ninth-grader Paul was required by the vice principal of his school to write an essay on "Why Jesus Loves Me" as punishment for disrupting class. The principal forbade Paul from wearing the Star of David to class, claiming it was a "gang symbol" (other children wear crosses). School officials have tolerated vicious anti-Semitic remarks directed at the children as well as physical assault. Their possessions have been defaced with swastikas and they have been given cartoons about the Holocaust.

Their mother and stepfather, Sue and Wayne Willis, have regularly protested the persecution of their kids, with very limited success. Sue Willis reports that the high school principal and an elementary school teacher both responded to her complaints "with words to the effect of 'If parents will not save souls, we have to.'"

It is tempting to dismiss these cases as anomalies, but violations of First Amendment prohibitions on establishing religion in the schools are not uncommon, especially but not exclusively in the South. *The New York Times* reports that in parts of Alabama "prayer has remained as common as pop quizzes in many schools." In Mississippi in 1996 a federal court intervened to protect Lutheran children from organized prayer and Bible readings in a predominantly Baptist public school system. In West Virginia, prayers are broadcast over the public address system before every home football game at Nitro High School, and everyone in the audience is expected to stand with head bowed, according to a recent report by *The Charleston Gazette.* "They say it's illegal, but we've always done it," Nitro athletic director Patrick Vance reportedly said. The *Gazette* also reports that during graduation ceremonies at Herbert Hoover High School in Clendenin, West Virginia, students recite the Lord's Prayer.

Organized, officially endorsed sectarian religious activities in public school are indisputably illegal; but they persist, partly because relatively few people have the strength and courage to challenge them. Members of minority faiths who are most likely to object are also most at risk when they do so. But anyone who publicly complains about illegal, school-sanctioned prayer or goes to court to stop it should expect to be ostracized, harassed and threatened with physical injury or death by God-fearing neighbors.

This is the climate of religious intolerance in which Congress will consider a constitutional amendment intended to legitimize organized group prayer in the nation's classrooms. The amendment, introduced by Oklahoma Representative Ernest Istook Jr., establishes a constitutional right to engage in sectarian religious practices on public property, including schools, and gives religious groups an entitlement to government funds. The Istook Amendment does state that "neither the United States nor any state shall require any person to join in prayer or other religious activity [or] prescribe school prayers." But the amendment would authorize student-led prayers, which often involve the *de facto* endorsement of school officials and can be quite coercive. Anyone doubting the threat to the free exercise of religion posed by student prayers need only attend public school in Alabama.

"I don't want the government involved in the religious upbringing of my son," Michael Chandler, plaintiff in *Chandler* v. *James,* has explained. "The state has no business telling my child when, where and how to pray." You'd expect conservatives mistrustful of government to sympathize with Chandler's concern. Instead, supporters of the Istook Amendment promulgate the dangerous fiction that religion has been exiled from the public schools and students have lost their rights to pray.

In fact, students have the undisputed right to pray individually or in groups during their free time; they can say grace before lunch, drop to their knees on the football field or pray silently in every class, as many do. Religious associations of students have the same rights as other student groups to meet on school property. In *Chandler* v. *James,* while the court enjoined organized, official prayer, it expressly affirmed the rights of students to express personal religious beliefs in their schoolwork or during graduation services, engage in religious activities during non-instructional time, announce meetings of extracurricular religious activities over the school's public address system and wear religious symbols. The federal courts have generally made clear that students have the right to exercise their religion in school; what they lack is the power to impose their religion on others.

Religious power, not religious rights, is what supporters of a school prayer amendment seek. In the name of rights, they seek the kind of power that subjects the children of minority faiths to religious persecution in the nation's schools. At least today that persecution is illegal and can be remedied in federal court, when the families at risk persevere. A constitutional amendment permitting organized school prayer would leave every public school student at the mercy of the religious majority. Introduce organized religion in the schools and you introduce sectarianism; and that is a prescription for tribalism, not virtue.

Andy
a moderate

Laura
a conservative
Republican

Sarah
a Native American,
liberal Democrat

Steve
a Libertarian

The Separation of Church and State
★ ★ ★

Dr. Bauer: Now we move into the constitutional controversy over allowing prayer in the public schools. What the Constitution says about religion can be interpreted a number of ways. The First Amendment says this: "Congress shall make no law respecting an establishment of religion, or prohibiting the free exercise thereof." The problem arises in the phrase, "establishment of religion." To try and interpret what that phrase means today, the Supreme Court has gone back to Jefferson. On the separation of church and state, everybody fights over what Jefferson really said or meant. What does the Christian Coalition's press release, "Library of Congress Skewers 'Wall of Separation' Myth," tell us about what they think Jefferson meant?

Laura: They think there shouldn't be much separation. They think public prayer should be allowed in all the schools. We've always had public prayer allowed in private schools. The thing they want is public prayer in the public schools.

Steve: They think the current situation is taking away their rights. They want to have religious symbols in public buildings, they want prayers said openly in the public schools, and they see that as a right that the Supreme Court has taken away.

Dr. Bauer: And that's because the Supreme Court has the responsibility of interpreting the Constitution, a document which can mean different things to different people. As we can see from our readings, there is kind of a warfare going on between two sides over what Jefferson really meant.

Andy: Why is Jefferson such a big deal?

Steve: Jefferson was famous for his stand on religion. He wrote the law in Virginia that separated church and state.

Dr. Bauer: Yes, he did. It was one of the issues he was most passionate about, because he knew people who had been put in prison in Virginia because they belonged to the "wrong church"—*not* the approved church established by the state. Jefferson's ideas on the need for the separation of church and state were the strongest influence on the framers and writers of the First Amendment.

Laura: But the Christian Coalition says that Jefferson was not a big fan of separating church and state because he allowed religious worship in government buildings.

Dr. Bauer: But you've also read Jefferson's own writing on the subject, "On Religion." It is a complete piece, no words are taken out of context, and it is very much like everything else he wrote about church and state. So which side is correct? What did Jefferson really have in mind about church and state?

Steve: Jefferson doesn't want one approved religion. He says that "difference of opinion is advantageous in religion." But that doesn't mean he's for the complete separation of church and state. It's just a matter of interpretation.

Dr. Bauer: Well, which interpretation is right?

Laura: Can't they both be right? Why does one have to be right and the other wrong?

Dr. Bauer: Because people act on their interpretation. And the Constitution is our fundamental law of the land. People's actions, then, are either against the law, or they're not. If there is a conflict between interpretations, then the Supreme Court has to decide which interpretation is stronger, more logical, fits the evidence, and, therefore is the law.

Steve: I can speak to my idea of which interpretation is right. In "On Religion," Jefferson says that "[the citizens of Pennsylvania and New York] have made the happy discovery that the way to silence religious disputes is to take no notice of them." Furthermore, government should stay out of religious disputes. I think if there were prayers in the public schools, the government would be right in the middle of trying to settle a bunch of religious disputes.

Dr. Bauer: Is this Jefferson's central argument on church and state? We know that ideas can be taken out of context, twisted, and used in any number of ways. But the most persuasive interpretation is the one that reflects the main idea. What is Jefferson's main idea?

Andy: Here's a line I just noticed: "Was the government to prescribe to us our medicine and our diet, our bodies would be in such keeping as our souls are now." I think he's saying that the government doesn't, and has no right to, tell us how to take care of our bodies, so it also has no right to tell us how to take care of our souls. And when there is an established religion, the government is doing just that—telling us how to take care of our souls. There should be no government activity that officially establishes a religion for all of us. That sounds to me like it would extend easily to saying there should be no prayer in public school or religious displays on public property.

Dr. Bauer: What do you all think of Andy's interpretation? Remember, we're looking for the main point.

Steve:	I agree with Andy.
Dr. Bauer:	Does anybody disagree? Is there any way to read Jefferson's "On Religion" and logically come to the conclusion that Jefferson would be in favor of prayer in public schools?
Andy:	Jefferson says that, "Had not the Roman government permitted free inquiry, Christianity could never have been introduced. Had not free inquiry been indulged at the era of the Reformation, the corruptions of Christianity could not have been purged away." I think he definitely wants government to allow freedom of thought about all religions, and that means government cannot pick one official, correct, and true church. That would restrain free thought.
Dr. Bauer:	This contrasts with Egypt, doesn't it? In Egypt, the government technically allows freedom of religion to Christians; yet their legal system is based on the Koran. Clearly, if the majority in the Egyptian government believe there is only one true religion, Islam, they do not really allow free inquiry. For example, when I was at the American University in Cairo, a professor at Cairo University—the state-run, public university—was stripped of his job and hounded out of the country for the crime of having a more liberal interpretation of the Koran than the official version. The Egyptian courts used a law that said Muslims could not legally be married to non-Muslims and divorced him from his wife although neither husband nor wife wanted a divorce. We can't even imagine this happening in the United States because we have a legal tradition of separating church and state.
Laura:	But Egypt has always had Islam as the official religion, and we've never had an official religion. I don't think that's even being debated, not even by the Christian Coalition.
Sarah:	I think the Christian Coalition wants to change the First Amendment so it will be open to a different interpretation.
Andy:	And they want Jefferson on their side. But so what? So what if Jefferson allowed religious worship on some public buildings? Why zero in on him?
Dr. Bauer:	Everybody tries to use Jefferson because, back in 1947, it was his writings that the Supreme Court used when they decided the very first case on the separation of church and state. The justice who wrote the opinion used an 1830 letter that Jefferson had written to a group of Baptist Church women. These women had asked Jefferson exactly what was meant by the First Amendment religion clauses. Jefferson wrote back and said that the First Amendment was supposed to erect a "wall of separation between church and state." So if the Christian Coalition can use Jefferson to further their own argument, that would knock some of the power out of all those Supreme Court opinions that have used Jefferson to separate church from state.
Sarah:	Do we end up in a war of words?
Laura:	We can look at the actual words in the Constitution.

Sarah:	But just like many parts of the Constitution, these are vague words: "establishment of religion." The Supreme Court has to decide what they should mean for the country, today.
Steve:	So the Supreme Court uses the framers' writings to help them understand the intent of language in the Constitution. Can't we also use our common sense? Follow the logical consequences of each opposing interpretation? If we mixed church and state, then the majority would always tend to favor their religion, and eventually it could become difficult to be a member of the wrong kind of church. That's the example we have from Egypt where certain groups are supposed to have religious freedom but they get pushed aside by the majority. Freedom of religion depends on keeping the church and state separated.
Dr. Bauer:	Some political scientists look at the religion clauses exactly that way. Instead of looking at what the framers wrote, they look at the way the two religion clauses might work together, logically. This stresses looking at the two religion clauses *together*: (1) "Congress shall make no law respecting an establishment of religion," (2) "or prohibiting the free exercise thereof." The two clauses may be dependent on each other. The Second Amendment also has two clauses that can be seen as dependent on each other: (1) "A well regulated Militia, being necessary to the security of a free State, (2) the right of the people to keep and bear Arms, shall not be infringed." What would the Christian Coalition say about that two-clause argument?
Laura:	They take exactly the opposite side of this and Steve's argument. They think that by the government separating the state from church, they are in fact establishing a no-religion zone that infringes on the Christian Coalition's freedom to exercise their religion.
Dr. Bauer:	Good. Now, since we're talking about Supreme Court decisions that are already decades old, there should be some evidence that freedom of religion is indeed in trouble. Is there any evidence of that? Is it harder to practice your religion freely since the Supreme Court made these decisions?
Laura:	The Christian Coalition thinks their right to pray in the public schools has been taken away.
Andy:	But that was never a right; prayer in public schools was a custom that hadn't been challenged in the courts. Whether it was lawful hadn't been decided on before, but now the Court has decided.
Sarah:	Just because you can't have official prayer, led by a teacher or whoever, doesn't seem to me a significant taking away of religious rights. Like the reading on school prayer says, you can always pray to yourself. You can pray before or after school. You can have all the religion clubs you want, after the school day is over. I don't see how that's losing the right to practice your religion.
Andy:	Jefferson wrote, "Truth can stand by itself." It doesn't need the support of the government to prop it up. Government doesn't have to support religion for religion to still be important.

Laura:	But the Christian Coalition argues that there is a hostile climate to religion.
Dr. Bauer:	Let's look at the evidence for that. Just because it is no longer legal for teachers or students to lead prayers publicly during the school day, is that evidence of a climate of hostility toward religion?
Sarah:	How would you test that out?
Steve:	We can test it out from what we already know. The Supreme Court has been ruling since 1962 that there should be no prayer in the public schools. In the years since then, has religion in America gotten smaller or larger? Are there fewer churches now then there were back then?
Sarah:	It seems to me that we have just as much, if not more, Christianity today than we did before the Supreme Court ruled against school prayer.
Laura:	Yes, maybe we have more churches. But what if society as a whole has less respect for religion?
Sarah:	A lot of factors may go into big social changes like that. Some of us may be less religious now, but others are more religious. We may be religious in more varied ways. We are a more diverse country today then we were when Jefferson was writing. Today, if you want the public schools to have respect for religion, there are a lot of religions to respect! For example, I don't know how many Christian Coalition members would be thrilled if I went into a classroom with my Native American traditions, burned sage, and chanted in my tribal language.
Dr. Bauer:	Is there evidence that, since the Supreme Court has been separating church and state, that society as a whole has less respect for religion? Let's take the case of whether or not a baby Jesus statue can be put on a courthouse lawn in a Christmas display. The Courts have said that the baby Jesus can be there as long as there are also symbols from other religions and secular Christmas displays, like a Santa Claus. Does this mean there is less respect for religion?
Steve:	No, I think it means there is equal, and more, respect for all religions, as well as equal respect for atheists. They pay taxes. It's their courthouse, too.
Laura:	But the Christian Coalition would definitely say "Yes." If Jesus has to share space with Santa and the Elves, the display is less religious.
Dr. Bauer:	What would satisfy the Christian Coalition?
Steve:	They want an amendment that says there will be no official religion, and everyone is free to practice their religion, but to practice it in places like public schools. That's what they want.
Sarah:	This could lead to "A Wing and a Prayer," which describes Jewish children being forced to participate when they didn't want to. The right to open, public school prayer led to those Jewish children being singled out. Their rights were taken away.
Dr. Bauer:	So you're balancing one right against another right.

Sarah:	And there is no balancing in this reading. It looks like the whole community, except for this family, is Christian. So the majority has all the rights, and the non-Christians have to go along. They were actually forced to pray.
Laura:	Now, the Christian Coalition would come back and say this is a false argument. They don't want to force anybody to pray.
Steve:	I can speak to that personally. I went to grade school in Iowa; Lincoln Elementary School in Davenport. My parents were atheists, and I was raised an atheist, so I was a little atheist third grader. And because I was the only non-Christian kid in the class, my teacher would single me out, make me do little drawings from the Bible at the back of the class when she taught Bible stories. Even after many Supreme Court rulings had declared school prayer against the law, the coercion to participate in the official religion was incredible.
Dr. Bauer:	That was a public school, Steve?
Steve:	Yes.
Dr. Bauer:	And what year would that have been?
Steve:	1983.
Andy:	You know, when I first looked at this article from the Christian Coalition, I thought all they wanted was to make sure some kid didn't get kicked out of school for praying on his lunch break. But after reading it a couple of times, I see what they really want. And what they really want is to make kids like Steve either participate in prayer so they can be just like the majority, or allow them to take the consequences of being ostracized until they change. Private schools exist now for people who want to pray publicly as a group.
Dr. Bauer:	To be fair to the Christian Coalition, they have a real sense of grievance. They had the power to pray publicly in all schools, and now they only have that power in school districts where parents don't complain and challenge them. Clearly they have that power in the school in Alabama discussed in your reading. They had that power when Steve was going to school in Iowa. But it is a tough thing to give up power.
Sarah:	Yes, but sometimes it is necessary to give up power to respect the rights of other people. The Bureau of Indian Affairs Schools used to have the power to make Native Americans into Christians. They took my grandfather and they forced him to be a Christian. That was the purpose of those schools: to take Native Americans and make them just like the whites. Separation of church and state was a joke on the Indian reservation. Becoming Christian was part of going to school. It was part of the assimilation process. My grandfather went into the Bureau of Indian Affairs School at the age of five, speaking his tribal language and practicing his tribal religion. When he left, he spoke English only, and had been taught to be a Christian. He was taken from his family and spent the next twelve years of his life being taught by the government what language to speak and what religion he should have.

Dr. Bauer:	And that was a public school.
Sarah:	It was run by the federal government with tax dollars. They used to have that power and now they don't. I'd call that progress.
Dr. Bauer:	This brings us to an interesting point. Congressman Henry Hyde thinks that if we bring back prayer into the public schools, it will benefit the whole society. Representative Bob Barr, a Republican from Georgia, argued that the killings at Columbine High School could have been prevented if public schools posted the Ten Commandments. During the same debate, Representative Tom DeLay, a Republican from Texas who is high in the leadership, said that the Columbine killings could have been prevented if the public schools would teach the Biblical account of creation instead of Darwin's theory of evolution. Despite Supreme Court rulings, Congress passed a law allowing schools to post the Ten Commandments.
Sarah:	I'm reading *Democracy on Trial* by Jean Bethke Elshtain, and she's big on this idea that we have too many differences—that it would be better if we were more alike. But that's ignoring people's different backgrounds. I think it's ridiculous to suppose that if we were all Christian we'd all get along much better. It didn't work for Europe during two World Wars!
Steve:	I'm seconding Sarah. If we're all supposed to be alike, it means it will be that much more likely that when someone different comes along, we'll attack that person.
Andy:	I think you could make the case that if we were more alike, there might be less hatred. As Dr. Bauer told us, in Egypt where the great majority follows Islam, and Islam is the basis for law, there is more respect for authority, less crime. I don't think we in America will ever get anywhere near that kind of single culture, but I see the point.
Dr. Bauer:	A number of conservative writers such as George Will point to a need for a common culture. They say if we had a common culture that said, "crime is bad, teenage pregnancy is bad, drug abuse is bad," we'd be better off as a nation than we are with a sort of "anything goes." Since Islam is taught in Egyptian schools, everyone is taught the same moral standard, and they create a common culture. In America, we tend to say, "You have a moral standard; I have a moral standard. Only religion imposes an absolute standard, and America's Constitution prevents us from establishing a religion and its moral standards, so everyone can follow his or her own idea." I think there's some truth to the conservative argument that the lack of a common religion prevents us from having a common culture with common moral standards.
Sarah:	That's true. It might be better if we could pick one standard of morality and go with it. The problem is, which standard would you pick?
Dr. Bauer:	That leads us back to Jefferson, who basically advises us to let all the religions flower, and those that have the most to offer society will come out on top—as long as we keep government out of that process.

Sarah: I would argue that we're still in that process. It's not that we have failed to find a moral and ethical and religious standard for the country. We're still looking for it.

★ ★ ★

For Additional Reading

Go to InfoTrac College Edition, your online research library at

http://web1.infotrac-college.com

Enter the following search terms using the Subject Guide or Key Terms.

freedom of religion   freedom of speech   free exercise clause

4 Civil Rights

MONICA BAUER

A PERSONAL PERSPECTIVE ON Affirmative Action

A TRUE STORY. WHEN I WAS GRADUATING FROM COLLEGE, I was one of three people from my school to apply for a special scholarship. It would have paid for all three years of seminary education, anywhere in the country, with room and board included. The scholarship came from Rockefeller family money and was given to only a few each year. There was never more than one winner in any given college. So the three of us who were applying sized each other up.

One of the applicants was an African American woman, one was a white man, and one was a white woman (me). We all knew each other because we had all been working around the chaplain's office and had taken some of the same classes. Every month, we would hear from the scholarship committee. First, we all made the national semifinals. Then we all made the national finals. The month the scholarships were to be announced was the longest month in my life. My friends were absolutely sure that, based on her race, the African American woman would win. After awhile, I started to think so, too. Meanwhile, it was likely that the white, male applicant was just as sure that, based on gender, either of the female candidates had a better chance.

Guess who got the scholarship? The white man, based on whatever criteria the committee happened to be using. All three of us ended up at Yale (I am still paying back my loans), and every once in a while we'd laugh about how tense that process had made us three people of good will, three future ministers! Imagine what those kinds of pressures do to people who incline toward racism or sexism?

Political scientists know that a recipe for tension is to distribute a scarce and valued commodity on a basis that appears to be unfair. The argument that one race or gender must suffer because of the actions of previous generations has never been persuasive to any but the staunchest liberals. If one of the objectives of affirmative action is to help all races and genders live and work comfortably together, then I believe it has failed.

As a person who may have benefited from affirmative action in the past, I have had to think long and hard about this issue. I have been discriminated against on the basis of my gender a few times, but, more often, I have been the target of anger because I might receive preference through affirmative action.

I know what it feels like to be denied job offers because of discrimination. When I preached my first sermon as an assistant pastor of a church in Connecticut, the ushers had to remove a protestor who came down the aisle waving a Bible and yelling, "Women should keep silent in churches!" When I was ordained in 1983, there were still many churches that were "just not ready" to have a woman pastor. Women are still more likely to be called to small, rural churches, where the pay is a fraction of that at the big, urban churches. It will take some time before the generational change wipes out the vestiges of sexism, even in my decidedly liberal church.

Still, I don't want to receive a job, or preferential treatment, through affirmative action. In my analysis, it poisons the atmosphere. Worse, even if you get your job solely on the basis of merit, if you are a member of a group that is targeted for affirmative action programs, people assume you benefited from affirmative action anyway.

As a graduate student in political science, I was part of a vast human experiment on awarding scarce and valued goods—a tenure-track job—in a manner perceived to be unfair. Because women, even in the recent past, were discouraged from attending graduate school, most college professors are still men. This is especially true for political science, which continues to draw far fewer women into graduate school. Thus, when political science departments have a vacancy, they sometimes feel pressure to hire a woman. Because most of those doing the hiring are men, they sympathize with the men in their applicant pools and may resent the direction in which they are being pushed by college administrators. Sometimes, the affirmative action dance can get weird indeed.

For example, I was once toyed with for months by a college search committee. The committee offered a position I very much wanted, first to an African American woman, then to a Hispanic man, both of whom turned it down for better offers. The department chair told me that the job would soon be offered to me. Then, at the last minute, he confessed that he could not hire me. The dean had decided I wasn't enough of a minority to qualify for affirmative action because they already had two white women on their faculty of seven.

Whenever I interview for an academic position, I make it clear that I want to be considered solely on merit. If I sense that it's an affirmative action hire, I don't apply. And yet, I know my department was thrilled to hire me, in part, because there was only one other woman in the department. This brings up an important point in the affirmative action arena: How can anyone know how much of a factor race or gender is, or has been, in the hiring process? Hiring is such an intricate process, and so many factors enter into a hiring decision, that it may not be possible to ever know those things.

That's why affirmative action was so important in the early decades of the civil rights era. The example I give my students is this: Put yourself in the place of an African American man in 1967 in Montgomery, Alabama. There is a vacancy at a department store downtown, a store that just a few years ago would not even allow you through the front door. You get dressed in your best suit, bring your excellent references with you, and apply for the job. The personnel manager grew up in an era when blacks and whites never did anything, work or play, side-by-side. She looks briefly at your résumé, asks you to leave your references, and promises to get back to you soon. Weeks go by. Finally, a friend tells you that a white man got the job. What will be the first thought that enters your mind?

The fact is, many people of color assume racism is alive and well in corporate America, but can't prove it in a court of law. It is this distrust, born of the legacy of hundreds of years of cruel injustice, that motivates African Americans, in particular, to defend affirmative action.

The readings in this section go far beyond the surface arguments about affirmative action, and invite you to think about different ways affirmative action has been used. A good social scientist will want to look at the ways affirmative action affects society in different settings. Is affirmative action in school admissions more or less important than affirmative action in hiring practices? Can affirmative action be defended as good for the society as a whole, even if it discriminates against specific individuals? Is affirmative action doing more harm than good to race relations, especially considering that the chief beneficiaries of affirmative action have been white women? What does the Supreme Court have to say, based on the Fourteenth Amendment, which promises "equal protection of the laws" to everyone?

We must trust each other to talk about this issue in our classrooms. If we assume that anyone who is against affirmative action is sexist or racist, then we can't have any real discussion. If we assume that anyone who defends affirmative action does so for selfish reasons, then we can't have any real discussion. And without discussion, I don't think we can reason our way through to the truth. What do you think?

Is Affirmative Action on the Way Out? Should It Be? A Symposium
James Q. Wilson

Opponents of affirmative action wish to describe the program as one of racial preferences that are not only disliked by the public but unethical and illegal as well. Supporters of affirmative action want to describe it not as preferences but as an effort to produce a more just society by giving a boost to people once victimized by discrimination. The public supports that, and many find it ethical and legal.

In one sense both views are correct. We do not care if the National Basketball Association is composed disproportionately of black players, if the doctors who delivered the septuplets in Iowa were black women, or if most naval aviators are white men. But many people do care if television commercials feature only white actors in a multi-ethnic nation, if an all-white (or all-Yankee) police department tries to serve a city that is mostly black (or mostly Irish), or if Tammany Hall offers only Italian candidates to the diverse voters of New York.

We judge these cases differently because in some organizations we think excellence at a specific task is the sole or dominant criterion for office, but in other organizations we think that some combination of excellence and social representation is important. We cannot say that we must never take race into account any more than we can say that we must always take it into account. We never or almost never take it into account in constituting organizations based on excellence (hiring NBA players or choosing violinists for a symphony orchestra); we sometimes take it into account in employing people in organizations whose functions combine excellence and representation (choosing people to run a charitable organization or to staff a police department); and we usually take it into account

in organizations where representation is the central function (making a television commercial or selecting candidates for an electoral ticket).

Unfortunately, few people make these distinctions. Some activists attack medical schools for not admitting "enough" blacks or Hispanics, even though few, if any, patients want to be operated on by anyone but the most talented surgeons. The federal government has insisted that a certain percentage of government contracts go to minority- or female-headed firms when the users of whatever is built do not know who built it, caring only about how well it was built. Admissions officers at selective public universities have created preferences for blacks by radically skewing the racial dimension of admission decisions, and have then sat idly by while many of these racial admittees have gotten low grades or dropped out of school.

By the same token, critics of preferences often do not state carefully how far their desire to ban them should extend. Can race be used by tax-supported colleges that are traditionally black? Can sex be used by tax-supported schools that are traditionally female? If the answers to these questions differ, why are race and sex dissimilar as selection criteria? Should we allow police chiefs to recruit blacks (or Asians, or Latinos) in greater proportion than their standing on some objective test would allow?

To me, police departments are an interesting case because they straddle the boundary between public agencies dominated by excellence and public agencies that require representation. Government in the United States does not—cannot—clearly distinguish between its elective, policy-making role and its appointed, policy-implementing role. The government is in part legitimate if it appears to its citizens to embody people with whom they can identify. But agencies differ in the extent to which the representational function is important. Nobody much cares who works for the Treasury Department, but a lot of people care who works for a police department and perhaps other agencies as well.

When I say they care, I am not suggesting that there is a black or a white (or Caucasian or Asian, or male or female) way to put out fires, issue traffic tickets, intervene in family quarrels, or enforce welfare laws. I only mean that people viewing the entirety of an agency that serves the public in a personal and important way want to feel comfortable that significant parts of the community that is served participate in that agency. Public service in this country has always been part of our political allegiance. In Boston the Irish were irritated by an all-Yankee police force; later, a nearly all-Irish Boston police department created concerns among Italians, and then among blacks.

Some forms of government hiring must be shaped in part by a desire to ensure that the public-serving part of the bureaucracy, as viewed by its citizens, serves, within limits, a reasonable representative function. A police department is an especially important case, because its officers embody the state; that is, they have a monopoly on the legitimate use of force. An agency that can arrest or even shoot people must represent the community to a greater degree than one that delivers the mail or saves homes from burning down.

Dealing with the representational aspect of policing would not be a problem if every department were equally willing to hire the best-qualified person regardless of racial identity and if all racial or ethnic groups were equally prepared to apply for departmental service. But the willingness to hire is constrained by the existing ethnic make-up of an agency, and preparation for admission is not equally distributed across racial groups. The members of some groups do less well than others on the kinds of tests (for example, of intelligence) and on their past histories

(for example, earlier convictions for minor crimes) than do the members of other groups.

Hence, at the outset, an agency must be nudged and some preferences must be given. Drawing the line between tipping the scale in favor of some members of underrepresented groups and still maintaining high standards is a difficult business—so difficult, in fact, that many police departments have tended to go to one extreme or the other.

The defenders of affirmative action recognize few bounds for their ambitions; they count numbers, and want quotas. The worst imaginable case is Washington, D.C., a city whose sorry police department was bitterly sketched by Carl T. Rowan, Jr., in a recent issue of the *New Republic*. On the other side, the opponents of such policies prefer that numbers be ignored and that only merit count, even though the public describes merit more broadly than simply having police skills. Not surprisingly, departments torn between these two kinds of pressures often resist any change until a court forces it, and then they embrace change beyond reason.

The case for some degree of representation in public-college admissions is much weaker than it is for police departments, since college professors neither arrest nor shoot us. Nor is race, taken alone, a very good guide to such representation as might be required. Helping blacks who do not measure up on tests often means helping those from middle-class families while ignoring whites from poor ones or Vietnamese who just climbed off the boat from Hanoi. I would support giving some preference to persons who have suffered personal disadvantage (for example, if they come from families that are recent immigrants or have low incomes) when they apply for admission to tax-supported universities, and I would do this even if the beneficiaries were (for example) blacks or Hispanics. The combined predictive power of SAT scores and high-school grades is significant, but not so great that we can be certain these criteria will identify all of the people who should be given a chance.

In the White House meeting between Bill Clinton and opponents of racial preferences, the President got this issue wrong. If we give preferences to athletes, he said, why not to blacks? There are two responses to this. First, athletic ability represents a personal achievement that, though different from doing well on the SAT, is like it in requiring native ability, arduous training, and personal effort. Second, the Supreme Court has held that race is a "suspect classification." Since it is, any program that uses a racial classification is subject to "strict scrutiny." The Court has issued a variety of opinions as to whether the use of race in an affirmative-action case would pass this strict-scrutiny test, sometimes saying yes and sometimes saying no, but since 1954 it has not wavered from the view that any racial classification is suspect and will be given a close look.

In taking this approach, the Court has given practical effect to what somebody said on another occasion: we did not fight the Civil War to make sure the University of Mississippi would admit good quarterbacks, we fought it to make certain it would admit blacks. To say that racial and athletic classifications are similar or that one can reason from the latter to the former is foolish. No court has ever held, or is likely to hold, that being able to throw a football 60 yards (or to have a father who gave the school a million dollars) places you in a class whose rights are protected by the barrier of strict scrutiny. Of course, one could argue for making both race and athleticism, the same, by getting the Court to say that race is no longer a suspect classification. But that would mean reversing 40 years of desegregation.

The case for some degree of representation in law, medical, and other graduate programs is weaker yet; indeed, to me, nonexistent. We recognize the greater emphasis on excellence as opposed to representation in graduate schools by not having a law-school band or a medical-school football team. And yet racial overrepresentation (that is, representation beyond what would be predicted from undergraduate grades and standardized tests) has been quite strong in graduate schools. Some people may say that doctors and lawyers play an important representational function, akin to that of elective officials or police officers, but I know of no evidence for that claim.

I have made all of these argument before, but to no avail. I should have recalled what I learned as a student of bureaucracy. No one should expect public agencies to make subtle distinctions of the sort I have been discussing or to be candid about the distinctions they do make.

Because I know how agencies operate, I supported Proposition 209 in California. In an ideal world, I would wish it had not been necessary. I would prefer giving police chiefs and welfare administrators (and perhaps even college administrators) a bit more flexibility. But we do not live in an ideal world; we live in one where, from time to time, secretive bureaucrats have to be given a sharp rap on the knuckles.

Is Affirmative Action on the Way Out? Should It Be? A Symposium
Glenn C. Loury

I have been criticizing affirmative-action policies for over fifteen years, in congressional testimony, in popular and scholarly articles, and in lectures nationwide. I was among the first to stress how the use of racial preferences sheltered blacks from the challenge of competing in our society on their merits. And I argued strenuously against the inclination of blacks to see affirmative action as a totem—a policy assumed to lie beyond the bounds of legitimate criticism, symbolizing the nation's commitment to "do the right thing" for black people. In short, I sought to expose the fact that the practice of affirmative action had been corrupted, to the detriment of those it was intended to help.

In the wake of a successful ballot initiative banning affirmative action in the state of California, I now find it necessary to reiterate the old, and in my view still valid, arguments on behalf of explicit public efforts to reduce racial inequality. In doing so, I offer no brief for the status quo. I am not defending racial quotas, or race-based allocations of public contracts, or racial double standards in the workplace, or huge disparities in the test scores of blacks and whites admitted to elite universities. These corrupt practices are deservedly under attack and should be curtailed. But I do defend the U.S. Army's programs to commission more black officers, the public funding of efforts to bring blacks into science and engineering, the attempts by urban law-enforcement agencies to recruit black personnel, and the goal of public universities to retain some racial diversity in their student bodies. The mere fact that these efforts take race into account should not, in my view, be disqualifying.

The current campaign against "preferences" goes too far by turning what, prior to Proposi-

tion 209, had been a reform movement into an abolitionist's crusade. True enough, the slogan "mend it, don't end it" was a cynical device, used by a President heavily dependent on black political support and seeking to avoid genuine reform. But taken seriously, the slogan describes pretty well what our national policy should be. That is, it is unjust discrimination for a wealthy person, on racial grounds alone, to win a public-works contract without having submitted the lowest bid. But if a state university seeks to recruit a modest proportion (say, 5 percent) of its entering class from the public and parochial schools in a nearby big city, intending thereby to admit more black students, no comparable injustice has occurred.

Proponents of color-blind policy must disagree with this, for their fundamental principle is that knowing the race of the persons burdened or benefited by a public action can never legitimately influence the desirability of that action. Indeed, they are hostile to the very idea of governmental racial classifications. And it is true that the Supreme Court has determined that racial classifications should receive heightened legal scrutiny.

But our moral queasiness about the use of race arises for historically specific reasons—namely, slavery and Jim Crow segregation. Those reasons centrally involved the caste-like subordination of blacks, a matter that, needless to say, was not symmetrical as between the races. Therefore, to take account of race while trying to mitigate the effects of this subordination, though perhaps ill-advised or unworkable in specific cases, should not be viewed as morally equivalent to the acts of discrimination that effected the subjugation of blacks in the first place.

It is important to distinguish here between legal and ethical modes of reasoning. I stipulate that an isolated individual's race, as such, is ethically irrelevant. That is, the weight given to an affected person's welfare when selecting a course of public action should not depend on race. Nevertheless, there are circumstances where the ability of a public policy to advance the general interest of all persons is enhanced by taking cognizance of the racial identities of particular persons. Under these circumstances, the steadfast refusal, in the name of legal consistency, to take into account the impact that a policy might have on the members of different racial groups can turn out to be an act of moral obtuseness.

To illustrate, consider the case I have made elsewhere ("How to Mend Affirmative Action," *The Public Interest,* Spring 1997) for "developmental affirmative action." I argue that the public goal of raising the competitive abilities of disadvantaged blacks can be appropriate, even though it is formulated in racial terms. This is because the effects of past racial oppression and, critically, of ongoing social segregation along race lines have been to leave many black families and communities relatively less well-endowed with the cultural and financial resources on which young people depend to acquire their skills.

"Merit" is not just something people are born with; it is the product of social processes that, because of our history and the ways we choose to associate with one another, have a racial dimension. Social policy should attend to racial inequality if the consequence of historical discrimination against blacks is not to be a permanent economic disparity. For these reasons, I suggest that racially targeted recruitment and training efforts in the workplace, and a willingness to experiment with unconventional selection methods in colleges and universities so as to find and develop the talents of black students, are legitimate undertakings.

Of course, the goal of reducing historic economic backwardness among blacks can also be pursued by policies that are race-neutral. But if a strict legal rule of nondiscrimination is to be symmetrically applied, then even race-neutral policies must be rejected if they are introduced with the intent of benefiting blacks. In Texas, the state legislature responded to the *Hopwood* ruling (forbidding the practice of affirmative action in college admissions) by passing a novel law. Texas now guarantees admission to any public university in the state to any high-school student finishing in the top 10 percent of his [or her] graduating class. This law is intended to benefit students with low SAT scores but good grades at less-than-competitive high schools—students who are disproportionately black and Hispanic. Yet if the explicit use of race in college admissions is an impermissible discrimination, then surely the intentional use of a proxy for race in order to reach a similar result should also be forbidden. The problem here is with the legal rule, not with the values of the Texas state legislature.

There is nothing in the sorry history of affirmative-action abuses that requires us to tie our hands with such color-blind formalism. Consider the common-sense observation that, in this country, an army where blacks are one-third of the enlisted personnel but only 3 percent of the officer corps is likely to function poorly. The U.S. Army cares about the number of black captains because it needs to sustain effective cooperation among its personnel across racial lines. That the racial identities of captains and corporals sometimes matter to the smooth functioning of a military institution is a deep fact about our society, one that cannot be wished away.

Now, monitoring the number of blacks promoted to the rank of captain, and formulating policies to increase that number, are activities that inherently involve taking account of some individual's race. Yet, depending on how they are undertaken, such activities need not entail the promulgation of racial double standards, nor need they seem to declare, as a matter of official policy, that racial identity is a determinant of an individual's moral worth. As the military sociologist Charles Moskos is fond of pointing out, the Army is the only place in American society where large numbers of whites routinely take orders from blacks. Ironically, the irrelevance of race to a person's moral worth may be more evident to the members of this institution than to some others precisely because the government has taken race into account in the conduct of its military personnel policies.

The color-blind principle, while consistent as a self-contained legal rule, is in my opinion neither morally nor politically coherent. For instance, it would seem to be an implication of this principle that we should discontinue all racial classifications associated with the collection of statistics by government agencies. Yet monitoring the racial dimension of social and economic trends is obviously a vital public function. These data are the sole source of our knowledge that discrimination has declined over the years, a key aspect of the case for reforming the practice of affirmative action. Without the data, the vast overrepresentation of blacks among imprisoned felons in this country could not be rationalized in such a way as to refute the charge of systematic racism in the administration of criminal justice. This illustrates how, despite the moral irrelevance of race at the individual level, there remains operational need to attend to racial disparity in the conduct of our public affairs.

The problem of enforcing anti-discrimination laws can even be used to illustrate the limits of the color-blind principle. Consider the targeted recruitment-and-outreach policies reflected in the familiar phrase from employment solicitations: "Please alert us to any qualified minority candidates." Both public and private employers engage in this practice because, among other reasons, they can better defend themselves against discrimination lawsuits should statistical disparities be invoked against them.

Thus, where the laws against discrimination are being enforced, one will find vigorous efforts being undertaken by employers to hire qualified members of racial minority groups. But such efforts are themselves inconsistent with the color-blind principle, even if no racial preference is given at the point of hiring. The laws of supply and demand ensure that when employers try especially hard to recruit qualified blacks, those blacks will enjoy more job offers, better market opportunities, and higher wages than their equally qualified white counterparts. So racially targeted recruitment involves racial discrimination, because it guarantees a labor-market environment in which the targeted group receives more favorable treatment. Color-blind employment policy, if faithfully and uniformly pursued, must mean the abolition of racial representation as a goal.

This shows the confusion of those color-blind advocates who offer the criminalization of employment discrimination as a *quid pro quo* for the abolition of affirmative action. Jailing employers for not finding enough black workers would only lead to a dramatic increase in the amount of covert reverse discrimination against white job-seekers. Indeed, since all anti-discrimination enforcement requires classifying, monitoring, and counting employees by race, the only fully consistent color-blind position is to advocate the repeal of the Civil Rights Act of 1964.

I respect the intellectual consistency, but doubt the moral and political probity, of those critics of affirmative action, like Richard Epstein of the University of Chicago law school, who advocate this course. That so few of the most stringent critics of racial preferences are willing to go this far reveals the continued salience of our peculiar, and asymmetric, racial history.

The "Talented Tenth" in Texas
William E. Forbath and Gerald Torres

The death of affirmative action in higher education here in Texas has occasioned a remarkable experiment—one that may, in the end, bring more black and Latino undergraduates to the University of Texas than ever before. Put forward by Latino and black lawmakers, the reform is a response to the far-reaching federal appeals court decision in *Hopwood* v. *Texas* in March 1996, which barred the University of Texas from considering race or ethnicity in its admissions system.

The new law, dubbed the "10 percent plan," entitles the top 10 percent of each high school graduating class to attend the University of Texas, Austin, the university's flagship campus, or any other state campus. "Texas is deeply segregated, regionally and neighborhood-by-neighborhood in its major cities," explains U.T. history professor David Montejano. "So the majority of our high schools are almost entirely white or black or brown. This law is color-blind, but it uses our bitter history of segregation to promote diversity. At the same time, it addresses the broader inequities that lead U.T. Austin to see few of the brightest kids of any color from the state's poorer counties."

Liberals and progressives have warned that the end of affirmative action would reinforce the elitist character of highly competitive public research universities like U.T. Austin. Instead, the end of affirmative action may erode that elitism, in ways that many of the liberals and progressives who call these universities home could find discomforting. We have grown accustomed to the melding of exclusivity and inclusivity embodied by affirmative action and conventional, highly competitive college admissions standards, although this system often chooses middle-class minorities (especially African-Americans,

Reprinted with permission from *The Nation*, December 15, 1997, 20–22, 24. © 1997.

less so Latinos) and relatively affluent white students as well. *Hopwood* forced champions of diversity to take account of broader inequities; ironically, this brought to light new chinks in the conservative case against affirmative action.

Texas has a Republican governor, George W. Bush; the G.O.P. also holds sway in the State Senate. Yet the state's enactment of the 10 percent plan may help save diversity in the face of *Hopwood*'s ban on affirmative action. The bill's sponsors made its purpose plain, so why did conservative lawmakers vote for it? Logrolling is part of the answer, but the plan also appeals to deeply held conservative and populist values.

Those who oppose affirmative action in favor of "merit based" admissions to higher education champion a system that relies heavily on SATs, LSATs, and their kin—all administered by the powerful Educational Testing Services of Princeton, New Jersey. Yet even their creators concede that SATs really measure what a student has learned far more than his or her "aptitude" for learning; and even if the SATs' predictive powers are as great as proponents claim, the tests seem invidious because how students fare correlates so strongly with their class background. The E.T.S., moreover, is just the kind of centralized social bureaucracy that conservatives, in most contexts, love to hate.

All this was in play at the Statehouse. One of the 10 percent plan's Latino supporters put it this way: "Imagine a boy from [poor and predominantly white] (authors' brackets) Levelland. He puts his shoulder to the wheel and works hard, listens to his teachers, and graduates first in his class. Why should some bureaucrats in Princeton, New Jersey, be able to tell him he's not good enough to go to the University of Texas?"

The 10 percent plan puts test scores to one side, but unlike affirmative action, it does so for everyone, and it does so in the name of a standard of merit even more deeply rooted than the

SATs: working hard, getting good grades and doing very well what's expected of you. For high school teachers in gritty towns like Levelland, in mostly black inner cities and in the state's solidly Latino border counties, the 10 percent plan provides a powerful new incentive to students whose horizons have been unfairly narrowed by class: Work hard and you can go to U.T.

Many of the students graduating in the top 10 percent of the state's poorer high schools will prove unready for U.T. The legislation allows U.T. to require summerlong remedial programs, but these may prove insufficient, and many may flunk out or never even enter the flagship campus. Many others may attend less expensive local community colleges or traditional black or Mexican-American campuses, like Prairie View A&M and U.T. Pan American.

If the number of black and Mexican-American undergraduates at U.T. Austin dwindles sharply despite the 10 percent plan, that may help spur the recruitment and private scholarship fundraising efforts already under way. It may even help muster the political will for broader initiatives to remedy the state's appalling inequities and underfunding of public school education.

Then, too, if minority enrollment plummets it may sour minority lawmakers on U.T. Austin. In the wake of *Hopwood* and the steeply declining minority enrollments it has caused at the university's law school, some are already asking why state money should support "elitist" institutions with no place for the children of the state's growing number of minority citizens. "If U.T. [Austin] (authors' brackets) becomes all white," one widely respected black senator from Houston has declared, "that won't reflect the face of Texas, and we ought to send the money where the people are."

One of our African-American colleagues demurs. "U.T. Austin is a first-rate university that trains the state's future leaders and professionals. It's a great public asset. For kids from inner cities, rural Texas and border counties who can cut it here, it's like coming to Athens. The end of affirmative action is going to whiten the place a lot, and that's tragic. But the answer is not giving U.T. Austin's money to other U.T. campuses or making U.T. Austin indistinguishable from them by diluting academic standards."

Affirmative action, our colleague goes on, "was always racial justice on the cheap, and for the middle class. It didn't mend the inner city or the horrible state of schools there. But it did get the best and brightest black students into elite universities. The 10 percent plan wants it both ways. It reaches more kids who are 'truly disadvantaged,' but with too little, too late. It's not even genuinely skimming the cream, because even kids in the top 10 percent of high schools in places like Houston's [predominantly black] (authors' brackets) 5th Ward—most of them, I mean—are going to lack the money or the incredible gumption to come, or are going to flunk out." Meanwhile, many minority students "with the best preparation are going to be excluded."

It's true that the 10 percent plan won't reach many well-prepared middle-class African-American students—at least those who go to well-funded and racially integrated high schools, where they may not graduate in the class's top 10 percent but still may be equipped for U.T. Austin. But many middle-class African-Americans also attend largely segregated high schools; an ironic dividend of residential segregation will be that many of the most hard-working and gifted of them will be admitted.

Moreover, some evidence counts against any grim certainty that the top 10 percent of students from the state's poorest high schools will flounder at U.T. During the early eighties, U.T. admitted a portion of each freshman class on a top 10 percent basis. According to admissions officials, each year about forty to fifty of those students had combined SATs below 800. By standard criteria, these students were the worst-prepared and most likely to flunk out. Yet most of them earned grades only slightly below the average of their entire class. As one admissions officer observed about these numbers, "The top 10 percent criterion does pick out students with grit and ambition."

The grit factor is part of the populist wager, and even skeptics must remember that with affirmative action outlawed, the alternative to the 10 percent plan might be to reach almost no black students at all. Consider U.T.'s law school, whose affirmative action program *Hopwood* struck down. Unlike undergraduate admissions, in the law school context restoring racial diversity with a color-blind program like the 10 percent plan seems virtually impossible. Thus, as a result of *Hopwood,* this fall's entering law school class includes only four African-Americans; last year's entering class (pre-*Hopwood*) had thirty-one.

The fall-off in Mexican-American students admitted to the law school has not been so sharp. This year's class has twenty-six, last year's had forty-two; and a modest commitment to admit more students from geographically underrepresented parts of the state may restore the balance. U.T. Austin's law school is a public law school with a mandate to educate state citizens for the bar. We are obliged to admit 80 percent of our entering class from Texas, and most of the law school's Latino students have come from South Texas. Without them that region would be more sorely underrepresented. Most of the school's African-American students, by contrast, have come from out of state.

In the face of *Hopwood* and California's "Civil Rights Initiative," which also outlawed racial preferences, Richard Kahlenberg (in his widely acclaimed book *The Remedy*) and others have proposed using class-based criteria— income levels, parents' education, etc.—to give disadvantaged candidates a leg up in applying to elite public institutions like U.T. and the University of California. Kahlenberg has argued

that the overlapping injuries of race and class insure that class-based affirmative action will disproportionately benefit black applicants and accomplish most of what race-based affirmative action achieved in its heyday.

But reality is not so obligingly progressive. The U.C.L.A. School of Law tried out class-based affirmative action this admissions season. Its experience suggests that in law school admissions, with large and highly competitive applicant pools, class-based affirmative action yields precious little racial diversity because it doesn't sort out the unique disadvantages tied to race. A few years before *Brown,* U.T. Austin School of Law prompted *Sweatt* v. *Painter,* which declared segregated legal education unconstitutional. In light of our caste-ridden history, the significance of race-based affirmative action is distinct and irreplaceable.

If class-based affirmative action seems unlikely to restore racial diversity at U.T.'s law school, the solution for the University of California's undergraduate institutions may not be imitating the 10 percent plan. California, we are told, is not so pervasively segregated. Perhaps only Texas's history and geography enabled the 10 percent plan to prevail and begin a process of trying to restore diversity on a new footing. In California, as in Texas, proponents of diversity must press for broad improvements and better funding for public education. But saving diversity at U.C. will still entail rebuilding support for some race-conscious measures.

The 10 percent plan is bound to be challenged in federal court. If it is, challengers will rely on *Hopwood* and its "color blind" reading of civil rights–era Supreme Court precedents. These precedents say that states cannot pass laws that use racial categories; nor can they pass racially neutral laws that have a racial impact if that impact is the very purpose of the law. An example often used is a hiring test adopted by a state agency because blacks were known or thought to fail the test frequently. Neutral on the face of it, the action was racially motivated and, therefore, unconstitutional. Of course, a state could adopt such tests for other, legitimate reasons. It could even do so knowing the tests would have a disparate impact on blacks as long as it did so in spite of and not because of that impact.

It's easy to see how such precedents could apply here. The Texas legislators knew the 10 percent plan would change the post-*Hopwood* racial composition of entering classes and the measure was before them for that very reason. Imagine if they adopted a plan and instead of increasing minority enrollment, the sponsors' announced aim was to diminish it, to restore a "strong white presence." If you think that would be unconstitutional, then a "color blind" reading of the precedents, following *Hopwood*, suggests the 10 percent plan is too. Or so plaintiffs would argue—but most likely, they would lose. Sound distinctions can be drawn between *Hopwood* and this case. Supreme Court Justice Antonin Scalia, for example, loathes looking beyond the actual language of statutes to divine a legislature's purposes; here, there is no racial categorizing, and geographic diversity is a legitimate purpose.

Beyond that, however, the broad support the law enjoyed in a conservative legislature may give pause even to the doctrinaire court that decided *Hopwood*, to say nothing of the federal circuit courts that have not yet confronted the question. That support embodies broad agreement—what John Rawls calls an "overlapping consensus"—that many important interests and ideals are served by keeping black and Latino students at great public universities and elite training grounds like U.T. and U.C. Insofar as this can be accomplished in a color-blind fashion, that's best; otherwise, the color-blind principle must accommodate other values, and a pragmatic balance must be struck. *Hopwood*'s unbending rule, its contempt for history and the real-world differences between Jim Crow and affirmative action, have no place in this difficult equation.

U.T.'s law school cannot resume affirmative action unless and until the Supreme Court undoes *Hopwood*. In the meantime, however, the Texas Constitution speaks to how the state's lawmakers ought to carry on with the 10 percent plan. That Constitution requires that the state support a "university of the first class"; it also mandates substantial equality of educational opportunity. If lawmakers defunded U.T., they'd be shirking the first obligation. But U.T. must serve the whole state; and so it cannot rest on the ruins of public education in general. That is what the second obligation entails, a system of public education that offers all citizens a real opportunity for a first-class education. A populism that settles for less is selling "the people" short.

FACE TO FACE

Student Interview with
Vincent Harding
Civil Rights Leader

Andy
a moderate

Laura
a conservative
Republican

Sarah
a Native American,
liberal Democrat

Steve
a Libertarian

What's It Like to Be a Civil Rights Activist?
★ ★ ★

Professor Vincent Harding—activist, friend, and comrade of Dr. Martin Luther King Jr. in the civil rights movement, adviser to the PBS series Eyes on the Prize, *author of* There Is a River *and* Hope and History—*now teaches at the Iliff School of Theology in Denver, Colorado.*

Laura: I'd like to ask how you became so involved? What led you to this point in your life?

Vincent Harding: I started to get involved a long time ago. My wife and I went south to participate in the civil rights movement in 1961. We had been married in 1960. She was a public school teacher, and I was working on my doctorate in history at the University of Chicago. I suspect that, in addition to some need to clarify the reality of being black people, our need to get involved was part of our religious commitment.

We were both members of the Mennonite Church, one of the "peace churches" at the time. We were both very much a part of the ethos of that church and of that peace movement; we wanted to focus on the need for racial justice and racial reconciliation. It seemed to us that, without ignoring the trouble at the University of Chicago where we were living, the major stage on which our national trouble was being acted out was the southern states. I'm not sure how much I was thinking about it in these categories at the time, but I certainly believe now that what we were involved in was not just a struggle for Negro rights, but for the expansion of democracy in America, and for a more perfect *union*.

Steve: Can you speak about what it was like to go from a culture like Chicago to race relations in the South—the noticeable differences and attitudes. Was it really completely different all of a sudden, or not as much as people might think?

Vincent Harding: You have to realize that Chicago was part of America, and there was no place in this country where race and racism and white supremacy were not issues. Simply, it was the very fundamental nature of the country. Malcolm X used to joke about it by saying the Mason-Dixon line was at the Canadian border. And other folks used to talk about *upsouth* and *downsouth*. So, there were differences, but there were also vast, and powerful, and troubling similarities.

Sarah: The civil rights movement seemed to be a real effort to bring white people and people of color together. We seem to have lost some of that spirit. What was it like, back at the beginning?

Vincent Harding: One of the ways in which people come together is through working together for something they mutually believe in; not having discussions about it, or conferences about coming together, but really working together. That is what happened in the South during the movement. One of the most exciting things about those days was to see southern white people and southern black people discover that they really belonged together. And then some went to jail together, some protected each other from death because they believed in this more perfect union. Now, after thirty or forty years have passed, these people who once came together, see each other, meet each other—it is like a family reunion. In spite of all the racial polarization around the country, these folks see each other and know that they are still deeply in love with each other because of all they have been through together.

Laura: Today, it seems like each group is only out for its own advantage. They want special privileges—very different from wanting to work together.

Vincent Harding: As you may have picked up from the segment of *Hope and History* that you've read, I am personally convinced that the whole idea of a civil rights movement is much too narrow a conception of what was going on. Because that leads to a *special interest* concept—what you're talking about. At our best, those who were involved in the movement were very serious about this idea of trying to create not "better things for colored folks," but a more perfect *union*. You see? A better *America*. Now, we assumed that there couldn't be a better America unless the needs of its poorest people, its most vulnerable people, were taken care of. But people weren't going around talking solely about what would be good for black people. Constantly the refrain was, "How can America really be America?" as in the Langston Hughes poem, "Let America Be America [Again]." So, part of the problem is that people are misreading what the movement was about. And for some people, I am afraid, it is almost a willful misreading.

If you say, "In the sixties, black people were out simply to get something for black people, and, especially, to get black people accepted into the middle class," then you can declare partial victory and go home. So, by the 1990s, you could say, "Okay, we got more black people living middle-class lives. Black people are in much better positions." Some black people are.

But if you take a much different position and say, "What people were struggling for in the 1960s was for the *expansion of democracy* in America," it's a whole different ball game, isn't it? Then, you see, that becomes an American task, not just for black people, or Chicanos, or whatever, it becomes the American task to get rid of racism. So, I don't buy the whole idea of *interest group politics* at the racial level. The only interest, at our best, that we were pursuing, was the interest of a new America—and a better America.

Laura: Throughout the nineties, what I've been hearing is the new, *politically correct* language—and I don't think that's going to help get rid of racism in this country. We have to be so careful these days not to offend, and I think it's driving us further apart. I guess I just wonder how you feel, because you don't use all the politically correct terms for race. You use the terms *black* or *colored,* not *African American*—and I guess I am wondering how you feel about the language shift that we've made?

Vincent Harding: Well, I feel a lot of things: The first thing I feel is that I want you to read the whole book, okay? And then you'll see what I do with language over two hundred pages, rather than just four or five. The second thing is that I am convinced that we can't be pushed apart unless we allow ourselves to be pushed apart. Which means, for me, many do not have the will to *resist* being pushed apart when political forces invite us to move away from each other.

If Sarah were your blood sister, you wouldn't let the language push you apart if you had grown to love each other. I think one of the problems is that we still have not learned how to be close enough so that we will want to stay together. We haven't really come together. That is our difficulty as a nation: that we don't yet know how to come together. When we really come together, it will be very hard for people to push us apart.

So, that is where I am pushing. I don't worry about anybody who can be pushed apart that easily by disagreements over what is politically correct. They weren't ever really together in the first place! I want to know how can we build that togetherness and then see what happens.

Andy: You talk in *Hope and History* about education and how it is presented and the hidden politics behind it all. How did it actually evolve in the South?

Vincent Harding: The southern system of *de jure segregation* was a powerful example of the connection between political ideas and educational practice. Those who were in charge of the system believed, many of them in their hearts, that black people were inferior to white people and that it would hurt their children to come into daily contact with black children. They therefore developed an educational system that kept white children and black children apart, and they had all kinds of legal justifications for it. And it is so important to remember that this system of segregation—which was fundamentally so evil and so flawed—in many parts of the country, but especially in the South, was legal. So, anybody who believes that whatever is legal is right should have some second thoughts.

It is also important to remember that those laws did not change because one day in 1954 Chief Justice Warren had a great vision and pulled his buddies together and said, "Don't you think it's time that education be in keeping with the Fourteenth Amendment to the Constitution? Let's write the *Brown* v. *Board of Education* decision!" It didn't happen that way. People had to push, had to sacrifice, had to say, "This is no good, we will not take this." These black parents, who saw their children being used by this educational system, had to stand up and say, "No!"

This taking a stand was one of the points at which the courts and political action came together. Because if you were living in South Carolina, which is where one of the first major cases came from that led to *Brown* v. *Board of Education,* you were living in the midst of a white-supremacist stronghold. If you were black, you didn't just go to court—"Well, tomorrow morning we will go to court!" You were *risking your life* to defy the law, and people had to do that. They had to decide whether it was worth that for their children, you see. And it was only as people made those decisions, very human, very risk-taking decisions, based on what they wanted for their children, that the courts were forced more and more to deal with segregation. But when, in 1954, the Court finally said, "Separate but equal is not constitutional and is not equal; we have to do something different," who was in charge of doing something different—desegregating the school systems? Do you know? The people who had operated the segregated school systems.

You then had a superintendent of schools who for 30 years had been running a segregated, now illegal, unconstitutional school system, and you were telling him, "Tomorrow has got to go another way—but you are still in charge." That's one of the reasons why, sometimes, if it looks as if a lot of things haven't changed, it's because a lot of people's minds haven't changed. Some are trying to figure out how to do what they did before, but do it legally, and do it without calling attention to themselves, and do it without getting the federal government involved.

Even a simple thing like the names you give to your schools sends a powerful educational message. What books you decide to use. Whether in 350 pages they have 3 paragraphs about Native Americans, 7 about African Americans, or more, or less. These are political questions. How do we decide who will be represented in the history textbooks? That's not simply an intellectual question or an educational question. That is fundamentally a deep question about your definition of *democracy.* Does democracy include all of the stories that are told?

Andy:	You just blew my mind away with the idea that because the same people who were running the schools before the *Brown* ruling continued to run them afterwards, not much actually changed. I think that is something I've never even considered before.
Vincent Harding:	Let me just complicate it a little more. After *Brown* v. *Board of Education*, what did the political system decide to do with these separate black and white schools? That was a powerful decision. *How* do you obey the law? Almost without exception, the political system obeyed the law by saying, "Oh, yes, of course, close the black schools. Put the black principal into a subservient role under some white principal someplace. Send the black superintendents someplace, but we are closing those segregated schools down because they're illegal now." Changing the law was a victory, but the way in which the people in charge decided to obey the law was a defeat.
Andy:	I really want to hear from you about some of your direct experiences in the sixties. What it was like?
Vincent Harding:	One of the interesting things was seeing how the dominant economic class of whites in the South dealt with the problem of civil rights. For instance, by the beginning of the sixties, in cities of the South, there was a merchant class that was feeling increasing tension with the old white-supremacist class. The merchant class was not made up of wonderful white, liberal integrationists. The merchant class was made up of people who were saying, "Listen, we are in favor of whatever is going to keep us making money. I am not going to put an ancient ritual of old-fashioned open segregation in the way of us growing and developing." So these people, in a whole variety of situations, became allies for certain kinds of change. If you owned a business in the city—
Andy:	—By merchants, you mean like gas station owners . . .
Vincent Harding:	No, no, larger than gas stations. Department store owners. Economic operators at the higher levels. We are not talking about small business people. If you owned a department store where the tradition was that black people didn't go to the lunch counter, and the black people determined that they would not be treated that way anymore, and their children would not be treated that way anymore, then the civil rights movement produced a moment of truth for these merchants. They saw that the day would come when the movement would organize a *sit-in* at their lunch counter. And all kinds of people who were not from the merchant class, but who were simply hot-heads, and rowdies, and white supremacists, would come in their store and beat those black people over the heads, and try to knock them down, knock them off their stools, and knock them out. Then policemen would have to come in the department store, and eventually federal government agents would have to come in there—you don't want *that*! You are a segregationist, but you are also a businessman whose bottom line is, how much profit do I make? So, what you are trying to figure out is

how to keep segregation going, but keep it quiet, calm it down some. You are not going to be able to go around with the white robes, in public, with signs that say, "This place is not for niggers." You can't do that anymore by the 1960s, partly because the new spirit was rising among the black people themselves, and partly for international reasons.

All over the world, your country is going around saying, "We are the leaders of the *free world!* And those Russian Communists, they are the leaders of the slave world." But the rest of the world sees people on your streets at home saying, "We are not free at all." And so more and more, even the president was saying, "Hey, listen, quiet that down. If you have to let them into your lunch counters, let them in. You don't have to love them, just let them in." Still no love—just let them in. This was the strange way in which the moneyed interests moved against the outwardly hard, racist interests, and said, "Cool it, please. We want our town to have a nice reputation so that we can have more jobs for your children. Let us handle these Negroes in a different way, not the old way." Remember. The slogan in Atlanta became, "Atlanta: The City Too Busy to Hate." And in some places that worked, and in some places that didn't work, and in some places the outright segregationists said, "No, we want to use our fists and our guns."

And so, you had struggles within the white community itself. Those are some of the stories that also need to be known. And they bring us back to Laura's question, because what happened in a lot of these places was that people began to come together because the government told them to. And that led people to do something that was very difficult: to come closer to each other without having regard for each other. Those working for democracy then asked, "What can we do to bring people together in a different spirit?"

Steve: All of my life I have heard about the sit-ins and the freedom rides, and I'd just like to ask, what was different about it from what we read in the textbooks? If you could pick a particular experience and perhaps tell us what it was like— the atmosphere, actually being there—what was memorable for you?

Vincent Harding: One time in Albany, Georgia, Martin Luther King had a federal injunction placed on him against leading any kind of protest activity. And he had to figure out whether he was going to obey the federal injunction or not. He and his advisers decided that since we were depending on the federal government then, as a kind of an ally, that at least in that situation, we probably ought to obey the injunction.

King had made the decision just that afternoon. Then something happened. A woman who was important in the movement—the wife of the assistant or leader of the local movement—had been kicked and knocked down by a policeman while she was visiting someone in jail. She was pregnant herself and eventually lost the child. But, that day, people were very, very angry. The demonstration that King had canceled had been planned for the next day. But people were just so upset and angry about the attack that it was clear there was a need for them to have an opportunity to express some kind of concern that evening—and Martin asked me if I would lead the demonstration to what was the combination jail and city hall.

It was a very scary sort of situation because by this time they had brought in state troopers to assist their local police. I remember it rather vividly. I think that by that time I had spent enough time around a jail, visiting Dr. King and visiting other people, that I knew the chief of police knew who I was. My role was a kind of negotiator for the movement, so the likelihood was that nothing was going to happen to me. But it was still a very exciting night, sort of scary, especially to be out there at night time when there were no cameras or anything around. Because those cameras helped protect you in those kinds of situations.

I remember thinking in jail about how I had almost not gone through with that demonstration. When we stopped a few, oh, maybe, 10 or 15 yards from the door of the city hall, I just sat there trying to figure out if I really wanted to do this. And one of the younger people was sitting next to me and she said, "Oh, Vincent isn't nobody going to get out and do it?" And so I said, "Yes, we are going to do it." We had a prayer vigil over there, and we were arrested and put in jail. It was a good experience.

Andy: That reminds me of a confession I have to make. I managed to do an internship in Congresswoman Diana DeGette's office. I don't know if you know Selena Dunham.

Vincent Harding: No.

Andy: She's the deputy director at DeGette's office and the liaison to the African American community. A great person. And she gave me an opportunity to go to my first African American bookstore for an event. As an intern, my job was to set up chairs, greet people, and all of that. And I had never been anywhere in north Denver—to Five Points—the "scary part" of Denver for white folks. And I was a little upset and a little worried about what I might find after all the stories I'd heard. And I wound up having the best time there! It was one of the neatest little bookstores, and the talks were about how to secure federal funding for that area—for urban renewal. As much as we talk about diversity, I had never been in a completely African American neighborhood before, and it surprised me that I had been worried about it.

Vincent Harding: I'd like to speak to you about the temptation you must have felt to sort of kick yourself for feeling worried about going into that area. In our society, we are *trained* not to be together, but to be apart. Therefore, it is absolutely understandable and expected that if we are put in a situation that we are trained to stay out from, that we are going to be scared.

The deeper question is, will we live with that, or will we recognize that there is something less than human about being scared to go into another part of the human community? And will we try to retrain ourselves and, especially, train and develop our children so that they are not continuing to re-enact all of this terrible separation that we live with in this society that leads to those kinds of feelings and thoughts? So, I'm glad you found your way to our black bookstore.

Steve: I have another question for you. The civil rights movement was largely known for being nonviolent. How did you and Dr. Martin Luther King view Malcolm X and the Nation of Islam in the North?

Vincent Harding: I think that one of the important things to keep in mind, comparing the Nation of Islam to the Southern Christian Leadership Conference, is that Malcolm X was deeply ambivalent about his movement, the Nation of Islam. He knew that his leader, the Honorable Elijah Mohammed, was almost never prepared to put his people on the line the way King was prepared to be on the line and to call others to be on the line. So, these were different kinds of spirits, really. The Nation of Islam had a much more interior kind of focus on cleaning up oneself. Their focus said, "Why go to white people if they don't want you?" Like many, many black people who would call themselves *Black Nationalists,* the Nation of Islam really went along with the idea that this was a white man's country. They wanted to separate and have their own nation.

But Martin Luther King said that this country belongs to whoever will work to change it, so we will *not* give it over and say, "This is a white people's country." King believed that we all have to change, and we all have to change each other, and we have got to change the country, and so the country belongs to us.

King was very open as a human being, and one of the best terms that you could use for him was that he had a generous spirit. And that spirit was there in his relation with the Nation of Islam, and certainly with Malcolm. The two of them did not really get to know each other, but he loved Malcolm. He liked his spirit; he liked his spunk; he liked the fact that he was willing to stand up and speak honestly. Martin disagreed with a lot that Malcolm said, but never would he allow himself to be in a situation where he might discredit or publicly criticize Malcolm. King really was a *mobilizer* of American commitment to change, and, in a sense, he was willing to put his arms around everybody who was working for change in society

They died three years apart, but by the ends of their lives, both of them were deeply involved in trying to figure out, "What is the future of poor people in this country? What do we do about the state of the poor?" Malcolm worried especially about the black poor but, certainly by the end of his life, was not limited to that. And King, as you know, was deeply involved in trying to bring all poor people together—from Native Americans, to Appalachian poor whites, to Chicanos. And I suspect—I know—that Malcolm was coming closer and closer to trying to work out some kind of connection with the southern movement and with King. One of the last trips he made, before he was shot, was to come down to Selma, Alabama, and speak for the Student Nonviolent Coordinating Committee down there. For both of them I think, the question became not, How do we differ from each other in our points of view? but, Where is our *common ground?*

★ ★ ★

Andy
a moderate

Laura
a conservative
Republican

Sarah
a Native American,
liberal Democrat

Steve
a Libertarian

New Ways to Think About an Old Problem
★ ★ ★

Dr. Bauer: Let's turn to the article by James Q. Wilson, past president of the American Political Science Association and a well-known political theorist and philosopher. He has an interesting view of affirmative action that is different from just about everyone else's. Wilson says perhaps we have been thinking about this whole question in the wrong way. Instead of an all-or-nothing attack or defense of affirmative action, we should perhaps think of using affirmative action in targeted areas that would benefit society as a whole. In other areas, affirmative action might be more harmful to society. Wilson talks about the quality of excellence benefiting the whole society—a quality that we wouldn't want to lose to a rigid application of affirmative action. And what example does he use?

Steve: The NBA. This kind of example really lays bare the issues behind affirmative action for me. No one in their right mind wants to put a racial quota of white players on the NBA. What we look for is excellence, and if a merit-based system produces teams on which there are more blacks than whites, then clearly, we are more interested in skills and excellence than we are in skin color. Who wants to argue that excellence is not a good thing? Who wants to say that we don't want excellence in our doctors, lawyers, the people who teach us in college, and those who will teach our children?

But in other areas, we may want to pay attention to racial balance. Wilson uses the police force as an example, and I know this for a fact: We have studies that show that communities respond better to a police force that reflects the ethnic mix of the community. So it makes sense if your city has 50 percent minorities to say, "Let's make sure that we have people of color on that police force." When you look at the interaction between communities and the police, race-based hiring makes sense. But if a doctor is performing surgery on you, that person should be there because of his or her excellence, not because they represent some part of the community.

Sarah: My point of view comes from being an American Indian. For a long time, decisions for American Indian people were made by non-Indian people. If the government thought something was best, it was done to us. Non-Indian lawyers represented Native Americans. From my experience, I have to say that it wasn't until American Indians started getting admitted to law schools, graduating, and representing our community, that we began to see some change. For the first time, we have Indians representing Indian people, and things are starting to happen. And this was a result of law school admissions.

I think the same thing can be said about medical doctors. There are people of different ethnic backgrounds that are a lot more comfortable with someone of their own background, because of the values or approach to medicine that they would take. So there's a need for doctors in those groups as well, right?

Laura: But don't those people also deserve to have the very best doctors?

Andy: I think that's Sarah's point. It's a subjective choice about who you would consider to be the best doctor. A Native American person may not want to go to the so-called "best" white doctor from Harvard, because she feels that, for cultural reasons, she would prefer a Native American doctor, whether a graduate from Harvard or the local state medical school.

We can look at the legal system and see that there are very few Native American lawyers. Then we take a step back and ask why are there so few Native Americans in law schools? Then back a step, and ask why are there so few Native Americans in college? That's why we need affirmative action in college admissions. That's where affirmative action has to start!

Sarah: You know, I am not in favor of quotas. I don't know what the answer is. But I know that just getting rid of affirmative action and saying, "The problem has been solved, we don't need any of these programs," that, to me, is a joke.

Dr. Bauer: Let's move on to the article by Glenn C. Loury. He is an African American conservative who took a lot of heat from the conservatives when he was no longer willing to defend the conservative view on affirmative action. In the words of Bill Clinton, Loury wants to "mend it, not end it." He wrote in 1998, a different climate from 1978 when *Bakke*[1] was decided. Back then, it looked as if liberal Democrats were putting together a hard-and-fast quota system of affirmative action. But starting with *Bakke,* and culminating in *Adarand*[2], traditional affirmative action is close to dead. What is Loury proposing instead?

Andy: Developmental affirmative action.

Laura: Can I ask a question? Is he saying that affirmative action belongs in some areas and not in others? He reminds me of Wilson, because he talks about the army's efforts and efforts in science and engineering.

Dr. Bauer: Here's what Loury says: "I am not defending racial quotas, or race-based allocations of public contracts." Notice these references to *Bakke* and *Adarand?* Then he goes on to say he is also not defending "racial double standards in the workplace, or huge disparities in the test scores of blacks and whites admitted to elite universities." What he does defend is targeted efforts to do a better job at helping minorities climb the ladder, in ways that are not designed to exclude people of other races.

Steve: He wants to keep the *Bakke* standard: that race can be used as one factor in admissions, but not the only factor. But in the *Hopwood* case, a court of appeals decision that the Supreme Court let stand, the Court said race couldn't be used as any factor at all. In the article, "The 'Talented Tenth' in Texas," the authors say race has been eliminated from consideration at all the public schools in Texas. So the law here is confused, and the Supreme Court isn't helping much.

Dr. Bauer: Justice Thurgood Marshall's dissenting opinion in *Bakke* contained remarks similar to Loury's who writes, "To take account of race while trying to mitigate the effects" of the legacy of Jim Crow laws and hundreds of years of discrimination, "though perhaps ill-advised or unworkable in specific cases, should not be viewed as morally equivalent to the acts of discrimination that effected the subjugation of blacks in the first place." He also says, "It is important to distinguish between legal and ethical modes of reasoning."

What is this difference Loury is talking about? If you study the law, you start to see that there are some things the law and the courts do well, and some things they don't. For example, sometimes, when you turn an ethical point of view into a law, you create a chain of past grievances. As Justice Powell asked in his *Bakke* opinion, if we start trying to settle old injustices, where would it end? That's logical, legal thinking.

But Glenn Loury says there is a difference between legal thinking and moral and ethical thinking. He writes, "there are circumstances where the ability of a public policy to advance the general interest of all persons is enhanced by taking cognizance of the racial identities of particular persons." Laura was right, wasn't she? Who does this sound like?

Laura: James Q. Wilson!

Sarah: But Steve still isn't buying it, are you?

Steve: No.

Andy: I'm not sure I agree with the traditional style of affirmative action, but we humans are crafty, and there are a lot of different ways to fix things. Some portions of affirmative action ruffle feathers on all sides, but I think the ultimate goal is for every person in America to feel that he or she has a stake in the success of our country. And to do that, they need to feel they are on an equal playing field with everyone else. And what is the best way to do that? I have no idea. But I think anything that can work toward the goal of getting people to feel a stronger sense of ownership of their nation is a goal we should work towards.

Sarah: Loury is looking for an ethical response that reaches out in training and recruitment. It's a compromise position, it seems to me.

Dr. Bauer:	Loury would rather spend time and energy training young students of color, so they are capable of getting into elite schools on their own merit, than defend a program giving them admission when they haven't earned it. But he insists the moral and ethical thing to do is to reach out and give these young students the extra help they need.
Laura:	There are programs out there for the disadvantaged. I grew up next to a housing project in Florida, and they had the Head Start programs. I guess I have a biased view about how that failed to help my community, that I think Loury is far too optimistic. We are not born equal, whatever race we are born into. We have unequal intelligence, talents in different areas. No government program will make us equal. I bet you guys wouldn't guess that I'm part minority myself. I'm actually one-sixteenth American Indian; my grandmother is one-quarter Indian.
Dr. Bauer:	Do you ever check off Native American on forms?
Laura:	No, I talked about that with my mother, but we would have had to trace it from the beginning of our family, and we never have. But we discussed how things might have been different for the kids in the family, getting into college and getting scholarships.
Sarah:	Well, you couldn't do that, because the federal law says you have to be one-fourth Indian to claim it as your race.
Dr. Bauer:	What Laura is talking about is very real. There has been some white resentment over affirmative action programs, especially among college students. That resentment centers around the idea that, had Laura been able to check off Native American on those forms, things would have been better for her.
Andy:	Almost like saying, "Those minorities have it easy."
Laura:	I don't feel that way. I'm the one who's had it easy. I don't think about it that much. I thought it was an interesting thing to have considered, being able to check off the box as a Native American. I actually hadn't thought about it for years, until today. But we did think about it when I was in high school and first thinking about college.
Sarah:	I think I would trade with you any special attention I've received for being a Native American, if I could have skipped all that I went through as a kid growing up and having to deal with my ethnic heritage.
Andy:	And considering all you went through, is it too much to ask that you get some slight amount of help? I don't think so. I don't think it's that big of a deal.
Dr. Bauer:	Andy, maybe you are looking at it morally and ethically.
Andy:	And I see there is a difference between that and the way laws have to work. Especially when you are applying the Equal Protection Clause of the Fourteenth Amendment.

Dr. Bauer:	Which is the concern in the *Hopwood* case. Let's end with "The 'Talented Tenth' in Texas."
Laura:	This was a very interesting case.
Dr. Bauer:	*Adarand* pretty much ended affirmative action in government contracts, and *Hopwood*, although not law outside of the federal sixth circuit, may eventually end affirmative action in graduate and college admissions.
Laura:	But in Texas, to make sure that minorities still get into the selective state schools, they made it mandatory that the state university system admit students in the top ten percent of every high school in Texas, no matter what their scores were on the SAT or ACT.
Andy:	In Colorado, some Democrat always introduces the same bill every year, and each time it is defeated by the conservatives in the legislature.
Dr. Bauer:	What is interesting about the bill in Texas is that it was passed by a Republican-dominated Texas Legislature and signed into law by the Republican governor, George W. Bush.
Laura:	The bill appears to collect the cream of the crop, but it's all relative. Maybe the top two percent of a bad school still won't be able to compete with the top ten percent from a really great school.
Dr. Bauer:	In this system, you allow the top ten percent from everywhere in, give them all a shot, and see who flunks out. Go back to the Glenn Loury article; he would talk about developmental affirmative action, making sure those local elementary, middle, and high schools were reaching out and providing extra help. I think Glenn Loury thinks it is unfair to the minority students to throw them into an elite college and leave them alone to sink or swim.
Laura:	They do have a summer program in Texas to help kids catch up.
Sarah:	They offered that to me. There's a summer program just for Native American kids.
Steve:	See, I like this Talented Tenth option, because it takes race out of the picture and puts the emphasis back where it belongs, on individual achievement. You may not have a great test score but still be an intelligent person, and once you get in, you can deal with it. And this is a kind of class-based remedy. It takes the top ten percent of the kids in the poor school districts no matter what their color.
Sarah:	That part I like, and I think it's an interesting approach. But I also think, and it says in the article as well, that this will not reach all the minority kids who have ability.
Laura:	But you can't make all the people happy all the time.
Steve:	If they want to go to the selective school, they should work harder and get into the top ten percent.

Sarah:	I don't see how this is so much better than traditional affirmative action.
Steve:	It is so much better because it doesn't say that you should get anything special just because you are a particular color. It is achievement-based. At some point, you need some way of measuring merit and achievement.
Sarah:	I think a more personal, individual evaluation is a better way to do it.
Dr. Bauer:	That would be ideal, but do you know how many applicants there are to the elite state universities? They just don't have the personnel to look at much more than grades and test scores. At smaller schools, the admissions people can look at individuals. And at the elite private schools, they try to look at the whole person; they have the capacity to look past traditional measures if a kid seems to have an interesting background. But the public universities don't have the money, which translates into the fact they don't have the time.
	A conservative would say, we live in an imperfect world. How much can government fix? How much should we ask government to fix? How could we possibly formulate rules to make things fair for everyone?
Sarah:	We can try!
Dr. Bauer:	And that's what Glenn Loury means when he talks about a moral and ethical dimension.
Laura:	But you'll never make everyone happy.
Sarah:	I think that's a cop-out, to say that because you can't make everybody happy, you shouldn't try to do the best you can do. It's worth working on. It's tough, and we may never get there, but let's keep trying.

★ ★ ★

1. *Regents of the University of California* v. *Allan Bakke* (1978). A civil rights reverse discrimination case in which the Court allowed the University of California Davis Campus Medical School to admit students on the basis of race if the school's aim is to combat the effects of past discriminations. The Court held, nonetheless, that Bakke must be admitted to the medical school because its admissions policy had used race as the sole criterion for a limited number of "minority" positions.

2. *Adarand Constructors, Inc.* v. *Federico Pena, Secretary of Transportation et al.* (1995). A case challenging a government program under which general contractors on government projects receive financial incentives to hire as subcontractors businesses that are owned by socially and economically disadvantaged individuals. The Court held that any race-based classification by any government (federal, state, or local) is subject to strict judicial scrutiny. Under this standard, racial classifications are constitutional only if they are narrowly tailored measures that promote compelling governmental interests.

For Additional Reading
Go to InfoTrac College Edition, your online research library at

http://web1.infotrac-college.com

Enter the following search terms using the Subject Guide or Key Terms.

affirmative action	Jim Crow laws	Proposition 287
Brown v. *Board of Education*	Martin Luther King Jr.	reconstruction
Civil Rights Act	poll tax	separate but equal
equal protection clause	Proposition 209	

5

The Rights of the Accused

MONICA BAUER

A Personal Perspective on Crime and Punishment

My interest in this issue began in the 1950s with Saturday morning visits to the Nebraska State Penitentiary, where my oldest stepbrother, Billy, was serving time on a bad-check charge. Billy couldn't afford to hire an attorney, so he was tried and sentenced without one. The Sixth Amendment to the Constitution guarantees defendants the right to counsel—to have an attorney speak for them— but in the 1950s, that promise was not enough to ensure justice for all. Billy had a constitutional right to counsel if he could *afford* it. (The Founding Fathers never dreamed that government would be in the business of supplying lawyers for the poor; after all, they wanted a small, limited government.) The right to a court-appointed attorney developed slowly through a series of Supreme Court cases. Had Billy been a murderer, instead of a petty thief, the state of Nebraska would have provided a court-appointed attorney under the precedent set in *Powell* v. *Alabama* (1932). Had Billy been charged with a federal crime, he would have had an attorney appointed for him under the precedent set by *Johnson* v. *Zerbst* (1938).

But it was Billy's bad luck (and his life was full of bad luck) to commit a *state* offense five years before *Gideon* v. *Wainwright* (1963), the case that, under the Fourteenth Amendment, applied the right to counsel to defendants in state courts. If Billy had been provided with an attorney, my guess is that he would have received probation. But as things stood in the late 1950s, Billy ended up doing hard time in the state penitentiary. Every Saturday we would take the hour-long drive from Omaha to the state capital, Lincoln, where we brought Billy his favorite food:

fried chicken. The pen, full of hardened criminals, made him crazy, and he actually escaped, only to be recaptured and spend an even longer time in prison. I was too young to be taunted by playmates, but my older sister and brother felt the full effects of the embarrassment and were taunted in school, especially when Billy escaped and his name was in the paper. The shame, I think, was one reason another brother eventually became a cop.

My brother Dan (not his real name) became a very good cop. His name ended up in the paper, too—for graduating first in his class at the police academy. Until the day she died, Mom kept his picture prominently displayed: Dan standing in our driveway, wearing his uniform, badge, and gun on his first day on the job. He spent twenty years on the force and became increasingly angry at the attention given to the rights of the accused. When African American cops in Omaha complained of racism in the ranks, my brother Dan was a vocal defender of his fellow white cops. Yet I knew from a lifetime of listening to his views that he was a racist himself, although he would never admit it.

Still, Dan was a pretty good police officer. Sincere and honest, he had a genuine desire to protect innocent people—he was especially happy to get a drunk driver off the road. Like most police officers, he never fired his gun in public. And the abuse he took day in and day out from the lowest type of human beings, wife beaters and drug pushers, was bound to affect his view of crime and punishment. Hearing his stories, I was able to understand how some police officers perceived the criminal justice system and their role in it. I never forgot that he took that abuse and placed himself in danger every day to protect all of us.

Dan became a police officer in 1975, nine years after the Supreme Court made ruled to protect the rights of those accused of crimes in *Miranda* v. *Arizona* (1966). Dan would rail against *Miranda*. He thought the ruling tied his hands and made it more likely that guilty people would end up back on the street. I used to tell him that the Constitution was designed to protect the accused—that we are all innocent until proven guilty. That just made him more angry. But I was right, and he knew it.

Unlike most of the rest of the world, in American law, the burden of proof is on the government to prove guilt, not on the individual to prove innocence. To gain a conviction, the state must prove guilt beyond a reasonable doubt. Until the moment the case is proved, the person under arrest or indictment has the same rights as any other citizen—one of them being protection against unreasonable searches, which is discussed in this section in the case of *Mapp* v. *Ohio* (1961).

My brother Dan hated the *Mapp* case, too, because that was the beginning of the exclusionary rule: If a search is conducted without a warrant for probable cause, the evidence cannot be used in court, or is excluded. Dan always spent part of his day getting search warrants from judges; he would complain whenever someone's case was dismissed because the evidence had come from an illegal search. Dan served half his career under the *Mapp* standard and half under *United States* v. *Leon* (1984), in which the Supreme Court ruled that there could be a "good faith exception" to the exclusionary rule. Dan's job got easier, and he was happy to see the Supreme Court rule his way for a change.

Dan and I had our more interesting arguments about the death penalty—the most serious use of the state's power to punish. Three years before Dan became a police officer, the Supreme Court had ruled in *Furman* v. *Georgia* (1972) that the death penalty, as it had been used up to that time, was "cruel and unusual punishment" and violated the Eighth Amendment. That made Dan angriest. When, a year after Dan joined the force, the Court ruled that the death penalty could be constitutional, provided it was applied in a manner that was not "arbitrary or capricious" (*Gregg* v. *Georgia,* 1976), Dan was pleased.

I am convinced that the justices who opposed the death penalty were correct when they labeled it "cruel and unusual punishment." Before you dismiss me as one of those far-left liberals who cares more about the rights of the accused than the rights of victims, let me say that I know all too well what it is like to be a victim of a crime. The last time I hitchhiked, I was 18 years old. A man let me into his car then pulled over to a side street and pulled out a handgun. He pressed it to my head (I can still remember exactly where, and how it felt cold against my skin as he pressed it against me to show he really meant business). Then he demanded all my money, and when he saw how little cash he was getting for his trouble, demanded that I take off my pants. Knowing what would happen next, I began to cry hysterically.

"Shut up, bitch," he yelled at me, but I couldn't stop. I distinctly remember thinking I was about to die because I couldn't stop crying. I think the robber and would-be rapist decided I was just too much trouble, so he told me to get out of the car. "Walk away, bitch, and don't turn around, or I swear I'll blow your head right off," he said as he pushed me out the door. I walked for about half an hour until I got to a pay phone and had enough courage to call the police.

I have no illusions that all criminals are just nice kids gone bad, like my brother Billy. But the discipline of political science keeps me from acting strictly from a revenge instinct. Because I know how powerful the desire for revenge can be, I take the rights of the accused very seriously—for I can easily imagine me sending the wrong man to the electric chair.

The police never found the man who robbed and threatened me. I didn't remember his face and could give only the most general description. But I was angry and I wanted revenge; I wanted to put that piece of scum in the electric chair and throw the switch myself. And angry as I was, if they had found a suspect, I know that I might have identified the wrong man—that my desire for revenge would have made me feel overly certain about the identification. On too many occasions, innocent people have gone to death row—some to be cleared and released after years wasted in jail, and some to be cleared only after their deaths.

A victim of crime, I am also a political scientist, and my reasoning and scholarship tell me that the death penalty is no deterrent, that its only function is revenge. Most of the rest of the world has decided that revenge is cruel and unusual punishment that reduces reasoning human beings to animals thirsting for blood to even the score. Why is our government still in the revenge business?

How do we weigh the rights of those accused against our need to feel secure? How do we weigh the rights of Billy against the rights of Dan, or the rights of the person who attacked me, against my right to feel safe or even my desire for revenge? Do you know anyone who has been touched by these issues? What role should emotion play, and what role should political science and reason play in deciding these issues? What do you think?

Mapp v. Ohio
Edited by Monica Bauer

SUMMARY OF THE EVENTS BEHIND *MAPP* V. *OHIO*

On May 23, 1957, three Cleveland policemen arrived at the apartment home of Ms. Dollree Mapp and her daughter. The officers had a tip: A person wanted for questioning in a bombing incident might be hiding in Ms. Mapp's home and keeping some of his personal effects there. When the officers arrived at Ms. Mapp's door, they demanded entry into the home, but Ms. Mapp refused and called her attorney. Meanwhile, the officers staked out the home and waited. Three hours went by, and then, aided by the arrival of four additional officers, the police physically broke into Ms. Mapp's home.

When Ms. Mapp demanded to see the search warrant, the police waved a piece of paper in her general direction and claimed they had a warrant. When Ms. Mapp was not allowed to see the warrant, she grabbed for it, and a fight broke out during which she was physically subdued. It later turned out that the police could not produce a search warrant because they had never asked the court for one.

The police then handcuffed Mapp and thoroughly searched her home, even going into her basement storage area. Although the police never found any evidence linking Mapp to the bomber, they did find some obscene magazines in her trunk. Mapp was then arrested and convicted of possessing obscene material.

In this decision, Justice Clark refers to an earlier case (*Weeks* v. *United States,* 1914) in which the Court had decided that federal law enforcement officers are bound to respect the Fourth Amendment ban on illegal searches. The *Mapp* case was about whether local law enforcement officers were also bound to accept such limits.

This case was part of the long process during which the Bill of Rights, which originally restrained only the federal government, would come to restrain the state and local governments as well.

Mapp v. Ohio
367 U.S. 643
Decided June 19, 1961
Mr. Justice Clark delivered the opinion of the Court.

Seventy-five years ago, in *Boyd* v. *United States* (1886), considering the Fourth and Fifth Amendments as running "almost into each other" on the facts before it, this Court held that the doctrines of those Amendments

> "apply to all invasions on the part of the government and its employees of the sanctity of a man's home and the privacies of life. It is not the breaking of his doors, and the rummaging of his drawers, that constitutes the essence of the offence; but it is the invasion of his indefeasible right of personal security, personal liberty, and private property. . . . Breaking into a house and opening boxes and drawers are circumstances of aggravation; but any forcible and compulsory extortion of a man's own testimony or of his private papers to be used as evidence to convict him of crime or to forfeit his goods, is within the condemnation . . . [of those Amendments]."

The Court noted that

> "constitutional provisions for the security of person and property should be liberally construed. . . . It is the duty of courts to be watchful for the constitutional rights of the citizen, and against any stealthy encroachments thereon."

. . . Less than 30 years after *Boyd,* this Court, in *Weeks* v. *United States* (1914), stated that

> "the Fourth Amendment . . . put the courts of the United States and Federal officials, in the exercise of their power and authority,

under limitations and restraints [and] . . . forever secure[d] the people, their persons, houses, papers, and effects against all unreasonable searches and seizures under the guise of law . . . and the duty of giving to it force and effect is obligatory upon all entrusted under our Federal system with the enforcement of the laws."

Specifically dealing with the use of the evidence unconstitutionally seized, the Court concluded:

"If letters and private documents can thus be seized and held and used in evidence against a citizen accused of an offense, the protection of the Fourth Amendment declaring his right to be secure against such searches and seizures is of no value, and, so far as those thus placed are concerned, might as well be stricken from the Constitution. The efforts of the courts and their officials to bring the guilty to punishment, praiseworthy as they are, are not to be aided by the sacrifice of those great principles established by years of endeavor and suffering which have resulted in their embodiment in the fundamental law of the land."

. . . There are those who say, as did Justice (then Judge) Cardozo, that under our constitutional exclusionary doctrine "[t]he criminal is to go free because the constable has blundered." In some cases this will undoubtedly be the result. But, as was said in *Elkins*, "there is another consideration—the imperative of judicial integrity." The criminal goes free, if he must, but it is the law that sets him free. Nothing can destroy a government more quickly than its failure to observe its own laws, or worse, its disregard of the charter of its own existence. As Mr. Justice Brandeis, dissenting, said in *Olmstead* v. *United States* (1928): "Our Government is the potent, the omnipresent teacher. For good or for ill, it teaches the whole people by its example. . . . If the Government becomes a lawbreaker, it breeds contempt for law; it invites every man to become a law unto himself; it invites anarchy." Nor can it lightly be assumed that, as a practical matter, adoption of the exclusionary rule fetters law enforcement. . . .

"The federal courts themselves have operated under the exclusionary rule of *Weeks* for almost half a century; yet it has not been suggested either that the Federal Bureau of Investigation has thereby been rendered ineffective, or that the administration of criminal justice in the federal courts has thereby been disrupted. Moreover, the experience of the states is impressive. . . . The movement towards the rule of exclusion has been halting but seemingly inexorable." *Elkins* case.

The ignoble shortcut to conviction left open to the State tends to destroy the entire system of constitutional restraints on which the liberties of the people rest. . . . Our decision, founded on reason and truth, gives to the individual no more than that which the Constitution guarantees him, to the police officer no less than that to which honest law enforcement is entitled, and, to the courts, that judicial integrity so necessary in the true administration of justice.

The judgment of the Supreme Court of Ohio is reversed and the cause remanded for further proceedings not inconsistent with this opinion.

Reversed and remanded.

United States v. Leon
Edited by Monica Bauer

SUMMARY OF THE EVENTS BEHIND UNITED STATES V. LEON

Alberto Leon was named in a search warrant for drugs with the following evidence of probable cause: (1) Leon was linked to another drug suspect, and Leon had previously been arrested in 1980 on drug charges; (2) an informant claimed to know that Leon had a large quantity of drugs in his home, but incorrectly identified Leon as living in Glendale, California, when his residence was in Burbank. On this level of probable cause, police received a valid warrant to search Leon and the other suspects for whom there was a great deal more probable cause. Drugs were found in Leon's home, and his attorney filed a motion that the evidence in Leon's home be excluded at trial under the exclusionary rule. At an evidentiary hearing, the local judge ruled that the Leon evidence should be excluded. The State of California appealed to the Supreme Court.

United States v. Leon

Supreme Court of the United States
Decided 1984
Justice White delivered the opinion of the Court.

This case presents the question whether the Fourth Amendment exclusionary rule should be modified so as not to bar the use in the prosecution's case in chief of evidence obtained by officers acting in reasonable reliance on a search warrant issued by a detached and neutral magistrate but ultimately found to be unsupported by probable cause. To resolve this question, we must consider once again the tension between the sometimes competing goals of, on the one hand, deterring official misconduct and removing inducements to unreasonable invasions of privacy and, on the other, establishing procedures under which criminal defendants are "acquitted or convicted on the basis of all the evidence which exposes the truth."

We have concluded that, in the Fourth Amendment context, the exclusionary rule can be modified somewhat without jeopardizing its ability to perform its intended functions. Accordingly, we reverse the judgment of the Court of Appeals. . . .

The substantial social costs exacted by the exclusionary rule for the vindication of Fourth Amendment rights have long been a source of concern. "Our cases have consistently recognized that unbending application of the exclusionary sanction to enforce ideals of governmental rectitude would impede unacceptably the truth-finding functions of judge and jury." An objectionable . . . consequence of this interference with the criminal justice system's truth-finding function is that some guilty defendants may go free or receive reduced sentences as a result of favorable plea bargains. Particularly when law enforcement officers have acted in objective good faith or their transgressions have been minor, the magnitude of the benefit conferred on such guilty defendants offends basic concepts of the criminal justice system. Indiscriminate application of the exclusionary rule, therefore, may well "generat[e] disrespect for the law and administration of justice." Accordingly, "[a]s with any remedial device, the application of the rule has been restricted to those areas where its remedial objectives are thought most efficaciously served." . . .

If exclusion of evidence obtained pursuant to a subsequently invalidated warrant is to have any deterrent effect, therefore, it must alter the behavior of individual law enforcement officers or the policies of their departments. One could argue that applying the exclusionary rule in cases where the police failed to demonstrate probable cause in the warrant application deters future inadequate presentations or "magistrate shopping" and thus promotes the ends of the Fourth Amendment. Suppressing evidence obtained pursuant to a technically defective warrant supported by probable cause also might encourage officers to scrutinize more closely the form of the warrant and to point out suspected judicial errors. We find such arguments speculative and conclude that suppression of evidence obtained pursuant to a warrant should be ordered only on a case-by-case basis and only in those unusual cases in which exclusion will further the purposes of the exclusionary rule.

Justice Stevens . . . dissenting in [Leon.]
It is appropriate to begin with the plain language of the Fourth Amendment:

> The right of the people to be secure in their persons, houses, papers, and effects, against unreasonable searches and seizures, shall not be violated; and no Warrants shall issue but upon probable cause, supported by Oath or affirmation, and particularly describing the place to be searched, and the persons or things to be seized.

The Court assumes that the searches in these cases violated the Fourth Amendment, yet refuses to apply the exclusionary rule because the Court concludes that it was "reasonable" for the police to conduct them. In my opinion an official search and seizure cannot be both "unreasonable" and "reasonable" at the same time. . . .

[H]owever, the Government now admits—at least for the tactical purpose of achieving what it regards as a greater benefit—that the substance, as well as the letter, of the Fourth Amendment was violated. The Court therefore assumes that the warrant in that case was not supported by probable cause, but refuses to suppress the evidence obtained thereby because it considers the police conduct to satisfy a "newfangled" nonconstitutional standard of reasonableness. Yet if the Court's assumption is correct—if there was no probable cause—it must follow that it was "unreasonable" for the authorities to make unheralded entries into and searches of private

dwellings and automobiles. The Court's conclusion that such searches undertaken without probable cause can nevertheless be "reasonable" is totally without support in our Fourth Amendment jurisprudence.

Thus, if the majority's assumption is correct, that even after paying heavy deference to the magistrate's finding and resolving all doubt in its favor, there is no probable cause here, then by definition—as a matter of constitutional law—the officers' conduct was unreasonable. The Court's own hypothesis is that there was no fair likelihood that the officers would find evidence of a crime, and hence there was no reasonable law enforcement justification for their conduct.

The majority's contrary conclusion rests on the notion that it must be reasonable for a police officer to rely on a magistrate's finding. Until today that has plainly not been the law; it has been well settled that even when a magistrate issues a warrant there is no guarantee that the ensuing search and seizure is constitutionally reasonable. Law enforcement officers have long been on notice that despite the magistrate's decision a warrant will be invalidated if the officers did not provide sufficient facts to enable the magistrate to evaluate the existence of probable cause responsibly and independently.

The notion that a police officer's reliance on a magistrate's warrant is automatically appropriate is one the Framers of the Fourth Amendment would have vehemently rejected. The precise problem that the Amendment was intended to address was the unreasonable issuance of warrants. As we have often observed, the Amendment was actually motivated by the practice of issuing general warrants—warrants which did not satisfy the particularity and probable-cause requirements. The resentments which led to the Amendment were directed at the issuance of warrants unjustified by particularized evidence of wrongdoing. Those who sought to amend the Constitution to include a Bill of Rights repeatedly voiced the view that the evil which had to be addressed was the issuance of warrants on insufficient evidence. As Professor Taylor has written:

> [O]ur constitutional fathers were not concerned about warrantless searches, but about overreaching warrants. It is perhaps too much to say that they feared the warrant more than the search, but it is plain enough that the warrant was the prime object of their concern. Far from looking at the warrant as a protection against unreasonable searches, they saw it as an authority for unreasonable and oppressive searches. . . .
> T. Taylor, *Two Studies in Constitutional Interpretation* (1969).

In short, the Framers of the Fourth Amendment were deeply suspicious of warrants; in their minds the paradigm of an abusive search was the execution of a warrant not based on probable cause. The fact that colonial officers had magisterial authorization for their conduct when they engaged in general searches surely did not make their conduct "reasonable." The Court's view that it is consistent with our Constitution to adopt a rule that it is presumptively reasonable to rely on a defective warrant is the product of constitutional amnesia.

The exclusionary rule is designed to prevent violations of the Fourth Amendment. "Its purpose is to deter—to compel respect for the constitutional guaranty in the only effectively available way, by removing the incentive to disregard it." If the police cannot use evidence obtained through warrants issued on less than probable cause, they have less incentive to seek those warrants, and magistrates have less incentive to issue them.

Today's decisions do grave damage to that deterrent function. Under the majority's new rule, even when the police know their warrant application is probably insufficient, they retain an incentive to submit it to a magistrate, on the chance that he may take the bait. No longer must they hesitate and seek additional evidence in doubtful cases.

It is of course true that the exclusionary rule exerts a high price—the loss of probative evidence of guilt. But that price is one courts have often been required to pay to serve important social goals. That price is also one the Fourth Amendment requires us to pay, assuming as we must that the Framers intended that its strictures "shall not be violated." For in all such cases, as Justice Stewart has observed, "the same extremely relevant evidence would not have been obtained had the police officer complied with the commands of the fourth amendment in the first place."

We could, of course, facilitate the process of administering justice to those who violate the criminal laws by ignoring the commands of the Fourth Amendment—indeed, by ignoring the entire Bill of Rights—but it is the very purpose of a Bill of Rights to identify values that may not be sacrificed to expediency. In a just society those who govern, as well as those who are governed, must obey the law.

Accordingly, I respectfully dissent from the disposition in [*Leon*].

Inadmissible
Michael Kinsley

The U.S. prison population has tripled in the past two decades, to more than a million. This country has more of its population behind bars than any other nation with reliable statistics. South Africa is second, the Soviet Union is third. Now that South Africa has a moratorium on executions, we're also the only advanced Western nation with a death penalty. It is absurd to say the answer to rising crime is locking up even more people for even longer periods, or chopping off more heads. But few politicians can resist.

Jeremy Bentham, who first elaborated the theory of prison as a deterrent to crime, might look at America's choked prisons and say we've got it all wrong. As James Q. Wilson and Richard Herrnstein, no softies, put it in their book, *Crime and Human Nature:* "It may be easier to reduce crime by making penalties swifter or more certain, rather than more severe." America's absurdly long prison terms often come at the end of a lengthy and random process that nullifies their power as a deterrent to crime.

One element of [the 1991] crime bill that can't be laughed off immediately, therefore, is [a] proposal to limit the exclusionary rule. This is the rule that evidence obtained in violation of a person's constitutional rights cannot be used against him in court, even if it proves him guilty. Or, as Benjamin Cardozo famously derided the exclusionary rule, it is the doctrine that "the criminal is to go free because the constable has blundered."

The exclusionary rule usually involves evidence obtained in violation of the Fourth Amendment right against unreasonable searches and seizures. Unlike a coerced confession, illegally seized evidence is just as probative as evidence seized properly. In the war of statistics about how often the guilty go free because good evidence against them can't be used, liberals are a bit disingenuous. It is true that the exclusionary rule is rarely invoked at a trial. But trials themselves are rare. Far more often, potentially excludable evidence will lead prosecutors to drop the case or negotiate a plea bargain for a shorter term.

Indeed, the best case against all the elaborate procedural safeguards created by the Warren Supreme Court is that they have created a level of protection for defendants that we can't afford to offer, and don't really offer. Practically all criminal defendants are actually tried in a much more rough-and-ready process—plea bargaining—in which there are no safeguards for the innocent or those whose constitutional rights have been violated, but where potential procedural claims are translated into shorter sentences. Meanwhile, legislatures increase the official sentences for crimes to counteract the plea bargaining effect.

So dump the exclusionary rule? Not so fast. There is a logical flaw in the argument that excluding wrongfully obtained evidence lets the guilty go free. That is, the guilty would also go free if the evidence hadn't been wrongly obtained in the first place. Conservatives complain about the burden of the exclusionary rule on cops and prosecutors. But the rule is burden only to the extent that it actually works in deterring unconstitutional behavior. The complaint, in short, is not with the exclusionary rule. It is with the Fourth Amendment itself. Eliminating the exclusionary rule would only lead to more guilty people being punished if it also led to more illegal searches, seizures, and confessions: an effect the rule's critics take great pains to deny.

In fact, the Fourth Amendment—as interpreted by the Supreme Court—could use some pruning back. Most guilty-going-free horror stories you read in attacks on the exclusionary rule involve a piece of evidence ruled inadmissible on some overly exquisite chain of logic involving some cop's failure to curtsy in the right direction. But cops also violate real Fourth Amendment rights that most people treasure and everyone—criminals included—is entitled to. And they would do it a lot more often if it weren't for the exclusionary rule (as they did before the rule was imposed in 1961).

Most calls for reforming or eliminating the exclusionary rule . . . come with deeply disingenuous alternative proposals for protecting Fourth and Fifth amendment rights. These generally involve internal police department disciplinary procedures and/or an enhanced right for victims to sue. You will not be surprised to hear that the record of police departments punishing their own for rights violations is laughable, as is the record of juries sympathizing with criminals who sue cops.

And isn't it odd for conservative antilegalistas to be proposing a whole new layer of bureaucratic and legal procedure? Addressing this concern, a recent Justice Department report notes—without apparent irony—that claims will be minimal since those whose rights were violated will not qualify for free legal counsel as they do in criminal trials. How very reassuring.

But the main problem with alternatives to the exclusionary rule is that if they worked, they would be just as burdensome to law enforcement as the exclusionary rule itself. The assumption has to be, therefore, that proponents assume they would not work. That certainly sounds like [Former] Attorney General Richard Thornburgh's assumption when he complains: "If police feel that someone's perched on their shoulder watching every action they're going to take, you're not going to get the kind of aggressive law enforcement that you need."

Andy
a moderate

Laura
a conservative
Republican

Sarah
a Native American,
liberal Democrat

Steve
a Libertarian

Balancing Law Enforcement and Individual Rights
★ ★ ★

Dr. Bauer: Steve, you're the resident expert in criminal justice. The exclusionary rule often seems to my students like some insane restriction on police power, designed to help criminals. Can you help us get a clear picture of just what it is?

Steve: The exclusionary rule is about taking "fruit of the poisonous tree"—evidence [the fruit] that has been obtained illegally [from a poisonous tree] cannot be used in a court of law [is poison]. The only way to obtain legally admissible evidence is by getting a search warrant or giving a reasonable argument at trial that you had probable cause to search. In the reading "Inadmissible," Michael Kinsley wrote, "the rule is a burden only to the extent that it actually works in deterring unconstitutional behavior." I'm not one of those criminal justice types that sees the Constitution as the enemy. A truly professional law enforcement agency should respect constitutional rights.

Dr. Bauer: Okay, so imagine I am a police officer, and I break down your door without a search warrant. And as I break down your door, I see a dead body; I see you standing over the dead body with a pistol in your hand. I cannot use what I saw as evidence at trial?

Steve: Correct. You might be able to say you heard something that gave you a probable cause to believe a crime was being committed inside. That's how it works in real life, and who is to second-guess the police officer about whether or not he had probable cause to bust down a door in a situation like that? As much as I would like to think we all abide by the Constitution and Supreme Court rulings, there are a million ways to get around the exclusionary rule.

However, there are still cases where the Court will enforce the exclusionary rule. There was a situation in California where a police officer pulled over a vehicle, and he conducted an unauthorized search of the trunk. He did not have probable cause to extend the search from inside the vehicle to the trunk, so he did not have probable cause to search the trunk. And he found a dead

	body in the trunk. That evidence was actually thrown out in a court of law, and they could not charge the driver with murder because the cop had no right to search the trunk of that vehicle.
Dr. Bauer:	That's a horror story on search and seizure, isn't it? Sort of a worst-case scenario where a crime has been committed, you have the probable murderer, but the evidence is thrown out of court because of the exclusionary rule. Now, if you think about it that way, it seems like it doesn't make any sense.
Andy:	More important than having an effective police force is protecting the constitutional rights of everyone in the country.
Laura:	I'd rather have an effective police force, thank you very much!
Dr. Bauer:	So, we have a controversy right away here: Are people's rights to privacy more important than law enforcement, or vice versa? That's the Fourth Amendment problem. Let me just quickly read the first part of the Fourth Amendment: "The right of the people to be secure in their persons, houses, papers, and effects, against unreasonable searches and seizures, shall not be violated; and no Warrants shall issue but upon probable cause. . . ." Now put yourselves in Ms. Mapp's situation.
Andy:	The police broke into her apartment and found stuff that they weren't there to find.
Dr. Bauer:	And how is Ms. Mapp treated in this process? Is she treated as a citizen with rights, or is she treated as if she has already been proven guilty?
Steve:	She is definitely treated as if she's been proven guilty. She asked for a warrant on several occasions, and they flashed a piece of paper in her face. They didn't let her examine it closely; they wouldn't let her attorney enter the house to consult with her. They basically just stormed in there and told her what they were going to do to her and her house.
Dr. Bauer:	Notice that Steve is describing this from Mapp's point of view. Search and seizure looks like one thing from the police point of view, and like something else from the citizen's. Do you think it was all right that Ms. Mapp underwent this kind of search? Inevitably, if we want tough law enforcement, the police are going to make occasional mistakes.
Sarah:	But, they were there to find something completely different from what they ended up finding. They were there searching for a suspect, and they found this obscene material. Even if they had a warrant, which they didn't, that warrant would have had some restrictions. No police agency is supposed to be able to just come and conduct random searches, then, if they find anything at all, prosecute you. The search has to be *particular*.
Dr. Bauer:	The police did seem intent on finding something, anything, that would justify an arrest. Did it seem to you that Ms. Mapp was a danger to the citizens of Cleveland at the time?

Sarah:	No, but the police must have thought she was. Thank goodness for "innocent until proven guilty."
Dr. Bauer:	Yes, some of the police attitude depends on whether they see people as citizens or criminals.
Laura:	If you want protection from the police, I think you have to put up with some amount of paranoia. If I were in law enforcement, I could see myself looking at people as potential criminals first, and citizens second. Rights are all well and good, but sometimes they have to go on the back burner when police are trying to stop crime.
Dr. Bauer:	Can you put a right on a back burner without taking it away?
Laura:	I think that if the choice is between letting a criminal go free and giving up a few rights, I sure don't want to let the criminal go free!
Steve:	Well, I'd say I don't see how you can put rights on back burners. You set some dangerous precedents limiting freedoms: "Well, we've done it before, so let's just put this other guaranteed freedom on the back burner for now and solve the immediate danger." In fact, if I were the judge ruling on that exclusionary case of that dead body in the trunk in California, I would take about one second deciding to exclude that evidence, and it wouldn't bother my conscience one bit.
	It must be like what defense lawyers face. They have a client who they suspect committed murder, but they know they are going to get him off. They are not defending criminals because they want to release them into society. Lawyers have a principle to uphold: Everybody is entitled to the best defense, the best legal thinking possible.
	You have to uphold your principles all the time. You can't just pick and choose situations, like, "Well this situation is obviously bad, so we can throw away some freedoms here; but this situation is okay, so we'll let people keep their protection from unreasonable searches." Principles are important, and they must be used consistently, or they lose their power to guide us. They become suggestions that you can either blow off or keep, depending on what you had for breakfast that morning.
Laura:	You are discussing the exclusionary rule in theory, though. When you are in a real-world arrest situation, I think a different procedure follows. When you have police involved, of course they are supposed to be going by the code of the law, but real life is not a court of law.
Andy:	Well, I think the idea that there are two separate things—laws and real life—is plain wrong. I have to disagree with your point that the police officer can do whatever he likes because he's in the real world. Police are trained to be in the real world. Does that mean no laws apply, and a police officer can search anybody just because he doesn't like the look on a face?
Laura:	That is not what I said, Andy. You are taking my words too far.

Andy:	Let's look at what the police should be able to do in the real world. I feel every single police officer needs to actually think about the fact that they are taking an individual into custody who is still a citizen accused of a crime. They need to have in mind that certain pieces of evidence can and cannot be obtained, and they need to follow the rules of law for the court of law.
Laura:	You know, I have a police officer in one of my classes who says you shoot to kill. You don't shoot to maim, you shoot to kill, to protect yourself and those around you. And I think that has to be the main concern for that police officer at that time.
Steve:	I don't disagree with you there. When somebody pulls a gun on you, of course you are going to shoot to kill. But how does that apply to the Fourth Amendment?
Laura:	All I'm saying is . . . sometimes, in certain situations, you have to put somebody's rights on the back burner while you are dealing with crimes. I think if any of us found something by accident during a criminal investigation, you wouldn't want to ignore it!
Dr. Bauer:	Well, let me bring this back to the reading and see if we can't focus a little tighter on this. Why would the Supreme Court believe that they need to throw out evidence gained through illegal searches? Because if those illegal searches were usable in court, it would give the police an incentive to trample on people's rights. Police work would be easy if all of us were searched all the time. But the Supreme Court thinks the protection of our Fourth Amendment rights is more important than making police work easy.
Sarah:	Privacy is an important right. If police are punished for taking away that right, that seems fair to me.
Andy:	The exclusionary rule takes away the incentive to search people without warrants, or without probable cause, because those searches don't count.
Steve:	The exclusionary rule is necessary because without it you are basically asking officers to figure out for themselves whose rights to respect, and whose rights to deny. First of all, law enforcement people are pitted in some sort of "us against them" battle with criminals. Their job is to go out and grab the bad guys, but still respect everyone's constitutional rights. It is just too tempting to go over the line without the exclusionary rule to remind you, "Hey, if I go over the line, the court will throw the case out, and my arrest will go nowhere." So there is some incentive for them, other than just expecting police will, out of the goodness of their heart, uphold the Constitution. We have to have the exclusionary rule.
Sarah:	In "Inadmissible," Kinsley says, "cops also violate real Fourth Amendment rights. And they would do it a lot more often if it weren't for the exclusionary rule (as they did before the rule was imposed in 1961)."

Dr. Bauer:	What would life be like without the exclusionary rule? If there were no exclusionary rule, do you think that would affect police behavior in search and seizure?
Sarah:	We'd be back where we were before 1961. People forget that the police force has, in the past, been pretty brutal. When you could use evidence from breaking down somebody's door without a warrant, they would break down that door, just like they did to Ms. Mapp.
Steve:	To me, if I were an officer, to me it would always be a very fine line how to approach searching somebody's house. At least the exclusionary rule is clear, and in that way I think it helps law enforcement.
Dr. Bauer:	Don't forget, the Supreme Court watered down the exclusionary rule in 1984—in a way that echoes some of Laura's arguments about the need to help the police. Steve, help us out, I know you've studied *Mapp,* and the 1984 case *Leon* v. *Ohio.*
Steve:	The court held in *Leon* that there was a good faith exception to the exclusionary rule. In *Leon,* an officer did some research for a warrant—he did some stakeouts of the premises and of the different individuals in the case; he had some evidence. But most of his case for probable cause rested on this anonymous tip that had triggered the surveillance. He took it to a judge, and the judge didn't really have any kind of tough standard for probable cause, so he issued the warrants. Later, it was decided that there was not enough probable cause, and without probable cause to search, the warrant would have been illegal. But the Supreme Court said it wasn't the officer's fault; he was acting in good faith with the warrant in his hand. The Supreme Court created a "good faith" exception to the exclusionary rule, and allowed the evidence from his search to be used in court.
Dr. Bauer:	The trick in dealing with search and seizure is to put yourself in the shoes of both the law enforcement people and the people being searched. When you do that, the *Mapp* and *Leon* cases look very different. Dollree Mapp is sitting there and suddenly her house is torn apart, and the most heinous crime they can get her on is possession of obscene magazines buried in a trunk in the basement. But if we turn to *Leon,* do we find a similarly sympathetic person who is the victim of an illegal search?

Nope. The police get a tip that two criminals are selling large quantities of cocaine from their residences. The informant has names and a possible area of the city where they live. When the police stake them out, they find people that match the descriptions given by the informant, plus, these suspects have previous records. Any sympathy for these guys? These guys who are searched after the police obtain a warrant? There's plenty of suspicion. |
| Steve: | The *Leon* case is almost tailor-made to give more sympathy to the police. They looked like they were trying to do their job right, and they found what they |

	were looking for—drugs and money—even though it turned out later that their informant hadn't given them enough probable cause to search that particular house.
Dr. Bauer:	It appears, then, that these two cases are very different. One has a sympathetic person whose house is invaded, broken into by police, and the other has drug dealers who get caught red-handed. What effect do you think this difference had on the Court?
Laura:	I don't think it should have had any effect at all. *Mapp* committed a crime, too. Obscenity was found in her home. I mean, what it comes down to is, a crime is a crime. I think the Court should have found that neither the evidence against Mapp nor against this Leon guy should have been thrown out. Steve was talking about principles earlier; well, that's my principle. Nobody should get away with crime, not with a little crime, not with a big crime!
Steve:	I'm going to stand firm on my principle of protecting freedoms and say that the "good faith exception" opens up a loophole I'd rather keep shut. I have to agree with Justice Steven's dissenting opinion. He says, "Under the majority's new rule, even when the police know their warrant application is probably insufficient, they retain an incentive to submit it to a magistrate, on the chance that he may take the bait. No longer must they hesitate and seek additional evidence in doubtful cases." In other words, there is now an incentive to take dubious evidence on a kind of "judge hunt," to see if you can't convince some judge somewhere that your flimsy evidence deserves a warrant! I have to disagree with this Supreme Court decision.
Dr. Bauer:	So, you agree with Justice Stevens that *Leon* considerably weakens the Fourth Amendment.
Andy:	I think it weakens the Fourth Amendment. In *Mapp,* you had officers that were disregarding the Fourth Amendment. As a result of the *Leon* case, you could very well have a judge acting with them. An officer just needs one more person, one judge, to agree to disregard the need for probable cause in the Fourth Amendment.
Dr. Bauer:	Police officers call it "judge shopping." If one judge turns them down for a warrant, they just keep shopping until they get what they want.
Laura:	The police can even obtain a warrant over the phone, now, right? From their car?
Dr. Bauer:	Sure, Laura, absolutely.
Steve:	And magistrates in large cities just sit by a phone; you call them up, give them the details, and they issue an oral warrant. The affidavit is just submitted orally and the paperwork follows.
Dr. Bauer:	Law enforcement officers are very savvy about which judges are likely to give them warrants. Some judges have a very loose definition of probable cause. What is a good definition of probable cause?

Steve: I think a good definition of probable cause is, "with the evidence you have, it is more probable than not that your suspects have committed the crime you want to charge them with."

Laura: And one person's probable cause is not somebody else's. I'd probably be the type of judge that would issue a lot of warrants, because I do want to give police the benefit of the doubt.

Steve: If I could say something to that definition, though? Although it might be open to interpretation, there have been numerous court decisions that gave guidance about it. It's not like we have a vague conception of what probable cause is. The police do know what amounts to probable cause in a certain situation. You go through the Police Academy, you are going to learn that in this type of situation, say, stopping someone on a street, you are going to need this, that, and the other, or a certain number of these factors, to have probable cause. So there is a past history of different court cases we, and the police, can look at that gives an idea of what standards they need to reach.

Dr. Bauer: Steve is talking about the "Terry Stop." In a 1968 case, *Terry* v. *Ohio,* the Supreme Court laid down rules for a police officer—in the real world as Laura was talking about earlier—who, with no time to get a warrant, needs to stop and search someone immediately. This "Terry Stop" allows an officer to pat someone down for weapons if, in good faith, the police officer believes his life may be in danger.

Andy: But this is just like the "good faith exclusion" in the *Leon* case. Who determines good faith? If a police officer says, "I think that all Hispanics in this neighborhood are shifty. Therefore, I have probable cause to search any Hispanic on the street." Or probable cause to search any home in the *barrio*. And I get on the phone to a magistrate who is also anti-Hispanic, and he gives me a warrant to search anyone in the barrio, and the court can't later throw out any evidence of any crime I happen to find. Even if a higher court looks at the warrant and says, "You guys didn't have probable cause," the evidence still counts because I can say I was acting in "good faith." I grew up in public housing, and under those rules, there are searches going on all the time. Most of those folks were innocent, but they had to put up with the complete loss of dignity that comes with being searched.

Laura: Well, I think there is something in this good faith element that we are missing here. There can be a true good faith exemption, for when an officer makes a genuine mistake. The officer does not know that he is doing wrong. For example, if you have a warrant for a house at a particular address, and you accidentally search the wrong address because your partner copied it wrong, that is a good faith exception.

Sarah: Could that have been applied to *Mapp* then? They thought they were at the correct house, but then they weren't, but then they found the stuff. So, they were acting in good faith when they entered the house?

Steve:	They would have been acting in good faith on entering the house, but once they found the person wasn't there, they would have had to stop the search because the warrant would have specified a particular person. Since they continued the search, no longer were they acting in good faith. People like Dollree Mapp would still be protected.
Dr. Bauer:	The second part of the Fourth Amendment refers to that. It says, "[N]o Warrants shall issue but upon probable cause, supported by Oath or affirmation, and *particularly describing* the place to be searched, and the persons or things to be seized." So, even if the officers in *Mapp* had had a warrant, it would not have said, "Search all of her photos and seize all of her porn."
	Let me get back to *Leon* and the good faith exception. Can't any police officer say in any court of law, under *Leon*, "Gee, I made an innocent mistake. I was acting in good faith, please don't throw out the evidence I seized." How can you test the truth of that statement? Under *Leon*, isn't good faith assumed on the part of the police officer?
Andy:	Yeah, always. The system always gives the benefit of the doubt to a police officer, especially if the suspect is a person of color.
Laura:	I'm sure a lot of police officers do use *Leon* to get evidence admitted . . . that's the way it works.
Andy:	We are to decide, Laura, if that is right or not.
Laura:	Exactly. I'm not disagreeing at all there.
Andy:	Should we really assume every police officer is entitled to a good faith exception to the rules? There are corrupt people in every part of society, including corrupt police officers. Look at the Abner Louima case in New York City, where some twisted cop used his power over a suspect to rape him with a broomstick and nearly killed the guy. For months, the cop denied he did it. He was expecting everyone to assume that a cop always acts in good faith. Thank God some of his fellow officers did the right thing so we know the truth. But if it was just Abner Louima, some poor Haitian immigrant, his word against that of the cop, how do you think that would have turned out?
Sarah:	The point is that the framers wrote the Fourth Amendment to protect citizens from police power. Police can protect us, but they can also persecute us, and the framers had recent memories of British persecution. The good faith exception opens a door that corrupt police could use. Who's to say that an officer won't break into Number 202, even though he knows it's supposed to be 102, and get all sorts of evidence on somebody he doesn't like? What the court should say is, "The warrant said 102 and you went to 202, so we don't care how many dead bodies you found. This does not hold up. You can try to get another warrant and conduct another search, but you're going to have to supply probable cause and do it right this time."
Dr. Bauer:	And that would be rolling back *Leon*?

Andy:	Right.
Laura:	I think I'm at a disadvantage here. I've never taken Constitutional Law, and I think I'm looking at it from a more realistic perspective.
Steve:	The Constitution can and does give a realistic perspective; it just sets a high standard. But you are undoubtedly right that in the everyday world, events don't follow the Constitution. For example, I have a friend who is in the Boulder Police Academy right now. They were explaining to him all about the Terry Stop. According to the Supreme Court, you can check for weapons, but you are not supposed to check for contraband or drugs. You can do a reasonable search for a weapon, a knife, or a gun, or something like that. That's what the law says. But his instructors tell him, most officers, since they are checking already, just go a little deeper and see what else they can find. I'm sure it will continue like that. This goes back to one of Dr. Bauer's first comments, that the Fourth Amendment is about balancing the rights of citizens against the needs of law enforcement. Law enforcement is always going to try and gain the advantage. The point is, as free citizens, we can't accept that! We need to be smart enough to recognize when our rights have been violated and use the courts to protect our constitutional freedoms.
Laura:	And if the police find something illegal in your house, Steve, I hope the Court uses the good faith exception and makes you pay for your crime! Maybe my perspective comes from recent experience. Someone broke into my house, two police officers came Friday evening to take a report of what was stolen. I opened up a drawer to get some clothes because I was leaving for the weekend, and out of the corner of my eye, I saw the police officer taking an inventory of my drawer! I just found that interesting. I thought, "Oh, when I opened this drawer, he was just kind of searching a little bit."
Dr. Bauer:	How did that make you feel?
Laura:	You know I was fine with it, because I shouldn't have had anything illegal in my apartment anyway. I honestly felt that way. I don't do drugs; I have nothing to worry about. I have no illegal guns.
Dr. Bauer:	So you wouldn't mind if the police searched your house every Wednesday?
Laura:	That is not what I am saying, no.
Andy:	But you have nothing to hide.
Laura:	I have nothing to hide, but that doesn't mean I'd welcome a search of my house. Still, I want the police to have every possible tool to find the people who stole my stuff. I agree with what President Bush did in 1991 to try and limit the exclusionary rule, and I really agree with the quote in "Inadmissible" from Cardozo: "The criminal is to go free because the constable has blundered." I still don't see the sense in that.

★ ★ ★

For Additional Reading

Go to InfoTrac College Edition, your online research library at

http://web1.infotrac-college.com

Enter the following search terms using the Subject Guide or Key Terms.

death penalty	Fourth Amendment	privacy rights
due process	Miranda rights	search and seizure

6 six Interest Groups

Who Really Writes Laws?

Editorial

Sen. Slade Gorton, a Republican from the state of Washington, had some highly skilled help in writing his proposal to gut the nation's Endangered Species Act.

Lawyers for the timber, mining, ranching and utility interests that have most often come into conflict with the Endangered Species Act did Gorton's drafting for him.

"Sen. Gorton laid out his thoughts to us, he asked for help and we gave it to him," Robert Szabo of the National Endangered Species Reform Coalition told *The New York Times* last week.

"No problem," said Gorton. "I don't think that's how good public policy should be made, but I'm perfectly willing to get the free services of good lawyers in drafting my views."

Of course, their services are not exactly free. The price they carry is having their clients' interests written into law. Those interests are absolutely inimical to the goals of protecting endangered species.

In a wonderfully perverse twist to the normal way things are done, Gorton did not have to pay retainers to these attorneys who did his drafting work. Instead, the members of the coalition in effect paid a retainer to Gorton: They gave him $34,000 for his re-election campaign last year.

This is only one example of the way things work in Washington now. The hired guns of corporate America regularly and openly sit at the table with Republican lawmakers and their staff members as they rework the laws that protect the environment and regulate business practices.

We don't mean to be naive about this. Lobbyists certainly worked hand-in-hand with Democratic lawmakers when that party was in power. In some ways, the Republicans are just being less hypocritical about it than the Democrats were.

The Democrats often tried to mask their ties to lobbyists; the Republicans revel in close links to the very industries whose activities make them most susceptible to government regulation.

These industries, of course, ought to have a chance to make their case in the debates over laws. When they actually draft the laws, though, they severely limit the opportunity for the interests of the general public to play an adequate role in adoption of the nation's laws.

The new Republican majority has talked a lot about reforming Congress. When it comes to cozying up to lobbyists, though, this Congress is headed in exactly the wrong direction.

"Beer"
Elizabeth Drew

In January of 1996, I asked Bill Paxon, a forty-one-year-old Republican congressman from Buffalo, New York, who headed the National Republican Congressional Committee for electing Republicans to the House, to list the most important people or groups behind the Republican's effort to maintain control of the House. He replied: Grover Norquist, the Christian Coalition, the National Federation of Independent Business, the National Rifle Association, and the National Beer Wholesalers Association.

The beer wholesalers?

David Rehr, the vice president for public affairs of the National Beer Wholesalers Association, a tall, slim, enthusiastic thirty-six year-old, with a flattish face and blunt, straight-up hair, explained the origins of his group's power and influence. "There are over eighteen hundred beer distributors," Rehr said. "We're in virtually every congressional district." This, he said, gives the organization both grassroots strength and the wherewithal, in terms of members, to raise money for candidates.

Rehr is a close ally of Grover Norquist, attending or sending a representative to his Wednesday morning meetings and going to many of his parties, and he also works closely with the Christian Coalition, the N.R.A., and the National Federation of Independent Business. Rehr sees the alliance as "the center-right coalition that is realigning America."

Like Norquist, Rehr believed that maintaining Republican control of the House was more important than the 1996 Presidential race, or control of the Senate. The House, where Rehr had access and success, was also the best investment. Rehr explained, "In a House race, two thousand to five thousand votes can make the difference, and you can have so much more

Excerpt from *Whatever It Takes*, by Elizabeth Drew. Published by Viking Penguin, a division of Penguin Books USA Inc. © 1997, 1998 by Elizabeth Drew.

impact on these guys. You meet the Senate guys—they love you for your money and your contacts, but they don't remember who you are." Explaining why the outcome in the House was the most important to his and like-minded groups, Rehr said, "It's like an inverse pyramid. The House is like a microcosm of America. It is the pulse of the country. While the Presidency denotes leadership by a single individual and party, it means less day-to-day. The Senate is somewhere in between. Senators have to run every six years, but House members have to run every two years, so House members live and die by their day-to-day decisions."

The beer industry, Rehr explained, used to concentrate on state governments, which when Prohibition was repealed were given the responsibility for regulating alcohol. But it turned its attention more to the federal government when the Reagan administration, through Transportation Secretary Elizabeth Dole, raised the drinking age from eighteen to twenty-one in order to reduce traffic fatalities.

Then, in 1990, something worse happened: George Bush and the Democratic Congress raised taxes on beer by one hundred percent. "That cost thirty-eight thousand jobs in the beer economy," Rehr said, "mostly wholesale, as opposed to retail." (For credibility, the beer wholesalers organization uses figures half the size of those put out by Anheuser-Busch, but all such industry claims are suspect.) As a result of the tax, Rehr said, people bought less beer, and of that, less premium beer, on which the wholesalers make more money. The beer wholesalers opposed the Clintons' health care plan, because it would have imposed coverage for workers in small businesses.

Rehr, the son of a postman, grew up near Chicago and once worked for former Minnesota Representative Vin Weber, still an influential Republican, and then for the N.F.I.B. He was brought into the beer wholesalers organization in 1992, he said, to "make sure the tax wasn't raised again, and to be sure that anti-beer legislation didn't pass the Congress and get signed into law." Another goal was to reorient the wholesalers organization more to the Republican Party, which was more likely to protect its interests, and to strengthen his group's political influence. He explained, "Before I got there, they were disproportionately Democratic-oriented. And the beer and alcohol industry used to think that if we had a few people there [in the Congress] and we had access, nothing bad would happen. My philosophy is you should elect people who will be your allies. Members of Congress are risk averse."

In January, 1993, Rehr instructed his organization's members to jam the White House telephone lines with calls opposing inclusion of a tax increase on beer in President Clinton's upcoming economic program to reduce the deficit. (Then–Treasury Secretary Lloyd Bentsen had floated the idea of an alcohol-tax increase.) The wholesalers association also then acquired a "blast fax" capacity, enabling it to send out quickly more than three thousand faxes to its members, asking them to call the White House; faxes were also sent to Members of Congress. No administration proposal to raise taxes on alcohol was made. Rehr called this "the fax firepower network." (In 1994, Rehr's organization won an award from the American Society of Association Executives—a trade association of lobby groups.) Like other lobby groups, Rehr's summons up an adverse development, no matter how likely, in order to stir concern, and activism, among the members. The issue of taxes on beer, Rehr said, "is a rallying issue even if it isn't on the table."

Rehr, who has the demeanor of a big, friendly dog, says, "What I do can be summarized 'Don't screw around with the beer wholesalers. If you pick a fight with the beer wholesalers, (a) it'll be expensive and (b) it could cost you your political life. We'll go against you with candidates and we'll support opponents. And you'll probably end up by not winning in the end.'" Rehr continued, "My view is if you're pro–small

business, we're with you, and if you're anti–beer wholesalers, anti–small business, we're your worst nightmare."

In 1994, the wholesalers, who have the fourth-largest trade association political action committee, contributed to forty candidates, seven of them for the House. (The three larger trade association PACs are two automobile dealer groups and the National Association of Home Builders.)

His members, the principal owners and operators of beer wholesalerships, earn anywhere from seventy-five thousand to more than a million dollars. "But we're politically united," Rehr said, "by being pro–beer consumption and small business." The beer wholesalers share some of the same antipathy as other small businesses toward certain government regulations—thus enhancing their political power. "Even if you have two hundred employees, when OSHA [the Occupational Safety and Health Administration] knocks on your door, you're a small business," Rehr says. In recent years, Rehr also helped stave off proposed legislation mandating that warnings about the effects of drinking beer be included in television and radio ads, or at the point of sale. His group supported the moratorium on new regulations passed by the House in 1995. (It died in the Senate.)

In 1994, Rehr worked closely with House Majority Whip Tom DeLay, a fierce opponent of government regulations—DeLay had owned a pest-control company before getting into politics and objected to regulations by the Environmental Protection Agency—in trying to fight off new OSHA regulations on ergonomics (repetitive stress injuries, in this instance from lifting cases of beer). Rehr, investing in a potentially valuable alliance, helped DeLay in his effort to become whip in 1995 by supporting his efforts to elect Republican candidates for the 104th Congress, especially new candidates—whose gratitude helped DeLay win his new role. Rehr said, "If you see a freshman and you say 'Tom DeLay' and 'David Rehr,' they'll say, 'Our guys.'" (As a congratulatory gift, Rehr gave

DeLay a large, framed whip, which hangs in his office.) After the 1994 election, Rehr helped several freshmen pay off their campaign debts—another time-honored way of winning legislative friends.

In 1996, Rehr's group was to give about eighty percent of its contributions to Republicans, with the emphasis on those who really needed the funds—thus incurring deeper gratitude—as opposed to those who have a safe district or a fat campaign treasure, or both. Rehr, like others, occasionally donated to candidates who didn't need the contribution, to ensure access. Democrats who have large breweries in their districts, such as Dick Gephardt, of St. Louis, where Anheuser-Busch is located, also received contributions from the wholesalers association, as did Vic Fazio, of California and as chairman of the House Democratic Caucus a man of some influence. "The beer industry is larger than the wine-making industry in California," Rehr said.

To enhance the power behind their efforts to keep the House in Republican hands, the interested groups stay in close touch. Rehr kept in regular contact with Bill Paxon and his staff, in particular the National Republican Congressional Committee's very smart executive director, Maria Cino; and with the Christian Coalition's top Washington officials, including a man named D.J. Gribbin, the head of the Coalition's Washington office, and a woman named Heidi Stirrup, who sometimes attends Grover Norquist's Wednesday morning meetings; and with Tanya Metaksa, executive director of the National Rifle Association's political arm. (Ralph Reed maintained his residence in Norfolk, Virginia, traveling to Washington frequently.)

The federal election law stipulates that interest groups aren't supposed to coordinate their efforts for or against a candidate, but what actually goes on appears to be a distinction without a difference. Rehr said, "The Federal Election Commission says you can't coordinate, but everybody talks to each other." He added, "We make a practice of not talking specific amounts with each other. We talk about who's targeted, how somebody's doing, but not in terms of 'Why don't you throw in three thousand and we'll throw in five thousand.'" This is a very narrow interpretation of the law.

On occasion, the alliance split over a candidate. "Sometimes Heidi and I disagree and fight with each other; usually we find an accommodation," Rehr said. The Christian Coalition and the N.R.A. parted with the beer wholesalers in refusing to support Tom Campbell, a moderate, pro-choice, pro–gun control Republican in a special election for a California House seat in 1995—in which both parties had a high stake. (Campbell won.) There's also some tension with the Christian Coalition because of its faction that opposes the drinking of alcohol. Since there are fewer and fewer Republicans—at least those who run for the House—who are economic conservatives but social liberals, the alliance doesn't split often, but sometimes a group's support will be less open and aggressive.

Rehr tells me that although the beer wholesalers group takes no formal position on gun control, it doesn't want the government to ban guns, because it sees that as amounting to taking things from people, and next there might be a prohibition on beer. There have been some tensions between the Christian Coalition and the N.R.A., because of a stream of the religious right that sees controlling guns as a moral issue. But all of these groups fit under Grover Norquist's "Leave Us Alone" umbrella.

Like the House members running for reelection themselves, in the early months of 1996 Rehr and his allies concentrated on getting as much money as possible to favored candidates by March 31st, the Federal Election Commission's first filing deadline of the year, so that when the F.E.C. issued its report on April 15th, those candidates would look formidable. "It's used as a mark," Rehr said when we talked in early March. "If the incumbent shows he or she has raised four hundred thousand dollars and has two hundred and fifty thousand or three hundred thousand dollars in cash on hand, it gives a potential opponent pause." (Bill Paxon, chairman of the House Republican campaign committee, said in early March, "We've been pounding on members to raise more money by the filing deadline; if they show a good balance, that could ward off opponents.")

This game of chicken was especially important at that point, when both parties were still recruiting candidates. The January report on contributions up to December 31, 1995, did scare off some potential opponents to Republican incumbents. Few thought then that the Democrats could retake the House, which also made the Democrats' recruiting difficult.

By early March, the beer wholesalers group had, in Rehr's words, "gone through all the freshmen and looked at who might have a difficult race, or might be targeted [by Democratic-oriented interest groups] and we've maxed out on all of them." In contributing parlance, "maxed out" means one has given the full amount allowed under the election laws—for a PAC, five thousand dollars in a primary and five thousand in the general election.

The Spanish Civil War of the 1996 elections was fought in January 1996 over filling the Senate seat of Bob Packwood, the Oregon Republican who had resigned in disgrace in September, 1995. The Christian Coalition, the N.F.I.B., the beer wholesalers, the N.R.A., and the Chamber of Commerce went into the state for the Republican candidate, Gordon Smith; labor and environmental groups provided people to help Smith's opponent, then-Representative Ron Wyden (the AFL-CIO contributed twelve people, plus twenty-five from its affiliates). Wyden won by a little over one percentage point. Rehr said, "The fact that Smith lost sent a wake-up call to Republicans in the House and the business community that they would see the same pattern used in seventy-five congressional districts across the country, and we couldn't sit back and let that happen."

"The Opposition"
Elizabeth Drew

Arrayed against the rightward groups was a collection of equally determined Democratic-oriented groups intent on regaining Democratic control of the House. Like the groups on the right, these people all knew each other. They were liberal, and they were out to make 1994 an aberration. Theirs were the voters who, unhappy with Clinton and thinking it mattered little who controlled the Congress, hadn't turned out then. The 1994 election was an embarrassment for these groups, so they were also working to restore their own political strength as well as to elect a more sympathetic Congress. Like their counterparts, they understood that this was about more than 1996: that if the Republicans retained control of the House they would probably be dug in for some time and have a stranglehold on domestic policy. A realignment will have taken place. Making the same calculations as their counterparts, many of them believed also that who controlled the House was more important than who controlled the White House.

This was particularly true of organized labor, which was making an unprecedented effort to elect a more friendly Congress. Its own political strength had been on the decline for more than a decade. In undertaking its special effort to dislodge the Republicans, labor wasn't so much "throwing its weight around," as the Republicans heatedly charged, as it was trying to gain weight. (Much of its trouble stemmed from its opposition to the North American Free Trade agreement, or NAFTA, in 1993, which Clinton championed. Not only was its opposition futile, but the battle caused many labor members to stay home or vote Republican in November, 1994.) Thus, at a special convention in Washington in late March, the AFL-CIO ratified the decision already taken by its leadership to spend $35 million on a special effort to dislodge the Republicans. In a fiery speech, the labor federation's new president, John Sweeney, elected the previous October as an insurgency candidate who vowed to reverse the decline in labor's political power, singled out Randy Tate and Greg Ganske, along with the House Republican leaders, as special targets of the effort.

When we talked a few days after his speech, Sweeney, a balding, white-haired, pink-complexioned man with blue, watery eyes and pronounced eyebrows, who was wearing red-and-blue suspenders, made it clear that the labor effort had a larger purpose than the immediate battle at hand. He said, "There's an opportunity for labor unions to organize to play a stronger and effective role in political battles." He added, "Our declining membership and less effective voice in politics—that was what my campaign was all about and our political activity is all about." He added, "We hope to be active in every single congressional district in the country, and we want to be more effective in politics for a long time to come."

When I asked him why he had singled out Tate and Ganske for mention in his speech, Sweeney replied, "Because they're among the most outspoken on anti-labor issues"—an observation that was debatable in Ganske's case. (He insisted that Ganske had supported a tax cut for the very wealthy. Ganske had tried to lower the income cap, but did vote for the final bill.) The more I spoke with union leaders, the clearer it became that, in their own version of Willy Sutton (who said he robbed banks because that's where the money was), they were choosing to fight in the districts with large numbers of union members. Both Tate and Ganske represented such districts.

Both Sweeney and Steve Rosenthal, the AFL-CIO's political director, were defensive about some points. They were at pains to say that the $35 million—or, Sweeney said, more if possible—they planned to spend on the fight for Congress amounted to only fifteen cents per member per month, and that money would come out of existing treasuries, not out of new dues assessments. Republicans argued, nonetheless, that labor was spending members' dues for a partisan campaign, which is illegal. Therefore, despite Sweeney's tip-off speech, and despite the obvious, union officials, including Sweeney, were at pains to say that they were simply engaged in an "educational" activity, or "issue advocacy." Because of the laws, they denied that they had "targeted" certain Republican candidates. . . .

Sitting in his office on the sixth floor of the AFL-CIO building on 16th Street, political director Steve Rosenthal said that labor, too, saw the House elections as the most important of 1996—more important than the contest for the Presidency.

Rosenthal, forty-three, had curly dark hair speckled with white, and large brown eyes, a thick beard, a barrel chest, a deep voice, and an easy manner. He looked more like a friendly revolutionary—with most of the revolution in his past—or a college professor than a stereotypical "labor boss." This former union organizer and political strategist, who most recently worked in the Labor Department under Robert Reich, was an amiable zealot. His mission was simple: take back the House for the Democrats. He had helped engineer Sweeney's successful race for president of the AFL-CIO, and since then he and Sweeney had been out to wreak vengeance on the 104th Congress. . . .

The charge against the 104th Congress, Rosenthal said, was "We believe that this Congress has waged the worst assault on working families in the last seventy-five years and they have tried to dismantle every protection that workers have had for fifty years." He listed attempts to reduce OSHA regulations to protect workers, efforts to change the nature of collective bargaining.

To Republican charges that forty percent of union members had voted for Republicans in 1994, Rosenthal's response was that that was the point of the 1996 exercise.

When I saw Rosenthal a few weeks later (on the wall behind him was the famous, unfortunate, photograph of Bob Dole lounging in bathing trunks in Bal Harbour, talking on a telephone), he said he thought that the Democrats had a thirty to forty percent chance to retake the House. "If you said at this point that the Democrats will retake the House, people would say you're crazy." He predicted (accurately, as it turned out) that for all the ruckus stirred up by the Republicans over labor's announced $35 million effort, it would be greatly outspent by the forces on the other side. I asked him how he felt about being called a "labor boss." He smiled and replied, "I prefer that to being 'irrelevant.'"

The AFL-CIO worked more closely with other groups than in the past. One was EMILY's List, which backed pro-choice Democratic women. EMILY's List, in turn, announced it would work closely with the Democratic National Committee in a joint project to mobilize women voters in five states; this number later grew to six, but the collaboration was to be less extensive or munificent than the EMILY's List people had hoped, as the contributions it expected from the D.N.C. went instead to more media advertising for the Clinton-Gore ticket. EMILY's List itself ended up working with state parties in thirty-one states. (EMILY's List made a point of raising money early so as to be able to persuade women candidates to run; the name EMILY stands for Early Money Is Like Yeast. "We make the dough rise," says Ellen Malcolm, the president of the group.) Others the AFL-CIO worked with were environmental groups such as the Sierra Club and the League of Conservation Voters; the National Abortion Rights Action League (NARAL); and the National Education Association. The AFL-CIO's training centers, used primarily to train union activists for the elections, also trained activists from the other groups.

EMILY's List, using work by pollsters Stan Greenberg and Celinda Lake, was particularly focused on getting non–college educated women to the polls. According to EMILY's List, forty-nine percent of the women who had voted Democratic in 1992 didn't bother to vote or went over to the Republicans two years later. Overall, fifty-nine percent of those who dropped out between 1992 and 1994 were women. The historic gender gap—women giving a higher percentage of their vote to the Democrats—only worked in the Democrats' favor if women voted in great numbers. There had been much talk in political circles after 1994 about "angry white men"—men who shifted to the Republicans in 1994. EMILY's List was making the point that there were angry white women as well.

Several environmental groups combined under their communal political arm, the League of Conservation Voters. The L.C.V. puts out a list of the "Dirty Dozen"—Members of Congress with the worst environmental records, as well as a scorecard. In 1996, they also mounted an "independent expenditures" effort, for the purpose of raising and spending more money than allowed for PACs under the campaign finance law. They were particularly interested in about a dozen House races—especially that of the highly controversial Helen Chenoweth, Republican of Idaho. The other major environmental group, the Sierra Club, also set out to raise unprecedented amounts, to concentrate on Republicans with poor environmental records, particularly those in races on the West Coast, where the environmental movement was especially strong. It targeted in particular Andrea Seastrand, Republican of California.

Both groups made a special effort in Washington State. Philip Clapp, of the Environmental Information Center, a legislative and political clearinghouse for environmental groups, said, "A lot of places that labor is going into have suburbs that labor doesn't get to, but environmentalists do." He listed Randy Tate's district as an example of where blue-collar workers are also environmentalists. The environmental groups met regularly to coordinate their efforts. (These groups had also gone into the Oregon special election.)

Earlier in the year, the AFL-CIO and its allied groups held two long meetings at the 16th Street headquarters to talk about who was doing what, to get a feel for the important contested districts.

The White House, in fact, put together a national steering committee consisting of representatives from the Clinton-Gore campaign, the Democratic National Committee, the AFL-CIO, the National Education Association, and EMILY's List. The group met semi-regularly at the Democratic National Committee headquarters to discuss what priority should be given which states, which of this coalition's partners were actively organizing in which states, who was doing what about direct mail or get-out-the-vote drives—a former campaign official explains, "all with a view toward accumulating enough electoral votes in November."

The *Mother Jones* Interview: John McCain

Jason Vest

Of all the dyed-in-the-wool conservatives one finds on Capitol Hill, Sen. John McCain of Arizona is certainly the least boring. Though he's predictably Republican in many ways—he's an ardent free-marketeer and pro-lifer, and he gets low marks from environmental groups—McCain has, in the past year, stridently stood up to the GOP leadership and worked with his erstwhile political opponents in the Senate for campaign finance reform and the tobacco settlement. Both efforts failed (largely due to lack of Republican support), but they helped increase McCain's public standing; his image as a courageous reformer has even led to speculation about a dark horse presidential candidacy in 2000. But critics say that image is carefully cultivated, and many accuse the press of going soft on McCain, who heads the powerful Senate Commerce Committee.

When *Mother Jones* dropped in on McCain at his Washington, D.C., office in mid-September, Lewinsky-mania was in full swing. Despite his well-known temper—he once reportedly got into a scuffle with his nonagenarian colleague Sen. Strom Thurmond (R-S.C.)—McCain was relaxed and smiling, displaying the forthright charm that has made him the darling of political reporters while trenchantly defending his right to accept campaign contributions from the likes of Bill Gates and Rupert Murdoch.

MJ: In September, the day after campaign finance reform was killed in the Senate for the third time, the news was buried on Page A16 of the *New York Times* under an avalanche of Clinton-Lewinsky reporting. What did you think when you saw the *Times* that day?

John McCain: It's an affirmation that this firestorm has sucked all the oxygen out of the political debate in America. I had some con-

fidence that we would at least pick up some more votes. Well, the president gave his speech—the apology/nonapology speech—and we took up the bill. It was two days of desultory discussion. It wasn't even a debate. Nothing in the media, no phone calls, no interest. We got the same 52 votes, and it was like dropping a stone in a well.

MJ: Did you expect it to end this way?

John McCain: You can understand people who want power and want to corrupt or destroy the constitutional balance. You can understand that, because that's why our Founding Fathers set up this system of checks and balances: There are always going to be people who want more power than is appropriate or healthy for the republic. But certainly, never in my life did I contemplate such a tawdry thing. Such an embarrassment.

MJ: Doesn't the current situation strike you as going a little too far?

John McCain: I don't blame Mr. Starr as much as I blame the law. The responsibility has to come back to Congress for formulating such a law, perhaps even the president for signing it.

MJ: How many of your colleagues could have withstood a Kenneth Starr?

John McCain: I don't know, because I don't know their personal lives. I don't socialize with many senators, much less House members, but let me tell you, I'm one who has undergone a special counsel. The special counsel's name was Mr. Robert Bennett in the Keating Five matter. [But] your point is legitimate, because Bennett was not given a charter to look at whether I had an affair 30 years ago with Cherie Snodgrass. [Laughs.]

MJ: Give me an example of why you think we need campaign finance reform.

John McCain: The so-called Telecommunications Reform Act of 1996, where every major telecommunications company was protected. Only one group was not represented while we formulated that particular piece of legislation, and that was—guess who?—the average American citizen, who has seen the cable rates go up 20 percent [in some cities], who has seen mergers and consolidations within the industry that have been found to be anticompetitive. You know how many people voted against that bill? Five.

As for the businesses [that lobbied for the bill], I respect those people, because they're trying to do the best they can for their stockholders, and they have fiduciary responsibilities. I don't blame them for trying, for enhancing their profits and protecting their turf. I blame us for falling prey to the influence of somebody like AT&T, which in 1996 gave $780,000 to Republicans and $456,000 to Democrats—which is not political schizophrenia, it's good business. If I were a CEO of a major corporation, I would do the same thing. I would say, Look guys, they're passing legislation. Get down there to Washington and make sure that we aren't harmed by it. So I don't hold animosity toward them. I hold animosity toward the system, which is completely broken. Where, in the words of [Sen.] Fred Thompson [R-Tenn.], there is no limit to the amount that you can contribute to any campaign in America.

MJ: How much difference did Thompson's investigation into fundraising practices in the '96 election really make?

John McCain: Two things happened with Thompson's committee. One was that we were unable to act in a bipartisan fashion. But there was also the factor that Republicans made sure that there was only one year under which Thompson's committee could operate, thereby allowing the administration to just walk it. And they were selling seats on trade missions. Not to mention everything else in government.

MJ: Your own party wasn't missing any dirt under the fingernails, either—

John McCain: Go no further. If this independent counsel is appointed, and I believe it will [be], either to investigate [former White House Deputy Chief of Staff Harold] Ickes or the vice president, you will see this scandal touch Republicans as well. Your point is very well made. Why do you think the Republicans made sure that the committee stayed in business for only a year?

It's the system. The system makes good people do bad things, and bad people do worse things. And we are dramatically diminished in the eyes of the people we represent when we are a product of a system that has become fundamentally corrupt.

MJ: The conventional wisdom is that money doesn't buy votes, it buys access.

John McCain: But access buys influence. You forget there's a corollary to that.

MJ: So how do you handle it?

John McCain: Because I'm chairman of the Commerce Committee, I see the CEOs of major corporations. Which has nothing to do with campaign donations—I have oversight of their businesses and I'll see the CEOs. I don't see the lobbyists, OK? If somebody calls—say if the CEO of PrimeStar wants to see me—I say, "Fine, tell him to come in." But if a lobbyist with PrimeStar calls and says he wants to come in, I say, "No, talk to my staff." But when Gene Kimmelman of the Consumers Union or Joan Claybrook of Public Citizen wants to talk to me, I say, "Come on in." What I try to do is listen to a balanced set of viewpoints, not dictated by campaign contributions or anything else, whether they're Republicans or Democrats or Libertarians or vegetarians. But there's nothing wrong with talking to people who are the experts on the issues.

MJ: Certainly. But it was reported earlier this year that when Microsoft's COO Bob Herbold came to visit you, he asked what Microsoft could be doing better in Washington and you told him to fire up a lobbying campaign.

John McCain: No, no. I said, "The way the game's played in Washington, you're gonna have to have a greater presence here in Washington," is basically what I said. In a perfect world I would say, "Stay out and don't have anything to do with [lobbying]," but you have to have a presence here in Washington.

MJ: Bill Gates has given you money, and so has Rupert Murdoch. Both have business before your committee. This is exactly the thing that most people would raise an eyebrow at. Why do you take their money?

John McCain: It would be nearly impossible for me to raise money without them. But the important point here is that the evil is soft money. There's nothing wrong, in my view, with taking a $1,000 contribution from anybody who wants to give it. And if it comes from Mr. Gates, or if it comes from my next-door neighbor in Phoenix, I think it's OK. I don't think the system was corrupted until soft money exploded, and I won't have anything to do with soft money.

MJ: A number of observers have noted that if Microsoft's antitrust issues were heard in your committee instead of the Judiciary Committee, Microsoft would get a much friendlier reception.

John McCain: They'd get a friendly reception in my committee because a lot of us have grave concerns about what the government's doing here. Our focus is not antitrust considerations—it's the health of the telecommunications industry in America. Our interest and our charter are directed toward the future of the industry.

MJ: So you're not worried about Microsoft warping the industry?

John McCain: I worried about IBM warping everyone. I worried about Apple warping everyone until they screwed up their marketing techniques. But I don't think Mr. Gates, or anyone, knows where this industry is going, as smart as he is. Of course I'm con-

cerned about it. My question is, What is the role of the federal government? I remember when the federal government brought a suit against IBM. And then 13 years later, it went before some judge and said it's irrelevant because of the rapid changes in the computer industry.

MJ: You not only have had combat experience in Vietnam, but you were also a prisoner of war. When you look at terrorism right now, with people like Osama bin Laden, do you have any reservations about watching strikes like that?

John McCain: You could say, Look, is this guy, Laden, really the bad guy that's depicted? Most of us have never heard of him before. And where there is a parallel with Vietnam is: What's plan B? What do we do next? We sent our troops into Vietnam to protect the bases. Lyndon Johnson said, Only to protect the bases. Next thing you know. . .Well, we've declared to the terrorists that we're going to strike them wherever they live. That's fine. But what's next? That's where there might be some comparison.

MJ: Now, about tobacco. . .

John McCain: Ah, part of my string of successes: campaign finance reform, tobacco bill, pork-barrel spending. I have a number of notches in my gun.

MJ: When you were handed that task, what was your first thought?

John McCain: I thought, "This is going to be a huge undertaking." But I thought that we could do it. I underestimated several challenges, but primarily I underestimated the willingness of the tobacco companies to spend as much money as they did, in such a concentrated fashion. Kathleen Hall Jamieson of the Annenberg Public Policy Center did a study that showed that more money was spent on this than any other [single-issue campaign], and they really saturated, including my state, by the way. One of the ones they saturated with was, "What's happened to John McCain? He's become a big-spending, big-government liberal—what's happened to John McCain?" After X million [dollars], people started stopping in the street and saying, "What's happened to you?" Like I had an automobile accident or a lobotomy. So it had great effect.

MJ: Did you see that as the beginning of something more ominous?

John McCain: I first saw that they would do anything, because they are bad people. They are really bad people. And I thought they would probably attack me personally, because if they could take me down, they could take anybody down. And they were running full-page ads in *Roll Call* with my picture. Why do you think they were doing that? Because they were influencing voters? No. They were influencing members.

MJ: In terms of influence, it seems that the religious right has succeeded in making sexual morality the pre-eminent national issue.

John McCain: My party is a majority, which means there are more elements to it, and which argues for a bigger tent. If we're going to get the center and hold the center, then we're going to have to be able to tolerate and even embrace, on occasion, disparate views. And I could make you a case, if you look at elections, that the so-called Christian right has been losing as many elections as they've been winning.

MJ: Yes or no: Are you going to run for president in 2000?

John McCain: I'm going to run for re-election in the Senate, and then I'm going to start the decision-making process. I have no PAC; I have no campaign team. I have been to New Hampshire, I think, twice this year. I've been to Iowa once or twice. I'm not one of those frequent visitors. And I just decided [that] after the election I would start talking to people to see if it's a viable undertaking.

MJ: Finally, speaking of presidential politics and ethics: What is character?

John McCain: Human foibles, whether they be a predilection, or immorality, or gambling, or mistreating your wife, or kicking dogs—that's a different kind, in my view, of morality. Whereas character—I'm trying to think who it was who said, "Character is who you are in the dark."

One of my greatest criticisms of this administration is that every time I talk to one of their people on an issue, you know what their opening phrase is? Three words: "We polled this." We polled this, so you should vote for school uniforms, you should be in favor of putting deadbeat dads' pictures in the post office, you should be in favor of whatever it is, the issue du jour. How many Americans do you think favored the United States, under the aegis of the United Nations, sending 480,000 Americans to fight and 54,000 of them dying in Korea? What if Harry Truman had said, Let's take a poll here as to whether the American people want us to send troops to Korea. See what I mean? That's my point. That's what character is, OK?

Jesse
a conservative
Libertarian

Krystal
a liberal
Democrat

Suzanne
a moderate
Republican

Turi
a moderate
Democrat

Will
a moderate

Is It True that Money Equals Power?
★ ★ ★

Dr. Bauer: There's a lot of money floating around Washington, and that leads us to how politicians raise money. They raise money from special interest groups. And that leads us to the editorial in the Madison, Wisconsin, *Capital Times:* "Who Really Writes Laws?" What, if anything, surprised you about this reading?

Suzanne: All of it! I mean, I just couldn't believe . . . I mean, I realized that Senators needed their staffs to help draft laws, but that they would take something written by someone else—a lobbyist—and use it, that bothered me a great deal.

Will: Not only that, but then they aren't that embarrassed to admit to the public that they *did* it. Like in this article, Senator Gorton wasn't too concerned.

Dr. Bauer: Senator Gorton happens to be Republican. Now what does the article say about Democrats? Do they never do this?

Will: They do it, but they at least try to hide it.

Turi: Those Democrats, man!

Dr. Bauer: Yeah, we are a sneaky bunch, aren't we? But, the Republicans are not all that upset about it because their special interest groups represent their constituency, and they are not upset about letting the world know. So, this bill comes fully drafted by lobbyists. For senators, it is sort of like taking a term paper from the Internet.

Suzanne: No, no. This is not like taking a term paper from the Internet. If the senator were taking the term paper from the Internet, he would have to pay for it. This way, he gets the work, and they pay him to use it! So, there is a difference here!

Dr. Bauer: You're right, that's a nice twist.

Jesse: One of these articles pointed out that it is not necessarily the money driving the policy, but the policy driving the money. The timber-mining-ranching interests are giving money to Gorton, who represents the state of Washington, which depends on timber and mining and ranching. Lobbyists give money, I think, based on what Gorton has already done, and they know that he agrees with their interests. They are not trying to sway somebody like Ted Kennedy! Lobbyists work with the people who already agree with them and whose interest groups have a big population in their state or district.

Suzanne: It wouldn't make good sense for a lobbyist to approach a different senator. I mean if you are going to try to get the senator to introduce the bill that you wrote, a good lobbyist will go to the senator who has some sympathy for your cause. That only makes good sense. But, it still strikes me as being "not quite right."

Jesse: Well, you would like to hope, I guess, that the influence of lobbyists is not the sole thing that any member of Congress uses to decide how to vote. But, I know that down at the state capital, it works the same way: The lobbyists bring in bills already written, and the only thing they don't have on them is the number and the sponsor's name. Even a lot of those probably have prepenciled in who they really want introducing a particular piece of legislation. Members just fill in the blank!

Krystal: It seems as if lobbyists are almost necessary to get things done. Well, how, in heaven's name, are members of Congress even going to be able to sit down and draft resolutions, and all of this rigmarole, and then how are they going to push it with all of their fellow members, and still have time to get anything done?

Suzanne: Krystal, it's his job. That's what the people from Washington elected him to do: to examine the issues that are important for him and his constituency, and then draft the legislation. Not to accept it as a piece from a special interest group.

Turi: Lobbyists make life easier for politicians. Because they have to do a whole lot less work, the politicians are probably a lot more agreeable to what the lobbyists want.

Suzanne: Going back to Dr. Bauer's saying those lobbyist-written bills are like pulling a term paper off of the Internet. All of us here are students. There isn't a soul at this table who would say, "It's okay, because my kid is sick, and my car is broke, and my boss is yelling at me, and so it is okay for me to download my term paper off the Internet."

Turi: You have to get out more! I know tons of students who cheat like that—for the same reasons politicians let lobbyists write bills. I'm not saying it's right, but it happens!

Krystal: But, you know, stealing something—stealing something from the Internet and presenting it as your own work—is different from being given something and being told, "You know, you can have this as your own work."

Suzanne: No, Krystal, it would not be all right for me to give Turi my term paper and allow her to present it in her class. That would not be—

Dr. Bauer:	But, how about if Turi said, "I got this from Suzanne"? This is what Senator Gorton is saying. He is not saying, "I made this up." He is not claiming credit; he is willing to say, "Hey, look this is *their bill*. I am sponsoring it; I agree with it. But, I didn't write it."
Suzanne:	Okay, but this is the problem with pluralism. Special interest groups are not all equal in power. And they have more power than ordinary people. Senator Gorton wouldn't take anything *I* wrote, no matter how skilled, or how firm my arguments were, or how right my stand was—
Krystal:	If you didn't have the money—
Suzanne:	Right. If I didn't have the money and the political clout to go with it, forget it! He is not going to be interested in me at all.
Will:	That's just what the editorial writer says at the end. When lobbyists draft the laws, "they severely limit the opportunity for the interests of the general public to play an adequate role in adoption of the nation's laws."
Suzanne:	I mean, I am not even sure Senator Gorton examined the bill and all its ramifications before he presented it.
Will:	Exactly. How do we know that? How can we be sure of that? Especially when he is getting a $34,000 kickback in the form of campaign contributions from that industry.
Suzanne:	Right.
Jesse:	Well, but there are a couple of different things to remember. He has to disclose that $34,000 on his Federal Election Commission disclosure form, so the people in his state certainly know where he is getting his money—on which side his bread is buttered, if that is the case. And, the other thing, he is voting consistently with an ideology that he has always held. He has determined that it is better for the state of Washington that timber jobs and mining jobs be saved, than that a particular endangered species be saved. And if you look at a Democratic issue, you will find the same thing: They vote consistent with their ideology, lobbyists or no lobbyists. Democrats will say it is better that we raise the minimum wage in Denver to $13 an hour than it is to help businesses keep labor costs low. It is the same from both sides.
Krystal:	We say we really want a representative democracy, and we sit here and constantly ask, "Where is the public? Where are the people?" Well, maybe the people are enrolled in these special interest groups; there are people who back these special interest groups in the state of Washington.
Dr. Bauer:	Sure, and that representation is a constraint on special interest group spending that is not often talked about in introductory textbooks: If an interest group wants the support of a member of Congress, but the group's proposal runs counter to the interests of the member's constituency, what is the likelihood that the member will take any amount of money to support that bill?
Turi:	Like Diana DeGette and the NRA, say, something like that.

Dr. Bauer:	Right. Flesh that out.
Turi:	Well, DeGette believes strongly that we need more gun control. And her constituents are very anti-NRA, so she said she would never take a dime from the NRA.
Dr. Bauer:	So the NRA isn't even going to approach Diana DeGette, because they know that her ideology is against them, and her ideology fits with the people in her district. This is what Jesse was saying—maybe the ideology of the member comes first, and lobbying influence comes second.
Krystal:	Isn't this the whole theory of pluralism? You have one representative who agrees with the NRA, and then you have another representative like Diana DeGette who you know is going to fight the NRA, and so you have a sense that it all evens out in the long run, perhaps.
Jesse:	The other thing, too, in defense of lobbyists, is that some politicians frankly need the help! One of our Colorado senators, Wayne Allard, is a veterinarian. He seems to be a smart enough fellow, but do you really want him drafting legislation his first year?
Will:	Two things still bother me: the fact that Gorton is just taking this bill from a lobbyist, verbatim, and the fact that lobbyists are not thinking beyond their own self-interest.
Dr. Bauer:	What we're really talking about is whether pluralism works or not. Political scientists who believe that our democracy is working say that it works, not because individuals are involved, but because groups are involved. And groups are supposed to fight for their own self-interests. In this model of democracy, a politician who speaks for an interest group is not such a bad thing.
Jesse:	Even if Slade Gorton is in the pocket of the timber industry, and Wayne Allard is in the pocket of NRA, so what? There are ninety-eight other senators who are not. Some of them are in the pocket of the Handgun Control group. And some are in the pocket of the environmental lobby who give money to reelect politicians who will protect the endangered species. They offset each other in the long run.
Krystal:	Then it becomes the people's responsibility to stay alert. If representatives that they have elected are not in sync with them, then it is their responsibility to know which lobbyists financially support their representatives, and vote accordingly.
Dr. Bauer:	Now that we have a better idea of what pluralism means, let's move to Elizabeth Drew's "Beer." Here we see an example of lobbyists working together. We have an interesting twist on pluralism, because we have groups that seem to have contradictory interests working together. They don't seem to be groups that ought to work together, yet they are. And if that is the case, then part of the theory of pluralism, of groups competing against each other, is a little shaken up. Something is going on here. Who are the beer lobbyists, why are they important, and who are they working with?

Krystal:	The Christian Coalition! The NRA!
Will:	They take what seems to be a narrow issue and show how it fits into the whole conservative package. By doing that, they can get different groups, each with its own narrow interest in what seems like night-and-day contrast to the others, to come together as a cohesive whole to lobby Congress.
Dr. Bauer:	Yes, there is a mobilization of support from the beer lobbyists, the NRA, and the Christian Coalition. But my question to you is, Do you really think the members of the Christian Coalition like the beer lobby? Do you think the ordinary rank-and-file members of the Christian Coalition have any clue that their lobbyist is making deals with the beer lobby?
Suzanne:	Probably not. It's that old saying, "Politics makes strange bed-fellows."
Krystal:	The people don't see it, but if you study politics, you know it has to be going on. Even on a small scale, at the level of campus politics, there is that kind of coalition-building to get things done—like when the Christian Student group is working with the Arab Student group to bring in a speaker that they both want.
Jesse:	Last year in the stadium campaign, we had probably the most diverse coalition of people you will ever see in your life under one roof. We had a couple hard-core Libertarians, like me. We had some very liberal Democrats, who just happened to be against this particular issue of funding a new stadium for the Broncos with tax dollars. We had four members of the Green Party; we had about a half-dozen people who were from labor unions. We had a lot of anti-tax Republicans and other smaller groups, like the American Constitution Party, and the U.S. Taxpayers Party. In a group of fifty people, we had at least thirty or forty different, distinct, and fairly narrowly tailored interests, all under the same roof, because that one issue brought us together. We couldn't talk about anything else! But, when we were talking about the stadium, we were almost always of the same mind.
Dr. Bauer:	So it is natural for groups who want power to work together in coalition, but does it surprise you that the [National] Beer Wholesalers [Association] were the fourth-largest trade association PAC in 1994? Had you heard of this PAC before? No. So my question is, how much do you think the voters know about special interest politics?
Jesse:	What they hear on the news, which is not much.
Will:	And they forget that because they have short-term memories.
Dr. Bauer:	So this is an insider's game. Why do special interest groups get involved in politics? Why did the beer people get all excited?
Will:	Basically, they got shafted; I think it was by some heavy duty taxes. And when it comes to losing money, you're right there. Losing money; a classic *high-salience issue!*

Krystal:	And that is usually when people get involved. When they feel they are getting shafted; that is when coalitions start.
Dr. Bauer:	All right, so in "Beer," we have the right-wing, special interest lineup. Who are these guys, the big heavy hitters in the right wing?
Turi:	The NRA.
Krystal:	The Christian Coalition.
Turi:	The NFIB.
Dr. Bauer:	National Federation of Independent Business.
Turi:	And then the beer.
Dr. Bauer:	The beer wholesalers. So, these are the top folks, plus lobbyist Grover Norquist's group—ATR, Americans for Tax Reform.
Krystal:	But out of these four, I had only ever heard of the National Rifle Association and the Christian Coalition!
Dr. Bauer:	Yes, most people don't know who Grover Norquist is, but he is a major player in Washington.
Jesse:	One of the things I want to point out is that these coalitions are kind of fragile. You never know when you are going to run into the next issue that is going to drive a massive wedge between different factions' members. Time may come when the beer folks want something very different from the Christian Coalition folks, and then, no more coalition.
Dr. Bauer:	Right. And all of this goes on below the radar of most voters. They really don't know. So, when we move to the next reading, "The Opposition," we have the lineup of the main liberal special interest groups, the left-wing groups. Who are they?
Jesse:	NEA!
Dr. Bauer:	National Education Association.
Jesse:	AFL-CIO.
Dr. Bauer:	Labor unions.
Jesse:	Greens, Sierra Club.
Dr. Bauer:	Environmental groups.
Krystal:	NOW.
Dr. Bauer:	National Organization of Women, feminists.
Turi:	The NAACP. The Urban League. African Americans.
Dr. Bauer:	It appears that the best case for pluralism says it is okay to have interest groups if you have opposing interest groups. It wouldn't be okay if we only had busi-

| Will: | An interesting point is that in addition to the money, these interest groups contribute workers and voters in the states or districts. |

ness interest groups, because then everything would tilt only one way. But as long as we have business groups on one hand, like the NFIB, and we have the labor unions like the AFL-CIO on the other, that appears to be fair. Can you tell that the stakes are high for both groups? Both groups are spending lots and lots of money in the 1996 elections.

Will: An interesting point is that in addition to the money, these interest groups contribute workers and voters in the states or districts.

Dr. Bauer: Yes, special interest groups aren't just all about money. They are also about mobilizing the voters. Both sides, in "Beer" and in "Opposition," have their grassroots organizers, loyal foot soldiers, trying to mobilize voters. One of the things that gives the beer wholesalers political power is that they are in every congressional district—businesses, employers, and employees in every congressional district. This is also why the teacher's union, the NEA, is so powerful.

Krystal: Whereas the GLBT—you know, the gay, lesbian, bisexual, and transgender people, and those sorts of groups—they may have a lot of members in the city, but not in the surrounding areas like suburbia or rural areas; they're not going to have as much power with their legislators, because they are so few.

Dr. Bauer: On the other hand, the voters that they do have are extremely loyal, single-issue voters, who will show up even if their legs are broken. And that is what both groups are counting on, aren't they? They are doing two things: They are raising money, and they are mobilizing their voters.

Suzanne: Where does the AARP fit into this?

Dr. Bauer: Well, the American Association of Retired People is also very powerful. Can you name a congressional district that does not have AARP members?

Suzanne: No. But I just wondered where it fits in the political landscape, you know, if you have a group on the left and another on the right . . .

Dr. Bauer: The AARP is interesting because it doesn't align itself with one party. It is a PAC that specifically pursues the financial security, or gain, of its members, and it tends to switch back and forth with a party's stand on issues—although they tend to favor Democrats.

Krystal: Like AIPAC, in a way, on pro-Israeli issues. As long as a congressional member running for office agrees with them, they will support that member, whether he or she is a Democrat or Republican.

Dr. Bauer: Yes, for those groups, it is the issue, not the party, that matters. Now let's look at John McCain's criticism of pluralism in the *Mother Jones* interview. I have cleverly structured this discussion so that after we have examined the classic "hoorah for pluralism," we can look at the other side. Senator McCain does not believe that the classic model of pluralism is working in America, and that is why he is the chief sponsor of the McCain-Feingold Bill that died three times

	in the 104th Congress, twice in the 105th, and is about to die again—and again, and again, and again. But Senator McCain is not letting go because he doesn't think that the system of competing groups is working. Why not? Why does he think we need campaign finance reform?
Turi:	Because money buys access, and ordinary people do not have the access to their representatives that big lobbyists have.
Dr. Bauer:	So, money is buying access, and access leads to influence. The theory of pluralism says, "Special interest groups are all right as long as everybody has a chance to buy access and gain influence." Who does McCain think is being left out?
Jesse:	The average-Joe-working-class American voter is being left out of the process.
Turi:	The poor and the middle class.
Dr. Bauer:	There is a famous story that the late Senator Hubert Humphrey told about who gets the attention of politicians. He said, "We talk a lot about how money doesn't buy votes, but what it does buy is access. If I come back from a meeting, and I have four phone calls, and I only have time to return one, and one of those phone calls is from a lobbyist who has given me money, who is going to get their phone call returned?" That is the problem with the classic, theoretical model of pluralism—it assumes that all players are equal and their interests will balance out in the end. Are business and labor equal?
Turi:	No, not at all. Business has a lot more money than the unions.
Suzanne:	But labor has more people. My husband was a member of the AFL-CIO, and we used to get these nifty newsletters from them, and I realized that they were giving money to candidates! My husband had to pay union dues to keep his job, and the union was using his dues to funnel money to political activities that I didn't agree with! That made me really angry. But, the point is, that they had the power to obligate us to give them money, and then they did what they wanted with it. So, AFL-CIO probably has significant financial resources—it just comes to them in small amounts, but it adds up!
Dr. Bauer:	In a typical campaign finance analysis, when you add up all the money spent, business outspends labor by quite a lot. Now the Republicans will say that you have to add the union's volunteers hours up too—
Jesse:	That is just what I was going to add. Union activists are a whole lot more committed. I mean, who are the big business activists? It doesn't go much below the CEO.
Dr. Bauer:	That's true, it's tough to get a crowd whipped up on pro–big business issues! But let me say this, the number of union volunteer activists has decreased markedly in the last 30 years. Recently, it's been more accurate to say, "Big business has the money, but labor *doesn't* have the money, and labor *doesn't* have the people." So, John Sweeney, the new president of the AFL-CIO, has

	made it one of his goals to work harder at the people part. But, I will tell you, it is hard. You people all work and go to school. How many of you have time to volunteer, even on a cause you really love?
Jesse:	Well, you don't have time, but you make time.
Krystal:	Exactly. That is how you have to look at it. It is not as easy as writing a check, but . . .
Dr. Bauer:	Well, you two have worked on campaigns, you're not normal!
Will:	Yeah, you two are activists!
Jesse:	I'll tell you what, there was a point last year when I basically left a picture of myself on my pillow so my wife would remember what I looked like! Between working full-time, school full-time, and probably working about 30 hours on the stadium issue, she never saw me; she thought the phone was growing out the side of my head!
Krystal:	That's true, the people you actually work with on campaigns become your family because you are donating so much of your time.
Dr. Bauer:	And that is what political activists are like, but they are small in number.
Krystal:	Exactly! I was the volunteer coordinator, and it was extremely difficult to get volunteers—and who blames them! They don't get paid, so they're not very consistent. How many of those people can you really get together and go out and knock on fifty thousand doors per weekend?
Dr. Bauer:	How many times did you have a list of people who had promised to volunteer—
Krystal:	And didn't show up!
Dr. Bauer:	I was taught at Campaigns and Elections National Training that if you ask twenty people to volunteer, five will say yes, and one will show up! You're nodding your heads, so that seems about right to you?
Krystal:	I would go even higher, and say that more people say yes, and when you call them, you get half a person.
Dr. Bauer:	It appears, then, that years ago, a group with lots of volunteers could beat a group with big money. Now, the interest group that can flood the TV and radio with ads, most of the time, will beat the heck out of the group of hard-working volunteers. You found that out on the stadium issue, didn't you, Jesse? So, McCain thinks that we need campaign finance reform, in part, because he doesn't believe pluralism is working. However, does McCain think that groups are evil because they hire lobbyists?
Will:	Of course not. He respects companies like Microsoft, because they are trying to look out for their stockholders.
Turi:	Absolutely. And groups make it easier for individual people to influence politicians. You know, you can't respond to one hundred thousand phone calls a

	day from all of these individuals who believe in one thing. It is easier to have one lobbyist say, "I am representing one hundred thousand people."
Dr. Bauer:	Right, mass politics has to work with groups. It doesn't work with individuals. The problem is that individuals don't tend to join groups, unless they are elites who know the usefulness of belonging to a group, or working class who are forced to belong to a labor group. But organized labor is only about ten to fifteen percent of the voting age public.
Suzanne:	People do tend to join the AARP. They have an advantage though: Their members are retired; they have time; and they have skills because they have worked all their lives—people who can write letters, make phone calls. I think that on any issue that affects the AARP, they are going to have a major, major say because they have resources—including money. There is no American Association of Middle-Aged People! They're too busy to go to meetings!
Dr. Bauer:	Again, this is a weakness in the classic model of pluralism. The elderly have a huge group that is fighting for their interests, but because the other age groups aren't organized, the influence wielded by the elderly is greater than that of other age groups.
Suzanne:	Young Americans could organize, but Turi, you don't have the time for political activity, do you?
Turi:	No. But I also don't think that there is a whole lot of desire, a sense of urgency, or commitment.
Krystal:	You have the CSA, Colorado Students Association, and other organizations similar to that on the national level, who lobby for students.
Dr. Bauer:	But do you know the clout of student organizations on Capitol Hill? Read a great book by Stephen Waldman called *The Bill*. It shows what little power students have over issues like financial aid.
Krystal:	I know. When financial aid was cut a number of years ago, members of Congress didn't get any calls from students saying, "Where's my financial aid?" If Social Security gets cut, what happens?
Suzanne:	March on Washington!
Dr. Bauer:	There you go. And that's why McCain says we need campaign finance reform "to level the playing field." To make it less likely that certain special interests are going to have so much more influence that they will crowd out everybody else.

★ ★ ★

For Additional Reading

Go to InfoTrac College Edition, your online research library at

http://web1.infotrac-college.com

Enter the following search terms using the Subject Guide or Key Terms.

coalitions	junkets	private interest groups
conflicts of interests	Keating Five	public interest groups
Federal Election Campaign Act	lobbying	single-interest group
independent spending	market share	soft money
influence peddling	muckrakers	Teapot Dome scandal
interest groups	political action committees (PACs)	

7

Political Parties

FACE TO FACE

Student Interview with
Richard D. Lamm
Former Governor of Colorado

Clint
a moderate

Mike
a Hispanic,
liberal Democrat

Robert
a moderate
Republican

Sonya
a Hispanic,
moderate Republican

Tony
an African American,
liberal Democrat

Do We Need a Third Party?
★ ★ ★

Richard "Dick" Lamm is a former Governor of Colorado and Democratic Party activist. Dick Lamm was also, for a short time in 1996, a candidate for the Reform Party nomination for president of the United States. Governor Lamm and the historian Stephen Ambrose have written about the possibility of a new political party.

Sonya: When we study political parties, the first thing we are all told is that a third party is not likely to work because we have a "winner-take-all" system. Isn't a new party impossible?

Dick Lamm: On a continuing basis, in a winner-take-all system, we're probably not going to have three political parties. In a "proportional representation" system, a small party that gets, say, ten percent of the vote, gets ten percent of the seats in the national parliament. That creates an incentive for small parties to stick around. But in our system, a party that gets ten percent of the vote in a congressional district can't get ten percent of the person elected. We have a "single-member plurality district" system—meaning whichever party gets the most votes, gets one hundred percent of the representation in Congress—or, winner take all. But this doesn't mean that we can't have vigorous third parties for a short period of time.

Tony: So what good is it to even think about a third party in American politics?

Dick Lamm: That's a good practical question. If I remember correctly, you're working for Mayor Webb's reelection campaign, aren't you? So, you're around politicians; you know that, ultimately, if Wellington Webb wants to win, he puts together a coalition. That's all American parties are—coalitions of groups that have different agendas but unite together to elect one candidate or a slate of candidates.

But some people are left out of both of our major parties, because no organization represents their ideas. The role of a third political party, and it's very important, is to bring to the public's attention new ideas that are being ignored by the other parties.

Clint: I don't think I'm represented very well by either political party. And most of my friends feel the same way. I think it's almost inevitable that a new party will have to form.

Dick Lamm: But it's not easy. In fact, I think it's harder than it's been at any time in American history because of Dr. Bauer's favorite subject, campaign financing.

Before Watergate, there was too much special interest money in American politics. After Watergate, my generation attempted to reform how money mixes with politics, but we didn't really change the system all that much. We now give the two political parties money from the federal treasury to pay for their national conventions and run their presidential campaigns. Because it takes so much money to run a campaign, especially for president, and because the major parties have that funding advantage, it's going to be harder to start a new political party.

Having said all that, I still think that neither political party in America is a . . . an honest broker of the national interest, and we need a new political party.

Robert: You used an interesting phrase—honest broker. That's what parties are supposed to do, isn't it? Represent the complex interests of a huge group of people, and translate these people's interests into laws. But as a Republican, I find that only part of my interests are being served by my party. Sometimes, it represents the opposite of my views.

Dick Lamm: It seems to me that the Republican Party has been drawn more and more to the right, and the Democratic Party has become more and more representative of large, organized groups. But I think that there's a new coalition out there of socially liberal Republicans and financially concerned Democrats. The coalition is there if we can find an issue to organize around.

Mike: So are you organizing this new party?

Dick Lamm: I'm not spending any time myself developing a new party. It's extremely hard work, and that kind of grassroots organizing is not what I want to do right

	now. Furthermore, until the right issue comes along, I don't think there actually will be a new party of substantial influence.
Dr. Bauer:	When you mentioned socially liberal Republicans and fiscally concerned Democrats, I immediately thought of a group that sprang up in the late 1980s, the Concord Coalition. It was headed by two former senators, Republican Warren Rudman and Democrat Paul Tsongas. They were trying to get the attention of both parties rather than create an new party.
Dick Lamm:	I belonged to the Concord Coalition. They were organized to draw attention to the budget deficit, and they did a good job of that. But now that issue is gone, and they have kind of disappeared. This is a pattern that we find in our history. In the 1850s, the Free Soil Party and other groups organized around such issues as slavery. The Progressive Party existed for awhile, then died out. At certain times, third-party coalitions burst onto the scene, then disappear when the issue is resolved.
Sonya:	What issues exist today that might convince us to join a third party?
Dick Lamm:	I think a part of it is going to be generational. It's hard to underestimate what little appeal the two parties really hold for young people, compared to when I was your age, in the sixties. There were so many issues that appealed to young people: feminism, civil rights, the environment, antiwar and prowar arguments over Vietnam. Everybody joined a political party for a *cause*. But now, with the possible exception of gays and lesbians—the last idealistic block of voters to come into the Democratic Party—it's the trial lawyers, it's the teachers unions, it's the special interests groups, each one with its hand out for some benefit that they hope to get from government. I simply think that you can't run a democracy when money buys both political parties. I don't think the status quo is sustainable.
Mike:	Perot made a big splash. That got some people thinking about a third party. But then, it began to seem as if Perot was not building a party so much as going on a giant ego trip. Still, he got people excited. Do you think if Perot had seemed less of a nut case that he would have done better?
Dick Lamm:	I don't think you can build a new political party around a personality. I think ultimately you have to have an issue. In South American politics there are "personality parties." I'm sort of proud that the U.S. doesn't get into personality parties.
Clint:	But Jesse Ventura just got elected as a third-party candidate, partly because he has such an appealing personality. Maybe that's the way to go—get more people that are exciting to run as third-party candidates.
Dick Lamm:	I think that Jesse Ventura is a really personable fellow and, arguably, the most interesting third-party candidate to surface recently. And Ventura is smart enough to realize that the trouble with the Reform Party was that it was a wholly owned subsidiary of its founder, Ross Perot. If Ventura gets the right issue, I think he can build up the Reform Party, and I think that's his goal.

Robert:	Didn't I read that you've been an adviser to Jesse Ventura since he got elected governor of Minnesota?
Dick Lamm:	Yes, he asked for my advice, and I gave it. For someone with so little experience, he's doing pretty well. He has a seventy-three percent popularity rating. But my own fear is that Jesse Ventura will wear a little thin. When your image in politics is unique and very exciting and newsworthy, you get a lot of attention. But at some point people may get sick of that emphasis on Jesse's personality. It's not my hope, but my fear.
Mike:	One of the functions of a party is supposed to be uniting the different branches of government. A Democratic governor ought to be able to work well with a Democratic legislature. But Jesse has no Reform Party people in his legislature. Isn't that an argument against voting for third-party candidates? If they win, how can they govern?
Dick Lamm:	That doesn't have to be a big problem. Lowell Weicker was elected governor of Connecticut as an Independent in the 1980s, and he worked well with his legislature. Jesse has coopted the two major political parties, and his popularity gives both parties an incentive to work with him.
Tony:	I can understand why Perot did so well in 1992: The economy was bad, and people were angry at government. But now, people seem pretty satisfied with the status quo. Under what kind of scenario do you see a third party picking up steam now that the economy is so good?
Dick Lamm:	You're wise to focus on the economy. That's the most salient issue to most voters. But the economy is headed for a train wreck, in my analysis, and neither party is interested in changing tracks. I think it's crazy to take 15.3 percent of your paycheck and put it into a pot of money, part of which goes to pay for Ross Perot's Medicare and Social Security!
	I think we need a new New Deal. And that new New Deal is going to be about the new issue of generational fairness, an issue that neither political party is flexible enough to address it. Young people are going to wake up, see how much power the elderly have, and realize that the young are paying for it. Unless one of the two parties really reforms itself, I think that your generation is going to get disgusted, and that's going to be the end of one of the parties.
Sonya:	Are you against Social Security?
Dick Lamm:	No, I'm against the federal budget turning into a retirement fund for the new elderly, who are often in good health and in secure financial shape. You know my generation's going to get back two to three times the money they've paid into Social Security, and you might not get your money back at all. And yet the polls show that Social Security and Medicare are still popular in your generation!
	Very rapidly, I think we're going to find that we have fundamental, structural problems in Social Security and Medicare. Clinton wants to spend the surplus keeping these programs as they are, which means the rich get benefits along with the poor. I didn't join the Democratic Party to transfer money from

the young to the old. I did join the Democratic Party to transfer money from the rich to the poor! I've got a ninety-one-year-old father, and you're paying for his Medicare. And your generation can't afford it. It's just not fair.

Sonya: But to even talk about reforming Social Security makes the elderly very nervous, and they vote. Young people don't. So isn't it kind of suicidal for any political candidate to come out and say, "We should only provide Social Security and Medicare to the poor, so that young people don't carry this huge future burden"?

Dick Lamm: Let me give you something to think about. I am fascinated by a statement by Jacques Chirac, the president of France. He said, "Politics is not the art of the possible, it is making possible what is necessary."

Robert: Once a third party rises up to deal with Social Security and Medicare, one of the two major parties is sure to take the popular position, and bam, there goes the new party.

Dick Lamm: That scenario of a new party rising until its issues are coopted by one of the major political parties is the historic process—and if nothing more than that happens, I'll be happy.

Let me make that very clear. I don't have any particular need to see a third party. I would be comfortable with a scenario under which the Democratic Party would reform itself. You know, it's just amazing to see how the Democratic Party, this great idealistic party that fought for ordinary people, has become a handmaiden of special interests.

It is just shattering to me.

★ ★ ★

FACE TO FACE

Student Interview with
Robert Beauprez
Colorado State Republican Party Chair

Clint	Mike	Robert	Sonya	Tony
a moderate	a Hispanic, liberal Democrat	a moderate Republican	a Hispanic, moderate Republican	an African American, liberal Democrat

What's It Like to Run the Republican State Party Organization?
★ ★ ★

Robert "Bob" Beauprez is the newly elected chair of the Colorado State Republican Party, as well as the head of a major bank.

Sonya: This is a basic question. When did you first get involved in the Republican Party?

Bob Beauprez: Actually, I started off as a Democrat. When I was about your age. My wife and I first registered as Democrats. That was in and around Watergate. The first president I ever voted for was George McGovern. And I thought I did the right thing.

As you've probably learned from your studies, where and when you grew up influences your politics. I grew up in a farm family. A Catholic farm family in Lafayette, Colorado. Mining community, heavily Democratic. If you registered as anything, you registered as a Democrat. A New Deal Democrat. Next door to our farm was a lady who had been the county and state Democratic chairman. She was Ms. Democratic Party in the state, a national figure, but to us, she was just Susie. Died a few years ago at the age of ninety-eight. She was kind of my adopted grandmother. I had all the reasons in the world to be a Democrat.

I remember the year that we had two very liberal Democrats running for office: Tim Wirth and Gary Hart. We paid very close attention to that campaign, and after church one Sunday, my wife Claudia and I went up to see Susie. And I said, "Susie, I'm a registered Democrat, voted Democratic in the last election, but I feel compelled to tell you that I'm listening to these guys and they're not saying what I'm thinking." And she said, "I know, but I've been a Democrat too long. I'm not going to change." She basically said, God bless, do what is on your mind. And so we changed our party affiliation, and I've been a Republican ever since.

Shortly after that, I worked in my first campaign. Second Congressional District, Boulder, up where I live. Wasn't successful then, haven't been successful since in *that* district, but gradually, I got more involved. I've been a precinct committee person, a district captain, which means you have to take on leadership of several precincts, chairman of the Second Congressional District in 1989–90, I think it was. And then I got very offended by party politics that had become factionalized with a lot of finger pointing that was offensive—that's just what it was—offensive. So, I backed away from party politics for awhile, but stayed involved in some campaigns, worked for George Bush.

And then a little over two years ago, with a party in Boulder County that was totally divided, they turned to me for help. They asked me to run for county chair, and, with some reluctance, I said I would. We made some progress: at least people began to behave civilly, to recognize that there were more issues they shared than separated them. So I became a county party chair, as well as a banker by day.

I had gotten to know our elected officials because I was president, now chairman, of the Independent Bankers of Colorado State Trade Association. When I traveled to Washington to meet our congressional delegation, Senator Allard said, "I think you ought to be our next state chair, because we've got a mess there, too." I said, "Hmmm, don't think so." Really tried to avoid that, but obviously I wasn't successful. Eventually, Senator Allard and the rest of the delegation said, "We are behind you. Go do this." So, here we are, less than two months into my first term.

Robert: How do you keep all the people from finger pointing, keep them all together?

Bob Beauprez: It's very difficult. I won't undersell that. We had some people who were bitter enemies. And they had long memories. They remembered every county assembly and public assembly where they yelled and screamed and finger pointed and just did hateful stuff to each other. Most of it centered around the delicate question of abortion and abortion rights. It's difficult. It's brutal. It's very personal, and it's not an easy issue. But it became almost the only issue. You were either on this side of the line or that side of the line. All or nothing. As if nothing else mattered. We were getting nothing done. There was no positive agenda.

It made me remember—all of you are too young to remember—the Vietnam War protests. I was at the University of Colorado in the late sixties.

And it was the war, every single day. Who was for it. Who was against it. No middle ground. Nothing else mattered. Period. And I thought, "Wow, life is more complicated than one issue." I didn't want to minimize the issue of the war, I don't want to minimize the abortion question, but we have other things we need to deal with, like how we're going to raise our kids. We have education issues, taxation issues, and we have employment issues. We've got Social Security, and Medicare, and the whole health care industry. A party either articulates those issues and moves forward, or gets comfortable wallowing in this muck! Nonproductive muck!

When I ran for the state chairman, I had meetings in fifty of the sixty-three counties, and many of them I visited more than once. Time and again I heard, "Bob, you have to unify this party." At first, I'd nod; then I began to ask, "What do you mean by that?" The moderates would say, "When you run those crazy right-wingers out of the party, then we'll be unified." And of course, the right-wing conservatives would say, "When you get those moderates to behave like real Republicans, then we will have unity." In other words, "When everybody agrees with me, then we will be unified." And it astounded me.

That is not unity, of course, that is intolerance. What is unity? I looked it up. Webster essentially defined it as a complex union of related parts. Nothing about everybody being in ideological agreement on everything. In fact, that's ridiculous! This country was founded on respect for difference of opinion. Furthermore, we encourage it—it is the foundation of liberty itself. It is fundamental to our freedom. Thomas Jefferson said, "How can we imagine that we would be alike in our thoughts, the most complex part of our very being, when no two of us are alike in face and form?" Why should we expect everybody to be the same?

Again, intolerance. Isn't that what's going on in Kosovo? It's wrong. Our best solutions come out of diversity of opinion and healthy debate. We ought to encourage debate! We ought to relish it! Celebrate it! I've really tried to get people to focus on that idea. You know, in large part, as long as all of us—Democrat, Republican, political, apolitical—look at unity as the *oneness of purpose* in this great United States of America, this great experiment in Western culture that we have all been a part of, as long as we focus on that and respect difference of opinion, the different ways to skin the cat, the different ways to get up in the morning and get through your day, then we can be healthy and wholesome and productive.

That's been my message. And yes, because of how I grew up, I think that the way my dad and granddad approached life is the best way: self-reliant, look inside, strong spiritual belief, protect the family, work hard, don't make excuses. I guess those are conservative ways, and they drew me to the Republican Party. Does that mean that the other guys, the Democrats, are all bad? No. I was tremendously inspired by John F. Kennedy. I still get chills when I see the video clip of him saying, "Ask not what your country can do for you—ask what you can do for your country." That's powerful. We should all say that.

Tony: How did you actually get the moderates and conservatives to work together?

Bob Beauprez:	I got a group together in Boulder County—a group that had been yelling and screaming at each other. I put the moderates over here and the conservatives over here. And I let them yell and scream at each other for three hours, two weeks in a row. And it was ugly. I would go home and ask my wife, "Why am I doing this? These people hate each other." And they did.

But finally one night, somebody paused long enough to take a breath. And one of the few elected officials we have in the whole stinking county up there was able to say, "You know, if we are ever going to get anybody elected in this county, we have got to arm them with issues that they can articulate and make a difference to the electorate." Great! We had quit calling names for a minute! I jumped up, grabbed a flip chart and a marking pen, and I said, "What are those issues?" And pretty soon they started to come out: education, transportation, land use, environment. We wrote nineteen of them. Most of them were local issues; some were national: Social Security, national defense.

We took our slate of resolutions to the precinct caucuses and invited them to tell us what we had done right, what we had done wrong. We amended some of them. Took them to our county assembly, which I had been told was a group of people who only knew how to fight with each other, and they adopted all of them overwhelmingly.

And then I took on the most sensitive issue. I was convinced that, as Republicans, there were some parts of the prolife question on which most of us could agree: in favor of parental notification and opposition to late-term and partial-birth abortion. We brought forward resolutions on those two issues, and they were overwhelmingly adopted, and we didn't have people yelling and screaming at each other and calling the other side less than human. We were civil. We walked out of there with tangible evidence that we had just demonstrated to one another that we really did agree on more than we disagreed.

Mike:	What's your strategy for repairing and uniting the Colorado Republican Party?
Bob Beauprez:	Well, it's much as before. You must know that it has not been a pretty sight in Colorado the last couple of years. I think that's largely because the state party, through its previous chairman, focused more on issues—some of them very sensitive and divisive—than it did on the broader message of unity of purpose. I see the job of chairman differently. It's fairly simple: At the end of the day, I am supposed to have more Republicans involved, more Republicans elected to office. If I do that, the elected officials that represent us will argue, line up, and ultimately vote about issues. That is not my job. I'm like the offensive lineman in football. I let the guys behind me decide what play to be run, then I put my head down and push real hard to advance the cause. When the Republican Party focused on who was worthy enough to be a Republican, we were waging war amongst ourselves instead of advancing an agenda.

My sense in traveling the state is that we have learned the error of our ways. There is a willingness in people to say, "Let's put all these differences aside." This doesn't mean that our differences, our principles don't matter. Quite the contrary, principles are critically important. But, we have to disagree in a civil, respectful way. Of late, we haven't behaved in a fashion that people respect. Shame on us. Too often, our politics were basically negative: "Vote for me because I am not as bad a scumbag as the other guy." That's ridiculous. You wouldn't want somebody to move into your neighborhood based on that criterion; you wouldn't hire a co-worker based on that criterion. Why would you elect someone to represent you based on that criterion? It's dumb. We have to recruit better people. We have to train better people. And we have to be respectable. And that should go for any public office, any political party.

Tony:

Since the national chair of the Republican Party, Jim Nicholson, is from your home state, do you feel any additional pressure to make the party in your state deliver when the presidential elections come around?

Bob Beauprez:

Maybe I should, but I honestly see it as an opportunity. Our last chairman, as you may know, Steve Curtis, was at odds with Jim Nicholson. I've never sat down and talked ideology with Jim Nicholson. I don't know where he stands and, for the most part, I don't care. I see his role much like mine: to advance the party, not to promote issues. That's the job of the candidate and elected officials. Still, do I feel some degree of pressure, or incentive to deliver Colorado for the presidency?" Absolutely. Not because of Jim Nicholson. But because I think that is one of the key ways I will be measured. And when we have an excess advantage of one hundred thousand in voter registration, frankly if I didn't deliver, that would be cause for concern.

Tony:

If the Republicans in Colorado have such a lead in registered voters, why was the governor's race won by such a narrow margin?

Bob Beauprez:

Shame on us! Shame on us. The previous state chair, Steve Curtis, did everything he could to hurt the Republican nominee for governor! Imagine, ten days before an election, and the state chairman says he's not sure he's going to support the Republican candidate for governor? This is what I meant earlier: We haven't behaved very well. We haven't played very smart. I think we are just now beginning to learn what it's like to be the party in the governor's chair. Governor Owens likes to say, and I believe him very sincerely, that he wants to be the governor of all the people. Certainly he knows that he is a Republican; we know he's a conservative. But I think he is very much aware that there are an awful lot of people in the state to whom he has an obligation and a responsibility—beyond partisan Republicans. That is part of the responsibility of being in a party, especially when the party is in the governor's mansion and holds the majority on both aisles in the state house.

There ought to be responsibility to not just run for office well but to govern well. I wouldn't pretend that you always see adequate evidence of that in politics, but when I meet with the leadership in the Colorado house and senate, and certainly in open dialogue with the governor's office, including the governor himself, I remind them all, they are supposed to govern well.

Last week, before the Columbine tragedy, I met with the leadership of the house, and I said, "You guys are making my job real difficult right now. You're going to be remembered as the legislature of guns and photo radar, and you ought to be remembered as the legislature of genuine tax reduction, a trans-

Clint:	portation plan, and full funding of charter schools. I'm not suggesting that everybody has to agree that those are the agenda items, but aren't they more positive than guns and radar? If you really felt compelled to deal with that other stuff, then deal with it and move on, for heaven's sake." But it has kind of consumed them. That is an error in leadership, I think.

Clint: Both parties talk so much about steering toward the middle of the road, that, except for the extreme ideologue, it's hard to tell if a politician is a Democrat or Republican. How do you respond to that?

Bob Beauprez: I think it's a fair criticism. I had my first meeting at the Republican National Committee a few weeks ago. The RNC is made up of other state chairmen like myself, a committee man, and a committee woman from each state—a group of 150 to 160 people by the time they assemble. And the message from them was very similar to what you just said: "Folks out there are turning off politics because they don't think it makes a difference." I've got four kids, and most of them are one side or the other of your age, and I'm not sure they think politics makes a difference. Especially when most of their adult lives they've had a president that—I am not really here to bash him because he is a Democrat—but I think he has been less than presidential. And that is a shame. I think the world and all of Jimmy Carter as a person, but I don't have that same respect for Clinton. When we have 240 million people to pick from, I find it a real shame we couldn't find someone whom we respect as a human being. How can we expect you to be interested in politics? We've had some bad apples in our party, as well, certainly. But our biggest fault has been our inability to bring forward a positive agenda. We have been reactionary. We've defined ourselves by what we are against instead of what we are for.

If I can use a personal example: I am a banker. Every year, I put together a strategic plan for the sake of my board. The plan says, "This is what we are going to do." It doesn't say, "This is *not* what we are going to do," but *"This is what we are going to do."* And that is the way I have lived my life for fifty years. When I was on the farm with my dad in the dairy business, we got up every morning and we went and did something. And I don't see that in politics.

We are moving into a political age that resembles an aristocracy of career politicians. And I think it's dangerous. I think our Founding Fathers had it figured out pretty well when they wanted a citizen legislature. They wanted those basic instincts, those "street smarts" to come to the state capitals, to the county courthouses, and to Washington, D.C., to run the country. I see people who go to colleges, get advanced degrees, believe themselves born and bred to be politicians. But I don't see that same savvy in them, because they've never done anything else but seek or hold an elective office. We've got them in our party, and the Democrats have them as well. And I think that's dangerous. If the politician doesn't stand for anything except being a politician, the parties need to focus on what they are really about. Set their agenda and then get on with it. Get on with it.

Dr. Bauer: Speaking of career politicians, when Scott McKinnis here in Colorado ran for the U.S. House of Representatives, he promised to serve only three terms. Now that he is in the Congress, has seen that the longer he stays, the more seniority he accrues and closer he gets to wielding power, Scott has changed his mind, and so have a number of Republican officials. Given what you have just said so eloquently, how do you feel about that?

Bob Beauprez: I've been opposed to term limits. I think, right problem, wrong solution. And I'll make sure I get back to Scott specifically. I think the right way to deal with the power of the incumbency is a more intelligent and active electorate. Vote the guys out of office if they are failing.

The Colorado state house, both Democrats and Republicans, are dealing with the dilemma of term limits because Coloradans voted for term limits. If a representative can serve for three two-year terms, he or she barely gets there and gets oriented before they have to run again. If reelected, the representative probably will be a committee chair, for heaven's sake, and the next reelection is looking at being kicked out because of term limits.

When I was in the dairy business, I served on the national board of directors for our trade association, and around the second year I was on the board, I thought I was about as smart as could be. I just knew it all. Around the third year, I thought, "Well, maybe I was a little presumptuous." Around the time I left, eight years later, I was finally getting the full breadth and perspective of what we were dealing with.

Now, take that experience to the national level. My advice to Scott, my advice to the Democrat Diana DeGette, would be the same: As long as you are comfortable there, as long as you still have the desire to serve, as long as the people return you to office, serve. We have seen effective, seasoned legislators sent back home for the wrong reasons—term limits—and the people suffer the consequences. Right problem, wrong solution.

Robert: Basic question: I am a Republican, and I want to run for the state house of representatives. What kind of monetary support and guidance can I expect from the Republican Party, and what would you expect from me as a candidate?

Bob Beauprez: This didn't always happen in the past, but this is my mission: If you come to us, green as grass, we will give you basic information, go through the nuts and bolts of what you need to qualify as a candidate, ask some of the personal, brutal questions that might give you pause about entering public politics—questions that will get asked later; you've seen examples. We will try to get you a mentor, another elected official who lives in a similar district and can share his or her experience with you.

We will conduct candidate campaign management schools—sometimes called "campaign colleges," but that's a gross exaggeration. The schools are just a series of meetings that would provide you, as well as whoever will run your campaign, with some guidance on how to raise money, how to organize precincts, how many campaign signs you order, is paper better than plastic. Simple, basic stuff.

We can give you access to data and information. The voter registration list from the secretary of state's office is public information. But we can help you sort those lists with specialized computer software. If you want a list of all of the Democrats, all the Republicans, we can give you that list. If you want a list of all the households that have at least one Republican registered, we can give you that list. If you want a list of everybody that is fifty and over, we can give you that data.

We also hold some other issues-based seminars. We call it the "Republican Leadership Program"—eight months during which we focus on some of the important issues in public policy. The Leadership program is intended to help a well-intentioned, but ideologically narrow, candidate develop more than just one issue.

Too many candidates from both parties sound like this: "I am coming to you as a candidate for the state house because of these shootings at Columbine. Tragic situation, and I am going to get guns out of the United States of America. Period. End of sentence. Don't bother me about how to fund roads. Don't bother me about how to create more jobs. Don't bother me about how to take people off the welfare rolls in downtown Denver and give them jobs. Don't tell me about poverty in San Luis Valley that is really a travesty. Don't tell me about the water that is escaping the state and going across our borders. I just want to get guns out of people's hands."

Finally, we hope we can give you some realistic idea of your potential for success. What it will cost. For example, if you come to us from a district that has twice as many registered Democrats as Republicans, we are going to say, "Why don't you take a vacation for a couple of months?"

Tony:

What is your best strategy for mobilizing the Republican Party so that you get more votes than the Democrats?

Bob Beauprez:

It's a combined effort. The Democrats do a much better job at turning out the vote than we do. They do a great job. Partly because of the Democratic Party organization, and partly because they have a good nucleus within the unions, some of which is a carry-over from the old labor union activism. Some of that is still alive and well; certainly the teacher's union is strong in Colorado. The last time we had an amendment on the ballot that the teacher's union didn't like, they mobilized their forces, and they turned out a lot of votes. They are very successful.

We will do it a bit differently. We'll do a lot of mailings, focus on the early balloting through the absentee or mail-in ballot. Some of the candidates will encourage the "die-hards," the "two-R household," where both the husband and wife are Republican. They will go down the list of everyone who voted in the last election, try to contact them either by phone or by mail, and remind them to vote. That's the cornerstone of our GOTV, Get Out The Vote, strategy.

In Boulder County, I took a different approach to GOTV. I did a mailing of fifteen thousand cards. And since I knew some of the candidates were focusing on the base, the active file, we focused on turning out the marginal Republican voters, one or two percent of those registered Republicans who hadn't voted in the last two elections. I can think of five races that are up my way that were lost by less than two hundred votes. That is not very many votes! Every vote matters, and we try to turn out as many voters as possible. But unless you do an enormous amount of analysis, you are never sure how successful you are.

Tony:

Because there are a lot of misconceptions, would you explain what the pay scale is for precinct committee people, precinct captains, county organizers, and state chairs?

Bob Beauprez:

It is volunteerism at its best! Some states pay their state chairs; Colorado doesn't. In the main, participation isn't about money. At a minimum, one would think of it as an affliction. That's why they call us political junkies, right? For some of the people involved in politics, it is their life's blood—they just have to. They have to be on the streets, delivering literature, on the phone, encouraging people to get out and vote, and when they lose, they get up in the morning, and they start again. It's an amazing process.

I have a limited staff at state headquarters. There are currently three paid positions. By the time we get close to elections, we will probably have half a dozen. But, the party organization is based on volunteers and elected officials. For their time and effort, the scrutiny they go through, the ridicule—sometimes deserved, sometimes not—that they endure and their families endure, the compensation is pretty minimal. For me, tonight has been one of those treasured compensations.

★ ★ ★

Key Concepts of Libertarianism
David Boaz

. . . I want to spell out some of the key concepts of libertarianism, themes that will recur throughout this book. These themes have developed over many centuries. The first inklings of them can be found in ancient China, Greece, and Israel; they began to be developed into something resembling modern libertarian philosophy in the work of such seventeenth- and eighteenth-century thinkers as John Locke, David Hume, Adam Smith, Thomas Jefferson, and Thomas Paine.

Individualism. Libertarians see the individual as the basic unit of social analysis. Only individuals make choices and are responsible for their actions. Libertarian thought emphasizes the dignity of each individual, which entails both rights and responsibility. The progressive extension of dignity to more people—to women, to people of different religions and different races—is one of the great libertarian triumphs of the Western world.

Individual Rights. Because individuals are moral agents, they have a right to be secure in their life, liberty, and property. These rights are not granted by government or by society; they are inherent in the nature of human beings. It is intuitively right that individuals enjoy the security of such rights; the burden of explanation should lie with those who would take rights away.

Spontaneous Order. A great degree of order in society is necessary for individuals to survive and flourish. It's easy to assume that order must be imposed by a central authority, the way we impose order on a stamp collection or a football team. The great insight of libertarian social analysis is that order in society arises spontaneously, out of the actions of thousands or millions of individuals who coordinate their actions with those of others in order to achieve their purposes. Over human history, we have gradually opted for more freedom and yet managed to develop a complex society with intricate organization. The most important institutions in human society—language, law, money, and markets—all developed spontaneously, without central direction. Civil society—the complex network of associations and connections among people—is another example of spontaneous order; the associations within civil society are formed for a purpose, but civil society itself is not an organization and does not have a purpose of its own.

The Rule of Law. Libertarianism is not libertinism or hedonism. It is not a claim that "people can do anything they want to, and nobody else can say anything." Rather, libertarianism proposes a society of liberty under law, in which individuals are free to pursue their own lives so long as they respect the equal rights of others. The rule of law means that individuals are governed by generally applicable and spontaneously developed legal rules, not by arbitrary commands; and that those rules should protect the freedom of individuals to pursue happiness in their own ways, not aim at any particular result or outcome.

Limited Government. To protect rights, individuals form governments. But government is a dangerous institution. Libertarians have a great antipathy to concentrated power, for as Lord Acton said, "Power tends to corrupt and absolute power corrupts absolutely." Thus they want to divide and limit power, and that means especially to limit government, generally through a written constitution enumerating and limiting the powers that the people delegate to government. Limited government is the basic *political* implication of libertarianism, and libertarians point to the historical fact that it was the dispersion of power in Europe—more than other parts of the world—that led to individual liberty and sustained economic growth.

Free Markets. To survive and to flourish, individuals need to engage in economic activity. The right to property entails the right to exchange property by mutual agreement. Free markets are the economic system of free individuals, and they are necessary to create wealth. Libertarians believe that people will be both freer and more prosperous if government intervention in people's economic choices is minimized.

The Virtue of Production. Much of the impetus for libertarianism in the seventeenth century was a reaction against monarchs and aristocrats who lived off the productive labor of other people. Libertarians defended the right of people to keep the fruits of their labor. This effort developed into a respect for the dignity of work and production and especially for the growing middle class, who were looked down upon by aristocrats. Libertarians developed a pre-Marxist class analysis that divided society into two basic classes: those who produced wealth and those who took it by force from others. Thomas Paine, for instance, wrote, "There are two distinct classes of men in the nation, those who pay taxes, and those who receive and live upon the taxes." Similarly, Jefferson wrote in 1824, "We have more machinery of government than is necessary, too many parasites living on the labor of the industrious." Modern libertarians defend the right of productive people to keep what they earn, against a new class of politicians and bureaucrats who would seize their earnings to transfer them to nonproducers.

Natural Harmony of Interest. Libertarians believe that there is a natural harmony of interests among peaceful, productive people in a just society. One person's individual plans—which may involve getting a job, starting a business, buying a house, and so on—may conflict with the plans of others, so the market makes many of us change our plans. But we all prosper from the operation of the free market, and there are no necessary conflicts between farmers and merchants, manufacturers and importers. Only when government begins to hand out rewards on the basis of political pressure do we find ourselves involved in group conflict, pushed to organize and contend with other groups for a piece of political power.

Peace. Libertarians have always battled the age-old scourge of war. They understood that war brought death and destruction on a grand scale, disrupted family and economic life, and put more power in the hands of the ruling class—which might explain why the rulers did not always share the popular sentiment for peace. Free men and women, of course, have often had to defend their own societies against foreign threats; but throughout history, war has usually been the common enemy of peaceful, productive people on all sides of the conflict.

Excerpt from "Conservatism"

P. J. O'Rourke

A conservative believes in the sanctity of the individual. That we are individuals—unique, disparate, and willful—is something we understand instinctively from an early age. No child ever wrote to Santa, "Bring me, and a bunch of kids I've never met, a pony, and we'll share." The great religions teach salvation as an individual matter. There are no group discounts in the Ten Commandments. Christ was not a committee. And Allah does not welcome believers into paradise saying, "You weren't much good yourself, but you were standing near some good people."

Virtue is famously lonesome. Also vice, as anyone can testify who ever told his mother, "All the other guys were doing it." We experience pleasure separately. Ethan Hawke may go out on any number of wild dates, but I'm able to sleep through them. And although we may be sorry for people who suffer, we only "feel their pain" when we're full of baloney and running for office.

To say that we are all individuals is not a profession of selfishness any more than it's a call to altruism. It is simply a measurement. Individuals are the units we come in, and the individual is the wellspring of conservatism. The purpose of conservative politics is to defend the liberty of the individual and—lest individualism run riot—insist upon individual responsibility.

THE INDIVIDUAL AND THE STATE

The first question of political science is—or should be—What is good for everyone?" and by "everyone," we mean "all individuals." The question can't be, What is good for a single individual? That's megalomania—like a New Hampshire presidential primary. And the question can't be, What is good for some individuals? Or even, What is good for the majority of individuals? That's partisan politics, which at best leads to Newt Gingrich or Pat Schroeder and at worst leads to Lebanon or Rwanda. Finally, the question can't be, What is good for individuals as a whole? There's no such thing. Individuals are only available individually. Complete sets are not for sale.

By observing the progress (admittedly spotty and fitful) of mankind, we can see that the things that are good for everyone are the things that have increased the accountability of the individual, the respect for the individual, and the power of the individual to master his own fate. Judaism gave us laws before which all men, no matter their rank, stood as equals (though this did mean no BLT sandwiches). Christianity taught us that each person has intrinsic worth, Newt Gingrich and Pat Schroeder included. The rise of private enterprise and trade provided a means of achieving wealth and autonomy other than by killing people with broadswords. And the Industrial Revolution allowed millions of ordinary folks an opportunity to obtain decent houses, food, and clothes (albeit with some unfortunate side effects, such as environmental damage and Al Gore).

In order to build a political system that is good for everyone, that ensures a free society based upon the independence, prestige, and self-rule of individuals, we have to ask what all these individuals want. And be told to shut up. There's no way to know the myriad wants of diverse people. They may not know themselves. And who asked us to stick our nose in, anyway?

In a free society some people will want to make money or art or love or a mess of their lives. Some people will want to help others. Some will want others to help them. And some people will complain about how chaotic freedom is and agitate for its restriction. We can hazard certain guesses about the common desires of mankind: three squares and self-esteem. But we may find that any given example of mankind is fasting to obtain enlightenment or deeply involved in masochism.

In a free society a person can want what he likes and do what he wants to get it as long as this does not occasion real and provable harm to a fellow person (light bondage and discipline are acceptable). Thus the two fundamental rules of a political system in a free society are (1) Mind your own business; (2) Keep your hands to yourself. The political leaders of our nation would do well to reacquaint themselves with these tenets. (Hillary, mind your own business. Bill, keep your hands to yourself.)

But how do we actually go about the construction of such a political system? We don't have to. The framers of the United States Constitution have already done a fair job of it for us.

The Constitution contains a plan for representative democracy that has, over the years, been successful in luring some of our most egregious national characters out of the private sector, where they would have done no end of damage to industry and commerce, and into public office, where they can be watched.

The Constitution promulgates our system of courts and laws, the purposes of which are to keep individuals who are too smart, too big and strong, too rich, or too pretty from running the rest of us ragged. It is an imperfect system, as the O. J. Simpson trial has proved exquisitely. But it beats deciding legal cases by means of armed combat—unless you're Nicole Brown Simpson or Ron Goldman.

The Bill of Rights protects freedom of speech, freedom of religion, and freedom of assembly, of course. You could hardly call yourself free without those freedoms. But even more important, the Bill of Rights protects your money, car, house, and stereo. The Fifth Amendment says, ". . . nor shall private property be taken for public use, without just compensation." Some alleged defenders of liberty look down their noses at property rights, believing them to be the sordid, mean, and grubby side to freedom. But think how little time you spend worshiping idols your neighbors abhor or gathering in mutinous crowds. And when was the last time you said anything more controversial than "Evan Dando sucks." Now think how much time you spend using your Visa card.

In fact, most day-to-day freedoms are material freedoms. Your career, your home, your workout at the gym, shopping, traveling, entertainment, recreation, any buying and selling, any hiring and firing, the baseball team you root for, and the prerogative of its players to stay out on strike until beach volleyball becomes the national pastime are all matters of property rights. In the old Soviet Union there wasn't any private property. Everything was public—like a public restroom, which is how the old Soviet Union looked and smelled. Dead-end jobs and zoo-cage lives, shoddy goods and mucky food and constant shortages of even those, complete lack of initiative and innovation in all things—that was what made the Soviet Union so depressing, not the fact that it was illegal to stand on a street corner shouting, "Marx bites his farts!"

And one other thing the Bill of Rights does is try to protect our freedom not only from bad people and bad laws but from the vast nets and gooey webs of rules and regulations that even the best governments produce. The Constitution attempts to leave as much of life as possible to common sense or at least to local option. Says the Ninth Amendment: "The enumeration in the Constitution, of certain rights, shall not be construed to deny or disparage others retained by the people." And, continues the Tenth, the "powers not delegated to the United States by the Constitution, nor prohibited by it to the States, are reserved to the States respectively, or to the people." And it is these suit-yourself, you're-a-big-boy-now, it's-a-free-country powers that conservatism seeks to conserve.

BUT WHAT ABOUT THE OLD, THE POOR, THE DISABLED, THE DISADVANTAGED, THE HELPLESS, THE HOPELESS, THE ADDLED, AND THE DAFT?

Conservatism is sometimes confused with social Darwinism or other such me-first dogmas. Sometimes the confusion is deliberate. When those who are against conservative policies don't have sufficient opposition arguments, they call the love of freedom selfish. Of course it is—in the sense that breathing's selfish. But because you want to breathe doesn't mean that you want to suck the breath out of every person you encounter. Frankly, it's a disgusting idea and not the kind of thing the average conservative would care to be seen doing on the street.

Conservatives do not believe in the triumph of the large and powerful over the weak and useless. (Although most conservatives would make an exception to see a fistfight between Norman Schwarzkopf and George Stephanopoulos.) If all people are free, George Stephanopoulos must be allowed to run loose, too, however annoying this may be.

But some people cannot enjoy the benefits of freedom without assistance from their fellows. This may be a temporary condition, such as childhood or when I say I can drive home from a bar just fine at 3 A.M. Or, due to infirmity or affliction, the condition may be permanent. Because conservatives do not generally propose huge government programs to combat the effects of old age, illness, being a kid, or drinking ten martinis on an empty stomach, conservatives are said to be uncaring or mean-spirited. In fact, charity is an axiom of conservatism. Conservatives like and admire manners, mores, reli-gion, family, friendship, and most fraternal and community organizations. And charity—being kind and helpful to others—is central to all these customs and institutions. Even the Crips, the Hell's Angels, and the Democratic Leadership Council claim to supply mutual aid to their members. Charity is one of the great responsibil-ities of freedom. But in order for us to be respon-sible and, hence, free, that responsibility must be personal. Of course not all needful acts of chari-ty can be accomplished by one person. But to the extent that responsibility should be shared and merged, it should be, in a free society, shared and merged on the same basis as political power, starting with the individual. Responsibility must proceed from the bottom up, from the individual outward, never from the top down, never from the outside in, with the individual as the squeezed-cream filling of that giant Twinkie which is the state.

You have to take care of yourself to the best of your ability to do so. Your family has to take care of you. Friends have to take care of your family. Neighbors have to take care of those friends. And a community has to take care of its neighbors. Government, with its power of coer-cion, red tape, and inevitable unfamiliarity with the specifics of the case, is a last and a desperate resort.

There is no virtue in compulsory government charity. And no virtue in advocating it. A politi-cian who commends himself as "caring" and "sensitive" because he wants to expand the gov-ernment's charitable programs is merely saying that he's willing to try to do good with other people's money. Who isn't? A voter who takes pride in supporting such programs is telling us that he'll do good with his own money—if a gun is held to his head.

When government quits being something that we only use in an emergency and becomes the principal source of aid and assistance in our society, the size, expense, and power of that gov-ernment are greatly increased. This in itself is a diminishment of the individual. And proof that we're jerks, since we've decided that politicians are wiser, kinder, and more honest than we are and that they, not we, should control the dispensation of eleemosynary goods and services.

But government charity causes other problems. If responsibility is removed from friends, family, and self, social ties are weakened. You scratch my back, and I'll get a presidential commission to investigate your claims of dorsal itch.

We don't have to look after our parents. They've got their Social Security checks and are down in Atlantic City with them right now. Our parents don't have to look after us. Head Start, a high school guidance counselor, and AmeriCorps take care of that. Our kids don't have to look after themselves. If they get addicted to drugs, there's methadone. If they get knocked up, there's welfare. And the neighbors aren't going to get involved. If they step outside, they'll be cut down by the 9mm cross fire from the drug wars between the gangs all the other neighbors belong to.

. . . Making charity part of the political system confuses the mission of government. Charity is, by its own nature, approximate and imprecise. Are you guiding the old lady across the street, or are you just jerking her around? It's hard to know when to offer charity without being insulting or patronizing. It's hard to know when enough charity has been given. Parents want to help children as much as possible but don't want to wind up with helplessly dependent kids. Parents want to give children every material advantage but don't want a pack of damned spoiled brats. There are no exact rules of charity. But a government in a free society must obey exact rules, or that government's power is arbitrary, and freedom is lost.

That is why government works best when it is given limited and well-defined tasks to perform. . . .

Excerpt from "Republicans in Need of New Appeal"
George Will

American political arguments often are retrospective, but elections usually are prospective. For Republicans to revive in time to win in 2000, they must understand how much has changed since 1995. . . .

. . . Republicans interested in recapturing the elan they acquired in the late 1970s and still had as recently as 1995 should begin by recognizing the depletion of their old stock of things to be against.

By 1995, when they captured Congress, the Cold War had ended, but they still had deficits and "big government" to deplore. . . .

. . . Republicans and Clinton are in complete accord that the first order of business is to "save" the biggest components of big government—the core of the welfare state, Social Security and Medicare. Which would be bigger, the government if Clinton got all his little additions, or the government if Republicans got the substantial defense increases they rightly favor, including ballistic missile defenses? . . . It is arguable that the Republican Party is the bigger-government party. . . .

Finally, "values." Many Republicans, cross about public support for Clinton, seem to think American values need protection from . . . Americans. As an electoral appeal, that needs work.

Granted, Clinton's silken charm makes one long for honest rancor. But Republicans who think people support him only because they have been irrationally charmed resemble Democrats who ascribed Reagan's popularity to his smile! A party in denial is in danger.

Reprinted from *The Washington Post*, February 21, 1999.

students

CHAT
ROOM

| Clint | Mike | Robert | Sonya | Tony |
| a moderate | a Hispanic, liberal Democrat | a moderate Republican | a Hispanic, moderate Republican | an African American, liberal Democrat |

Can the Libertarians, Moderates, and Social Conservatives in the Republican Party Get Along?
★ ★ ★

Dr. Bauer: Let's start by looking at one of the smallest American political parties, the Libertarians. Many Republicans think a lot like Libertarians. Both parties favor the individual's rights over the needs of the government, and that idea can be traced back to the Founding Fathers.

Tony: I think the Founding Fathers did stress individual rights, but as soon as Libertarians begin talking about abolishing most of government because spontaneous order will just pop up without a government structure, they lose me and the Founding Fathers! I can't think of anything our Founding Fathers said that came close to "We don't really need government, because people will just decide to obey an unwritten rule of law."

Dr. Bauer: How about the notion of limiting government? That really is the linchpin in the David Boaz selection from *Libertarianism: A Primer.* Boaz says government is a dangerous institution.

Tony: That's the sort of idea that puts people in army surplus fatigues and sends them running around in forests on their weekends.

Dr. Bauer: Let's not take the easy way out. Libertarians have some opinions worth considering. They are against social engineering. They say that laws should protect the freedom of individuals to pursue happiness in their own ways without government structuring and directing society toward a particular outcome. That means government shouldn't try to manipulate us to make us "better."

Robert: Aren't they basically saying that if I want to smoke pot in my house, I should have that freedom?

Dr. Bauer: Logically, yes. But if you smoked pot, got into an automobile seriously whacked out and hurt or killed someone while driving, that is not a respon-

	sible use of your freedom and Libertarians would reject it. You don't have the right to hurt anyone else. Libertarians decide what is right and wrong by the effect an action has on other people.
Robert:	But if I am in my house or at a party enjoying whatever, then there is nothing wrong with that because I am not infringing anyone else's rights.
Dr. Bauer:	Yes, that's why Libertarians think drug use and prostitution should be legal—a limited government stays out of the individual's private life. Who benefits when government is limited? Libertarians defend the rights of "productive people" to keep what they earn. Their vision of society includes productive and the nonproductive people. If I'm productive, why should I pay for the nonproductive people? Don't they have a point?
Mike:	To an extent. But I don't think all tax money goes to welfare. Taxes also pay for roads and protections I need to make and keep money—like regulating the stock market and the banks. Without that kind of help from government, I would buy a Hummer and go live up in the mountain wilderness like a true *rugged individualist*.
Dr. Bauer:	So our government does things that benefit the productive person, as well as the nonproductive?
Tony:	Yes. And they should. If I am doing well, why shouldn't some of my tax dollars go to inoculating a one-year-old child against typhoid and whooping cough—give that child an opportunity to lead a productive life as well? All children are potentially productive members of society if only they can get a little help when they need it!
Robert:	But Libertarians would ask why your tax dollars should support a sixteen-year-old unwed mother and her three kids sitting on the couch watching television.
Sonya:	Yes, that's different from roads we all need and medical care that everyone should receive. No sixteen-year-old girl should be getting money, doing nothing to earn money, just sitting on the couch with three kids.
Clint:	You have the right to try and make it on your own, but you don't have the right to make me support you.
Tony:	Libertarians seem pretty sure about who's asking for a handout. What happens when previously productive people stop being productive because they're sick or old or can't find a job? Boaz wrote, "Modern Libertarians defend the right of productive people to keep what they earn, against a new class of politicians and bureaucrats who would seize their earnings to transfer them to non-producers." Don't we all see a point in our lives where we will make the transition from producers to nonproducers? Or do Libertarians intend to die at fifty?
Robert:	Or, do they all have such great retirement plans and 401(k)s that they're not going to need any help from the government?

Clint:	Maybe if they aren't giving all their money to support nonproducers, they will have enough to fall back on if they get sick or when they grow old. Have you seen what they take out of every paycheck just to pay for Social Security? Maybe if I could keep that money, I could invest it and not need Social Security or any government help.
Dr. Bauer:	Libertarians would say, if you want a good retirement, be virtuous, put something away every month, don't buy stuff on a credit card, and then we won't have to take care of you in your old age.
Sonya:	They have a point.
Tony:	What happens to those who spend their entire lives in minimum-wage jobs? All the money they earn gets spent on a place to live and something to eat. They can't afford to put money away for their retirement. They are productive, but still poor! They certainly deserve an opportunity to retire and enjoy the remainder of their years.
Dr. Bauer:	At your expense? You're okay with that?
Tony:	Yes! For someone in that situation, I'm okay with that. If Bill Gates wanted to take Medicare payments, I'd get angry.
Dr. Bauer:	Well, he's eligible, but that's another topic. Let's move on to P. J. O'Rourke's article about conservatism. Does he sound like other conservative writers or conservatives you know? What is missing in P. J. O'Rourke that you find in other conservatives?
Robert:	Humor.
Dr. Bauer:	Missing in P. J. O'Rourke?
Robert:	That's a joke! I know he's a big deal political humorist!
Dr. Bauer:	P. J. O'Rourke says there are "two fundamental rules of a political system in a free society"—only two! One is, "Mind your own business"—as in that bumper sticker, "Focus on your own damn family"—and two, "Keep your hands to yourself."
Sonya:	O'Rourke didn't seem like a conservative to me, he seemed like a Libertarian. He's missing the preaching about morality that a lot of conservatives get into. They can't just be financially conservative, they have to tell you what you should or shouldn't do: whether you can have an abortion, whether you can be gay, the morally correct ways to raise your family. I don't find that in O'Rourke.
	He cares more about the community than Libertarians do. He's against government charitable programs because he says, "If responsibility is removed from friends, family, and self, social ties are weakened." And he says, "Conservatives like and admire manners, mores, religion, family, friendship, and most fraternal and community organizations. . . . Charity—being kind and helpful to others—is central to all these." He says our social problems could be better solved through private charities like churches.

Dr. Bauer:	I want you to imagine for a second how much each of you would give voluntarily to charity if all the social programs that P. J. O'Rourke doesn't like in our government disappeared tomorrow. How much of that slack do you think you—your family, friends, church, fraternal and community organizations—could take up in charitable giving?
Clint:	None. If government stopped helping the elderly, people would stockpile their money. The more they gave to charities, the less money they would have to take care of themselves.
Dr. Bauer:	Interesting point. So if the government's social safety net disappeared, people might be even less generous to charities!
Mike:	In your scenario, are we still paying the same taxes we pay now?
Dr. Bauer:	No. In my scenario, P. J. O'Rourke's ideal universe, there are minimal taxes and minimal government spending.
Robert:	Well, there's a tax deduction for charitable giving now, and hardly anybody does it! You take away the incentive, which doesn't work now, and you have a program that's even less effective!
Dr. Bauer:	O'Rourke says that conservatives aren't mean-spirited—they believe in charity. What do you think of that?
Tony:	The conservatives won big with welfare reform, but the charities can't possibly help all the people who will lose their benefits. The Salvation Army has said that because donations are not keeping pace, they just can't handle the influx of requests they're getting.
Robert:	I think it's a whole different mind-set, a cultural change that would take time. And it's not going to happen in a year! I mean, we can sit around this table and say, "I would not, or I cannot, give to charities." But, if that's the only way that elderly people are going to get food, or preschool kids are going to get fed and inoculated, then sure we are all going to pony up, because that is the only way society is going to work.
Dr. Bauer:	Before we leave P. J. O'Rourke, who is a lot of fun to read, let me give you another observation from him: Government takes wealth from those who produce it and gives it to those who don't. Does he sound like a Libertarian here?
Robert:	In a way. But the Libertarians want to eliminate taxes altogether and O'Rourke believes they should be lower. That's what makes me a Republican, too, and not a Libertarian.
Dr. Bauer:	P. J. O'Rourke is a fiscal conservative; the fiscal conservatives are interested in lower taxes. The Republican Party today is made up of fiscal conservatives, social conservatives, and some Libertarians. I usually refer to the social conservatives as the religious right, short for the religious right-wing of the Republican Party. We use the term *right* for conservatives, and *left* for liberals, because the French revolutionaries, who sided with the poor, sat on the left

side of the French Parliament, and the King's supporters, mostly the wealthy and the religious leaders, sat on the right.

And this leads us to the George Will article "Republicans in Need of New Appeal." One of the leading conservatives in the country, George Will represents a blend of social and fiscal conservatism. So, in other words, he is not P. J. O'Rourke. Yet he seems here to be perfectly happy to let the Moral Majority movement, which had been the core of the religious wing of the Republican Party, disappear.

George Will has been talking for about ten or fifteen years about bringing morality back to politics, which is why I was so shocked by this article. In the second to the last paragraph, he talks about values: "Many Republicans, cross about public support for Clinton, seem to think American values need protection from . . . Americans! As an electoral appeal, that needs work." So, what is Will saying?

Clint:	The Republican Party needs to change—to do something to get these people back.
Dr. Bauer:	Which people?
Clint:	The people who have become more socially liberal.
Sonya:	He also says, "A party in denial is in danger."
Dr. Bauer:	What does he mean by that? Who is in denial?
Sonya:	The socially conservative Republicans—the ones that are angry about Clinton. They deny Clinton's appeal and the reasons for his success. That is not a way to survive.
Dr. Bauer:	Because politics is about compromise, flexibility, and bargaining.
Robert:	And that is why religion should stay out of politics—because you shouldn't compromise your religion.
Mike:	Maybe they do need to create a new party just for the social, religious conservatives.
Robert:	Or find a new occupation for them—such as running a church where people who want their guidance can go—instead of forcing their morals on other people.
Dr. Bauer:	What about the notion that political parties rise and fall as issues rise and fall. George Will says that Republicans rose to power on certain issues. What happened to those issues?
Tony:	They faded. The Cold War ended, and judging partly from Will's article, Americans no longer think that we need Republicans in order to have a fiscally sound government. Clinton deserves credit for balancing the budget. When Will asks, "Which would be bigger, the government if Clinton got all his little additions, or the government if Republicans got the substantial defense increases they rightly favor. . . ?" He answers his question with, "It is arguable

Dr. Bauer:	that the Republican Party is the bigger-government party." So the Democrats can no longer be labeled the "tax-and-spend party." That era is gone.
	After the 1994 elections, Clinton said that "the era of big government is over." Now, it may not be. But when George Will, one of the most important Republican conservative columnists, says that the Republican Party is the bigger-government party, we have got to take that seriously!
Sonya:	But notice most of the big government spending favored by Republicans is for defense.
Tony:	What happened to the Republican Party is that Clinton took a lot of their issues. The era of big government is over; the Supreme Court has taken all the steam out of affirmative action; welfare has been reformed; the budget has been balanced. So what can the Republicans be for?
Mike:	If everything that the Republicans wanted, everything they stood for, happened, why aren't they happy?
Dr. Bauer:	That is a great question!
Clint:	Because they can't take credit for it. Clinton and the Democrats are taking all the credit!
Dr. Bauer:	The Republicans take credit for winning the Cold War.
Clint:	But the perception is that the Democrats accomplished the social and fiscal reforms people wanted—so the Republican Party is not winning.
Sonya:	Also, you asked what Republicans can be for. After big government and taxes, the only remaining issue is religion and morals, that is, values. If Will says discussion of values lacks appeal, what are the Republicans going to grab onto to get their person in the White House and keep control of Congress?
Dr. Bauer:	That certainly seems to be George Will's question. Historically, political parties try to look for the next big issue so they can ride it like a surfer rides a wave. I don't know what the next big issue will be for the Republican Party, or whether they will be able to unite all of their factions behind that issue. But more importantly, neither does one of the most influential Republicans in America.

★ ★ ★

Excerpt from *Locked in the Cabinet*
Robert Reich

I'm off to the Hill.

Any meeting with more than two members of Congress is a free-for-all. They're all entrepreneurs these days—angling for credit with their constituents, favors for big donors, attention from the national media. Members of the House are especially difficult to harmonize, because the districts they represent are literally all over the map. And Democratic House members are even more unruly than Republican House members (unruliness is part of the Democratic ideology). So my expectations for this meeting are low.

It was supposed to begin at noon and they're still filing in, forty-five minutes later, yakking and yelling at one another, grabbing cheese and baloney sandwiches from a table at the entrance, tossing each other Cokes. It's a regular high school. The caucus room in the basement of the Capitol building is tightly packed with rows of aluminum folding chairs. But the room is too small to contain all the members now pushing to get in, which makes this even more of a zoo.

"May I have your attention?" Dick Gephardt is now the House minority leader, with the near-impossible job of maintaining a semblance of order. He's a mild-mannered man whose politics are on the liberal edge of respectability, which means he supports a minimum-wage hike but won't stick his neck way out to get it.

"May I have your attention, *please?*"

They quiet down just enough for Gephardt to heard over the din.

"We're here to talk about the *minimum wage,* and here's the Secretary of Labor."

A no-frills introduction if I ever heard one, followed by a few claps. Most of the members continue chatting among themselves.

I spend the next few minutes shouting out factoids: The value of the minimum wage has steadily dropped since 1969 (when it was about $6.50 an hour in today's purchasing power) to today's $4.25. More than four million people work for the minimum, they're mostly adults, sixty percent are women, and forty percent are the sole breadwinners in their households.

I refer to several large charts I've brought along for the occasion, but I needn't have bothered. The assembled legislators aren't watching. I then ask if there are any questions.

"Mr. Secretary!" yells Barney Frank of Massachusetts. Barney's political views lie to the left of the rest of the Massachusetts delegation, which puts him in the Twilight Zone.

"Yes?"

"You said that if Congress wants to go *higher* than seventy-five cents an hour the President will consider it. How high will he go?"

A trick question. I remember Leon's admonition, so I hedge. "It depends on you guys coming to a consensus about what you want."

"*I think I hear what you mean, Mr. Secretary.*" Barney normally speaks in a nasal yell. Today his volume is even higher than usual. "*You're saying that if we could get a con-sen-sus on a hike of a dollar an hour, the President would sign on?*"

The room is suddenly quieter.

"It's really up to all of *you.* We look forward to working with you on it."

"So your answer is *yes!* We agree among ourselves to raise the minimum by a *dollar* an hour, and President *would support it!*"

"Yes, but only if—"

"That's *wonderful* news! *You made my day, Mr. Secretary.*"

The room erupts in cheers mixed with howls of protest. A gaunt-looking congressman sitting in the front row lifts up a thick report he's been thumbing through and smashes it to the floor. "God-*damn* it," he explodes and promptly walks out of the meeting.

Gephardt tries to restore calm. "Please. *Please.* Let's hear everyone out." He nods to an exasperated member who's jumping up and down.

"Take a good look around this room," the animated congressman begins. "Why do you think there are so few of us left? Why do you think the public rejected so many of us last November? Because this party couldn't let go of old Democratic ideas that are *obsolete,* like *raising the minimum wage.*"

Applause mixed with catcalls and boos.

Gephardt points to another hand in the air. "Rosa?"

Rosa DeLauro from Connecticut stands to address the group. "We Democrats *have* to stick together, and we *have* to stick up for the little guy." Rosa is passionate. "I don't care whether it's seventy-five cents or a dollar and half. What's important is that we *do* it. There's nothing more basic to the Democratic philosophy than the idea that people who work hard should get a fair day's pay."

Wild cheers. Several members stand and applaud.

"Tim?"

A young congressman in a well-tailored suit bounces up. "I'll wager anybody in this room," he begins in a soft Southern drawl, "if we come out for a minimum-wage increase, *I'm* not gonna be here two years from now, regardless of whether I vote for it or against it, because the voters in my district just aren't gonna *elect* a *Democrat* again." His voice rises, and he waves his arm in the air. "Haven't we learned *anything?*" At this very moment, Republicans are introducing a tough welfare bill, cutting off unwed mothers under eighteen. They want *less* government, and the people out *there*"—he points vaguely—"want less government too. But here we are proposing *more government,* folks. This is the *ster-ee-o-typ-ical* Democratic response to *everything.*"

Simultaneous applause and hisses.

Fifty hands are in the air, all demanding airtime. Gephardt's attempt at order is breaking down. Members begin interrupting one another.

"I can't *believe* we're arguing over whether to *raise* the *minimum wage,* for Chrissake! We're *Democrats.* In 1989 we—"

"Forget 1989. In 1994 we had our *goddamn heads* handed to us. If we do this—"

"What the *hell* are people arguing about here? This is a *no-brainer. You* tell *me* how someone is gonna make a living on four dollars and—"

"Whatever we do, let's do it *together.* If we go out there and start pissing on each other again, we'll—"

Gephardt finally gets them to quiet down.

"Now *listen,* all of you," he says wearily. "You *heard* the Secretary of Labor." Gephardt points to me. "The President is willing to take the *lead* on this minimum-wage bill, and I think we owe the President our full support."

Boos, applause.

Gephardt winks at me. I don't know exactly how it happened, but I think the President just took the lead. Leon won't be pleased.

Gephardt continues. "Now, the President is going to propose a specific increase in the minimum wage, and he plans to do it very *soon.* And whatever it is, we have to be *united* behind him. I propose that we form a committee to decide what we want to recommend. . . ."

Half the group are already on their way out of the room. The other half are arguing with each other. No one can hear what Gephardt is saying. He gives up.

Why is this such a big deal? Even if the current minimum wage were hiked by a full dollar, its purchasing power would barely reach what it was in the early 1980s. Technically it's not even an *increase.* It's simply an adjustment to take account of the corrosive effects of inflation. A lot of *other* things get adjusted for inflation—Social Security checks and tax brackets, to take but two that affect the middle class and the wealthy. So what was really going on here?

The answer, I think, is that today's debate among these House Dems isn't about the minimum wage itself. It's a choice about their strategy for 1996. It's about the Lesson of 1994. Should *they* fight or move right?

Clintons Seek to Repair Rifts for Democrats
Richard L. Berke

With an eye to the November elections, to the 2000 Presidential campaign and perhaps to his own legacy, President Clinton has embarked on an aggressive drive to repair divisions between the liberal and moderate wings of the Democratic Party.

The effort is being championed not only by Mr. Clinton but by Hillary Rodham Clinton, who had largely kept a low profile in Democratic politics and policy discussions after attacks over her role in the health care debacle in 1994.

But last week, Mrs. Clinton convened and presided over the first of what is expected to be several meetings at the White House at which prominent Democratic thinkers discuss ways of finding common ground on issues like trade, education, and Social Security.

Several participants said in interviews that although the purpose of the session was to engage the party in a deeper philosophical debate, an underlying theme was more practical: how best to position Democrats for the 1998 and 2000 elections.

In a memorandum describing the meeting, one of the participants, Ruy Teixeira of the Economic Policy Institute, a labor-backed group here, wrote that Mrs. Clinton and others "may see the uniting of the party" around a new political approach "as important to Clinton's legacy."

Another participant, Benjamin R. Barber, a political science professor at Rutgers University, said, "There is a sense that this is a stage where the Democrats can begin to heal their rifts."

When President Clinton first took office in 1993, he alienated many among the party's moderate wing with his stands on issues like homosexuals in the military and increased spending for social programs. Later, he veered so far to the right—on matters including welfare and free trade—that liberals complained that they had been abandoned.

While political labels have grown fuzzy in modern American politics, moderates in the Democratic Party generally favor programs that promote competitive, market-driven economic policy and, on social programs, are less-inclined than liberals to concentrate on Government-sponsored remedies to protect the disadvantaged.

The Clintons are trying to address something of a national identity crisis for the Democrats. The most reliable Democratic voters—those who are most likely to go to the polls in November—are those who are most devoted to the party's traditional liberal ideals.

In their discussions, the Clintons are struggling to come up with compromises that will satisfy those liberals without turning off the more moderate voters, particularly in the suburbs, who are not as loyal to the Democrats. The support of these voters is considered crucial if the party is to regain control of Congress and Governorships in pivotal states.

The appeals for unity reflect a recognition that Mr. Clinton's effort to fashion a Democratic Party around moderate positions is not in itself enough to insure the party's dominance in the future. But many of the participants acknowledged that the effort could fall apart.

In his memorandum, Mr. Teixeira said the gathering might have been propelled by a recognition among moderate Democrats that "the liberal-labor wing of the party is not going away and is, in fact, key to winning in 1998, as well as 2000." Another reason for the meeting, he said, could be Vice President Al Gore's ambitions, including "agendas around Gore's candidacy for President."

Sidney Blumenthal, a senior White House aide who organized the meeting, declined to discuss the immediate political implications. "This was a step in the long-term development of a new progressive politics in America that has been begun by the President," he said. "And it reflects that the center of political and intellectual vitality lies here in what we call 'the third way.'"

This "third way" strategy, championed by Mr. Clinton and Prime Minister Tony Blair of Britain, is founded on the notion that political parties should not feel limited to the traditional right or left approach to governing.

The meeting called by Mrs. Clinton of more than two dozen Democrats—it included White House aides but was dominated by people outside the Administration—marked an intensified move by the Clintons to reposition the Democratic Party. The session included several allies of Mr. Gore, including Elaine C. Kamarck, a lecturer at Harvard University, and Bruce N. Reed, the White House domestic policy director. It also included Barry Bluestone, a professor of political economy at the University of Massachusetts. He is close to Representative Richard A. Gephardt, the House Democratic leader, who may challenge Mr. Gore in 2000.

"Nobody in the party wants Al Gore and Dick Gephardt tearing the party to pieces," said Mr. Barber, the Rutgers professor.

Mr. Barber added that because many issues discussed fell in the traditional purview of First Ladies—like education, health and children—the session was also an opportunity for Mrs. Clinton to re-emerge on policy matters "without re-asserting herself in an overtly political way."

The participants said the session was friendly, although some discussions grew intense. "Everything was cordial, but people were willing to disagree on certain points like charter schools and Social Security," said Fred Siegel, a professor of history at Cooper Union and a fellow at the Progressive Policy Institute, a centrist group. "Those were the flash points."

Participants said they were struck by the degree to which Mrs. Clinton was in control. "She was clearly the guiding spirit and very, very fully engaged in the discussion," said William A. Galston, a deputy assistant for domestic policy during Mr. Clinton's first term.

Though Mr. Galston said the focus was far in the future, he added, "If the Democratic Party is united and has clear answers to the central policy questions today, that will certainly help a nominee such as the Vice President, who will be strongly defending the Administration's record."

Another person at the meeting, speaking on the condition of anonymity, said Mrs. Clinton's role had led him to think that she was signaling her involvement in 2000.

"It struck me as part of this that Hillary's going to play a major role in the Gore campaign," he said. "There were people from Hillary's staff, Clinton's staff and Gore's staff. It looked to me like a kind of pre-preparation for the year 2000."

After the meeting, participants—not including Mrs. Clinton—met over lunch at the Democratic Leadership Council, an organization of centrist Democrats that claims credit for much of Mr. Clinton's agenda in the 1992 Presidential campaign.

Al From, the president of the council who for years battled with liberals, put forth a more accommodating tone at the gathering. "We are not going to be a protectionist party," he said. "But there are issues like labor law reform that we haven't taken enough of an interest in that we need to look at."

Several participants, including liberals, said they endorsed Mr. From's concept of broadening those who benefit from the improved economy, an idea that became something of a mantra of the meeting.

"Some people described it as 'expanding the winners' circle,'" said Nick Littlefield, a Boston lawyer and a former top aide to Senator Edward M. Kennedy of Massachusetts. "I described it as making sure that everybody shares in good economic times. The important thing is that we focus less on the notion of 'a third way' because I don't know what that really means."

Instead, Mr. Littlefield said that much of the discussion had focused on identifying shared values and enunciating them in the 1998 campaign.

"Everybody was saying, 'Wouldn't it be great if there could be specific themes other than H.M.O.s and tobacco and campaign finance?'" he said.

In a memorandum to Mr. Blumenthal before the meeting, Jack Donahue, an associate professor of public policy at Harvard University, suggested that the most important area for the party to find common ground would be a "mend it, don't end it position on public education," rather than a "scorched-earth assault" on public schools.

The more liberal contingent included Richard Rothstein, a researcher at the Economic Policy Institute; Richard C. Leone, president of the Century Foundation, and Paul Starr, editor of the *American Prospect*. Moderates included Will Marshall of the Progressive Policy Institute and David Osbourne, a consultant. Those considered between the two branches included Ralph Whitehead, a specialist on media and politics at the University of Massachusetts, and Barbara Whitehead of the Progressive Policy Institute.

White House officials at the session included Paul Begala, a senior aide; Maria Echaveste, a deputy chief of staff; Michael Waldman, the chief speechwriter; Morley Winograd, Mr. Gore's senior policy adviser, and Minyon Moore, the head of public liaison.

Not all Democrats support the drive to establish "a third way."

"Clinton has never really tried to be a party leader," said Terry Michael, a former communications director for the Democratic National Committee. "And I'm just wondering what this 'third way' thing will amount to. If they're simply trying to find another label and run away from the term 'liberal,' that's going to turn off much of our base."

Clint
a moderate

Mike
a Hispanic, liberal
Democrat

Robert
a moderate
Republican

Sonya
a Hispanic,
moderate Republican

Tony
an African American,
liberal Democrat

Can the Moderates and the Liberals in the Democratic Party Get Along?
★ ★ ★

Dr. Bauer: Some people in the Democratic Party are not happy, a fact we see in the selection from *Locked in the Cabinet* by former Secretary of Labor Robert Reich—a traditional old-fashioned Democrat. In political science terms, Reich is considered a "New Deal Democrat." Dick Lamm, whose interview is at the end of this chapter, said that he started out as a New Deal Democrat, believing in the legacy of FDR. During the Great Depression, Franklin Roosevelt remade the Democratic Party into a party that championed the poor. Is it fair for me to say that Robert Reich is a New Deal Democrat?

Tony: He appears to believe that the government should increase the minimum wage, interfere in the market economy. He wants government to help those people making the least money.

Dr. Bauer: Yes, Reich is a conservative's worst nightmare—he wants to engineer society to benefit certain people. But why all the fuss among the Democrats in the House? Shouldn't Democrats always be in favor of increasing the minimum wage?

Sonya: Democrats sold their souls to big business and can't support the poor the way they used to. The businesses backing them now hate raising the minimum wage.

Dr. Bauer: Except—what's the end of the minimum-wage-hike story? It is not in the reading. Does anybody know what happened?

Sonya: The minimum wage went up a dollar, even though Clinton proposed only ninety cents.

Dr. Bauer: Yes, it went up! So we have to be careful when we describe Democrats as having sold out to big business, because if they had. . . .

Tony: They wouldn't have fought for a minimum-wage increase at all.

Dr. Bauer:	Yes. There is still a New Deal wing of the Democratic Party, and they embarrassed the other wing of the party, the "New Democrats," so much that they forced them into increasing the minimum wage.
Robert:	In making that kind of decision, did they have to weigh the political support of people who were working at minimum wage against the loss of support from businesses?
Dr. Bauer:	There was a cost to their votes, and they worried about it. What was the cost? It wasn't losing PAC money from businesses.
Clint:	House members—especially Southern Democrats—were afraid it would cost them the support of conservative Democrats and, therefore, their seats in Congress. Right?
Dr. Bauer:	Yes. Reich quotes a southern Democrat who says, "If we come out for a minimum-wage increase, *I'm* not gonna be here two years from now, regardless of whether I vote for it or against it, because the voters in my district just aren't gonna *elect* a *Democrat* again." Where do the Democrats get the notion that they are an endangered species because the people don't want these liberal programs?
Robert:	History?
Dr. Bauer:	Recent history.
Tony:	The 1994 elections—when the Republicans took control of the House and Senate in a landslide by opposing big government that meant more regulations, more interference, and a higher deficit. Democrats got scared that if they voted for what seemed like old-fashioned tax-and-spend Democratic proposals, they would lose their seats the way the liberal members did in 1994!
Dr. Bauer:	Yes. See how quickly party politics have turned in just a few years? In 1995, at the time of the Reich article, the Democrats had answered the question, "Should we fight or move right?" with, "We have got to move way to the right, because if we don't, we are going to lose our districts." And what did we just read from George Will about the Republicans in 1999?
Mike:	They have to move left, toward the center.
Sonya:	Everybody is moving to the center.
Dr. Bauer:	But there are complications. Where are the members from who are really in favor of increasing the minimum wage?
Tony:	Connecticut? The Congresswoman, Rosa DeLauro.
Robert:	She said, "We Democrats *have* to stick together, and we *have* to stick up for the little guy. . . ." The basic Democratic Party oath.
Dr. Bauer:	Where else?
Sonya:	Barney Frank from Massachusetts.

Dr. Bauer:	Yes. That tells us that there's a regional difference within the Democratic Party. And there's a regional difference in the Republican Party. Where do most of the social conservatives come from in the Republican Party? Are they concentrated in a region?
Tony:	They are more concentrated in the South.
Dr. Bauer:	You bet.
Mike:	Regional differences affect the Libertarians, too. They have a stronger following out in the West, home of the rugged individualist.
Dr. Bauer:	So, we have two parties, but each party represents a coalition of different wings. There are internal fights in both parties, and some of them are regional fights: Southerners versus Northerners, Easterners versus Westerners. This is a big country. It is awfully hard for a country this size to have political parties that unite a majority of the nation. But both political parties are trying to be national in scope and power. The southern wings of both parties are more conservative; their northern wings are more liberal.
Tony:	And no one is paying attention to the West in either party.
Dr. Bauer:	Except for California because it controls so many electoral votes. Remember, the electoral college actually elects the president and vice president. Electoral votes are apportioned to the states by population. By tradition, a state's electors cast their votes in line with the plurality of the state's popular vote. Both parties try to capture the majority of votes in the electoral college by fighting over the large-population states. The big states that are neither solidly Democrat nor solidly Republican are called the battleground states. That's where the parties really battle it out.

Lets move on to Richard Berke's article, "Clintons Seek to Repair Rifts for Democrats." In this article, we see that there are more than regional differences in the Democratic Party—there are some ideological differences. What is the biggest ideological rift that Clinton is trying to repair so that his friend and vice president Al Gore can become president in 2000? |
Clint:	The one with organized labor?
Dr. Bauer:	Yes, the labor unions. Berke reports that, in an analysis of the Democratic Party, there is some "recognition among moderate Democrats that 'the liberal-labor wing of the party is not going away and is, in fact, key to winning in 1998, as well as 2000.'" A portion of this rift is regional because there is less organized labor in the South, but by and large, labor, itself, is a definable faction within the party. They were a powerful group in the old New Deal coalition but lately are feeling abandoned because Clinton fought for a bill that they opposed.
Tony:	NAFTA.
Dr. Bauer:	Thank you. The unions are livid about the North American Free Trade Agreement. Clinton came in and took a bill that helped companies relocate to

	cheaper labor markets, a bill George Bush wanted passed and couldn't get it passed.
Tony:	And labor thinks their support put Clinton in office. When Clinton turned his back on them and supported NAFTA, that was a stab in the back.
Dr. Bauer:	And he didn't just support NAFTA, he pushed NAFTA through Congress. He said, "This is a priority for me."
Mike:	He drove NAFTA.
Robert:	It never would have gotten through Congress without that huge effort from Clinton.
Dr. Bauer:	The Democratic Party is still divided over labor issues and is still licking its wounds. Labor is part of the Democratic "base." Berke doesn't use the term *base* directly, but he describes what it means. He says, "The most reliable Democratic voters—those who are most likely to go to the polls in November—are those who are most devoted to the party's traditional liberal ideals." That describes the base: those most likely to vote for your party—traditionally loyal.
Tony:	Democrats also refer to African Americans as part of their base. Republicans will point to white, middle-class males as being part of their base.
Dr. Bauer:	Or religious conservatives.
Clint:	Then the party base must include the people who will vote straight ticket. If voters don't know anything about the background of a candidate, they'll say, "Oh, she's a Democrat, I'll vote for her" or "He's a Republican, he must be good."
Robert:	Aren't the base people also the twenty to thirty percent on each side that you don't have to worry about? They are going to vote for you?
Dr. Bauer:	Unless you make them angry.
Robert:	Which is what Clinton did to labor.
Dr. Bauer:	Right.
Clint:	And then the base just won't vote.
Dr. Bauer:	Exactly. Remember, in the Reich article, the Southern Democrats worried about the lessons of the 1994 elections? The consequence to the House members backing Clinton was . . . ?
Tony:	Low voter turnout for the Democrats.
Dr. Bauer:	Right. The Democrats did not get out to vote. Which Democrats in particular? Union people. Labor stayed home in 1994. Labor felt sold out by Bill Clinton and those who voted with him on NAFTA, and they showed it. And what was the end result of labor not voting?
Tony:	We got a Republican Congress.

Dr. Bauer:	See how this works? The base is trapped. If the base stays home, the party loses; if the party loses, the base gets nothing. But that doesn't mean the base won't stay home.
Sonya:	So, if they don't get what they want, they would rather stay home to make their point. Like in that election when liberal Democrats stayed home instead of voting for Humphrey?
Dr. Bauer:	1968. The liberal Democrats stayed home. . . .
Tony:	And then we got Nixon. Wow!
Sonya:	So they might screw themselves, but they teach the party a lesson at the same time.
Dr. Bauer:	Exactly. When the base stays home, the party loses—that's what happens—so you do have to worry about your base. The Republican Party base is fiscal conservatives—they'll vote, but will they vote as actively as the Christian right? How far can the Republican Party move toward the center without losing its religious right base?

This is the same problem that the Democrats have: How far toward the center can they move without losing their liberal base? The Democratic Party experience in previous elections has shown the consequences of losing any part of your base. The party leaders began to realize that by being divided, first they got Nixon, then they got Reagan, then they got Reagan again, and then they got Bush—maybe the time had come for compromise between the conservative and liberal Democrats. Think of how many elections the liberal left voters lost before they changed their minds. Maybe you have to be beaten up electorally quite a bit, lose a lot, before the base says, "We are going to have to adjust our core values."

The Republicans won big in 1994, but they lost in 1996, and they lost in 1998. If they lose in 2000, perhaps their base, the religious right, will come to its senses and compromise. |
Tony:	But they can't because "God has no room for compromise."
Dr. Bauer:	They have a much tougher base problem than the Democrats had. When the Democrats were trying to get labor liberals and the moderates back together, how did they do it?
Sonya:	The wooing: "I just ticked off my girlfriend, I better buy her some flowers."
Dr. Bauer:	The beginning of compromise.
Tony:	That's why Al Gore and Richard Gephardt are meeting a lot, and why Gephardt has come out in favor of Gore. Each represents a different wing of the party, and they're trying to publicly mend the rift so that all the Democrats will get out and vote and they can keep control of the presidency, which Gore wants . . .

Dr. Bauer:	And regain Democratic control of the House in 2000 so that Dick Gephardt can be Speaker. And Dick Gephardt is labor's boy.
Tony:	Big time.
Dr. Bauer:	Big time. Writing his article before Gephardt announced that he would not run for president in the year 2000, Berke reported the fear that Gephardt would run and split the party.
Tony:	It would have split it right down the center and left the Republicans to pick up the pieces.
Dr. Bauer:	Which is one of the major reasons why Gephardt is not running. It appears now, in early 2000, that, in terms of dealing with their base and trying to move the party to center, the Democrats may be in better shape. Some labor unions have endorsed Bill Bradley for president in 2000, but the fight between Bradley and Gore does not promise to be bitter—the kind of fight that tears a party apart.

★ ★ ★

For Additional Reading

Go to InfoTrac College Edition, your online research library at

http://web1.infotrac-college.com

Enter the following search terms using the Subject Guide or Key Terms.

caucus	New Deal Coalition	patronage
closed primary	open primary	political machines
dealignment	party	realignment
direct primary	party in the electorate	state party committees
divided government	party in government	ticket splitting
national party chair	party identification	two-party system
national party committees	party organization	

8

eight

Public Opinion

Advice to Poll Consumers
Herbert Asher

To death and taxes should be added public opinion polls, an integral and unavoidable part of American society today. Public opinion polling is a contemporary manifestation of classical democratic theory; it attests to the ability of the rational and wise citizen to make informed judgments on the major issues of the day. Polling makes it possible for political organizations to demonstrate that public opinion is on their side as they promote their ends. News organizations are also enamored of polling in part because polls seem to elevate the citizen (and thus the media audience) into a more prominent political role; in effect, the polls transform the amorphous citizenry into a unified actor in the political process. Poll results that are not supportive of government actions provide the media with stories of conflict between the government and the people, just as points of contention between the president and the Congress or between the House and the Senate become a media focus.

As the technology of polling has been continually refined, upgraded, and made more available, many institutions, organizations, and private groups have gained the ability to sponsor and conduct polls. These organizations can readily hire pollsters for surveys that will promote their aims, or, if they want to be absolutely sure that the poll results will be favorable, they can conduct their own surveys. Such self-serving polls are replete with loaded questions, skewed samples, and faulty interpretations similar to the surveys done by the Tobacco Institute and by the Michigan Tobacco and Candy Distributors and Vendors Association to try to head off higher cigarette taxes and antismoking legislation (Morin 1989; Perlstadt and Holmes 1987).

Reprinted with permission of Congressional Quarterly, Inc., from *Polling and the Public: What Every Citizen Should Know,* 4th ed., by Herbert Asher (Washington, DC: Congressional Quarterly Press, 1998), 170–175. © 1998 by Congressional Quarterly, Inc.

Adding to the proliferation of surveys, the major news organizations have heavily invested in their own in-house polling operations. The resulting increase in the number of polls they conduct justifies their investment and enables them to keep up with the competition—that is, for certain news stories, such as presidential debates, a news organization that fails to conduct and report a poll on who wins is open to the criticism of incomplete news coverage. The unseemly contest among the media to be the first to "call" the outcome of particular elections illustrates how the pressures of competition and ratings promote the widespread use of polls. The media operate under the assumption that the public reactions to major news events are meaningful and that public opinion polls enhance the news value of a story.

HOW TO EVALUATE POLLS: A SUMMARY

Polls are a significant way for citizens to participate in society and to become informed about the relationship between the decisions of government and the opinions of the citizenry. As more organizations conduct polls and disseminate their results, whether to inform or to sway public opinion, citizens should become wary consumers, sensitive to the factors that can affect poll results. Gaining this sensitivity does not require familiarity with statistics or survey research experience. Consumers need only treat polls with a healthy skepticism and keep in mind the following questions as tools to evaluate poll results.

One basic question poll consumers should ask is whether a public opinion survey is measuring genuine opinions or nonattitudes. Are respondents likely to be informed and have genuine opinions about the topic? Or is the focus so esoteric that their responses reflect the social pressures of the interview situation, pressures that cause respondents to provide answers even when they have no real views on the subject at hand? The answers to questions about nonattitudes are not easy to find, for as W. Russell Neuman (1986) argues, there is often not a clear demarcation between attitudes and nonattitudes. Indeed, Neuman coined the term *quasi-attitude* to designate something between an attitude and a nonattitude, and he points out that citizens' responses to survey questions are "a mixture of carefully thought-out, stable opinions, half-hearted opinions, misunderstandings, and purely random responses" (Neuman 1986, 184).

Another question to consider when evaluating polls concerns screening. Have the researchers made any effort to screen out respondents who lack genuine attitudes on the topic? Unfortunately, reports frequently omit information about screening questions and their effects—that is, often one cannot tell what proportion of the total sample has answered a particular item and what proportion has been screened out. To do a better job of reporting this information, news organizations should, at minimum, provide the number of respondents who answered a particular question. When this number is substantially smaller than the total sample size, they should explain the discrepancy.

When screening information is not presented, citizens are forced to form impressionistic judgments about whether the measurement of nonattitudes has been a problem in the survey. Of course, some issues of public policy that have been hotly debated and contested by political elites, even issues such as tax reform, may not be of much interest to many Americans and thus may be highly susceptible to the measurement of nonattitudes.

Citizens are in a better position to evaluate the potential effects of question wording than the presence of nonattitudes. Because the media usually provide the actual wording of questions, readers (or viewers) can judge whether any words or phrases in the questions are blatantly loaded, whether the alternatives are presented in a fair and balanced fashion, and whether a question accurately reflects the topic under study. If a report of a survey omits question wording, particularly on items dealing with controversial issues, the consumer should be wary and ask why.

Question wording is just one reason a complete questionnaire should be made available with a survey report. The questionnaire also is helpful when a survey contains many questions on a topic but reports the results for only one or two items. Without the complete questionnaire, a poll consumer is unable to assess whether the selective release of results has created any misleading impressions.

Another reason to examine the entire questionnaire is to assess the potential effects of question order. This is seldom possible, however, since press releases (other than those issued by news organizations) and news stories rarely include the complete survey form, but citizens should be aware that the way earlier questions are asked can affect responses to subsequent queries. This is a subtle phenomenon for which most citizens have little intuitive feel, yet the strategic placement of questions is one of the most effective ways to "doctor" a survey. While each individual question may be balanced and fair, the overall order of the questions may stimulate specific responses preferred by the sponsor of the survey. One clue that this problem exists is the refusal of an organization, such as a political campaign team, to release the entire poll results.

The next question consumers should address is sampling. Although it is the most mysterious part of polling for most poll consumers, sampling is probably the least important for them to understand in detail. Sampling error is *not* where polls typically go astray. Reputable pollsters pick good samples and typically report sampling error and confidence levels so that citizens can form independent judgments about the significance of results. To make sure that a sample properly reflects the aims of a poll, a poll consumer should pay close attention to how the sample is defined. And certainly the consumer should confirm that the sample is a scientifically selected probability sample rather than a purposive one that an investigator selected for reasons of convenience.

One aspect of sampling that citizens should not overlook is the proportion of the total sample to which a particular finding applies. For a variety of reasons, such as the use of screening questions or the need to study analytically interesting subsets of the original sample, the proportion of respondents on which a result is based may be substantially smaller than the overall sample. Thus one should know not only the sampling error of the total sample but also the sampling error of the subsets.

Interviewers and interviewing are aspects of polling that can influence outcomes, but they are aspects not easily questioned. It is almost impossible for citizens to evaluate the effects of interviewing on poll results because reports usually provide too little information about the interviewing process beyond the method of interviewing (for example, telephone or personal) and the dates of the interviews. The poll consumer normally assumes that an interview was performed competently, undoubtedly a safe assumption with reputable polling firms. But consumers should note that an interviewer with the intention of generating biased responses has many opportunities to achieve that end while asking questions. The best way for the poll consumer to gain some sense of potential interviewer effects is to be a poll respondent who carefully observes the performance of the interviewer—an opportunity that may or may not come one's way.

The final questions to ask when evaluating a poll relate to the end products, analyses and interpretation. Most citizens do not have access to raw poll data; instead they must rely on the analyses and interpretations provided by the media and other sources. But do these sources of

information have a vested interest in a particular poll outcome? If so, poll consumers should scrutinize poll results even more carefully. For example, a poll sponsored by the insurance industry purporting to demonstrate that the liability insurance crisis is due to the rapacious behavior of trial lawyers should be viewed with greater skepticism than a similar poll sponsored by an organization with a less direct interest in the outcome. Likewise, election poll results released by a candidate should be viewed more cautiously than those released by a respected news organization.

After evaluating the source of a poll, the consumer then faces the more difficult task of ascertaining whether the pollster's conclusions follow from the data. This task is problematical because often, as noted earlier, only a portion of the relevant evidence is presented in a news story or press release. Or a poll may have included many items on a particular topic, yet the report may present only a subset of those items. Without knowledge of the total questionnaire, one can only hope that the analyst has reported a representative set of results, or speculate on how different items on the same topic might have yielded different results. Likewise, reports might include results from the entire sample but not important variations in the responses of subsets of the sample. Lacking direct access to the data, the citizen is left to ponder how the overall results might differ within subsets of respondents.

The interpretation of a poll is not an automatic, objective enterprise; different analysts examining the same polling data may come to different conclusions. Although this may occur for a variety of reasons, an obvious one is that analysts bring different values and perspectives to the interpretation of polls. Often there are no objective standards on what constitutes a high or low level of support on an issue; it may indeed be partly cloudy or partly sunny depending upon one's perspective. Thus, poll consumers should ask themselves whether they would necessarily come to the same conclusions on the basis of the data presented. Just because the poll is sponsored by a prestigious organization and conducted by a reputable firm does not mean that one has to defer automatically to the substantive conclusions of the sponsors. And if a poll is conducted by an organization with an obvious vested interest in the results, then the poll consumer is certainly warranted in making an independent judgment.

Excerpt from "Torn Between His Lawyers and Political Aides, Clinton Chose Strategy of Denial"

Jill Abramson

On January 21, the morning the accusations about President Clinton's relationship with Monica S. Lewinsky first appeared in the news media, the political consultant Dick Morris was in New York City when his pager went off. The call, Mr. Morris said in an interview, was from the President.

That morning, there had been heated deliberations between lawyers in the office of the White House counsel, Charles F. C. Ruff, and the White House communications and political team, according to several current and former White House aides interviewed in the last week.

A White House adviser said the lawyers wanted the President to say very little and insisted that the word "sexual" not appear in Mr. Clinton's first official statement about Ms. Lewinsky, which was due to be released by Michael D. McCurry, the White House press secretary.

Several political and communications advisers, who had weathered previous accusations involving Mr. Clinton, were pressing for as much early candor as possible, the "more rather than less approach," as one of them labeled it in a recent interview.

Apparently torn himself over the best approach, the President reached out once again to Mr. Morris, the political consultant who had helped orchestrate his comeback from the brink of other disasters, including the 1994 election that delivered the House to the Republicans. Mr. Morris, whose position as a Clinton insider had been shattered by his own sexual misconduct in 1996, said he had not been surprised to get the call.

The President told Mr. Morris that he had "slipped up" with Ms. Lewinsky but that the charges against him were untrue, Mr. Morris said. The adviser offered to take a poll to see what the attitude of the voters would be if the President admitted an affair with Ms. Lewinsky.

Before the poll results were back, Mr. Clinton proceeded shakily through a first day of questions, with a vague statement (the President "never had any improper relationship" with Ms. Lewinsky), and an oddly present-tense response in a PBS interview ("There is no sexual relationship—that is accurate."). In the following days, backed in part, Mr. Morris said, by his polling, the denials only became more forceful. . . .

By then, Mr. Morris said, he had reported his polling results back to the President. The public would forgive admission of a sexual dalliance, but not that the President had been untruthful about it in his sworn deposition in the Paula Jones sexual misconduct case. . . .

Reprinted with permission from *The New York Times*, August 24, 1998. © 1998 by The New York Times Company.

Excerpt from "Politics and Policy: How Public Opinion Really Works"
Daniel Yankelovich

Sometimes a truth is so simple and obvious that it eludes detection for years. So it is with public opinion. We have grown so accustomed to seeing public opinion quantified in polls (77% say they support "national health insurance," for example) that we make an unwitting—and, as it happens, false—assumption. We assume that public opinion is some kind of phenomenon like wind velocity, whose variations can be measured, and that the measurement is valid.

Public opinion is in fact less like a physical process than a biological one, evolving in seven stages. Unless one knows public opinion's stage of development on an issue, poll numbers will usually mislead. Any political leader who really thinks 77% of voters support national health insurance is deluding himself. As I demonstrate in my book *Coming to Public Judgment,* once one sees public opinion in this light, one can never go back to the old way of looking at it.

Public opinion on any issue develops slowly over a long period—at least ten years for a complex issue. It evolves from incoherent globs of opinion toward fully integrated, thoughtful, and considered public judgment. On issues in early stages of development, the quality of public opinion is raw and unformed. Many people express strong feelings, but vehemence does not mean settled views. Opinions at this stage are unstable, flip-flopping at the slightest provocation. People have not thought through the consequences of their views. Today, for example, most of the public remains mired in wishful thinking on protectionism and health care, resisting any attempt to confront with realistic information the costs and trade-offs each entails. Political candidates who act on the results of opinion polls on these issues will soon feel the ground give way under their feet.

At the opposite end of the developmental spectrum are issues on which public opinion has had a chance to mature. When public opinion has progressed through all seven stages, its quality is impressive. People's views are solid and stable, not mushy. They hold them consistently and coherently, accepting responsibility for the trade-offs involved.

Many issues have reached this stage, but I want to cite one that may seem surprising. Many policymakers fear that the American public, under pressure from the recent recession, is reverting to a pre-World War II form of isolationism. But the American people have actually thought through the isolationism vs. internationalism issue. Having gone through all seven stages, they agree with those who urge that with the end of the Cold War, the nation should give greater priority to our domestic concerns—without, however, abdicating our responsibility as leader of the free world.

Unfortunately, opinion polls as presently reported don't indicate which stage a particular issue has reached. Leaders attempting to communicate with the public without this information risk gridlock and frustration. Why? Because to communicate with the populace, a leader has to know where people are coming from, where they stand in their thinking now, and where they are headed.

—*Stage 1: Dawning Awareness.* Here people become aware of an issue or some aspect of it. Budding awareness launches the long and tortuous journey toward public judgment.

—*Stage 2: Greater Urgency.* The second stage is a move beyond awareness to a sense of urgency about an issue. . . .

—*Stage 3: Discovering the Choices.* In the third stage the public begins to focus on alternatives for dealing with issues. The timing of Stage 3 varies by issue. On some, choices become clear almost immediately. But on most they do not.

Some issues can fester for years before concrete, feasible choices appear.

The public comes to focus on choices that leaders offer without insisting upon alternatives to consider. Often the proffered options are not the best choices and certainly not the only ones. Stage 3 represents progress, however, because it begins the process of converting the public's free-floating concern about the need to do something into proposals for action. . . .

—*Stage 4: Wishful Thinking.* This is where the public's resistance to facing trade-offs kicks in. Most of the time on most issues, the public raises a barricade of wishful thinking that must be overcome before people come to grips with issues realistically. In opinion polls it is easy to get people to express approval for a cornucopia of improved services and even to claim that they would accept modest increases in taxes for them. But saying this in a survey and accepting in reality are wholly different matters.

It is difficult to know whether the public's tendency toward wishful thinking is stronger now than in earlier periods of American life. I suspect it is. The public's ritualistic incantation of "waste, fraud, and abuse" may be a rationalization to avoid the need to confront societal problems, even though it has grounding in reality.

Mainly, though, the public erects its wishful-thinking barricade to public-policy proposals because people feel excluded from decision-making on matters that affect their lives. It is a truism that people act most responsibly when they are personally engaged. To make sacrifices ungrudgingly, people must understand why these are needed, and they must have some say in the types, forms, and conditions of sacrifice they are asked to make. A significant part of the public's resistance to facing reality reflects the perception that a serious disconnect separates today's leaders from the voters. . . .

—*Stage 5: Weighing the Choices.* Here the public does what we call choice work: weighing the pros and cons of alternatives for dealing with an issue. In practice Stages 4 and 5 overlap, with people thinking through how they feel at the same time that they continue to resist coming to grips with the hard choices.

Wrestling with complex issues—abortion, the death penalty, immigration, censorship, environmental protection, homelessness, as well as health care—requires getting in touch with one's deepest values and often realizing that these may conflict with one another on a particular question. People naturally resist having to compromise or abandon cherished values.

Stage 5 is hard work, and work that the public must do for itself; there are no shortcuts. In earlier stages the media and experts do most of the work. The media specialize in consciousness raising, and they do it well. Leaders and experts formulate the policy choices. But the public must invest the effort to grasp the choices, understand their consequences, and wrestle with the conflicts of values these choices entail. . . .

—*Stage 6: Taking a Stand Intellectually and Stage 7: Making a Responsible Judgment Morally and Emotionally.* As the two stages of resolution, these can be considered together. These stages are linked, but different. People are quicker to accept change in their minds than in their hearts. Most Americans, for example, accept in their minds the idea of equal opportunity for minorities in the workplace, but they haven't quite taken the final critical step toward accepting it wholeheartedly.

The same is true for First Amendment guarantees of freedom of expression. In their minds, Americans support freedom of expression unreservedly, recognizing how essential it is to preserving America's priceless heritage of political freedom. But the reason that laws and courts are indispensable to First Amendment protection is that offensive speech, flag burning, and pornography create such intense emotional and moral revulsion that, in the heat of the moment, the public can easily disregard its intellectual commitment. Intellectual resolution requires people to clarify fuzzy thinking, reconcile inconsistencies, consider relevant facts and new realities, and grasp the full consequences of choices. Emotional resolution requires people to confront their own ambivalent feelings, accommodate themselves to unwelcome realities, and overcome an urge to procrastinate.

In arriving at moral resolution, people's first impulse is to put their own needs and desires ahead of ethical commitments. But once they have time to reflect on their choices, especially if the larger society provides moral support, the ethical dimension asserts itself, and people struggle to do the right thing, often successfully. . . .

CHAT ROOM

Clint	Mike	Robert	Sonya	Tony
a moderate	a Hispanic, liberal Democrat	a moderate Republican	a Hispanic, moderate Republican	an African American, liberal Democrat

Playing a Serious Game with Numbers
★ ★ ★

Dr. Bauer: Our first article is a very small part of an important book, *Polling and the Public: What Every Citizen Should Know,* about public opinion. It describes how the public can evaluate polls by asking several questions—the most basic being whether a poll is "measuring genuine opinions or nonattitudes." What does he mean by that? What is a "nonattitude"?

Mike: The answer a person gives when she or he doesn't really know anything about the question.

Dr. Bauer: Does anybody remember the famous example about nonattitudes in the classic bad poll? It was actually an experiment . . . the polling question was about the Supreme Court.

Clint: Pollsters made up a name for a nonexistent Supreme Court justice and asked people to rate his performance.

Dr. Bauer: Were people willing to admit that they hadn't heard of the justice and weren't able to rate him?

Clint: No. They were given rankings to choose from, and instead of choosing "No opinion," they chose "Supreme Court Justice Johnson is the best justice on the Court."

Dr. Bauer: Has anybody in this room ever been polled?

Robert: I've been polled a few times on different subjects. But the political poll was like twenty minutes long and had a lot of questions and a scale of one to five. Halfway through, I was confused about which measurement I was working with—least favorable to most favorable or like to dislike. They kept changing the scale. It was a strange experience.

Dr. Bauer:	Sounds like they were trying to measure the depth of your opinion, too. Instead of simple yes or no answers, they wanted to know *how much* you liked or didn't like something, so they used scaling. It's a more accurate way to measure opinion, but it can get confusing.
Robert:	Yeah, they took me in a lot of different directions.
Tony:	I've been on the other end of polls in campaigns—I've done some phone polling myself. The first contact—when I ask if the person is willing to participate—is very interesting. A lot of people said, "No, I don't have time." And some people got excited and said, "Oh, good! I've never been polled before, and I've always wondered where they get their results."
Dr. Bauer:	As you found out, there are a number of people who won't participate in a phone poll. And the refusal rate has gotten higher every year, so much so, that pollsters worry that the people who do answer polls may not represent a random sample. If that's true, the whole premise behind polling, that we can find the opinion of the general public through a random sampling of a small percentage, is in real trouble. Robert, did participating in the poll make you feel as if someone was listening to you? As if you and your opinions were important?
Robert:	I felt more like I was being probed for information.
Dr. Bauer:	Like the aliens coming down—
Robert:	Yeah, as if either I gave them the answers they wanted or they'd just keep at me.
Dr. Bauer:	Was this a push poll, Robert?
Robert:	It totally felt like it.
Dr. Bauer:	Does everybody here know what a "push poll" is?
Robert:	A poll in which the interviewer is telling you what to say, but you don't know it.
Dr. Bauer:	Yes, they're leading you in a direction, usually a negative one. Was your poll experience like that?
Robert:	Totally. Totally.
Dr. Bauer:	Tony, since you've done some polling, give us an example of how to word a question that you want to use to *push* someone into giving you a negative opinion about the opponent?
Tony:	I'm trying to think. . . . Okay, first, "What is your average household income?" If you respond with "Somewhere around $30,000," they respond with, "Are you in favor of Bill Clinton, who just passed the largest tax increase in the history of the world—increasing taxes on the middle class so that he can spend that money to fund partial-birth abortions in foreign countries?"
Dr. Bauer:	Good! Another way to do a push poll is to use order bias, which Asher also discusses in the reading. The interviewer asks, first, if the person has a favor-

able or unfavorable opinion of the incumbent. Almost everybody has a favorable opinion. Then the interviewer says something really nasty about the incumbent, and follows up with the question, "*Now* what do you think of the incumbent?"

Robert: How would they actually use a push poll?

Dr. Bauer: A push poll tries to create opinion, rather than measure it. It's not a true reflection of public opinion. But a normal poll can also be used to create opinion, can't it?

Clint: Sure. Because a normal poll reports what the majority of people think, the solid numbers in the report might persuade people to change their opinions so they fit in with the majority. And it looks so scientific. People like the appearance of facts.

Mike: Then, if you get the numbers you want, you can use polls to create a "sheep mentality" so the rest of the population will agree with, and join, the majority opinion.

Dr. Bauer: Political scientists call this a "bandwagon effect." We see this at the start of the 2000 presidential race—almost a stampede to support Republican G. W. Bush, Jr., with record fund-raising early in the primary season as everyone piles on the bandwagon to go with the winner. But the only race G. W. Bush has won outside his native Texas is in polling.

Robert: One time when I was being polled, the interviewer asked all kinds of questions about my income, race, religion, even if I was married, or had a college degree. What was that all about?

Dr. Bauer: Those are "screening questions." Pollsters use them to separate, or screen, people into different segments, smaller subsets, of the population. The more a poll tries to focus on smaller segments of the population—the middle class or college students—the larger the poll's margin of error will be. The margin of error—within so many percentage points of what everyone would say if you could ask everybody—is supposed to tell you how accurate the poll is. And the margin of error is based on the size of the sample.

For example, suppose we are sampling everybody in Denver on abortion, and we use the screening question, "Are you Protestant, Catholic, Jewish, or other?" The answer to this question creates four different subsets. If we want to report the opinions of people who are Jewish, we hit that screening question, go to all those who answered Jewish, and report their opinions. How large is the Jewish population in Denver?

Robert: Not that big. There are certainly a lot more Hispanics, African Americans, even maybe Native Americans. Compared to places on the East or West Coast, Denver has a pretty small Jewish community.

Dr. Bauer: Here's my point: The probability of learning the public opinion of a small subset of the community, such as Jews in Denver, is pretty small. What are the chances that the people who report that poll in the media will tell you that they are using subset findings of a whole sample? And that the margin of error for a small subset of a population is double or even triple the margin of error for a poll that surveys all Denver residents? The margin of error could be as high as thirty percent when you take a subset of a larger random sample! That's pretty close to useless information. This is one of the ways that polls can mislead, by using subsets. What other groups can be subsets?

Sonya: People in New Hampshire or California taken from a nationwide poll. But the public has no way of knowing what the margin of error was for just New Hampshire or just California.

Dr. Bauer: That's right. They give you the margin of error for the national poll but not for the subset state.

Clint: Another subset used is household incomes.

Dr. Bauer: Good; pollsters will report that "middle-class voters think this" or "upper-income voters think that" but never report the margin of error for those subsets. Any other subsets that we ordinarily find in polls?

Sonya: Race or gender.

Dr. Bauer: Those are frequent subsets. A lot of polls recorded in the press break down their results into these subsets.

Mike: Can we add age to that?

Dr. Bauer: Yes, younger voter versus older voters. This is quite common, isn't it? Anytime you see a subset, you should be skeptical of the poll's findings.

Robert: Aren't some of those subsets more important than others? Like, older subsets are more important than eighteen- to twenty-one-year-olds? Because seniors vote. Shouldn't we take their opinions more seriously when we are looking at who is likely to win an election?

Dr. Bauer: If you're using polling as a tool for winning elections, to find out what people who are likely to vote think about a candidate, yes. But there is another use, and that is to decide what policy an elected official should support to maintain his or her popularity. To help us dig deeper into how this type of polling has profoundly changed American politics, let's turn to the article, "Torn Between His Lawyers and Political Aides, Clinton Chose Strategy of Denial." What policy did the White House come up with in response to polling done about the Monica Lewinsky scandal?

Tony: They tried to shape the debate. If you have a sense of what the public reaction is likely to be on a given issue, then you can shape your communication to use just the right words to explain yourself.

Dr. Bauer: This is called "damage control" and is used when an official has made a decision on an action. For example, Bush had decided that he was going to do anything he could—including bomb Iraq—to get Iraqi soldiers out of Kuwait. He virtually said he didn't care about public opinion, he was going to do it. Then the Bush White House polled to see how they would shape the decision, what words Bush would use to describe the action to the public. That's why the Bush White House never talked about the price of oil; if they were going to war, "stopping aggression" was a phrase that worked much better in the polls.

Clint: The White House also tried to decide which position the president should take: whether he should deny his relationship with Lewinsky or admit to it.

Dr. Bauer: Yes. Which use of polling is more dangerous to democracy: to use polls after the decision to take an action or to use polls to make the decision?

Robert: I think it's much worse to let polls tell you what to do. You're asking the entire country, through the poll, to tell you how to run your business. And that's not right. That is not why we elected that person.

Tony: I am going to have to agree with Robert that using polling to determine policy can be the scariest use. On most policy questions, the public isn't nearly as well informed as the policy makers who are paid to spend time researching the issue in depth. And certainly in polls you are not going to get to the heart of the tough part of a question. For example, on Social Security: If you call people and simply ask them are they in favor of saving Social Security, the vast majority will say yes. If you ask them if they want to use some of the budget surplus, they are going say yes. But, if you don't tell them what other things the surplus could go toward, then the public isn't fully informed. So, to rely on that public opinion poll would give you only half the real picture. Because if I said we could use some of that for education, you might think twice before agreeing that the whole surplus should go to Social Security.

Dr. Bauer: Yes, that's true. Now let's return to the Clinton decision and take a look at that. Based on a poll, Clinton made a decision to hang tough on this sex scandal that then drags on for seven long months. My question to you is, was the poll that Dick Morris did for the president accurate? What was his conclusion in the first poll?

Tony: According to the *Times* article, he concluded that Clinton should deny that there had been a sexual relationship.

Mike: The public would forgive an admission of his sexual acts, but not that he lied in his deposition. He had already testified in the Paula Jones case that he had not had a relationship with Monica Lewinsky, so he had to continue to deny it. If he admitted to having lied, the public would turn on him.

Dr. Bauer: Was that accurate? Did that turn out to be true?

Robert: Surprisingly, no.

Sonya: By a large margin, the public chose to forgive him—even for lying.

Dr. Bauer:	So Morris's advice at the beginning of the whole scandal changed history. White House political aides advised Clinton to come clean right away; he chose denial because of Morris's poll. If he hadn't, there might not have been impeachment. Why do you think Morris's poll was inaccurate?

This question leads us right into the next reading, "How Public Opinion Really Works," which gives us some insight into why Dick Morris's original poll was such garbage. This reading outlines seven stages of public opinion—seven stages of thinking about an issue before the public comes to a real, as opposed to an easily changeable, opinion. What does he call the real public opinion, do you remember? He calls it "mature opinion." Immature public opinion is not grown up, it's easily influenced. Yankelovich says that if pollsters sample public opinion before people have gone through these seven stages, the poll will not reflect a real opinion. In other words, the poll will get a nonattitude. Let's follow the impeachment process through these stages. What are the seven stages? |
Sonya:	One, dawning awareness; two, greater urgency; three, discovering the choices; four, wishful thinking; five, weighing the choices; six, taking a stand intellectually; and seven, making a responsible judgment morally and emotionally.
Dr. Bauer:	When Dick Morris was doing his original polling, in what stage was the public?
Tony:	Dawning awareness.
Dr. Bauer:	Exactly! And how well formed is public opinion at the dawning awareness stage?
Clint:	It's *not*.
Dr. Bauer:	It's not well formed, yet people will cough up an answer to a pollster. See how dangerous this gets? At what point did we get to greater urgency in the Clinton scandal?
Tony:	Probably around the time we learned about the Linda Tripp tapes. By that time we had heard a lot of gossip, but the tapes made people think there might be more concrete support for the rumors.
Dr. Bauer:	And the next stage, discovering the choices—when the public discovers that it can have this, or it can have that, but it can't have both.
Sonya:	That could have been when people started talking about consequences if it turned out that Clinton had lied and there had been a sexual relationship with Lewinsky. Public opinion changed when people first started talking about taking action against him.
Mike:	The choices seemed to be to impeach or to censure—two very different choices with different consequences for the whole country.
Robert:	And we were making choices about word meanings—"Is oral sex really sex?"

Dr. Bauer:	Good point, Robert! And that led us into stage four, wishful thinking. First we heard about the blue dress with the DNA stain, and then when we learned that it had been oral sex between Clinton and Lewinsky, there was this burst of support from the Democrats saying, well, it was just oral sex, so Clinton didn't lie when he said, "I never had sex with that woman." Some might say that was wishful thinking. I remember the Democrats, especially, were eager to believe that Monica Lewinsky was blackmailing Clinton, that she was a stalker, and it was all her fault.
Mike:	There was a lot of wishful thinking that this was just going to go away. We didn't want to deal with something so personal.
Dr. Bauer:	When did the public begin to weigh the choices in the impeachment mess?
Tony:	When Congress began releasing the transcripts from Clinton's grand jury testimony and from Lewinsky's grand jury testimony. It appeared that the Judiciary Committee was going to move for action under the Articles of Impeachment. That is when the public had to weigh choices.
Dr. Bauer:	Yes, I think the people took their cue from the House when the Judiciary Committee began to weigh choices. And then we get to stages six and seven, which are interesting because Yankelovich makes a strong distinction between taking a stand intellectually and taking a stand ethically, or in your heart. When did the public start to take their stands?
Clint:	During the impeachment itself. The moral question was whether Clinton should go down because he lied about sexual misconduct. Intellectually, people thought Clinton was doing a good job running the country.
Dr. Bauer:	Yes, and I think this was making the House managers crazy—the public believed intellectually that Clinton was doing a great job, and the House managers were saying, "Wait! The public is at stage six! We want them to be at stage seven, making moral judgments!"
Robert:	Yankelovich says that stages six and seven are very similar and have to be weighed together. And so basically people were saying to pollsters, "How do you impeach somebody who is doing such a great job for something—marital infidelity—that is so common among American men?"
Dr. Bauer:	Okay, but again, that is an intellectual statement. It ignores the ethics.
Tony:	I don't think so. I think the intellectual and emotional came together in stage seven. Intellectually, the people said America is doing fine, our economy is much stronger than any other nation's, my job pays me well. Emotionally and ethically, it is much more important to me that my family continues to do well under Clinton's administration than that we remove him from office for marital infidelity.

Dr. Bauer:	Okay, so let me throw something out to you, and see what you think. I thought when I read this article that the House impeachment managers making the argument in the Senate didn't have time to take public opinion through all seven stages.
Tony:	I think they did, because, essentially, it began in January with Clinton's initial statement, pounding on the podium, that he had not had sexual relations with that woman. I think that gave the Republican managers plenty of time to start at the very first stage of dawning awareness. There were months, plenty of time for them to do polling through each of the stages, before they got to the impeachment hearings.
Clint:	I disagree. I think the people just got tired, they hit overload hearing the same arguments over and over and over, and the public just didn't take the time to think it all through. Plus, every time they saw polls that said Clinton was okay, the economy was still strong, it reinforced the idea that they could just support the president and stop thinking about it.
Dr. Bauer:	So, you're saying that when people saw polls that said Clinton should stay in office, they jumped on the bandwagon. You have a point. We know that the House managers kept trying to make the trial in the Senate last longer so they could change public opinion. That was the purpose of getting more witnesses to testify in person. They knew from their polls that public opinion was so rock steady for Clinton, they would have to work extremely hard to change it. Had they read this article, do you think they might have been more likely to conclude that they were measuring mature public opinion, that it had already gone through these seven stages, that perhaps they were in a losing cause and should wrap it up?
Tony:	I definitely think that by the time we finally reached the Senate trial, America had reached stage seven and emotionally would not detach themselves from Bill Clinton—they wanted him to stay in office. There was no movement whatsoever by then that showed the American public was willing to have him removed. So, I think if they had been paying attention to what we have before us in this article, they would have let it go. Instead, they gambled a lot on trying to change public opinion, and mature opinion is very hard to change. The trick, then, is to know when public opinion is easily influenced and when it has matured to a point that nothing short of a national disaster will budge it.

★ ★ ★

For Additional Reading

Go to InfoTrac College Edition, your online research library at

http://web1.infotrac-college.com

Enter the following search terms using the Subject Guide or Key Terms.

margin of error	public opinion	scientific polling
political socialization	push poll	tracking poll
polls and bias	sample size	

9

nine

Voting and Elections

A PERSONAL

PERSPECTIVE ON

Elections

MONICA BAUER

THE FIRST TIME I RAN FOR OFFICE, I GOT TALKED INTO IT. IN 1984, I was the pastor of a little church in Crete, Nebraska, a town known for two things: Doane College and a giant Alpo dog food plant. Not much politics in Crete. But 1984 was an important year for the people of rural Nebraska; it was the peak of what was being called the "farm crisis." That meant that hundreds of farmers in Nebraska— thousands all over the nation—were filing for bankruptcy and watching their lives fall apart. Some parishioners, and friends of my parishioners, were so upset by the farm crisis, they were considering suicide. The causes of the crisis are too many to go into here, but, in essence, the federal government, which had been regulating what crops farmers could grow and what prices they could charge for their crops, was not regulating what it cost to grow them. Costs doubled, then tripled, while the federal government's farm subsidy program froze farmers' goods at prices decades old. That was good for American consumers, who enjoy one of the cheapest and best food supplies in the world. But it devastated all but the giant corporate farms, who were buying out the family farmers desperate to salvage something. I smelled injustice.

As a small town pastor, I did what I could. I joined a statewide, interfaith committee that addressed the farm crisis, but after every meeting, it was clear that there was very little we could do except complain to a government that didn't seem to care. I went to a national conference on economic justice; the speakers

181

urged people to get involved in politics—decisions were made in the political arena. Some of us might even run for office ourselves.

I was 30 years old, had never run for dogcatcher and had never done anything in a political campaign more complex than make a few phone calls for Jimmy Carter when I was in college. I had never gone to a meeting of a local political party and had never met a real politician. Given my limited background, a Bachelor's degree in European history and a Master's degree in divinity (I had yet to study political science), I thought I would volunteer to do research for the state headquarters of my political party. It looked like the 1984 election would be a repeat of the previous election in 1982 when the incumbent congressman had been opposed by a guy who had sold bread and brownies door-to-door from a little red wagon to finance his "campaign." He played it strictly for laughs and parlayed his doomed candidacy into a position of local humor writer for the *Lincoln Star.*

What happened next duplicated a typical pattern in a race against a congressional incumbent, but I was too dumb to know it. The minute I showed the slightest interest in helping to defeat the incumbent, the state party chair began courting me. We had long talks about the farm crisis; she told me that there was no one with half my dedication who was going to challenge the incumbent. Two candidates had already filed to run against the congressman in 1984, and they were both certifiable fruitcakes.

The first choice on the ballot was a guy who worked at the local Taco Bell and claimed to have solved Einstein's last problem, the unified field theory. The second choice was a guy who was unemployed and claimed he wanted to run for Congress to draw attention to the real problem with the Reagan administration: too much sugar in Reagan's diet due to the jelly beans he was renowned for having on his desk. One of those two was bound to be the Democratic nominee for the U.S. House of Representatives, allowing the congressman—who had refused a seat on the House Agriculture Committee because he really wasn't interested in agriculture (the First Congressional District of Nebraska is about eighty percent farm country)—to coast to another easy win.

"He won't even have to debate anybody! He won't have to run at all! We won't even get a chance to hear the issues," the party chair complained. I saw the injustice of it all.

"Why won't the experienced politicians run against the congressman?" I asked. The party chair sat me down in a room at the state party headquarters, where a number of up-and-coming politicians managed to lie to me with straight faces for about an hour. One at a time, each explained to me why they could not possibly run. These state senators, some of them very nice people, told me variations of the same story: "I'd like to run against the congressman, but my ———— (fill in the blank: mother, father, kids, dogs, cats) make it impossible for me to run at this time." I had entered the world of practical politics, but I didn't know it.

Almost in unison, they turned to me and said, "Why don't you run, Monica? We'll help you all we can!"

Very flattering to a political novice, and most flattering when the governor himself, Bob Kerrey (now Senator Kerrey), asked me to run. I was ushered into his office for an appointment that had been arranged by the state chair. I remember the governor looking at my résumé, asking me a few questions, then saying, "I think you'll be a great nominee, a real asset to the party. You go ahead and run, and I'll help you all I can."

If only I had taken some political science classes, I would have known what a setup this was. Most congressional districts are drawn up by the majority party of each state legislature and are designed to favor one party or another. The First Congressional District of Nebraska, too, favors one party—the Republican Party—quite heavily. At the time, the voter registration in the district ran about sixty percent Republican to forty percent Democrat. This meant that, all things being equal, the Republicans would always win that seat, no matter who ran for the Democrats. Furthermore, the reelection rate for all House incumbents hovers between ninety and ninety-eight percent each election cycle. The party chair knew this, as did all the state senators and the governor, all the people who had told me to run and said they would help me out. In slang terms, this is called a *sacrificial lamb* race. *Baa, baa, baa.*

Here is what I learned in that first try for office: You can't raise money without showing special interest groups polling results that show you have a chance of winning. If you have no previous experience that would get your name before masses of people, chances are, if you were to cough up the five thousand to ten thousand dollars it cost (in 1984) to run a poll in the twenty-seven-county First Congressional District, your results would be like mine. My poll produced the important and useful information that only about ten percent of the district recognized my name. A much larger percentage recognized the name of the congressman who had been in office, making the local papers, for eight years. Most of those folks, even the registered Democrats, seemed to like their congressman pretty well.

I took my poll results to Washington. Just about every special interest group I was willing to ask for money was not willing to give me a dime. "It's clear from your poll," they would say, "that you are going to lose. We don't give money to people who are going to lose."

There were a few exceptions, God bless them. The Farmer's Union gave me money. I have fond memories of driving through rural Nebraska going to Farmer's Union meetings. Once I even won the door prize and walked away with two-dozen farm-fresh eggs—and about $100 in campaign contributions. Some of the local unions gave me money because my daddy had been a union man all his life and I made a good speech and promised to help them out in the increasingly unlikely event I should ever get to Congress.

All in all, I raised just short of $50,000, enough for one small campaign office, three staff people, and one television commercial. Written and produced by me, the ad aired four or five times, mostly late at night, when time was cheaper to buy. Can you guess how much the commercial helped my campaign?

The congressman never took me seriously, except to say that since I had a two-year-old, it might be better if I stayed home with my child instead of running for Congress. In typical front-runner style, he refused to debate me. The Congressman spent $250,000 that year to defeat me, and he did it with ease.

As the underdog, the only tool I had was the possibility of getting a boost from the press. If I couldn't afford to buy ads, I would have to aggressively go after what is called "free media"—press coverage. I hired a great media director (who is now the lead reporter and news director for Nebraska Public Radio), who got me hooked up to almost every radio station in the state. I would do at least three radio interviews a week. I wrote what seemed like a million press releases, and some of them wound up in the paper, next to a little grainy photo of me. I noticed that the press wouldn't print much of my serious stuff about the farm crisis, but they got excited when I attacked the congressman. So I attacked, and attacked, on every possible issue—whatever would get me press attention.

As for my political party, I had had the notion that "the party" would help me campaign. But American parties are not organized groups, they are just names on voter lists. Local parties are shoestring operations, virtually all volunteer; the state organization sometimes has one or two people. I had thought that I could count on all the Democrat voters to support me out of party loyalty—at least I'd get forty percent of the vote! But party loyalty has been dying a slow death for a long time in American politics. Most Democrats, when faced with the choice of voting for the name they knew (the congressman's) or the name they had never heard of before (mine), happily cast their votes for the Republican incumbent.

The Democratic Party didn't give me a dime. Not a nickel. When I beat the two nut-case candidates in the primary, I was given a big pat on the back and a list of registered Democratic voters from whom I might solicit campaign cash. I was also given the opportunity to speak at twenty-seven county party dinners with then-Senator Jim Exon.

Senator Exon was a kindly fellow, who seemed to know every person in the state by name; studying how he operated was like taking a graduate course in practical politics. I noticed he had very little success keeping the interest of a crowd if he talked about important issues, such as the then mushrooming national debt or the farm crisis. Senator Exon campaigned one-to-one; he impressed people with his blend of country-style charisma and charm. He genuinely seemed to care for everyone he met, even me. I had almost none of Exon's country charm, just a lot of facts about people who were so financially burdened by a system the government had set up that they were thinking of suicide long into lonely nights.

Since then, what my family refers to as the Disaster of 1984, I have continued to work in practical politics. I ran for state representative in Massachusetts, and lost, in large part because of a drumbeat of criticism throughout the campaign from a local, small-town newspaper. I was vice chair of a local Democratic Party town committee, served on a planning board, was a delegate to several state party conventions, and worked on a number of campaigns. On occasion, I vote for moderate Republicans instead of the Democrats. I am still part of the ten percent of the electorate that is politically active. I consult and specialize in writing persuasive literature for local candidates. Every semester, a student asks me if I will ever run for office again. What do you think I always answer?

The Close: Effective Issues and Smart Messages for the Final Days of Campaign '98

Democratic Perspective

Frederick S. Yang

The end-game strategy of the closing weeks obviously depends a lot on how effective individual campaigns have been in the previous months and weeks. Hopefully, by then, Democratic candidates will have accomplished the following objectives to best position themselves for the stretch run: (a) laid down a solid foundation on personal qualities, (b) staked out aggressive positions on the key issues of this election—education, HMO reform and Social Security and (c) mobilized their campaign organization to turn out the Democratic vote.

Objective #1—What Makes You Tick? Even before the mid-summer furor over the Clinton-Lewinsky situation made it almost mandatory, candidates—even the best-known—were well-advised to provide some insights into their values. Too many times, candidates only complete half the sale—telling voters what issues they care about, not why. Issues are excellent vehicles to communicate a candidate's beliefs, such as caring about the future and understanding the value of keeping a promise. And by establishing themselves on the personal level early on, candidates have a better chance of withstanding the inevitable negative attacks that are likely to come in the closing weeks.

Objective #2—What Are You Fighting For? The polling data indicates that the Democratic agenda on critical issues of public education, HMO reform and Social Security resonate strongly with the electorate. Equally as important, these issues provide the opportunity for Democrats to readily draw clear and powerful distinctions with Republicans, which is an important advantage given the clutter of political communications in the closing weeks. Consider this polling information:

Reprinted, with permission, from *Campaigns and Elections,* a Congressional Quarterly, Inc., publication, Oct./Nov. 1998.

Social Security: Few Americans support Speaker Gingrich's risky plan to use the budget surplus to fund major tax cuts (24 percent) versus the Democratic plan to use the entire surplus to make Social Security more financially secure (69 percent). Indeed, fully 63 percent of Americans—including two-thirds of independents—believe the budget surplus will *not* be large enough to fund tax cuts and Social Security (July 1998 NBC/WSJ poll). Needless to say, given that seniors comprise a disproportionate share of mid-term turnout, Democrats should make Social Security a prominent issue at the close of the campaign.

HMO Reform: Democrats are on very strong ground castigating the Republicans for gutting the bipartisan Dingell-Ganske patients' bill of rights legislation. Simply put, Americans do not trust the insurance industry to reform HMOs. They look favorably on new, common-sense government regulations. On the main point of contention between Democrats and Republicans, the American public says by an overwhelming 69 percent to 18 percent margin that patients should have the right to sue their HMOs for improper care, rejecting the GOP argument that such a provision will raise the cost of health insurance (July 1998 NBC/WSJ poll).

Education: In the mid-June NBC/WSJ national survey, improving public education ranked just behind Social Security as a voting issue for this November's congressional elections. And in the same survey, a majority of Americans opposed a proposal to provide tax-payer-funded vouchers for private school tuition, which suggests that Democrats' rock-solid support for public schools (versus the GOP proposals to jeopardize public education) is another winning issue.

Objective #3—Who Votes? Obviously, Objectives #1 and #2 relate directly to turning out voters, which is in some ways perhaps the *most* important objective for Democrats in 1998. Democratic turnout tends to lag behind Republicans in mid-term elections. An effective program focused on identifying actual Democratic voters and getting them to the polls can make the difference.

The good news for Democrats is that the key issues of education, Social Security and HMO reform resonate extremely well with the "base" vote *and* the all-important swing vote. In other words, there is little need for the Democratic message to be substantially different when it comes to the sometimes contradictory strategic tasks of motivation (Democratic voters) and persuasion (swing voters).

But the ultimate success or failure of Democrats in 1998 will rely equally, if not more, on winning the "ground" game versus winning the "air" game, which means the main task of campaigns at all levels is putting a premium on election day turnout.

So while pundits focus on the television ads and the campaign back-and-forth, the real action that will likely determine control of Congress and of numerous state houses will be occurring under the radar.

Republican Perspective
Glen Bolger

For Federal candidates, the 1998 elections are about six broad message areas: Social Security, taxes, education, the balanced budget, health care, and Bill Clinton. While it's possible that something may occur between the time this article is written and the moment this publication hits your mailbox, this is the general direction we're headed.

Taking a purely election-oriented perspective on each of those six issues, here are key points on each:

Social Security: First and foremost, it's important for Republicans to remember that Democrats demagogue this issue. They will do and say anything to scare senior citizens. Democrats like to use phones to deliver a late "hit" message to senior citizens. To counteract the demagoguery, Republican campaigns must have a part of their campaign plan dedicated to senior citizens. That page in the plan should include both tactics (mailings, phones, television) as well as messages. Tactically, mail is an excellent way to reach senior citizens—they read voter mail at a higher level than any other age group. The strongest message you can use is that you want to take Social Security off-budget so that Congress can no longer raid the Trust Fund for programs like foreign aid and welfare. It is also important to stress that the surplus should be used to protect Social Security.

Taxes: This issue is pretty simple—Republicans are for cutting taxes, Democrats aren't. The tax issue unites *base* Republicans and *soft* Republicans. Issues like ending the marriage penalty tax, reforming the IRS and making the tax code fairer, flatter, and simpler all resonate strongly. Republican candidates should have a tax component in their paid media message.

Education: What a difference a coherent message makes! Two years ago, Democrats controlled the education issue. Now, voters generally perceive no difference between the two parties on the issue. Heather Wilson's control of the education issue in the New Mexico CD-1 special election kept Phil Maloof from uniting his soft Democratic vote and helped cost him the election. As I've been saying for two years, it is important that Republicans not beat up on teachers. Instead, we've got to align with kids, parents and teachers *against* bureaucrats who are wasting money. Messages like discipline, basics, money in classrooms, competency testing and other reforms resonate. Doing well on education can help a Republican cut down the gender gap among younger women.

Balanced budget: It is important to drive home the message that we need a Republican Congress to keep a check on the president and Democrats in Congress to make sure they don't increase spending, ending the balanced budget. Voters aren't convinced that the budget is balanced—and they sure don't trust the Democrats to do it. GOP incumbents should take credit for the balanced budget, while open seat candidates want voters to choose which candidate will do a better job on the balanced budget.

Health care: This issue has lost some of its zip for the Democrats. This isn't to say that voters aren't concerned about managed care. However, when the only substantive difference between the Republican plan and the Democratic plan is an independent review versus the right to sue, the lines are blurred for voters. Republicans backed HMO reforms to cover patients for reasonable emergency room visits and to allow patients to pay slightly more to go outside the HMO network to see the doctor of their choice. This makes sure HMOs do not restrict what doctors tell patients about treatment options.

It's also important to remind voters that Republicans fought for—and passed—health care portability.

Bill Clinton: Despite his good job approval ratings, President Clinton's personal numbers are extraordinarily weak. Our polling also shows that Republicans can't wait to get to the voting booth to send a message to Clinton. Direct mail fundraising that capitalizes on Clinton's hypocrisy is bringing in significant returns.

At the same time Republican candidates are benefitting from Clinton's woes, they should be careful not to appear "holier than thou"—or be a "johnny one-note" solely on this issue.

Elections are about contrasts between individuals. Those contrasts can be issue-oriented, ideological-oriented, character-oriented, or experience-oriented.

It is still incumbent on each campaign to determine the best contrasts to make and focus its "home stretch" message based on those differences.

Candidates Need to Run as Publicrats

Jerry Cammarata

The idea hatched by our Founding Fathers that the public good ought to be put before adherence to party identity was not only right, it also worked—and it works today in government and, happily, even in electioneering.

The American people are tired of partisan combat. The era when families were either Democratic or Republican from generation unto generation is long gone.

Just look at the topsy-turvy politics all around us. Rudolph Giuliani is mayor of New York City—a Republican re-elected to a second term by a huge margin in a city where Democrats outnumber Republicans five to one, and in a town that has been a Democratic garrison since Aaron Burr helped found the Tammany Society. Not long ago, Pat Buchanan drew what votes he got in the last round of presidential primaries from restless union members fearful of the implications of free trade. More recently, over one-third of House Democrats bucked their party's leadership and voted for the partial-birth abortion ban. Of course, there are also the "Blue Dog" Democrats of Congress, who are among the most ardent of the fiscally conservative, balanced budget advocates.

What is a politician to do? A politician—and a campaign manager—is to get the message: voters have figured out that party labels are anachronisms to be ignored. The only platform most Americans are interested in these days is a commitment to good government, and the only ideology they look for in a candidate is a doctrinaire adherence to the philosophy of What Works.

Voters now want Publicrats in office.

Think about the recent history of the broadest issues facing the nation. Is campaign finance reform only a Republican or Democratic issue? Are restrictions on lobbying inherently conservative, liberal or Perotist? Does the stabilization of Social Security and Medicare have to be a right-wing or left-wing cause? Can only one party say kids who are graduating from high school should be able to read, write and calculate well enough to get a job or go to college? These questions miss the point—which is precisely the point. Voters don't care what label candidates put on these issues. They're much more interested in finding constructive solutions.

The irrelevance of partisanship is also the reason Ross Perot garnered 19 percent of the vote in the '92 presidential election. It's the reason the convention delegates of the Perot-inspired Reform Party almost universally trashed every candidate running for the Republican and Democratic nominations in 1996: none of the logs cut as presidential timber were taking specific stands on meaningful government, school, election and fiscal reform issues. The delegates left with tension headaches and the average voter yawned his or her way through that election.

Publicrat campaigning not only works, though: it's good for the country. Campaign professionals ought not be mere "buyers" for parties that become generic political department stores. They have a responsibility to select not just marketable candidates, but candidates who will provoke substantive debate as candidates and who will shape thoughtful policy if elected.

The party loyalists may point out that those original representatives who were making high-minded pledges in 1776 did not have to run for their seats—though they may have had to run for their lives. However, the first chief executive to lead the new democracy they created did have to face an election, twice in fact.

In 1796, as George Washington was nearing the end of his second term as president, he published a document which has come to be known

Reprinted, with permission, from *Campaigns and Elections*, a Congressional Quarterly, Inc., publication, Oct./Nov. 1998.

as his "Farewell Address." Though written as a speech, Washington never actually delivered it orally.

"The spirit of party," Washington wrote, "serves always to distract the Public Councils, and enfeeble the Public Administration. It agitates the Community with ill-founded jealousies and false alarms; kindles animosity of one part against another, foments occasionally riot and insurrection. It opens the door to foreign influ-ence and corruption, which find a facilitated access to the government itself through the channels of party passions."

Washington gave the above advice to a new nation, but also to future generations of candidates and political consultants—and he remains the only president ever to win the unanimous vote of the Electoral College

Now that's something to think about.

CHAT ROOM

Clint
a moderate

Mike
a Hispanic,
liberal Democrat

Robert
a moderate
Republican

Sonya
a Hispanic,
moderate Republican

Tony
an African American,
liberal Democrat

Getting Out the Vote, and Making Your Base Happy
★ ★ ★

Dr. Bauer: We have a reading about the final days of a campaign. The first thing to notice is that 1998 is an off-year election, so the authors direct their advice to U.S. House of Representative races, Senate races, and even some local races. Let's take a look at this. Is there much difference between the Democratic perspective and the Republican perspective on how to win elections?

Clint: No, you mobilize your base; you get out the vote. Run a ground war, not an air war, which means focus on the grassroots—knocking on doors and mailing literature.

Tony: But you can't mobilize your voters without issues. Stick to issues.

Dr. Bauer: How do you know which issues are important?

Sonya: The ones that have been important in every election for years, like education. When wasn't education important?

Dr. Bauer: When the Evil Empire was still alive, education was not a big issue—foreign policy was the most important. In fact, some of the issues in the articles are new. What is the Republican list of big issues?

Tony: Social Security, education, health care, taxes, balanced budget, and Bill Clinton.

Dr. Bauer: Until we got to Bill Clinton, we could see that both sides are using the same polling data. One of the things pulling the two parties to the center, is their use of sophisticated polling techniques that were not available fifty years ago. If you are doing polls and coming up with the same list of issues, how do you differentiate the two parties? How are the Republican candidates supposed to handle that one issue that is not also on the Democratic list?

Sonya:	The one issue that is different is Bill Clinton, but the article says not to be a "johnny one-note." The author does not advise running solely on Bill Clinton.
Dr. Bauer:	Right. And what was the Republican perspective on Bill Clinton as they went into the 1998 election?
Clint:	His personal numbers are extraordinarily weak.
Dr. Bauer:	Aha!
Robert:	Republicans are upset by his hypocrisy.
Dr. Bauer:	In 1996, Bob Dole said in effect, "Wake up, America! How come you don't hate Bill Clinton the way I do?" It didn't work. And in 1998?
Tony:	They haven't learned their lesson. They are still screaming, "Wake up, America! Why don't you hate Bill Clinton the way we do?"
Clint:	Because voters feel he's doing a good job.
Mike:	The polls are at seventy percent approval.
Dr. Bauer:	Yankelovich might call this wishful thinking on the part of pollsters, and this happens to Democrats as well as Republicans. If they are desperate enough to find something negative in polling data, they will. Notice what Glen Bolger writes: "Despite his good job approval ratings, President Clinton's personal numbers are extraordinarily weak." Republican pollsters want to forget about the job approval rating because it doesn't fit the picture they want to see. Instead they want to look at responses to a subset of questions like, "Do you find Clinton honest?"
Sonya:	Or, "Do you think he is moral, a good person?"
Dr. Bauer:	And do we think he's moral?
Robert:	Of course not!
Dr. Bauer:	Do we care?
Mike:	No, look at his job approval.
Sonya:	Seventy percent of people don't care.
Dr. Bauer:	This is one of those unusual moments when you can look at the Republican Party's campaign advice to Republican candidates a month before an historic election. In 1998 they ran the 1996 campaign over again. And we know what happened—an historic loss for the Republican Party. Newt Gingrich was telling people—and it's one of the reasons Newt is not Speaker anymore—that the Republicans would pick up thirty or forty seats. Republican political consultants said the same thing. Based on what?
Sonya:	Their dislike for Bill Clinton. And historical precedent. The party not in the White House usually picks up seats in the midterm election.

Dr. Bauer:	Bill Clinton and history. That was going to hand it to them. Nothing else differentiated the Republican enough except an opposition to Bill Clinton and, perhaps, taxes. No wonder the Republican Party was having difficulty formulating their message in 1998.
Sonya:	But taxes wasn't on the Democratic list.
Dr. Bauer:	And what do the polls tell us? Has this issue gotten better for Republicans since 1998? Is there a big anti-tax feeling in the country?
Clint:	The economy is still good, so it doesn't matter. People are making money.
Tony:	If they can afford to pay their taxes, usually, people are willing to do their fair share.
Dr. Bauer:	There is a lot less anti-tax fervor now than in the late seventies or the early nineties, when the economy was bad. As we saw in George Will's article [Chapter 7], Republicans are still in the market for an issue that will give voters a reason to vote Republican. Can you win an election campaign if your party says exactly the same things as your opposition?
Clint:	Maybe you need to have the better candidate—someone personable and articulate, a good actor who can put a better spin on those same issues.
Dr. Bauer:	So, you don't really need different issues? You just need a really good campaigner?
Tony:	You have to be an incredibly good campaigner to get around the constant question in every media interview, on every talk show, in every debate: "What differentiates you from your opponent?"
Robert:	If you pick an issue, you have to pick an issue that affects the majority of the American voters.
Mike:	I think your message has to affect the majority of Americans who *vote*. That's now about forty-nine percent of the people eligible to vote. They are the only ones who matter on election day. That's why so many of the current issues are about senior citizens: Social Security reform, HMO reform. Polls indicate that a higher percentage of senior citizens vote than other age groups.
Clint:	Qualifications can make you different.
Dr. Bauer:	Yes, these help differentiate candidates in a primary when a number of politicians from the same party are running against each other for the party's nomination. But you can make up for a lack of qualifications if you have passion and message. If we asked Pat Buchanan why he ran for president, what do you think he'd say?
Tony:	Oh, he'd have a definite, strong message: against immigration, for the American worker and the exodus of manufacturing beyond the American borders. Pat Buchanan has always been passionate about those issues, he's run every campaign on those same issues.

Dr. Bauer:	He's what is called an "ideological" candidate. Ask ideological candidates why you should vote for them, and they always have an answer. They know why. Pat Buchanan knows, Gary Bauer knows, Allen Keyes always knows. Jesse Jackson always knows. Bill Bradley. Does Bill Bradley always know? What's Bill Bradley's message as he runs against Gore for the Democratic presidential nomination in 2000?
Tony:	Campaign finance reform.
Dr. Bauer:	That's important to me, but I don't think the average voter cares. It's not what political scientists call a high-salience issue. *Salience* means importance; a high-salience issue is one that has so much personal importance that it may motivate my vote. What is an example of a high-salience issue?
Clint:	The economy.
Dr. Bauer:	Yes. And when the economy is going well, as it is today, candidates are stuck looking for another high-salience issue. Democrats ran on education, saving Social Security, and the environment. They also ran, most of the time, as pro-choice and anti-religious fundamentalism. And the Democrats won big in 1998.
	Basically, the lists of issues used by both parties are attempts to figure out which issues have high salience for *likely voters*. Both parties want to appeal to "swing" voters. Party loyalty doesn't exist for them; swing voters are motivated only by high-salience issues. To appeal to them, you appeal on issues.
	And that brings us to "Candidates Need to Run as Publicrats," by Jerry Cammarata. What is his message?
Sonya:	That the candidates need to address voters who put the public good before party labels like Democrat or Republican.
Clint:	That party labels are out of date. Voters are registering as independent, because they don't care about one platform or another, and they're "tired of partisan combat."
Sonya:	Negative ad campaigns.
Dr. Bauer:	Yes, those are part of partisanship, aren't they? A classic way to run and win has been to criticize the opposition—the candidate and the party. Campaign managers call these ads "comparative"; other people call them "negative" ads.
Tony:	I'm sure everyone has seen the ads that come from the Republican National Committee or the Democratic National Committee: "We're for health care reform and giving senior citizens the right to choose their doctors. Call ——— and tell him you're tired of his stand against senior citizens." The ad supposedly focuses on an issue, but it's still a partisan effort to attack an opponent.
Dr. Bauer:	Those party ads can be very pointed and very nasty. And negative campaigning certainly has an effect. So, what is it that voters are longing for?

Sonya:	Cammarata says the candidates have to find "constructive solutions" no matter what label they put on the issue.
Tony:	The philosophy of "what works"—that's the only ideology voters look for in a candidate.
Dr. Bauer:	Another word for that idea is *pragmatism*. Pragmatic politics. Do we have any examples of people who have gotten out of the party box and are thought of as nonideological—politicians who just do What Works?
Clint:	Perot and Ventura. Ross Perot got nineteen percent of the vote and inspired what is now the Reform Party. Jesse Ventura of Minnesota ran as a Reform Party candidate for the governorship—and won. Neither one of them took hard positions on the standard issues. They ran on what they believed.
Dr. Bauer:	And do we know what they believed?
Robert:	No, but Cammarata says that none of the Republican or Democrat candidates in 1996 was "taking specific stands on meaningful government, school, election [and] fiscal reform issues" either.
Tony:	I don't think that's true. I think the parties are saying different things, and it's the Reform Party that doesn't say anything! Let me tell you my experience when we did presidential debates in class. I was part of one debate on abortion, and of course, I represented Democratic Clinton–Gore. Someone else represented Republican Dole, and someone else represented Reform Party Perot. A lot of these debates rested on delivering a simple message. When students asked a question about abortion, the Clinton–Gore response was, "Safe, legal, rare." Just those three words. Boom. There's your message. The Dole response: "Opposed, except for rape, incest, mother's life in danger." Simple message. And obviously different. The Perot response would be, "Well, you know we haven't really taken a stand. Actually, we think the economy is the most important thing."
Dr. Bauer:	Perot used to say that he "wanted to get under the hood." Does anyone have any idea what he would have done once he got the hood up?
Sonya:	No idea!
Dr. Bauer:	But you knew it was going to be something good, right? How did we know it was going to be something good?
Clint:	Because he said so.
Dr. Bauer:	Absolutely right. Because he said so. And nineteen percent of the people in 1992 said, "Wow, he says he's going to do good things."
Robert:	Well, I think he went out on the limb. He said what he thought, instead of the canned Democratic and Republican speeches. Perot said, "I don't know all of what's wrong, but when I get in there, I'm going to use common sense and fix it."

Dr. Bauer: When we have identifiable, ideological political parties, we know what they represent. We may not like it, and it may lead to division and negative campaigning. But, by and large, we know what the candidates and their parties stand for. I'm concerned that the new publicrats too often represent cults of personality; that, since they have no firm ideology except What Works, sometimes they can operate as demagogues rather than leaders of coalitions. And their appeal may not be healthy for a democracy.

★ ★ ★

For Additional Reading

Go to InfoTrac College Edition, your online research library at

http://web1.infotrac-college.com

Enter the following search terms using the Subject Guide or Key Terms.

campaigns	reapportionment	voters and participation
gerrymander	redistricting	
incumbency advantage	turnout	

10 ten *The Media*

Just the Facts? A Symposium

Jonathan Alter

One of the most enduring visual images of the news business is the "zipper"—the electronic display belt (most famously in Times Square) that relays breaking news to passersby. "Pearl Harbor attacked," "FDR dead," "Space shuttle launched" —the zipper has always been concise, clear, and as "objective" as it is possible to be.

Until now. At the corner of 49th Street and Sixth Avenue in Manhattan, Fox News has a zipper that I like to watch when I have the chance. Many of the bulletins that move across the zipper include a cute little two- or three-word comment thrown in afterwards. The zipper has a little extra zip, usually from the conservative side where Fox and its owner Rupert Murdoch stand, and occasionally I get a chuckle out of it. Call it the respect of one wise guy for another. After all, for a decade I've been one of the authors of *Newsweek*'s Conventional Wisdom Watch, which each week makes snippy little comments about figures in the news. Before that, I laced my *Washington Monthly* articles with plenty of "attitude."

But I'm starting to have some second thoughts about my role in the "Attitude Revolution." It's one thing for magazines to try to be clever. Columnists and talking heads (I'm guilty of being both) can offer their opinions. But zippers are supposed to stay zipped up. The news sections of newspapers, like television anchors, are supposed to deliver the news straight. Textured reporting is welcome, but snide assessments of motive belong in feature pieces and magazines. Phrases like "In an effort to divert attention . . . " and "In an attempt to appear presidential . . . " should not be in the news section.

How did we get here? How did the walls start breaking down? I've got a few pet theories:

The end of the Cold War: The seriousness of the bipolar struggle tended to inhibit attitudiniz-

ing in the news pages. Starting in World War II, the press tended to define news as what government officials said or did on a given day, because those words and actions were at least distantly tied to our survival. Today's media climate is a return to the prewar racy standard, which was called "ballyhoo" during the 1920s. With the end of the Cold War, the stakes are smaller, which means we're more free to indulge in silly partisanship and triviality.

At the same time, the duality of the global struggle—and the duality embedded in a legal system that came to dominate much of American life—made people think that offering two sides to a story somehow made it fair. The clash of competing forces defined news—and led the way to truth. Or so the theory goes. The inadequacy of that adversary structure has become clearer since the Cold War ended, even as it insinuates itself deeper in the media culture.

Technology: The Internet lends itself to attitude and opinion—to the idea that everyone has his or her view, and that they are of equal value. And the fragmentation of media because of cable technology means that there's a lot more time to fill. Straight, "objective" news can't fill it. Just reporting straight news doesn't get you ahead in the intensely competitive world of TV news. Sad to say, audiences prefer chewing over old, sexy news to hearing fresh news that doesn't make the blood race. Newspapers have a different problem. They no longer bring people the headlines, which readers have heard on TV or radio. So they include more packaging, analysis and attitude in order to stay alive. That's not all bad; good analysis is important in a confusing world. But spin is cheaper to produce.

Baby boomers: When they were young, baby boomers wrote for college and underground papers that were more like the foreign press— long on opinion and shorter on facts. Boomers were often intensely political when they were young, and many stayed political even when real ideological differences faded. Axe-grinding that began over weighty issues like Vietnam has now extended to trivia. Moreover, some of those who became journalists also grew up believing that "stenographic" reporting was a bit below their ambitions, especially if they wanted to go on TV to analyze the news (I plead guilty again). For the academically inclined (and a growing number of them ended up in journalism), the whole idea of "objectivity" was contrary to deconstructionism, the still current academic fashion in which texts all contain hidden messages of bias and privilege. The unspoken logic: If "objectivity" is impossible, why try?

The cult of attribution: The decline of "objectivity" is partly an understandable reaction to journalism that sometimes made a fetish of attribution. One reason I was never comfortable working on newspapers was that I disliked having to attribute perfectly obvious facts to someone else. At most papers, basic statements of fact ("The sky is blue") were required to have a ludicrous level of attribution ("according to the National Weather Service"). A looser standard of attribution has mostly been a positive development in American journalism. *The New York Times,* for instance, is a better written, more interesting newspaper than in the past in part because of new standards of what's permissible in the news sections.

The wrong lens: The problem is that the *Times* and other news organizations are losing sight of what news is. In September, for instance, President Clinton signed an executive order offering (not just proposing) important new protections to 120 million Americans in HMOs. The *Times* gave the story three paragraphs on page 21. What was once a clear definition of news—a decision that affects large numbers of people—is no longer big news because it's not "hot." It doesn't lend itself to conflict, spin, secrecy, scandal and personal attacks or quirks—the new standards of news.

The public is hypocritical about all of this. Viewers complain about the poor news diet, but routinely zap cable shows (the networks are a different story) every time they turn away from Monica Lewinsky. Even so, there is a growing unhappiness about the direction of news coverage. Readers and viewers want "objectivity" back. The first step toward doing that is to understand where "objective" journalism came from in the first place.

Just the Facts: How Objectivity Came to Define American Journalism, by David T. Z. Mindich, is a good place to begin. Mindich opens with the common but important caveat that there is no such thing as "true objectivity" and that the word should always be used with quotation marks around it. He quotes Sydney Gruson of *The New York Times:* "Pure objectivity might not exist, but you have to strive for it anyway." Christiane Amanpour, a now-famous reporter for CNN and CBS, recently gave a speech updating the old standard. "Objectivity," said Amanpour, "means giving all sides a fair hearing, but not treating all sides equally. . . . So objectivity must go hand in hand with morality."

As Amanpour suggests, some of the changes in the old, unthinking standard of "objectivity" have resulted from hard thinking about the issue, not just a desire to get ratings and readers with a few clever remarks. There are not "two sides" to the atrocities she reports on. Sometimes there are six sides to a story—or only one. And the conventions of the news business have been easily manipulated by people in power to inhibit the reporting of the truth. The charges of Sen. Joseph McCarthy, for instance, were reported "objectively."

Mindich doesn't deal with McCarthyism or other 20th century cases; he's more interested in the 19th century origins of "objectivity," and those origins are illuminating. Because this is an academic (though clearly written) book, he breaks down "objectivity" into its journalism textbook components: detachment, nonpartisanship, inverted pyramid, facticity and balance. Each arose as a journalistic convention as a result of particular developments in American history.

Detachment and non-partisanship come from the Jacksonian and immediate pre-Civil War eras. James Gordon Bennett, the founder of the *New York Herald*, ran a splenetic and vicious penny paper, but he was the first major newspaper owner who was associated with no party. He went back and forth, endorsing the Democrat in one presidential election, the Whig in another. More important, in agitating against another newspaper editor who advocated duels and once beat up Bennett himself, he pioneered the idea of peaceful, if vitriolic, means of resolving disputes. This kind of nonviolent non-partisanship was tremendously popular. And by mid-century, detachment and independence were beginning to sell as party papers faltered.

Soon the old strictly chronological, narrative newspaper style, where the news was buried in the 25th paragraph, also began to fade. It was replaced by the inverted pyramid, the structural underpinning of a modern news story, in which the most important facts come first, in a "lead," with other facts presented in descending order of importance. According to Mindich, this approach grew out of coverage of the Lincoln assassination in 1865. Lincoln's Secretary of War, Edwin Stanton, the greatest press censor in American history, also originated the inverted pyramid. While war correspondents still filed flowery narratives, Stanton, who had total control of all new information, telegraphed the first terse bulletins from the war department. Stanton was also the first to use the conventions of "objectivity" to bolster authority. By the 1880s, it was standard for newspapers. The telegraph, which placed a premium on speed and economy of style, became an important technological tool of "objectivity."

I've noticed that the inverted pyramid is distinctly out of fashion on the news programs watched by the most viewers—TV news magazines. The basic story structure on *Dateline* is right out of 19th century journalism: a strong narrative with the news—the payoff—buried far down in the story in order to maintain suspense and keep people watching after the commercial breaks.

The purchase of *The New York Times* by Adolph Ochs in 1896 is often seen as a landmark in the development of "objectivity." While William Randolph Hearst and Joseph Pulitzer pioneered yellow journalism, the *Times* was developing a sense of "balance" that would heavily influence journalism in the 20th century. But Mindich examines the case of Ida B. Wells, a former slave turned crusading journalist who showed how flawed the *Times*' "balanced" coverage of lynchings turned out to be. It's Wells' critique of phony balance—two sides to every story—that has informed the better critiques of objectivity today.

So how to balance the need for "objectivity" with good writing, good analysis, and good humor? Not easily. We should want reporters to analyze, reach conclusions, and write with style. The only answer I can envision is to erect a stronger firewall between anchors and commentators, between news shows and entertainment shows and between the news sections of a newspaper and the rest of the paper. The risk is boredom, lost ratings, and lost circulation. The reward would be greater confidence in what people watch and read. The good news is that truly partisan, biased news organizations don't make big money in the media game. In the last quarter century, the big profits have generally gone to reliable papers and networks with a reputation for some objectivity in their news sections. *The Wall Street Journal* and ABC News are more profitable than *The New York Post* and Fox TV. Smart news executives know this, and are watching the balance carefully.

Just the Facts? A Symposium
David Ignatius

It is endearing of Charlie Peters to sponsor a symposium calling for more objective, less opinion-laden journalism. Can this be the same beloved, raccoon-eyed editor who used to hector his editors when they offered up an overly fact-laden piece: "Where's the gospel?" The same man who infuriated dozens of America's leading journalists by writing his own opinions into their pieces? The same man who coined the term "rain dance" to describe his efforts to put more of a writer's heart and soul into a piece?

You have to wonder: Can our own mischievous, opinion-drenched Huck Finn really have turned into Tom Sawyer? Or Robert Pear?

A chary editor might have suggested to Charlie that, instead of a symposium, this topic might make a good "Tilting" item (long the preferred way to deal with the boss's momentary obsessions). Or perhaps another volume in Charlie's autobiography. But as it happens, Charlie has something going for him in this new crusade for "Just the Facts." He's right.

Let me begin (inevitably) by defending my own newspaper, *The Washington Post.* The danger of too much opinion and spin on the front page isn't something we've just discovered. The *Post*'s top editors during the '90s, Leonard Downie and Robert Kaiser, tried hard to suppress tendentious writing and gratuitous analysis in news stories. Kaiser, in particular, became exasperated at those introductory clauses that begin so many newspaper stories: "In a move intended to deflect the House impeachment inquiry, President Clinton yesterday announced . . ." Or: "Despite growing criticism of his divisive record as House Speaker, Newt Gingrich yesterday proposed . . . " Such leads had become all too common at the *Post.* They were a product of the emphasis over the last two decades on interpretive, analytical journalism (encouraged by, let's be frank, a certain humble West Virginia lawyer and his band of anti-elitist Harvard grads).

Kaiser decided to do something about this trend toward manipulative, opinion-saturated "news" leads. He banned them. Specifically, he enunciated something that came to be known at the *Post* as the "Kaiser Rule." Reporters were forbidden to begin a story with any kind of explanatory clause, whatsoever. I'm sure people can find examples of this rule being violated, but on major front-page stories, it stuck. To reporters who complained that their analytical stories had been neutered ("Jeez, Bob, Clinton was deflecting attention . . . ," etc., etc.), Kaiser would answer with a memorable dictum first postulated by the *Post*'s editor in the '50s, J. Russell Wiggins: "The reader deserves one clean shot at the facts."

That may be a good motto for the new, new journalism. Don't tell people what to think. Present readers with information, as cleanly and clearly stated as possible, along with context that gives them a chance to make up their own minds what it means.

To be sure (as we used to say when I worked at *The Wall Street Journal,* where every front-page story was supposed to have a "to-be-sure graph" that allowed the possibility that the thesis of the surrounding story was false), there's a place for analysis. The front page of any great newspaper needs good analytical writing that helps people make sense of the world. And it needs vivid, colorful writing that brings home the intensity and visceral reality of events to readers.

That's the business that newspapers are in now—at a time when people usually know the basic facts about a big story before they pick up the paper, from television, radio or the Internet. Our job is explaining the world—providing meaning and context and a way of ordering the world. That's what a newspaper front page is, essentially—a daily ordering of the world that establishes the seven or eight topics the editors think are most worthy of a reader's attention.

That's a subjective and interpretive mission, inescapably. But it's not an excuse for violating the Kaiser Rule. Readers do deserve one clean shot at the facts.

The *Post* has taken some grief in the profession for Downie's and Kaiser's emphasis on traditionalism. The buzz on the street has been that the *Post* was less experimental, less daring, less open to "personal" writing, less "fun." Some of this criticism was misplaced; some of it was probably valid. But it's worth noting that the changes in the *Post* resulted from Downie's and Kaiser's deliberate efforts to steer the ship away from the rocks that Charlie Peters is now sighting. Indeed, I have to ask where Charlie was during all those years the *Post* was getting drubbed by media gossips for being a little *dull*.

The biggest danger I encountered in my years as an editor was a reflexive cynicism among some reporters that led them to assume they knew what a story was about, before they had actually done the reporting. They would begin with an assumption of who the good guys and bad guys were, and then organize the facts around that hypothesis. Sometimes, reporters were so confident about their *a priori* hypotheses that they would make only the most perfunctory, last-minute efforts to contact the "bad guys." ("Mr. Jones couldn't be reached for comment." "Mr. Jones failed to respond to a reporter's inquiry.")

This sort of cynicism is so common that it has become a journalistic stereotype. But it's actually the opposite of the fundamental journalistic values of curiosity and skepticism. The reason you call people for comment (and keep calling them until you get them) is because you want to get it right. A good reporter lives in terror of the possibility that his elaborately constructed hypothesis is *wrong*—that the last phone call he makes will reveal that the real story is some-thing different from what he had assumed. Interestingly, in my experience, the very best reporters rarely exhibit the stereotypical cynicism and arrogance that people have come to associate with the profession. Bob Woodward isn't that way. David Broder isn't; David Remnick isn't; Kate Boo isn't; David Maraniss isn't. These people couldn't gather the stories they do without being genuinely curious about the world and open to new information.

The reflexive cynics in our business tend to be the burn-outs: the has-beens or never-weres. Most of all, they're the television people, who affect a world-weary know-it-all-ism that the public has, quite rightly, come to loathe. If ever there was an unearned cynicism, it's the kind found among these TV celebrities and pundits. Many of them haven't chased a fire truck, let alone covered a war.

A final impediment to giving readers one clear shot at the facts is the journalistic tendency to keep score—especially in covering the White House. There seems to be an unquenchable need to record, on a daily basis, whether the president is up or down, whether he had a good week or a bad week, whether he continues to be "dogged by scandal" or has "triumphed over his critics." This running box score is often nonsensical; there is no real event whatsoever being described, only an imaginary battle for influence. And often the scorekeeping obscures what actually is going on—the particular legislative debate or foreign-policy crisis that reporters see as a backdrop for the real issue: Is he up? Is he down?

What reporters really mean when they write this daily form sheet on the presidency is: What do my colleagues in the press corps think? What's the consensus opinion of the handful of people I talked to today? To call that sort of work "bad journalism" is charitable. It isn't journalism at all. There isn't a fact in sight.

Just the Facts? A Symposium

Timothy Noah

Two imperatives in contemporary journalism are at war with one another. One imperative says: Be smart! Be analytic! Be like *The Washington Monthly* or *The New Republic* or *The Weekly Standard*! The other imperative says: Don't say anything that will make your readers—or, more important, your sources—mad! Don't lose significant leaks from government sources, which still matter a lot, to the competition! The first imperative boils down to being subjective; being so intelligently and fair-mindedly will benefit a reporter's career over the long run.

The second imperative boils down to being rigorously neutral. This is no longer the path to glory in a journalistic career, but analysis-free reporting remains a useful skill—sometimes you just want to know, Did the bill pass? Did the Red Sox win? What is the disagreement between party A and party B all about?—and solid careers can be built on it.

The trouble arises when a reporter, torn between the imperative to be smart and the imperative to not rock the boat, tries to have it both ways. One common corruption arising from this dilemma is to be snide. Nobody can prove you think that the Clinton health-care bill is a nightmare of red tape, but you can still communicate the general idea. "There are ways of saying it, without actually saying it," a seasoned *New York Times* reporter once told me. Another corruption is to sculpt your analysis to resemble prevailing biases so perfectly that no one is likely to complain. (When readers or sources bitch about "biased" reporting, what they almost always mean is reporting whose biases they disagree with.) Thus you can portray a Ralph Nader or a Jesse Helms as a hopeless boob simply because he isn't working within the mainstream.

Ultimately, it's best for reporting to strive to be neither "analytic" nor "neutral," but simply to be fair-minded and truthful based on a detailed examination of the matter at hand. A good reporter who is well-steeped in his subject matter and who isn't out to prove his cleverness, but rather is sweating out a detailed understanding of a topic worth exploring, will probably develop intelligent opinions that will inform and perhaps be expressed in his journalism. It is very difficult to be a blowhard on a subject one has studied extensively and from many angles. The extent to which the reporter spells out his assumptions and follows them to their logical conclusions may vary, but whether the result is a work of "opinion" journalism or "objective" journalism matters less than that the writer's objective is to inform, not to impress.

students

Clint
a moderate

Mike
a Hispanic,
liberal Democrat

Robert
a moderate
Republican

Sonya
a Hispanic,
moderate Republican

Tony
an African American,
liberal Democrat

Opinions and Journalism
★ ★ ★

Dr. Bauer: A good place to learn about current journalism and the journalists who write about politics is the next series of readings. These come from an influential magazine called the *Washington Monthly*. Thirty years ago, this magazine began a mission to put more excitement into writing about politics. Their editors demanded that reporters write with style and passion. This was called "attitude journalism"—as opposed to the old-fashioned model, "objective coverage." The question asked in these readings is, has attitude journalism gone too far?

Tony: I think it's gone way too far. The media uses political reporting to show how clever they are. This is another one of my pet peeves! Somewhere along the line they lost the idea that they are supposed to report the news rather than just promote themselves. They should try harder to be more, not less, objective!

Dr. Bauer: What does it mean to call reporting "objective"? Jonathan Alter says in his article that during the twentieth century, newspapers sold more copies if they appeared to be reliable, credible, and objective in their reporting; objectivity came to define American journalism. Alter repeats a quote from Sydney Gruson of *The New York Times*, who said "Pure objectivity might not exist, but you have to strive for it anyway." Why had objectivity been under attack by attitude journalism?

Robert: Objective journalism can be less entertaining than writing with passion.

Dr. Bauer: An objective story should follow the criteria that you can find in any journalism textbook today: detachment, nonpartisanship, the inverted pyramid of the story, facts, and balance. Sometimes, those elements can make even stories about politics boring.

Tony:	I have a problem with the criterion of balance in objective journalism. The newspaper should not have to interview someone from the Klan every time they run a story about civil rights. And I wouldn't want to be fair and objective if I were reporting on child molestation. If something is clearly wrong and against the social fabric, then I don't think it's necessary to report on both sides.
Dr. Bauer:	In other words, we don't crave balanced stories if we already know where the moral truth is.
Mike:	How can you report something that is absolutely wrong in a balanced way? Like segregation? Alter gives the example of the newspapers giving balanced reports on lynchings at the start of the twentieth century. Let's hear the facts, just the facts, and never say that lynching is wrong! I like attitude journalism, I think there's a lot to be said for reporting that raises people's consciousness about issues.
Dr. Bauer:	I think it's important to point out that attitude journalism began in the sixties, precisely because young reporters decided they knew the moral high ground on stories such as civil rights and the war in Vietnam. Reporters began to feel a moral obligation to say what they thought was going wrong with society.
Sonya:	I think it's important to know how the ideal of the objective story got to be the standard. Here's what I learned in my journalism class. The inverted pyramid style came along during the era when reporters used to send their stories by telegraph. A telegram would start with the most important facts and succeeding paragraphs got less and less and less important. In case they got cut off, the newspaper would still have the most important part of the story. This style also allowed editors to cut the bottom of the story if they needed to and still have left the primary elements at the top. The important thing was to get the facts up front.
Mike:	The problem with putting the facts up front in television news is that the viewer will listen to the information and then change channels! Viewers don't stick around to see the rest of your show, your ratings drop, and it's not good for the company. That's why TV dropped the inverted pyramid style and mixes important information throughout a report.
Dr. Bauer:	Right, the objective standard is being shaped by the need to keep viewers.
Mike:	Absolutely.
Tony:	I'm convinced the media revolves around making money, whether it's catering to the short attention span of television viewers or manipulating readers of a newspaper. The next big political story, watch how the newspapers chop it up. Every big story has a jump cut to another page buried deep in the paper so you have to turn past the department store ads and past the liquor store ads to get the other half of the story. Advertising has taken over the world. The dollar is more important than the news.

Sonya:	You can't criticize the media because it has to make money! How else are newspapers and television stations supposed to pay their reporters?
Dr. Bauer:	Sonya's right. Unless we want to pay big subscription fees, similar to the ones paid for premium cable channels without commercials, we can't keep criticizing the media for trying to make money. But we can try to figure out how much the incentive to make money distorts what we read and hear. Alter offers a partial solution: "We should want reporters to analyze, reach conclusions, and write with style. The only answer I can envision is to erect a stronger [fire]wall between anchors and commentators, between news shows and entertainment [shows] and between the news section of the newspaper and the rest of the paper." But look at the next sentence.
Sonya:	"The risk is boredom."
Robert:	That's right. Excitement sells, boring doesn't.
Dr. Bauer:	The good news is, Alter says at the very end, partisan, biased news organizations don't make as much money as the "reliable papers and networks with a reputation for some objectivity in their news section[s]." Making money can go hand in hand with reliability and objectivity as long as objective news is written in a way that doesn't put the readers to sleep.
Tony:	I don't know. If you're a partisan reporter, eventually you'll get a call from the *Today Show* or from *Larry King Live,* and they'll put you on as an expert. And they'll advertise your paper, and you'll become one of the talking heads being rewarded for bias.
Dr. Bauer:	I agree with you that biased individuals are more colorful, more apt to appear on the Sunday talk shows, become celebrities, and make more money. But notice that Alter isn't referring to the biased reporter. He says biased news organizations don't make big money.
	Now, I'd like to open this chat up a little. Did anyone have a favorite piece you want to talk about?
Tony:	Yes, I'd like to discuss the quote David Ignatius reports from Wiggins, editor at the *Washington Post:* "The reader deserves one clean shot at the facts." [Laughter.]
Robert:	I've got that highlighted five times!
Tony:	Yeah, I couldn't agree more. I wouldn't mind one—
Robert:	Just one shot.
Tony:	I wouldn't mind reading a straight story. If it's about bombing Iraq, I wouldn't mind reading just about bombing Iraq and not, "In an obvious attempt to distract the public from the impeachment proceedings, the president is bombing Iraq." [Laughter.]

Dr. Bauer:	This is interesting. We have our strongest Democrat, Tony, and our strongest Republican, Robert, in complete agreement. They both keep searching for more straight news. Editors can give you more straight news and less attitude journalism by following the "Kaiser Rule." Robert Kaiser, an editor for the *Washington Post*, banned bias from news headlines and lead sentences. What is a biased lead, an opinion-saturated lead?
Clint:	It's the first sentence in a news story that might read something like, "In a desperate effort to change the subject and deflect the public's attention away from their recent loss on impeachment, Republicans proposed a tax cut today."
Dr. Bauer:	A perfect example. When I was running for Congress, news stories always led with, "Underfunded, long-shot candidate Monica Bauer [laughter]—gave a poorly attended speech [laughter] . . . "
Sonya:	". . . in an attempt to gain more voters."
Dr. Bauer:	No, it was always ". . . in a futile attempt to gain more voters." [Laughter.]
Mike:	Ignatius also pointed out how much of Washington journalism is about keeping score on the White House—it was a good week, it was bad week, dogged by scandal, or triumphant over critics. It just depends on what kind of spin they want to put on it.
Tony:	That's why every TV newscast begins with, "The president's approval numbers are down half a point today as news came out that war was being threatened in the Balkans." I don't want to keep score when I'm reading government and politics.
Dr. Bauer:	I think this must have driven the Republican House managers nuts during the impeachment trial. Every single lead about the impeachment trial began with "President Clinton's approval rating remained at sixty-five percent today while the House Managers tried to explain why he should be impeached." Isn't that so?
Tony:	Yes, exactly.
Dr. Bauer:	How about the notion that the Washington media go to the same few people they know in Washington and report their views as the "Washington consensus." This practice is on blatant display Sunday morning during the famous talk shows on politics, such as *Face the Nation* or *This Week*. How many of you have ever watched more than one of those shows in a single morning?
Tony:	I have.
Dr. Bauer:	What do you learn from these shows?
Tony:	After awhile, they begin to sound exactly alike. You hear essentially the same four or five people no matter what channel you watch. After this person is finished talking to Tim Russert on *Meet the Press*, he or she, or an assistant, or

Sonya:	a surrogate speaker, or someone repeating the same party line, is on *This Week* with Sam and Cokie. Then they hit the cable circuit, and then they begin hitting the MSNBC shows, then they go off to the Larry King show. So it feels like we're getting the same information from the same five people regardless of the issue.
Sonya:	I think one of the reasons why these Sunday morning inside-politics shows are so successful is that their panels are made up of classic movie characters. There's the wacko conservative, and the feminist, and the extreme liberal, and they're all chosen to represent something. It's just like a movie, and you're entertained.
Robert:	I don't want to be entertained. I want to know what's really going on. That's why Timothy Noah's article is my favorite. He says that it takes hard work to be a good reporter, and that's why so many reporters would rather write attitude journalism. It's harder to get the details of the story on your own; it's easier to talk to the same five people over and over, and add your own attitude spin.
Dr. Bauer:	It's harder to work in an objective style, isn't it?
Robert:	Yes, and they should put only hard-working, good reporters on these Sunday morning shows. Noah says, "A good reporter who is well-steeped in his subject matter and who isn't out to prove his cleverness, but rather is sweating out a detailed understanding of a topic worth exploring, will probably develop intelligent opinions that will inform and perhaps be expressed in his journalism. It is very difficult to be a blowhard on a subject one has studied extensively and from many angles." I want a deeper analysis than somebody's flippant remarks.
Clint:	Deeper analysis can be boring, though.
Sonya:	And a deeper analysis is not an objective straight shot at the facts, which is what you were arguing for earlier, Robert!
Robert:	Sure it is.
Sonya:	It's analysis. An analysis is not fact.
Dr. Bauer:	Can you have an analysis that is opinion free?
Sonya:	No.
Robert:	Okay, I've modified my stand some and I'll admit that an analysis is an interpretation of facts. On the Sunday morning shows, I would listen to analyses from reporters who know their stuff, had researched the facts. Their analyses—intelligent and thoughtful, taking all the sides into account—is the only opinion I want to hear.
Clint:	Robert only wants opinions from people with credibility. People who know an issue so well that it gives their opinions more weight.

Dr. Bauer:	You're saying you want educated opinions.
Robert:	Yes, from someone who's actually dug through the subject matter.
Clint:	But how many times do reporters actually research their stories?
Robert:	David Ignatius touched on that when he talked about TV news celebrities doing a lot of reporting on different topics. One of the reasons why everyone respected Edward R. Murrow's World War II reporting was because he did it from a basement in London while planes flew overhead and bombs dropped around him.
Dr. Bauer:	Recently, I hung out while a person in my department was being interviewed. When the camera wasn't running, I heard the reporter say to my colleague, "I don't know anything about this field. I don't have a clue. Please tell me before the camera starts running what this is about, so I can ask you some good questions." Mike, you're our working TV journalist. Is that unusual in local news?
Mike:	No, it's not. Too few reporters need to cover so many stories that it's absurd to expect them to be knowledgeable about every story they do. One day they could do a story on a murder and the next day, a story on budget cuts. There's no specific beat, no area of concentration, for most local reporters—they do general news. Producers come up with an idea in the morning, pick a reporter, and say, "Go do it—be an expert on this story in two hours." That's five stories a week that you haven't got enough time to research. So most local reporters go into stories blind. The reporter does some research, calls people, gets the information from the person being interviewed before the interview—"Okay, just tell me about ———." They do, and you quickly write questions about what you just heard. Between the workload and demand every day, that's how it's put together. That's just the way it is.
Sonya:	Well, I think we all need to develop an idea of what "good reporting" looks like, so we can recognize it when we see it.
	★ ★ ★

Just the Facts? A Symposium
Suzannah Lessard

The problem with the more subjective elements in journalism today, in my view, is not inventiveness per se but cynicism. During the '80s it became extremely unfashionable to believe in anything or anyone who had anything to do with political life. It was as if the slightest taint of hope or admiration, or of in any way taking seriously what transpired on the political stage, would automatically brand a journalist as credulous. And credulousness, in the atmosphere of those times, held the horror of terminal disease. This came about, perhaps, because the Reagan propaganda about America was so patently and dangerously delusory and yet pervasive that any positive note might automatically seem to join the Pollyanna chorus.

Whatever the reason, this legacy is destructive. One H. L. Mencken is probably enough for all time. Imitations are really a kind of comedy act that are more about the writer than they are reflections on current affairs. The value of inventiveness in journalism is that it brings to reflection the full spectrum of responsiveness and the variety of the ways in which we see things. Faith, hope, and charity are elemental ingredients in that mix.

But this is not to say that we must have writers who are positive about what is going on. The distinction has to do with a richness of tone. One can excoriate in a tone that implies that things could not be any other way, and one can excoriate in a way that admits, implicitly, the possibilities of what could be. It's the latter tone that is capable of grief, of authentic outrage, of compassion, all of which "betray" belief of a kind.

Idealism—one could call it an underlying tone of love, as opposed to scorn or contempt—is always risky and exposing. We see it still appearing calmly but courageously in the writings of older commentators who do not, on the whole, avail themselves of creative devices. Among the more inventive generations it's almost obsolete, and we are all impoverished for it. It can't be true that inventiveness necessarily leads in this direction: Great fiction is always work that arises out of love, however ghastly the events and characters depicted. The argument that the cynicism only reflects the debasement of the political world is arrant nonsense. It's a rule of thumb that where humanity is gathered in significant numbers the full Shakespearean panoply is present.

Just the Facts? A Symposium

Joseph Nocera

To my mind, the big problem with American journalism is not so much that it is snarky, or that opinions have crept into news stories, or that it is more often about attitude and showing off than about facts—though all of that strikes me as plainly true. Rather, it is that journalism—especially the journalism practiced by political print reporters, which is the concern of this magazine—has lost its way. Once, these were the people through whom politicians made their cases to the nation; now, thanks to Larry King et al., they have been stripped of that role, and they simply don't know what to do anymore.

So they practice "gotcha" journalism. The cover process rather than policy. They get caught up in spin, and who's-doing-what-to-whom and all the rest of it. It's a kind of journalism of nihilism—for it doesn't really believe in anything except itself. Journalism has become, to an astonishing degree, self-referential, like a tribe cut off from the rest of the world. When Maureen Dowd, the current queen of the tribe, and others of her ilk sneer at those who would like to see a journalism that actually cares about things the country cares about, that's when their cards are most on the table. The notion has become practically incomprehensible. Note, also, by the way, how the only people she ever quotes in her Ain't-I-One-Smart-Cookie op-ed columns are her fellow journalists.

The late Theodore White gets blamed a lot for starting us down this path. He, of course, was the first political writer to add detail and color to political reporting—to make process come alive. And it is certainly true that other reporters picked up his techniques—and then drove them into the ground through sheer overkill. But what has long been forgotten is that White had a tremendous—and completely unembarrassed—passion for the country, for its people and its problems, its strengths and weaknesses. And he was never afraid to display that passion in his books. He would, for instance, regularly include lengthy chapters interpreting the latest census data in his *Making of the President* series, as well as chapters that had nothing to do with process and everything to do with the problems facing the country. The craft it took in writing those chapters was astonishing, for this was material that was difficult to bring to life. But it was important, and he *cared,* so he made the effort. When the day comes that Maureen Dowd can bring herself to leave Monica and Bill behind and writes a column about the census, you'll know that political journalism has begun to find its way again. Me, I'm not holding my breath.

Just the Facts? A Symposium
James Fallows

The problem the *Monthly*'s getting at is not confined to news stories with loaded lead-ins. ("Dogged by criticism of his role in the Lewinsky case, President Clinton today raised a man from the dead with the slightest touch of his hand.") It's just as common, and has an even longer history, in the portentous-sounding but vapid zingers that end the typical TV or radio news report. ("The president may have conquered death today. Whether he can beat Kenneth Starr tomorrow . . . *is not so clear.*") And whether used at the beginning of a story or the end, such fillips are not the real problem. The menace is the incredibly shallow, incurious, and cynical view of life that lies behind them.

Within limits, the effort to put attitude into a news story is a worthy one—or, at a minimum, one this magazine should be slow to condemn. In one way or another it has urged for years that reporters use as many tools as they can to share what they've seen—what they know—with the reader. It was in this very magazine, a mere 25 years ago, that I wrote (at the suggestion of the editor) a review of Ward Just's book of short stories, *The Congressman Who Loved Flaubert.* The point of that review, and of other *Monthly* articles *passim,* was that a Flaubert-like, novelistic sensibility can add to a full understanding of public life. This was in contrast to the preceding "just the facts" wire-service ethic that led some of the funniest people in the press to write dull, constipated stories and to use euphemisms like "tired and emotional" to describe politicians who were drunk and stuporous on the Senate floor.

Yes, there should be places where the facts come through straight and plain. The lead of a story is usually such a place. Yes, there should be clues to the reader about what is a clear-as-we-can-make-it factual summary and what is the extra interpretation. But trying to move beyond the straight facts is not the big problem here.

The problem, I think, is that the people writing these stories are less interested, and therefore less interesting, than reporters really need to be. The mark of a great reporter is boundless curiosity—a desire to find out all there is to know. Name your era, and anyone we think of as a great reporter from that time was distinguished by omnivorous curiosity. Stephen Crane in Cuba. Charles Dickens roaming through America. John Hersey in Hiroshima. James Agee in the South. The grossly underrated John Gunther, in his *Inside* series of books. They made their mistakes, but they wanted to learn every single thing they could about as many topics as they could.

Today's most famous journalists, by comparison, (a) spend a much larger proportion of their time spitting out opinions and predictions, especially on TV, rather than taking in new material, and (b) are curious about a much narrower slice of the world. It's somewhat exaggerated, but basically fair, to say that today's pundit and star political-writer class is not driven by fascination about the world in general, or even about politics in the broadest sense. Rather, its members are fascinated by one specific question: which politicians are gaining or losing power. That's why they package every public event in a "Dogged by criticism . . . " wrapping. That's why they spend so much time on pointless prediction and speculation about future shifts in strength. That's also why they're so cynical, since boiling life down to this one simple struggle is as deadening as any other reductionist view. (Imagine a coroner who let his dealings with other people be reduced to calculations of how long before they showed up on his slab.)

The game of musical chairs that leaves some people in office and some out is a legitimate topic. But it makes up about 2 percent of what's significant and interesting in life. As long as it occupies most of the imagination of the political-writer class, their claim on the public imagination will shrink.

It's progress that most of us no longer view journalism as simply the gathering of facts. Some facts are more important than others. We know that what readers should get isn't the facts but the story. A newspaper should help us decide what events mean, and to do this, writers and editors have to interpret, opine, explain, disregard, and emphasize. In short, they have to write and edit. But what's wrong is when newspapers try to hide this aspect of what they do. When they cloak themselves in the myth of objectivity. The reader, in his quest to get the story, is entitled to know what particular point of view the particular story in his hands is told from. Only then can he be an informed news consumer, able to get out of this particular tale what's in it and well advised about what else he still needs to know.

So it's not the point of view, but the smuggled-in point of view that's got to go. Last fall, a front-page *Los Angeles Times* story reported that as part of the last-minute budget deal, then-Sen. Alfonse D'Amato won approval of a provision requiring health insurance companies to cover post-mastectomy reconstructive surgery. The paper then immediately explained that D'Amato did this to undercut the strong support among women enjoyed by his election opponent, Charles Schumer. It was just assumed without comment that D'Amato had only this motivation. No consideration was given to the idea that D'Amato might be actually concerned about women not being able to afford reconstructions. If D'Amato was indeed so coldly single-minded, that at least is something the paper needed to support with some facts, such as his past voting record on women's health issues. But to flatly ascribe the basest motive to him in passing is precisely smuggling opinion in. As this episode shows, this journalistic offense cuts across ideological lines—liberals are just as guilty as conservatives.

Financial reporting often keeps its agenda hidden. Last October, when a computer problem halted trading at the New York Stock Exchange for about an hour, all the papers gave precise accounts of the standstill with one glaring exception: not one mentioned the brand of computer that failed. This is like reporting a plane crash without mentioning the type of plane, an extraordinary level of incuriosity, helping to protect that company's stock price, but not helping anybody understand what went wrong or what other computer systems are likewise vulnerable. Also, when around the same time, the yield on 30-year Treasury bonds dipped below 5 percent for the first time ever, most of the reporting came wrapped in the alarm the development prompted among stockholders and bond buyers, but generally did not explain that this was very good news for a much larger group of Americans—those trying to secure a home mortgage.

And sometimes it's public sentiment that cows newspapers out of raising questions. For instance, the coverage of John Glenn's space mission (with the notable exception of *The New York Times* editorial page) was positively boosterish. News stories gave no meaningful space to the idea that Glenn's involvement was pure PR. And even though the shuttle suffered the potentially dangerous loss of a protective panel during launch, none of the papers the next day mentioned NASA's previous "special" astronaut, Christa McAuliffe.

Perhaps the height of illicit editorializing in newspapers is the news photo. With all the pictures available of the likes of Bill Clinton or Newt Gingrich, is it ever really necessary to run a picture of them with a dopey expression or a finger in the ear? In a recent *New York Times* "Week in Review" section, alongside a story about politicians speaking their minds about other countries, was a looming picture of Al Gore, cropped so close that none of his hair is visible and you can see the sweat that's bubbling out of every giant pore in his face. The verbal equivalent of the picture—"Gore, looking like a crazed criminal with something to hide, said,"—

would never pass muster. Therefore, the picture shouldn't either.

What to do about smuggled-in point of view? Well, readers should ask themselves, "Whose interests are being served by this story told this way and whose are being left out? And they should communicate what they find out to the papers via letters to the editor and via the papers' on-line sites. When editors learn that readers are becoming more sophisticated about what's missing, their stories are more apt to include it. For instance, now that the big papers know that readers are aware of the political role of spin and counterspin, they more often tend to include in their political stories a discussion of the possible spins. (An excellent example was *The New York Times* piece last August breaking the news that President Clinton was considering using as a defense against perjury his claim to be wielding a certain definition of sex. The story was not only a White House trial balloon, but it explained that it was.)

And the beat system in force at most papers should be modified. Much of a story's hidden point of view comes not from some sort of grand conspiracy but from when reporters have too much familiarity with the culture of the institution(s) being covered, so much so that assumptions held by participants in the culture creep seamlessly into the journalists' reporting and writing. Correspondingly, an able reporter who is less familiar with the cultural assumptions is more apt to question them and look at them in a fresh way. A reporter coming off a Pentagon tour might ask great questions at City Hall, and vice versa. To maintain a paper's institutional memory, you still need reporters with lots of experience on a beat, but they should generally be paired with another reporter with commensurate experience but in another area. In other words, half of a papers' reporters should be kept cycling through.

students

Clint a moderate	**Mike** a Hispanic, liberal Democrat	**Robert** a moderate Republican	**Sonya** a Hispanic, moderate Republican	**Tony** an African American, liberal Democrat

Politicians as Crooks, Liars, and Thieves
★ ★ ★

Dr. Bauer: My favorite reading in this series was the article by Suzannah Lessard. She echoed a theme that was also seen in the last half of the David Ignatius article: that the media has become too cynical. What does that mean?

Tony: A cynical reporter has an immediate negative response to a story—an assumption that something sinister lies behind an event, that the politician has something to hide. Cynical reporters say to themselves, "This guy's lying. I need to find out what his real motive is for telling us that he wants to fix Medicare."

Dr. Bauer: That's pretty good. What's another good definition for cynicism? Or what is the opposite of cynicism?

Sonya: Idealism?

Dr. Bauer: Idealism, right. Lessard says idealism in a story would give it "an underlying tone of love, as opposed to scorn or contempt." Many reporters within the Washington press corps, whether they're Republican or Democrat, appear to be cynical, meaning they don't believe anyone in government is trying to make things better. And their immediate bias is always, What is the hidden story? What does it do to ordinary people who read that kind of journalism week after week after week?

Clint: It makes us cynical.

Dr. Bauer: Yes, Clint. A lot of time has been spent analyzing the liberal or conservative bias of the media. But I don't worry so much that the press will turn me into a Republican because I read a lot of conservative commentators. But I do fear becoming as cynical about politics as the Washington press. I worry that my students read only a cynical point of view. When you talk to other students about politics what is their sense of American politics?

Clint:	That politics is a total joke. That politicians are corrupt, and they don't know what they're doing.
Dr. Bauer:	So why bother to participate?
Clint:	Exactly!
Dr. Bauer:	Yes, that worries me. And it worries Suzannah Lessard. No one in the news media wants to sound like a "Pollyanna"—the fictional children's book character who always looked on the bright side of everything. To sound like a Pollyanna is to be naïve, and, in the real world, often to be naïve is to be suckered. The worst thing a reporter can do is sound naïve—so naïve that he or she might actually believe any good statement or good intention from a politician.
Sonya:	This fits with my experience. The biggest critics of politicians I've met are my broadcasting classmates. They're already cynical about politics; they describe politicians as "all crooks."
Dr. Bauer:	To me, that's a bias and inappropriate, because their minds are closed to the slightest chance that some politicians are involved for the right reasons.
Tony:	Speaking of cynicism, I'd like to raise one of my pet peeves! When I go out during campaigns and hold up a sign for a candidate, particularly someone who has never run for office before, I hear, "That person is scum." They never heard of the candidate. They don't even know what office she's running for, but because she *is* running for an office, she is obviously scum, because back in 1974 Nixon lied.
Dr. Bauer:	We've had more recent experience than Nixon of a president who lies!
Tony:	Yeah, but it doesn't mean that they all lie. When I read a story about a doctor who lied, I don't immediately imagine that all doctors lie. But I think Watergate did create that atmosphere of distrust. I think most people didn't care that Clinton lied, because they expect him to! I think that's bad news for American politics, I really do.
Dr. Bauer:	Have you ever read about a political leader in a magazine or newspaper, and the article inspired you to believe that politics might do some good in the world?
Tony:	I can't ever remember an instance. Maybe reading the Constitution.
Dr. Bauer:	People like the Constitution. It's our American scripture. But do we like politics in general?
Tony:	You mean the people actually hired to uphold the Constitution?
Dr. Bauer:	That's right! Good point. The Constitution is sacred, but politicians are scum. The Constitution was written by politicians, to be used in a political system. So how can we love the document and hate the people that give it breath and life?
Robert:	Do you think it's gotten worse since the media began to hold a spotlight on politicians? I mean, they can't go out and mow their lawn without some

reporter writing, "Bill Clinton went out and mowed the lawn today . . . and he missed about three spots." [Laughter.]

On a good day, they might write, "He did about an average job of mowing today." I see what you mean about the press being too cynical to ever say anything good about politics.

Dr. Bauer: Your remarks reminded me of Joseph Nocera's article. He talks about what he calls "gotcha journalism"—journalism that is based on finding scandals and flaws in politicians. There's a great quote in this article, one that relates to the topic of cynicism. Nocera writes, "The late Theodore White gets blamed a lot for starting us down this path. He, of course, was the first political writer to add detail and color to political reporting—to make the process come alive. And it is certainly true that other reporters picked up his techniques—and then drove them into the ground through sheer overkill. But what has long been forgotten is that White had a tremendous—and completely unembarrassed—passion for the country, for its people and its problems, its strengths and weaknesses." That's what I'm missing. Do you get that from anybody that you read? A love for this country that translates into a discussion of politics? It's almost as if love of country and politics have been separated by an ax. But, in fact, most people go into politics because they love the country. Most journalism students will not believe that, but it's true.

Sonya: But even in your classes, you've said people go into politics for their egos.

Dr. Bauer: But it's a combination. If you have an ego, but you don't have a passion for this country, then you go into investment banking and make a whole lot of money. [Laughter.]

Sonya: But you don't get the prestige.

Robert: Who has more prestige, Bill Gates or Bill Clinton?

Sonya: Right now? [Laughter.]

Robert: It's Bill Gates who's worth sixty-four billion dollars versus Bill Clinton who earns less than the worst baseball player!

Dr. Bauer: But the story here is that sometimes people go into journalism for ego as well.

Robert: "I want to be famous like Woodward and Bernstein."

Dr. Bauer: But you think they don't want to work as hard today as they did in the sixties?

Robert: Not even close.

Dr. Bauer: What do you think, Sonya?

Sonya: I disagree. Yes, some journalism students say, "I want to go on TV and be like Katie Couric, and make seven million dollars a year and be in everybody's living room every morning." And others are willing to put in the eighty to one hundred hours a week that it takes to be a truly great reporter.

Robert: Not the ones I see.

Dr. Bauer:	They represent the "incredibly shallow, incurious, and cynical view of life" that James Fallows talks about, and he thinks it makes journalists lazy. If you've already made up your mind that all politicians are scum, then you don't have to do the work.
Mike:	The Scott Shuger article said that cynical reporting has even spread into news photos. He said this was a sneaky form of bias that would never be allowed if it were in writing.
Robert:	Yeah, that was funny.
Tony:	That's so incredibly true.
Dr. Bauer:	Shuger uses an example of an Al Gore photo. Some of you were in the class where I handed out a *Newsweek* poll about Al Gore that was run in 1997, speculating about how Gore would do in the New Hampshire primary. And it had a picture of Gore. Do you remember what that looked like?
Clint:	It looked like a mug shot!
Sonya:	Didn't they draw in sweat?
Dr. Bauer:	Yes . . .
Sonya:	Like fake sweat coming out from his head?
Dr. Bauer:	Yes, they did, they actually *added art* to the photo to make it look worse. If one of your pet peeves is hidden bias, look for the photos, especially during any election—you'll get a strong sense of who the press thinks is the front runner.
Tony:	Very true. And if the unflattering photo in the newscast looks similar to the photo the opponent is using in his commercials, the slant is obvious. Candidates always give their most flattering photos to the press. But the press can choose to use that photo or not. Obviously, a bad photo was not supplied by the candidate's own staff!
Sonya:	I have an issue with that picture they've have been running a lot of Clinton with that pouty face. The media is suppose to be so liberal and so biased, but if they're so pro-Clinton, why do they choose the most disgusting, pathetic-looking picture of him?
Mike:	They're sending a message about Clinton without having to put it into words. And I know from my TV experience, that pictures are ten times as powerful as words. But Shuger gives a good suggestion. He says we should all write and complain when we see that kind of hidden bias. At my station those complaints are taken very seriously. The problem is, hardly anyone bothers to complain to the media. They may bitch and moan to their friends, but they don't bother to write a letter to an editor of a newspaper, magazine, or television show.

| Dr. Bauer: | It's hard to keep idealism in a profession where a cynical approach to politics is the norm. But without a little idealism in our news coverage, we never pay attention to the parts of our political system that actually work. I agree with Clint. I think this generation has been taught by the media that politics is a joke and politicians are crooks. "Gotcha journalism" was raised to a high art during the whole Monica saga and turned off still more people to American politics. It scares me when I hear Sonya say that her friends majoring in broadcasting are already cynical. We all need to be aware how a cynical media has affected the way we think and feel about politics. |

★ ★ ★

FACE TO FACE

Student Interview with
Jene Nelson
Executive Producer of Denver's "9News at 10"

Clint
a moderate

Mike
a Hispanic,
liberal Democrat

Robert
a moderate
Republican

Sonya
a Hispanic,
moderate Republican

Face to Face: Student Interview with Jene Nelson
★ ★ ★

*Jene Nelson is the executive producer of Denver, Colorado's "9News at 10,"
the local newscast with the largest audience in the United States.*

Dr. Bauer: Tonight, our interview focuses on the media, particularly local television news coverage, and the impact that local news has on politics. We have two media-savvy students in our group: Mike works at Channel 9, and Sonya interned in editing last summer.

Let's begin by asking about your political coverage. Candidates do things—they send you press releases; they beg you for coverage. How do you decide who to cover? How do you decide what is news in a political campaign?

Jene Nelson: It's not as simple as it might seem. In the previous U.S. Senate campaign, Ben Nighthorse Campbell, Terry Considine, and Matt Noah all ran, all competed for coverage. Matt Noah was the antiabortion candidate, and he ran very graphic ads on television. That got a lot of coverage. Why? you might ask. The issue itself was controversial and heated.

Essentially, we look for interest and timeliness. Different news days dictate different coverage. If a political candidate has an interesting thing to say, and it's a slow news day, there's a much better chance we'll do that story. But if it's one of those news days when everything seems to happen on the same day, a politician will have to do something very special to get air time.

We just look for a good story. When Gill Ford announced he was running for Mayor of Denver against Wellington Webb, that was our lead story at ten. Then we did some follow-ups to that story because it was controversial. I'd like to do a story on the District 10 city council race, because it's particularly interesting. A gay community activist is challenging an incumbent, and the gay activist has the backing of the police union because the union is angry that the incumbent voted against them on past issues. Now, that's an interesting race!

Robert: If you have three senatorial candidates, do you try to give them all equal coverage, or do you cover the one who provided a media event and gave you the best pictures that day?

Jene Nelson: We try to do equal coverage on any of our stories. Obviously, if someone is taking a plunge from the top of the Speer viaduct tied to a bungee cord, it might be hard to top that because we are a visual medium. So, if one candidate did something spectacular, and there were good pictures, that would be hard to balance.

This is an extreme example, but one story I like to tell happened during the Bush–Clinton presidential race. We did a story on the five o'clock news when then-candidate Clinton was in town and held a pep rally. We had great pictures of the rally that seemed to report, "Gee, Clinton's swell." Then we followed with a CBS poll on how far ahead Clinton was. At that time we were an ABC affiliate using a CBS poll, so it looked like we were bending over backwards to make Clinton look good. Then we followed with twenty seconds on "here's George Bush campaigning in Oklahoma, and boy did he sweat." That was the story the pictures told, it *was* the news that day, but it looked wrong. Running those stories was the mistake of a producer not terribly experienced in the fine art of balance. An experienced producer would have looked at that composite and said, "You can't do that." You can't do three minutes on one candidate, and only twenty seconds on the other, especially in a state with a lot of Republicans.

Clint: Especially when the twenty seconds showed a negative image of Bush sweating.

Jene Nelson: Yes, that was not pretty. You didn't want to answer the phones that day!

Mike: The media has been charged with having a liberal bias when it comes to elections and election coverage. Just being around the station, I think, in general, reporters and producers try to get both sides of the story, but time constraints don't always allow them to. Do you think the media have a liberal bias?

Jene Nelson:	Sometimes a reputation for bias is harder to overcome than the bias itself. We try to bowl straight down the middle, and I gauge Channel 9's coverage by the number of calls we get from both sides. If one caller says, "You're for the Republicans" and one caller says, "You're for the Democrats," then we know we are doing our jobs. I think a lot of times it is easy to blame "the liberal media." And do we slip from time to time? Once in a while, bias probably slips in—but not necessarily for the liberals.
Mike:	What about the assumption that the media is controlled by big business and money—specifically the money you get from advertising? If your advertisers like a particular candidate, do they pressure you to go easy or complain when you get too tough?
Jene Nelson:	I can't speak for the media in general, but I can speak for "9News," and I've been here nearly ten years. The news producers and reporters never feel pressure from advertisers. Several times in the past we have done stories that were critical of people or companies that advertise on our station, and we were fully backed by our management. That's what it means to be a professional journalist.
Sonya:	How much of an effort do the producers make to be sure that the reporters and anchors know what they're talking about when they cover elections and politics in general?
Jene Nelson:	Well, I'm fortunate to work with Ed Sardella, who's a political junkie and knows far more than I ever will about the inner workings of politics. He prepares. It's incredible to watch him prepare for elections. You could quiz him about the most minute details, ballot initiatives, the inside story of what's in a bill, and he will know.
	Ed Sardella has anchored here at Channel 9 for more than twenty years. He is a senior editor as well, the author of several books on news writing, does workshops, and is quite famous within the business. Most stations in major media markets will have at least one knowledgeable, experienced anchor like Ed. The other anchor is Adele Arakawa. She's been with us for about five years and has been in the business for more than—well, I can't say how many years, or she will kill me. But, she, too, is a professional.
	We also have reporters who specialize. Politics is their area of expertise, and we rely heavily on them. Finally, it's the producer's responsibility to stay on top of politics, particularly if it's making news, or we're not going to be able to properly assign a reporter or produce an accurate story.
Sonya:	Do you try to assign reporters that specialize in politics to political stories?
Jene Nelson:	We use "general assignment" reporters—a sort of jack-of-all-trades and, sometimes, the master of few, but, again, at our broadcast, we are fortunate to have crews who are familiar with just about everything. So, I feel comfortable assigning any story to any of my reporters. We also have some real specialists—Sheri Sellers is our medical reporter; Mark Kohlberg is our consumer

reporter—but I would also feel comfortable assigning them stories outside of those topics

We're lucky. If you were in a different market where the standard weren't as high as it is here in Denver, you might run into a station where people didn't have a clue.

Dr. Bauer: Have you ever worked at one of the smaller market stations?

Jene Nelson: I've been with two.

Dr. Bauer: And what was that like?

Jene Nelson: There is a vast contrast between small- and large-market stations. I like to tell this story, too. I once worked at a station so small it covered two cities, Pueblo and Colorado Springs. They call that a dual market. I went from there to a television station in Las Vegas, which, even though it is still not a major market, I thought was a move up, and I was very anxious to make a good impression. So, I went over to the main anchor and tried to discuss the news with him. He looked at me and said, "I don't care what you put in your newscasts. Just make sure it is right on the TelePrompTer." He went on to make hundreds of thousands of dollars in his career, was widely popular, and he frankly had *no interest* in news in general, never mind politics! He was very forthright that he was a *news reader,* that was what he did. We had to watch and edit very carefully whatever he said. He also had a lot of friction with the female anchor, because she was a diehard journalist. It was a very interesting place. The producers had final word on anything that went over the air. If an anchor wrote something and the producer wanted to change it, the producer did—which was scary, considering the median age of producers in that market was around twenty-five.

Mike: When you assign someone to a political story, do you take into account their political views? Do you send a Democrat to cover Democrats, or a Republican to cover Republican events, or vice versa?

Jene Nelson: This is the honest truth: I don't know anybody's political views or party affiliation. I haven't the first idea. I can have suspicions, but it's part of our job to be unbiased, to cover stories in a nonpartisan fashion.

Dr. Bauer: What happens when the number of phone calls you get on a story indicates bias? How much attention do you pay to people calling up and complaining about the news?

Jene Nelson: We have a program called "9News Listens" that encourages viewers to call in. Whenever we show that full-screen graphic that says call, or write, or fax, we get a lot of response! And we listen. If we don't, we get the same complaints over and over again.

I think people feel particularly strongly about politics. They want to make sure that their side is being treated fairly and their party is represented fairly. The only thing a producer or reporter can do is look back on the stories you ran and know that you were accurate and fair.

Sonya:	If you haven't been, do you ever go back on the air and do a correction, or add-on, or expand on a story that was aired previously?
Jene Nelson:	If we are wrong on a story, or if people were just outraged on a story, yes, we do corrections. It depends on what kind of error it was and how many calls we get. I'm trying to think of what it was last week . . . We misspelled *Juan* on a graphic of San Juan. We had *J-a-u-n* on that map. I just thought, "Oh, no, no, *no.*" I'll ask the assignment desk—the editors take the lion's share of the calls during the newscast—if we're getting a lot of calls. If we get only three calls on a typographical error, then I probably won't do a correction, because I think it might be even more distracting to go back and say, "Gee, three of you called, and here is why you called, and boy, are we dumb!" If we get more calls, we may want to admit to a typographical error.
	If we aired a *factual* error that's important to the story, I don't care if there are no calls, it gets corrected. The public has a right to expect accuracy and fairness from professional journalists. You need to be right. And if you are *not* right, you need to *make it* right.
Clint:	When I watch your political reporting, I sometimes see a print reporter, some guy who works at the *Denver Post* newspaper. How does that work, cooperation between a newspaper and a TV station?
Jene Nelson:	We have a partnership with the *Denver Post.* As you probably know, most people get their political news from TV, and newspapers are having a tough time making money. A number of TV stations have partnered with a local newspaper, and that's good for the paper and good for us. It gives us more expertise, especially in local politics, than most local TV reporters have. Fred Brown, over at the *Post,* lives, eats, and breathes politics—a terrific resource.
Dr. Bauer:	I was a congressional challenger in a district that was registered sixty percent as the other party. I had no hope of winning, and my lack of media coverage reflected that. I watched the Diana DeGette race and noticed that her challenger received about the same level of coverage that I had ten years ago. Local political experts often decide early whether a candidate has a chance of winning. Can you talk a little bit about how you decide to cover congressional challengers in particular? How do they get on the air?
Jene Nelson:	Getting news coverage is tough. We always cover debates, but most incumbents won't debate challengers. Having an aggressive campaign manager, someone who just stays on the media, will send out press releases, and make sure there is an organized, continuous effort—that could help. In large markets that have several congressional districts, we probably won't do candidate profiles that give everyone running an equal amount of air time. Although I know it's hard for challengers to raise the money, if they really want to get their campaigns on the air, they need to buy commercial time.
Clint:	And this is one of the things we worry about in politics: How does everyone get covered?

Robert:	If the candidate were to bungee jump off the Speer viaduct, she'd get some coverage. Maybe.
Jene Nelson:	Exactly. *Maybe,* depending on the day. It would be nice if you had bodies to send *everywhere* and unlimited time to cover politics. We have *twelve minutes of news time every night*—that's what's left after you take out commercials, weather, and sports. My basic job is to take a look at that twelve minutes and ask, what can we talk about tonight that is going to matter the most to the most people? Or, what are *they* going to talk about? What do *they* want to know? If there's a political story that is important to a lot of people, it will get covered. But candidates who want air time so people will vote for them may not be important to a lot of people.
Robert:	In the competition with other newscasts, how do you decide what gets you the highest ratings?
Jene Nelson:	Again, we are blessed with a viewership that is higher than the other major networks combined. Possibly because of our lead, I don't look at what the others are doing. I keep other stations in my peripheral vision, but when I see people watching the competition and saying, "Oh boy, Channel 4 has this, and Channel 7 has that," I don't think that's a great way to produce our own news. And as the number-one station and the leader in the marketplace, I don't think we need to do that—we can't learn from them. We need to look at our viewers and decide what the important stories are to them. We look at the competition only secondarily.
Dr. Bauer:	When you look at the Nielsen ratings, don't they give you a breakdown of the demographics of your audience?
Jene Nelson:	We just had our Nielsen report as a matter of fact, and the newsroom does not get demographic breakdowns. Typically, if we want to see demographics, our sales department will do that for us. There is also other data that I won't even get into, that tells us what our viewers are doing—the average viewer likes to garden, hike, is between this and that age, is a fan of *Seinfeld,* or was a fan of *Seinfeld,* and on Thursday night likes to go out and drink martinis. You can get that detailed!

I choose what to cover based on viewer interest and press responsibility. For example, the fighting in Kosovo is not a local story. But a human drama is playing out in Kosovo. We are making history there. So, I do something on Kosovo every night in our newscast, because I think it has huge ramifications. Our children will be studying what we are watching unfold. Of course, it helps if there's a local angle on a national story. If some people over there are local, then we could argue that it becomes a local story, too.

You know, you can sit and talk to producers who will say, "We have to do stories that matter to people." Well, lots of stories matter to people. "We have to have a lot of pacing." Well, I've done newscasts that had six stories, but they've been six great stories, and I've also done newscasts that had twenty-three stories. I often equate producing to a buffet line. You look at your choic- |

es, and you put together the best, or the most nutritious, meal that you can for the viewers. Sometimes it's a low-fat meal, sometimes you want two desserts. It depends on what news is available and if you can make it appealing.

Dr. Bauer: How do you deal with incumbents who don't want to talk? In the Lamm–Campbell Senate race, Dottie Lamm kept trying to get Senator Campbell to come out and talk. And he pretty much ignored her, which is a typical front-runner strategy. What do you see as your role in that? There are voters out there; there is a challenger who is trying to get the incumbent to talk; the incumbent is sitting back. Do you pursue people in office and try to get them to comment, or do you take "No comment" for an answer?

Jene Nelson: It depends. For example, if an allegation were made, if Candidate A said about the incumbent Candidate B, "This person is a low-down dirty dog and gets drunk and kicks his poodle on the weekends," then we would in fact pursue Candidate B and ask, "What do you have to say in response to this?"

But if Candidate A says, "I think we ought to do this," and we ask Candidate B for a response, and Candidate B says, "No comment, I am not going to debate with Candidate A," then we can't do much more. Everyone has a right to say "No," to refuse an interview. We can only report that "Candidate B declined to comment." And sometimes Candidate B's declining to comment speaks much louder than anything he might say! I think it is important to ask the question; we just can't force somebody to give an answer. Tonight, for example, there's an interview I really want us to get, and I don't know if we will, but we can't make somebody talk to us.

Sonya: What advice, if any, would you give to a viewer who isn't educated in politics and is getting information strictly from your newscast?

Jene Nelson: We have supplemental information available on the Web. I know not everyone has a computer, but they have access to one through public libraries. We started a "9News" Web page, and we have everything outlined on that page, especially during election season. In the last election, the Web page was wonderful; it was a whole voter's guide.

Education is up to the viewers. In twelve minutes, we can't teach everything there is to know about political issues. We can't go in-depth, but we can give an overview and let viewers know what's out there for them to explore. You can get a lot more about a story on PBS than on a local network affiliate, because they have more time to spend on their stories—they don't have commercials breaking in.

Clint: I'd like to ask how you deal with scandal. We had a "Clintonesque" scandal here in Colorado when Governor Romer was being pursued by this Washington, D.C., guy who apparently had videotape of the governor kissing some woman who was not his wife. How did you decide to cover the scandal of him and his aide having some sort of affair?

Jene Nelson: That coverage was straightforward. When the allegations started coming out, Roy Romer called his news conference right there at the Denver airport. In

	other instances, we call and confront the person with the allegations against him or her and give them a chance to deny it or tell their side of the story. We say, "We hear this . . . . Do you have anything you would like to say about this matter?" If they are pursued and hounded, they will hold a news conference.
Sonya:	Governor Romer's sex scandal was only on the news for one or two news cycles, because Romer was smart and called a press conference to talk about it, rather than repeat the Clinton strategy of stonewalling.
Jene Nelson:	If somebody speaks directly to the allegation, the story dies a lot sooner than if they keep dodging the bullet, because there's no intrigue left. When somebody talks, there's really not much for us to say. After Roy Romer said, "Yes, I have had this relationship. Yes, my wife Bea knows about it. It was an affectionate relationship, not a sexual one," what is left to say? We could have decided to go and see what Bea Romer had to say, or asked his lover what she had to say, but at that point, it was almost a dead issue. Because where do you ethically go with that?
Dr. Bauer:	Were you here when former Colorado senator and presidential candidate Gary Hart went through his sex scandal disaster?
Jene Nelson:	I was not here. But I was in Colorado at KOAA-TV Pueblo–Colorado Springs and covered it there.
Dr. Bauer:	How would you contrast the way each politician handled his scandal?
Jene Nelson:	I'm trying to think back. I remember that Senator Gary Hart was running for president; he announced right here in Denver. There were a lot of rumors that Gary played around. Then he essentially dared the *Miami Herald* to get something on him. They got pictures and went with the story. He had, again, a wife who stood by him at all the news conferences, but then later on, he pulled out of the race. His political career was over, and he didn't even run for reelection to the Senate.
	It was a scandal that he couldn't recover from; it just killed him. I think we live in a different world now. We are less worried about who is having a fling with whom and more concerned about job performance. I think the fact that President Clinton, in the middle of a horrendous sex scandal, still has a high job approval rating reflects that.
Mike:	I have a couple of questions about election night coverage. How do you decide when somebody has won?
Clint:	Yeah, how do you *call a race?*
Jene Nelson:	We have a political analyst, Floyd Ciruli—you've probably seen him on the air. That's his job. Politics is his life. Every election night that I've been here, Floyd has been here as well. Even when you don't see him on the screen, throughout the campaign and election he's right here, telling us how the candidates are doing, breaking things down, saying, "This means that," doing polls for us, analyzing turnout, doing predictions based on his knowledge of past races here in town.

Dr. Bauer:	Has he ever made a mistake on a political race?
Jene Nelson:	Not that I recall. A producer can only do so much. I rely on the staff. And luckily, they are a lot more professional than that bozo down in Las Vegas who just read everything from the TelePrompTer!

★ ★ ★

For Additional Reading

Go to InfoTrac College Edition, your online research library at

http://web1.infotrac-college.com

Enter the following search terms using the Subject Guide or Key Terms.

leak	presidential press coverage	selective perception
media	press conference	sound bite
political bias	scoop	

11 The Legislative Branch

MONICA BAUER

A PERSONAL PERSPECTIVE ON Congress

IN JANUARY 1997, I WAS SITTING IN A CRAMPED OFFICE FULL of half-empty boxes on Capitol Hill. Buzzing around me were two small girls, aged four and seven. An older girl was playing hide-and-seek with them around an overstuffed sofa. A tall, thin man called out to the two little ones: "Frannie, Raphaella, come on! You don't want to miss your mother's swearing in, do you?" An older woman smiled and said how much her late husband would have loved to have seen this. I caught the eye of Diana DeGette, the congresswoman-elect, and we exchanged a knowing look. Diana's stepmother, Nell DeGette, was right: Diana's father would have loved to have seen it, as would her mother, who had died seven years before. This was Diana's day to be happy, but there was a touch of sadness about it, too.

The congresswoman-elect was my friend. We became friends when she started dating my best friend from college, a tall, thin boy from New York with the preposterous name of Lino Lipinsky de Orlov, Jr. He had started at Brown University at age sixteen. I was the opposite: short, round, from Nebraska, and a twenty-two-year-old sophomore. We had both left high school early, but he left for acceptance at an Ivy League school, and I dropped out to become a musician. I was one of the few people ever accepted as a transfer student with a GED. In short, I had nothing in common with anybody at Brown, and I was badly in need of a friend. My name was Monica Elizabeth Teply Mills, and I was about to make my name shorter.

While Lino helped me find my way around Brown, I found my way around a divorce and built a new life. The Brown University dorms brought us together, side-by-side in a coed suite. A friendship began that has lasted more than twenty-three years.

Lino, a political junkie who worked on the student newspaper and eventually became its editor, tried to get me into campus politics. I ran for student government on a platform of *agape,* the Greek word for "selfless love." Running for office was Lino's idea; the losing platform was completely my own. Lino's advice, then as now, was right on the money. I ignored him at my own peril: *Agape* didn't cut it in 1977.

In 1979, when we all graduated and I married Neil Bauer, Lino was in the wedding party. If I could have had a best man, I would have picked him. He went off to NYU Law School, and I went off with my new husband and new name to the Yale Divinity School. When our daughter, Joanna, was born, Lino was one of the first friends to visit us in New Haven. That's when he asked me if I could come visit him in New York. He had somebody he wanted me to meet. A fellow law student and president of their class, she came from Denver, Colorado. Her name was Diana DeGette. In 1984, I was an ordained minister in the middle of a run for Congress. I gave up a weekend of campaigning to perform their wedding.

In 1992, both Diana and I ran for state representative in our respective districts: mine in Massachusetts, where I had settled after leaving the ministry and becoming a political science professor; hers in her hometown, where her family had roots going back four generations. I ran against an incumbent (a bad habit) and lost. Diana ran in a new district where there was no incumbent and she was the party favorite . . . and won.

One afternoon in November 1995, while listening to NPR on my car radio, I heard Pat Schroeder, the legendary congresswoman from Denver, make the surprise announcement that she would retire after serving twenty-four years in the House. I drove like a maniac straight home and called Lino and Diana. "Of course, you are going to run," I said. Well, it turned out she did.

In August 1996, I became a small part of Diana's primary election campaign. My duties included driving the candidate to and from an emergency root canal and babysitting Frannie and Raphaella on primary election night. And that's why my husband, fifteen-year-old Joanna, and I were sitting in the office of a new member of Congress in January 1997 about to watch the swearing in.

Most voters see Congress as a cesspool of corrupt politicians. Because of the size of congressional districts, it is rare that any of us ever personally meets our member of Congress unless we make an effort to do so. And the news about Congress and the representatives and senators whom so few of us know personally is usually bad news. Congressional dogfights are covered by the press until *conflict* is the only word we associate with Congress. The words *politician* and *scandal* have been linked so often in the public press, going back to the very founding of the government, that it seems most people would rather their son or daughter marry a garbage collector than a career politician. It hasn't helped that we have had divided government—a recipe for congressional frustration. When things go wrong in American society, it is simple and easy to blame those "politicians in Washington." And when things go well, the best Congress can hope for is a little bump up in public approval, but no permanent change in its image. I want my students to see past all that.

My friend and graduate-school mentor, John Hibbing, understands the difference between the public image of Congress and the reality of the people who work for us there. When he was a graduate student, he wrote his doctoral dissertation on why members of Congress leave. He interviewed dozens of men and women of goodwill from both parties and came away with a respect for them as people and as legislators. He passed that respect on to me when I studied with him at the University of Nebraska. In his most recent book, *Congress as Public Enemy: Public Attitudes Toward American Political Institutions* (co-authored with Elizabeth Theiss-Morse), John argues that the public has contempt for Congress because it is doing what it is *supposed* to do—that is, bargain, compromise, respond to local interest groups, and move as fast as the constitutional constraints of a bicameral system with a presidential veto will allow. Criticizing Congress for being partisan, slow, or making deals is like criticizing an apple for being red or because it doesn't taste like chocolate.

When Diana DeGette was sworn in as a new member of Congress, I knew she was joining one of the least-respected groups in American society. I also knew that, since she was not a publicity hound, she would get very little media coverage. As a pro-choice congresswoman, she would have pro-life pickets showing up at her house. As a major proponent of gun control, she would get letters that verged on death threats—and sometimes go over the line. (I know from personal experience: I got letters like that from NRA activists when I was just a candidate for Congress.) She would have to work crazy hours and squeeze in time for her kids. She would have to hire staff, thereby making enemies of those she didn't hire, and occasionally have to fire staff, thus making more enemies.

Her Denver friends might be offended when she doesn't have time to return their calls. Her Washington friends might be more interested in her for political than social reasons. She would lose some of each over time.

In return, she would have the chance to change public policy the only way it gets done: in the trenches, knowing the details, being just a little bit more tenacious than the people who don't want your side to win. I don't worry about Diana—she's a born legislator the way some people are born athletes—I worry that my students may never meet anyone like her and never imagine that a congressional career can be more than sleaze and scandal. And never imagine that members of Congress have mothers who die of lung cancer, fathers who die of heart attacks, and kids who get sick. And a husband who still, occasionally, wants to spend time with that person he met, the young law-school class president who took him on his first hike through the Rockies.

National Busybodies: Congress

P. J. O'Rourke

Feeling good about government is like looking on the bright side of any catastrophe. When you quit looking on the bright side, the catastrophe is still there. The euphoria of the Bush inauguration wore off, and the government remained in its usual form—whatever that is—and persisted in its usual actions—whatever they may be.

The three branches of government number considerably more than three and are not, in any sense, "branches" since that would imply that there is something they are all attached to besides self-aggrandizement and our pocketbooks. I never determined how many sections there really are to the federal system. It probably can't be done. Government is not a machine with parts; it's an organism. When does an intestine quit being an intestine and start becoming an asshole? Nor did I ever determine any valuable rule for examining the branches of government, except one: If you want to know what an institution does, watch it when it's doing nothing.

On one of those warm and luminous spring days when the soul would fain soar free and the conscious mind wanders in reveries of—at my age—reseeding the lawn, I went to Capitol Hill and spent the day indoors watching the House of Representatives.

The House chamber—which, according to the Capitol building's tour brochure, is "the largest national parliamentary room in the world"—isn't as big as an old fashioned downtown movie theater nor as elaborately decorated, though the carpet is just as loud. The walls are covered in fussy Victorian paper on a background the color of fake Wedgwood china.

Reprinted with permission of Grove/Atlantic, Inc., from *Parliament of Whores: A Lone Humorist Attempts to Explain the Entire U.S. Government* by P. J. O'Rourke. Published by Atlantic Monthly Press. © 1991 by P. J. O'Rourke.

Editor's Note: This classic essay is a decade old but remains relevant in its description of Congress.

There are lots of brass whim-whams and a remarkable number of doors (which do not, however, result in many quick exits from political life). Above the doors are medallions bearing bas-relief profiles of mankind's great and reasonably great lawgivers: Moses, Solomon, Alfonso X, Solon, Hammurabi, Pope Innocent III. No U.S. congressmen are included.

The only impressive part of the room is the three-tiered dais where the Speaker of the House sits with his minders and butt boys. And this is only slightly more impressive than the set for the "Here Comes the Judge" skit of the old "Laugh-In" show. The speaker occupies a large chair in front of a large flag, and bracketing the flag are two huge gilded fasces. These pre-date Mussolini—at least I hope they do.

A visitor's gallery runs around three sides of the place, to let the public come hear the commonweal talked away. On the fourth side, above the speaker's dais, is a steep and narrow balcony, a pigeon's paradise for journalists. Electric tote boards hang below the gallery rails showing what is being voted on and giving a running tabulation of the yeas and nays so Congressmen can tell which way their own wind is blowing. The ceiling is bordered with the seals of all the states—a plethora of sunrises, wheat sheaves, spear-carrying ladies in Liberty caps and tamed Indians.

The House convened at the gentlemanly hour of 11:00 A.M. and the session began, as sessions customarily do (unless something big like a war or a farm-price-support bill is afoot), with "One Minutes." These are speeches of said duration that any member may make on any subject. As a tool of political debate the One Minute cannot be very effective, at least not on the day I was there—only eighteen congressmen were in the place, and they were waiting to make One Minutes of their own.

The Democratic One Minute speechmakers had gotten together to exploit the approach of Earth Day. Each Democrat brought a poster to the microphone; each poster bore a quotation from George Bush on subjects ecological; and across each quotation was printed, in red stenciled lettering, "PROMISE BROKEN." The point was, I think, that President Bush had promised to clean up the environment, and now, a year and a half after his election, the environment was still not clean. The Democrats, with their posters propped on easels, looked like Amway salesmen touting pyramid franchising schemes. Although, in fact, more than half the members of Congress are lawyers, so that comparison is very unfair to Amway.

For the sake of political balance Republicans interpolated themselves among the Democrats. But the Republicans lacked an issue *du jour.* Thus ten Democrats fumbling with posters alternated with ten Republicans simply fumbling. Of the Republicans:

No. 1 was inaudible.

No. 2 wanted the Florida barge canal returned to Florida.

No. 3 was against international terrorism.

No. 4 was in favor of tiny, beleaguered Lithuania.

No. 5 had a new plan to end the budget deficit.

No. 6 was very much in favor of tiny, beleaguered Lithuania.

No. 7 was irked by tort law.

No. 8 eulogized a dead city councilman from Syracuse, New York.

No. 9 (I missed this one. I had to go to the bathroom.)

No. 10 was in favor of the census.

The members of the House are, to a man (and twenty-nine women), ridiculously bad at public speaking. Indeed, they don't speak at all; they read from prepared texts and are ridiculously bad at

reading. Every clause is an exclamatory declaration. Every verb is in the present tense. Every subject is second person plural. You can tell, without watching, when a congressman has reached the bottom of a page—there will come a dramatic caesura, a full stop that lasts, no matter its violence to sense, until that page has been turned and the words at the top of the next page kenned.

We are in a position! To mandate the expenditure! Of great amounts of money! By state and local governments! But we are not! [rustle of paper] Giving them financial aid!

said a Democrat from Massachusetts.

In every speech there is, however, one little section the congressman has managed to memorize. His head will come up from this typescript. He will boldly gaze at his (in this case nonexistent) audience. And, with only one or two deep breaths to buoy his confidence, he will recite his piece.

Our polluting ways! Are destroying our waterways!

said a Democrat from Mississippi.

The Democrats ended their "promise broken" presentation, but the One Minutes continued. Money laundering, Frank Lorenzo, U.S. trade policy, radioactivity, Stalin, Hitler and discrimination against people who have Hispanic surnames were denounced. Earth Day was praised. The navy was scolded for blaming a battleship gun-turret explosion on a person who lived in a member's district. Blue Cross was taken to task for something about bone marrow. It was questioned whether banning China from a conference on global warming was a fit punishment for the events of Tiananmen Square. It was noted that President Reagan had been a very popular president. A member stated that the number of homeless in America exceeds the population of Atlanta. (It doesn't.) A member from

Kentucky announced the presentation of a Kentucky Earth Day Award, the recipient being himself. A dead senator was praised. So was an animated cartoon meant to combat drug abuse. An ecology-conscious Republican—in a very Republican piece of ecology consciousness—said he'd just come back from the Bahamas, and, boy, were the beaches littered. He proposed a tax on non-biodegradable items that litter beaches. Lax enforcement of the ivory trade ban was rebuked. And a parliamentary inquiry was made under the One Minute Rule about why there were so many One Minutes today.

A few more members of Congress had strolled in by now, for a total of twenty-five or thirty on the House floor. Two hundred regular citizens were in the visitor's galleries. And one member of the press—me—was in the press section. The congressmen stood in the aisles chatting. The public perched on their seats staring. And I just sat doing nothing. I was not even, to judge from my notes, taking notes.

Finally the One Minutes ended, and somebody moved that this be National Crime Something-or-Other Week, which motion carried. After that a clerk read a bill called H.R. 644 to amend the Wild and Scenic Rivers Act by designating the east fork of the Jemez and Pecos rivers in New Mexico, read it so quickly that I could understand nothing about the bill except what its name stated. Then the speaker of the House recognized someone. (A telling concept, "recognized." The average representative has been in office for over nine years, so there aren't many strangers here.) This wasn't the real speaker speaking, however; this was the speaker pro tem, who is anybody the speaker wants it to be—usually someone who needs to have his picture taken in a large chair for campaign purposes. Another reporter came into the press section, peered down at the speaker pro tem, said, "Who the fuck is that?" and left.

The person whom the speaker pro tem recognized, a Democrat, extolled the Wild and Scenic Rivers Act, saying it was clearly an act that designated—as wild and scenic—rivers.

A Republican got up and said the Wild and Scenic Rivers Act was a swell bill and H.R. 644 was a heck of a fine amendment to it, or words to that effect, except many more of them. He finally sat down.

A Democrat who was actually from New Mexico said the same thing again and, in a fit of bipartisanism, thanked everybody there (although, as I pointed out, hardly anybody was) for supporting H.R. 644. "The Pecos River originated in the geologically significant Sangre de Cristo Mountains," said the Democrat, not wanting us to confuse these with any geologically insignificant mountains, which may be found elsewhere. "There was threat of development," he said. (That is, people making livings, building homes, staking out a future for themselves and their children—as a good environmentalist one shudders at the thought). And, said the Democrat, an amendment to the amendment was needed to ban the strip-mining of pumice stone within a quarter mile of these rivers. You would think that if a river were designated as wild and scenic, a ban on strip-mining within a quarter mile of it would go without saying, but apparently not.

A lone Republican objected to the amendment to the amendment, and someone objected to the objection. A dozen congressmen wandered away, and a desultory debate ensued among the remaining members. From this debate I learned that the mining of pumice stone along the Jemez and Pecos rivers always was and wasn't ever highly destructive to plant and animal life, that mine operators invariably did and obviously didn't restore the mined areas to their original condition and that mining claims in the area are adequately regulated and completely unsupervised by existing laws. The strip-mining ban passed by a voice vote of about fifteen yeas and one nay, after which one of the congressmen noted in passing that the House of Representatives had just legislated the stone-washed denim industry out of existence.

Meanwhile a number of children on a school tour or something had been led onto the floor and allowed to sit in some of the many empty congressmen seats. They fidgeted briefly and were led out. A vote on H.R. 644 itself was called. Voting in the House of Representatives is done by means of a little plastic card with a magnetic strip on the back—like a VISA card but with no, that is, absolutely *no,* spending limit. These cards are inserted into slots in boxes mounted on the back of the aisle seats—one box for yes, one box for no and one box (the one very few congressmen had any excuse for using) for present. The congressmen had fifteen minutes to vote. Pretty soon there were congressmen coming in through the doors in strings of ten or a dozen, like picnic ants, until 90 percent of the representatives we have had appeared on the floor. No opposition candidate back home was going to accuse them of letting rivers be nonwild or unscenic. H.R. 644 passed 391 to 1.

The clutter of members milled around clasping hands, gripping shoulders and patting arms as though they were campaigning for election by each other instead of by the somewhat mystified public in the balconies above. The leader of the Democrats in the House (and sometime presidential hopeful), Richard Gephardt, stepped to a microphone on the floor and announced that, it being almost three in the afternoon, legislative business was finished for the day—finished for the week, too, since this was a Thursday. Congressman Gephardt then listed some of the wonderful things Congress would do when it reconvened on Tuesday next. Newt Gingrich, the number-two man among Republicans in the House, went to another microphone on the floor and said to congressman Gephardt (though they could easily have heard each other without amplification), "Since you did all those tough One Minutes, when will we see the clean-air bill out of committee?" This was apparently a very funny thing to say, because they both laughed for a long time. Then all the representatives who'd given those One Minutes pestered the speaker pro tem for permission to "revise and extend their remarks." That is, they wanted carefully typed versions of their speeches rather than ver-

batim transcripts to go on record so that they won't sound as stupid in history as I've made them sound in journalism.

The congressmen then drifted away, except for one or two who were going to speak to a completely empty chamber in what are called "Special Orders." These are speeches made only for the sake of the *Congressional Record* and the C-SPAN television coverage of Congress. As I left, a representative from Illinois was holding forth to the ether—with all the gestures, tropes and intonations appropriate to a demagogue swaying thousands—on the virtues of a high-school basketball team in his district, state champions with a record of 36 and 0.

Was this an average day in Congress? No. On an average day Congress isn't there at all. Congress only meets about 145 days a year.

This is not to say that congressmen are lazy. I followed one around for a day—a highly respected congressman from a fine political party representing an excellent district of a lovely state (and one who would just as soon not have his name in a book by me). The congressman had an 8:00 A.M. breakfast meeting in the Cannon Building (named, as all three House of Representative office buildings are, after former speakers of no distinction) with an informal group of ideologically like-minded colleagues. They discussed ways to stifle that beggar's army of liberals that dominates the House, but I don't think they came up with anything surefire. At 8:30 there was a second breakfast meeting, in the Rayburn Building, this time for the executive committee of a private club on Capitol Hill where influence gets pedaled, horses get traded, logs get rolled and metaphors get tired.

By 9:30 the congressman had to be down the hall at a Housing and Community Development Subcommittee hearing. Testimony was being given about the squalid living conditions in apartment complexes run by A. Bruce Rozet, one of the nation's largest developers of federally subsidized low-income housing. The Republicans on the subcommittee were furious at Rozet for renting apartments with "boarded windows . . . broken fire doors, crumbling walls and incredible filth." The Democrats on the subcommittee were furious at the Republicans for pointing out that Rozet was a major Democratic campaign contributor and served as a Jesse Jackson delegate at the 1988 Democratic convention. A former tenant of a Rozet development was just plain furious. And if the tenant's testimony about how the squalor in her apartment got so squalid is anything to go by, A. Bruce Rozet was probably furious at her:

> I am a recovering drug addict. I became addicted to crack-cocaine three years ago. I started using crack at Glenarden Apartments. . . . During the time using, I was going to school for data entry. I would come home and study but would become sleepy. So I thought that if I would smoke a little crack I could stay up and study longer. But there was not much success in that, then my addiction progressed more . . . and eventually I started running a crack house.
>
> I invited drug dealers in to sell drugs, store guns and money. In turn they would give me money and drugs. Then things became out of hand. . . . As a result of constant fighting and other distasteful conduct, my apartment became destroyed and unfit to live. (Examples of this would be: All of my doors were knocked off the hinges. My furniture became dirty and broken. . . . The commode was stopped up from human waste, which led them to use cups and other cooking utensils for the toilet. In general there was large holes knocked through the walls, light fixtures destroyed throughout. All of my clothing were scattered everywhere. I never used the closet.)

Amazing stuff. But the congressman didn't have time for amazement. He was due in the Longworth Building at 10:00 A.M. for a meeting of the Merchant Marine and Fisheries Committee. This committee intended to "mark up" (that is, fool around with) six different pieces of legislation that, if approved by a majority of the

committee members, would be sent to the House of Representatives to be fooled around with some more.

One bill authorized spending half a billion dollars to keep America's practically nonexistent merchant fleet in tip-top shape. Another bill gave $600 million to the National Oceanic and Atmospheric Administration for, I guess, Americans who find themselves up in the air or out to sea. A third bill "explicitly requires states to adopt or revise new coastal water quality standards based on EPA-promulgated water quality criteria." Which means, I think, that if you go to the beach this summer and the ocean is too cold for swimming, you can complain to the government. The fourth bill was a nonbinding resolution urging the president to work with Congress to "establish a comprehensive national oceans and Great Lakes policy." (Keep them filled with water would be my suggestion.) The fifth bill was exactly the same as the sixth bill except more carefully worded, to make sure that whatever the sixth bill did remained under the purview of the Merchant Marine and Fisheries Committee. And nobody knew what the sixth bill was supposed to do. It was called H.R. 4030, the reauthorization of the coastal-zone management act, and according to the summary handed out to committee members, its provisions all seemed to be obvious—"Defines 'coastal zone'"; weird—"recognizes sea level rise"; or weirdly obvious—"amends Coastal Zone Management Act findings and policies to indicate that development in the coastal zone must occur with environmental safeguards." The bill also "authorizes awards for excellence in coastal zone management" and, of especially vital importance to the nation, "changes the name of the National Estuarine Reserve Research System to National Estuarine Research Reserve System." Some nineteen amendments to this bill were also proposed, including one to name the award for excellence in coastal-zone management after the Merchant Marine and Fisheries Committee chairman.

This chairman was exceedingly old and supported on each side by members of the committee staff. These behaved toward the chairman like the "flappers" of Laputa in *Gulliver's Travels,* whom the abstracted Laputians employed to strike them now and then and remind them what they were doing.

A representative from Louisiana pointed out that under the terms of the technical language in H.R. 4030, 50 percent of his state was coastal wetland and thereby federally prohibited from any use by humans.

A representative from Alaska waved H.R. 4030 in the air and shouted, "Anybody who knows what's in this bill raise his hand."

Would half the population of Louisiana have to move to Arkansas? Would the committee ever figure out what it was voting on? Would the chairman stay awake? I'm sure the congressman would like to know, too. But we had to go. The House of Representatives was meeting at noon.

You already know what a meeting of the House of Representatives is like.

At 1:00 P.M. the congressman went back to his office in the Longworth Building to meet volunteer firemen from his congressional district. They were shy and husky men in wool-blend sport coats that gaped at the back of the neck, and they gaped a bit themselves to be in the actual private office of a real congressman. (Members of the House have, on average, about six hundred thousand constituents and are thus governmentally no more important than a mayor of Indianapolis. But the Indianapolis Motor Speedway isn't on the back of a fifty-dollar bill.)

The congressman is genuinely likable—as most politicians are, whether they ought to be or not—and the firemen genuinely like him. The congressman was interested in the volunteer firemen. Politicians *are* interested in people. Not that this is always a virtue. Fleas are interested in dogs. And—though the congressman had suffered a torch juggler's schedule all morning and was due across the street at the Rayburn Building in fifteen minutes—he treated the firemen to the same gracious and unhurried welcome that you or I would give to the Joint Chiefs of Staff if they happened to drop by our house.

The volunteer firemen were in Washington for a national convention. Besides sight-seeing and middle-aged, convention-style high jinks, they were pushing legislation in Congress. I believe they wanted everything in the country fireproofed. The congressman was frank with them. Politicians are not only likable and interested in people, they even tell the truth sometimes. (Though whether this says a lot for the politicians or very little for the truth depends.) The congressman told the firemen that he, too, thought everything should be fireproof. But before he decided how to vote, he would have to find out how much making America nonflammable would cost the public. The firemen gave him a fireman's hat.

At 1:15 the congressman went to be briefed on the European Bank for Reconstruction and Development. Why an American congressman needs a briefing on a bank for frog swallowers, bucket heads and various kinds of garlic nibblers who are already so reconstructed and developed that they're buying the United States in wholesale lots is a good question. If you find the answer, the congressman would like to hear it.

By 2:00 the congressman was back in his office, lunchless and working with his staff. When a congressman sits down with the people who work for him, the result is a sort of college-finals cram session. Congress meddles in every part of American life and then some. Congressional legislation reaches beyond the grave with estate taxes and back into those clouds of glory that Wordsworth says we trail when it touches upon abortion issues. A congressman needs to be informed about it all. During this particular week in the spring of 1990 the following bills, motions and resolutions were burrowing, meandering, sneaking, breezing, slipping or being pushed through the legislative process:

1. A five-year omnibus farm bill to pay the people who own the ground where we dig the hole that we pour our tax dollars down

2. A commodities futures trading commission reauthorization act to make sure the com-

modities market is as well regulated as, say, the savings and loan industry

3. A proposal to further complicate the above-mentioned commodities market complications

4. Consideration of who gets to be on the commission that will accomplish numbers 2 and 3 above

5. A food safety act to fund research into whether it's safe to eat food

6. Pesticide control to control the controlling of pests

7. Rural-development legislation to preserve rural life in the parts of America that remain rural because they're undeveloped

8. Supplemental appropriations for 180 miscellaneous items that Congress forgot to appropriate money for, including $1 million for family planning in Romania

9. Regular appropriations for everything else

10. A defense bill to defend us from the Soviet Union

11-14. Four treaties with the Soviet Union to do the reverse

15. A nonbinding *kvetch* about our allies not paying their fair share of number 10

16. A bill to sell fighter planes to Koreans (though whether these are the Koreans in Korea or the Koreans who own grocery stores in Harlem, the bill does not say)

17. A bill to close unnecessary military bases unless those bases are overseas or in a congressman's district

18. A bill seeking "alternative nondefense uses for defense facilities"—aiming our ICBMs at Sally Jessy Raphael, for example

19. A housing bill to house people such as the young lady who testified at the Housing and Community Development Subcommittee hearing about not using her closets

20. A homeless housing bill to house people even worse than her

21-25. Four bills regulating U.S. exports, assuming we have any

And that, one would think, is about the limit of the human capacity for expertise. To be con-

versant with twenty-five disparate issues at once is as much as we can ask of a person. However, it is less than 10 percent of what we ask of a congressman. During this same week in 1990, 250 other items were also on the congressional calendar, including:

the federal budget
money laundering by organized crime
local bank check-cashing rules
whether the same truck can haul food and garbage, too
fish hatcheries
highway safety
outer space
children's television
airline ticket prices
phone service for the disabled
phone service for the rest of us
national forests
cable TV
whether Puerto Rico should be a state or a nation or what
indoor air quality
outdoor air quality
oil spills
oil shale
groundwater
coastal water
water resource development
tariffs
the economy of the Caribbean
tax-free retirement plans
Panama
Eastern Europe
El Salvador
South Africa
the Washington, DC, subway
civil service pay reform
whether federal employees can wear political campaign buttons to work
crime

price-fixing

immigration

the line-item veto

math and science education

vocational education (not to be confused with math and science education or job training)

job training (not to be confused with vocational education or getting a job)

public health

private health

family planning (other than that done in Romania)

child care for when the family planning doesn't work out

parental leave so that those parents who failed to practice family planning and now need child care can get some time off from work to screw the baby-sitter

nutritional labeling

guaranteed job security for federal employees who peach on their bosses

voter registration

veterans who were exposed to radiation

small businesses

whether presidential primaries should be held in groups, like AA meetings or something

how much free mail members of the Senate should be allowed to inflict upon the public

and, of all things,

paperwork reduction

We expect our congressman to know more about each of these than we know about any of them. We expect him to make wiser decisions than we can about them all. And we expect that congressman to make those wise and knowledgeable decisions without regard for his political or financial self-interest. Then we wonder why it's hard to get first-rate people to run for Congress.

So here was the congressman I was following, a good and conscientious congressman desperately trying to master all 275 of these issues during the approximately two hours a day when he didn't absolutely have to be somewhere else. What could he do but cheat? Congressmen have crib sheets. They're called voting cards. They are eight inches long and four inches wide—just the right size to slip into a suit coat's inside pocket. They look like this:

Bill Number: H.R. a billion-zillion

Title: Fiddlemeyer-O'Houligan Unbelievable Grocery Bill

Info: Amends the federal anti-trust laws to make the price of everything reasonable, like it used to be, and includes provisions requiring kids today to listen up when their dad talks to them

Committee Action: Passed by the House Means and Ends Committee 3/17/90

Home: Constituents will murder you in November if you oppose it.

Administration: President will kill you right now if you support it.

Remarks: A toughie

Prior Votes: The 100th Congress was going to pass it, but a lobbyist ate their copy of the legislation.

Recommendation: Hide in the cloakroom during floor vote.

After his staff work the congressman went into a brief flurry of signing correspondence, well, not actually signing it—there's a machine that does that—but a brief flurry of looking at correspondence to make sure the machine hadn't signed anything horrifying. Then the congressman rushed to the Cannon Building for a 4:00 P.M. meeting of his "class"—the congressmen of his own party who were first elected the same year he was. A congressional class is one of the hundreds of groups and subgroups within the Congress that constantly coalesce and disperse like the stuff inside a lava lamp, and to about the same effect. At 5:00 P.M. the congressman attended another political get-together, this one for important members of his party from all walks of life (except, presumably—though I may be hasty in this presumption—jail).

From 5:30 until 9:00 the congressman had to be at the National Fire and Emergency Services Dinner at one hotel while, from 6:00 to 8:00 he had to be with the governor of his state at another dinner in another hotel on the other side of town. But a good politician can be two places at once when it comes to public appearances, just as a good politician can be no place at several different times when it comes to public issues.

Myself, I was completely exhausted by 7:00 and went home, leaving the congressman, twenty years my senior, looking as animated and energetic as a full school bus—shaking hands and trading chat with governor, firemen, ambulance drivers, other congressmen and even, at one point, his own wife.

This, according to the congressman's staff, was a "light day." The congressman normally spends three such days a week in Washington—Tuesday through Thursday—then flys halfway across the nation to his congressional district and spends Friday, Saturday and Monday doing more of the same at lectures, dinners, town-hall meetings and his two constituent service offices. He takes one week of vacation in August, one week at Christmas and one week at Easter. And he does all this for $125,100 per year, which, for all the public's caterwauling over the congressional pay raise, is less than what a shortstop hitting .197 makes.

The public—or things such as *Newsweek* that pass themselves off as the public—have also caterwauled about the size and cost of congressional staffs. This congressman has nine staff members: an administrative assistant, or AA, who is to the congressman as a master sergeant is to the lieutenant in an army platoon; three legislative assistants, or LAs, who hack through the legislative tangles and walk across the political mire of all the bills before Congress; two support

staffers to man phones, word processors and signature-writing machines; two case workers in the district offices to cope with voters; and one field representative to visit shut-ins, plus a few unpaid interns and volunteers.

The inefficiency of government as compared with private enterprise is, everywhere, an item of faith. Even the most socialistic of pundits bothers us with this simile. But a company with six hundred thousand customers would have more than nine employees. And pay them more, too. A congressman's allowance for hiring staff is $441,120. And the members of this staff, in return for salaries of between $20,000 and $80,000, have to do all the exhausting and exasperating things the congressman does without the gratifications of getting on the evening news.

Thus we Americans have struck a remarkable bargain. We pay $566,220 a year—less than a dollar apiece—for a congressman and his staff, and in return they listen to us carp and moan and fume and gripe and ask to be given things for free. Because this is, in the end, what legislators do. They listen to us. Not an enviable task.

The congressman whom I was shadowing, who is not the best-known member of the House and who does not represent a famously querulous district, gets thirty-eight thousand constituent inquiries a year, mostly letters, all of them answered within ten days. Some of this is crank mail, but not enough. Crank mail at least amuses the staff, and good crank letters go in the "Chuckles File." But these are answered, too. One constituent wrote every week for months saying that the CIA was using low-level pulsed microwave radiation to read his thoughts. Finally, the congressman suggested that he line his hat with tinfoil, and the fellow has not been heard from since.

Most of the inquiries, however, involve real things—all the things already mentioned that Congress is considering and all the things it has or will or might consider and all the world's other things besides. There are protests; appeals; calls for legislation to be passed, revoked and amended; letters on behalf of cousins who want to immigrate, sons who want to go to West Point and daughters who want civil service jobs; and problems with Medicare, the Veterans Administration, the IRS, the FHA, DOT, OSHA, AFDC, ABCDEFGHIJKLMNOP. There's something that must be done about each of these, say we voters; what's more, our Social Security check was late again last month. And out to every inquiry goes a respectful, responsible, dutiful reply, a reply that is as helpful as possible.

I read a week of the congressman's mail, more than seven hundred letters. There were exactly two thank-you notes in the pile.

FACE TO FACE

Student Interview with
Congresswoman Diana DeGette
(D-CO)

Jesse
a conservative
Libertarian

Suzanne
a moderate
Republican

Turi
a moderate
Democrat

Will
a moderate

What's It Like to Be a Member of Congress?
★ ★ ★

Will: What do you think your responsibilities and duties are as a member of Congress?

Diana DeGette: To represent my constituents and to improve public policy that is important nationally. For example, my work on kid's health care is important to people in my district, but it is also important to people all over the country. So I try to strike a balance between caring for the needs of my local constituents and dealing with national issues.

Turi: How do you decide what you need to focus on?

Diana DeGette: How do I pick my issues? Number one, my committee and subcommittee assignments give me the biggest opportunity to have an impact on an issue. That's why I've concentrated on health and environment issues, because my subcommittee has oversight over those issues. Number two, I pick issues in which I have an intense interest. Otherwise I won't delve into them as deeply as I could. It's very hard to focus on a few issues, especially early in a career,

	because you can focus on anything under the sun. But I think the most important thing for a member of Congress is to be focused. The people who are most successful in Congress are the ones who are most focused.
Will:	So how do you deal with the other issues that you may not be an expert on?
Diana DeGette:	I do my homework, and I hired a top-notch staff. It's very important to do both, because I need to vote on a variety of issues on a daily basis. For example, last week we had a bill on education one morning, then in the afternoon we debated Kosovo, and that's just one day. On issues that I don't deal with on a daily basis, I read summaries and turn to staff members who have expertise in areas I don't. I also think it's important to find a mentor, someone you generally agree with on issues, and turn to them when a bill has to do with their area of expertise. For something as big as Kosovo, I did a lot of reading, had several briefings from my staff, and then Secretary of State Albright came down to the Hill and gave a briefing to the whole Democratic caucus.
	Last week we had a hearing in my subcommittee on the date-rape drug. If there's a hearing or a markup of a bill in one of my subcommittees, I do background reading and get briefed by my staff. Already I'm beginning to develop areas of expertise so that I don't need as much prep time as I used to on certain issues.
Jesse:	How do you get along with other members of the delegation? Is the partisanship so thick that it's hard to work together and remember that you're all Coloradoans?
Diana DeGette:	I get along well with most members of the delegation on a personal basis. We have a small delegation, only eight of us, counting our two senators, and my view has always been that if we don't work together, we will lose out to other states with bigger delegations, like California.
Dr. Bauer:	We have been reading about campaign finance and campaign finance reform. How do you feel about these issues?
Diana DeGette:	Under the current law, there are some big loopholes. If a tobacco company wanted to give me five thousand dollars, I'd have to report that on a Federal Election Commission disclosure form. Then, after a vote was taken on a tobacco bill, the press, my constituents, could look and see who got money from what group, and they could publicize the link between money and politics. Rather than face that, I could say to a tobacco company, "Instead of giving me five thousand dollars, why don't you just spend fifty thousand dollars on an 'independent expenditure campaign'? That won't show up on my disclosure forms, and I'd get a lot more help toward reelection." That's the problem with the campaign laws.
	If you eliminate PAC money, as some have suggested, but continue to limit contributions from individuals to one thousand dollars apiece, two things happen: One, candidates with no personal wealth are shut out of the process. Under *Buckley* v. *Valeo*, the Supreme Court ruled that rich candidates could spend as much of their own money as they chose, while ordinary people like

me, without PACs to help us, would be unable to run. Two, eliminating PACs encourages massive independent expenditure campaigns. Special interest groups are going to find some way to contribute to campaigns; if they can't contribute directly to a campaign because we've shut down PACs, they will run their own campaigns for or against candidates. These independent expenditure campaigns are legal, and there are no limits on the money raised and spent for them.

The two reforms I do support are better and faster disclosure and the elimination of soft money—the unlimited and unregulated donations corporations and individuals make directly to the political parties. But, of course, the parties usually turn around and use them for individual campaigns, so it's just a way to get around the law.

Will: Is there any PAC you would refuse to accept contributions from?

Diana DeGette: I do not accept contributions from the tobacco industry. If the NRA should, by some mistake, send me a check, we would send that one right back. We scrutinize every donation that comes in to make sure this is a group we would be proud to be associated with.

Turi: How does raising funds affect your daily life in Congress?

Diana DeGette: The original idea behind the FECA reforms of 1974 was a good one: to keep big donors from having too much influence over Congress. But the individual contribution limit is so low, and the costs of campaigns so high—much higher than in 1974—that there have been unintended consequences. I had to raise almost a million dollars in 1996, and that's approaching the average amount spent on a competitive race. Even a PAC can only give five thousand dollars in the primary and five thousand dollars in the general election. That's almost peanuts, now, but it was big money in 1974, when the FECA amendments were passed. Where are candidates going to get the money? The impact has been that some members of Congress spend almost all their time raising money, especially people in districts where the party registration is close. I have a rule: I don't miss congressional business to do fund-raising. But I'll run into a colleague on the way to a hearing, and I'll ask, "Are you going to the hearing?" and he or she replies, "No, I'm going across the street to make my fund-raising calls." People are skipping hearings on congressional business to do fund-raising. I try to do all my fund-raising when Congress is in recess. Luckily, I have a district that is considered safe for a Democrat, and I do fund-raising a little bit at a time, so that two months before November elections, I don't find I suddenly need two hundred grand. But the fund-raising I do, I do very efficiently!

Senators only have to run every six years, but their races are even more expensive. I was talking to a person who is being recruited to run for the Senate, and she was told she would need to raise nine million dollars!

Jesse: How has serving in Congress changed your life?

Diana DeGette:	I came to Congress from the state legislature, so I had a general understanding about procedures. Still, it took me awhile to learn the rules. I was very concerned that as a freshman in the minority party, I wouldn't get a chance to get much done. I was pleasantly surprised that I was able to pass two or three bills my first year. What's no surprise is the almost complete lack of bipartisanship. Even in the Colorado house, where all my friends still complain about how bad it is, there was a camaraderie that I don't feel in the U.S. Congress.
Will:	How has serving in Congress affected your family?
Diana DeGette:	My husband had to get a new job, my kids had to get a new school. We rent a house in Maryland during the school year and come back as a family to live in our Denver home in the summer. I fly back for votes during the summer. We all miss Denver. But it's also exciting. One time, I brought my nine-year-old daughter with me on Air Force Two, and Al Gore came back and started talking to my daughter. He asked her if she wanted to pick the movie on the flight, and she chose *Madeline,* so that's what we all watched on Air Force Two all the way from Washington to Denver.
	I've taken my kids down to the Capitol, and they've met Miss America, the president of the Girl Scouts, so there are good things and bad things.
Will:	What's a typical day like?
Diana DeGette:	There is no typical day. When we're in session, my husband takes the kids to school. I start out with a couple of meetings with staff, and the House goes into session at 10 A.M. I sometimes have two committee hearings, but they're scheduled at the same time, so I run back and forth. In the meantime, there will be votes on bills and votes on amendments, so I will be going back and forth to the floor to vote. Layered on top of that, different groups of constituents drop in. For the last few weeks, we've had a different group come into the office every half hour. So it is really crazy.
	Then if we're not voting late, I try to get home by six, so I can help my two daughters with their homework and get them to bed. But if we're meeting late, which is increasingly the case, my husband has to do that.
Suzanne:	Tell us a little bit about your committee work. How many committees do you sit on?
Diana DeGette:	I sit on the Commerce Committee, and what you need to know is there are four committees—Ways and Means, Appropriations, Commerce, and Rules—called *exclusive* committees because their workload is so large and important. If a member sits on one of those, he or she is not allowed—is excluded from— a second committee assignment. I was really fortunate to get on Commerce as a freshman; it was a plum assignment that was given to me by the Steering Committee of the House Democratic Caucus. I sit on two subcommittees, the Health and Environment Subcommittee and the Finance and Hazardous Materials Subcommittee. This term, I've added a third subcommittee,

Oversight and Investigations. The Commerce Committee has jurisdiction over anything that deals with interstate commerce. John Dingell, the Democrat who had been chair of that committee for many years before the Republican takeover in 1994, set out to make the jurisdiction of that committee as broad as possible. If you ask John Dingell what our jurisdiction is, he'll say, "The world." On the Oversight Committee, we'll have the administrators of government agencies come in and tell us what they're doing. Recently Carol Browner, the head of the Environmental Protection Agency, came in to discuss hazardous waste. We had a great hearing with Alan Greenspan to discuss how the president's Social Security program would affect the stock market. So it's a very broad jurisdiction.

I hire people with experience on my committee. My legislative director used to work for another member on the Commerce Committee and has real expertise in health care. Each member of my staff has expertise in another area under my committee's jurisdiction.

Will: Could you comment a bit on how it felt to be involved with the impeachment and party-line voting, and whether you take public opinion into account when you vote on something that important.

Diana DeGette: I think impeachment is the second weightiest action Congress can take, after declaring war. I think the vote on impeachment was a vote every member had to think through for him- or herself. I know that on some issues, a member of Congress ought to reflect the constituency, but in a situation as serious as impeachment or war, I thought I needed to look deep inside myself, into my own core of values, and ask myself what decision I needed to make.

It was important for constituents to air their views on the impeachment hearings. The president is elected by all the people, and Congress can't forget that or take it lightly. We were getting over one thousand phone calls a day into our office—more than on any other issue. We had to hire temps just to answer the calls. I want to hear what my constituents have to say, and I want them to know I'm listening.

On the other hand, if we had a president who had committed high crimes and misdemeanors that posed a risk to our constitutional form of government, I think members have a patriotic duty to impeach even if it's against the public will. That's why our government is set up the way it is. I looked at impeachment from the perspective of a former constitutional lawyer. I researched the Constitution, read the Rodino Report from the Nixon hearings, researched the old case law, and came to my own conclusion that Clinton had not been guilty of a crime against the state, which is the original definition of a high crime.

When it came time to vote, unlike other occasions when the party leadership will make its wishes known, none of the Democrats was pressured to vote one way or another. House Minority Leader Dick Gephardt called us all into his office in small groups of four or five, and instead of telling us how to vote, he said, "Tell me what you're thinking. What information do you need? How can I help you?" It became an educational process. The party leadership brought in constitutional scholars to talk to us, but at no time did they pressure us.

I was told by some moderate Republicans that they were pressured by their leadership to vote for impeachment, and I think that's really awful. The process became so partisan in the end because the Republican leadership set the rules. Many Democrats and moderate Republicans thought a more appropriate punishment was censure, not impeachment, and they wanted to have the option of voting for censure. But the Republican leadership has the power to decide which amendments can be debated on the floor and which get buried. They decided not to allow a vote on censure to come to the floor. They were afraid, and rightly so, I think, that it would pass.

That behavior is going to cause rancor in the Congress for a decade to come. People have a bitter, bitter taste in their mouths that they weren't allowed to vote their conscience on this matter. I understand that the party in charge makes the rules. But when people are casting a vote that might be the most important vote of their career—and for only the third time in history that Congress even considered impeachment—to stand in the way of people voting their conscience is pure politics in its worst form. I can tell you it is still affecting the way things get done in the House, and I think it's going to affect the 2000 elections.

Suzanne: If the founders could see our modern Congress, what would they say?

Diana DeGette: I think the founders would be amazed. Some things are a lot more representative. Technology makes news travel instantly. More and more people are e-mailing their representative, so we can communicate much faster. People bemoan the lack of morality in politics, but twenty or thirty years ago, Congress was a bunch of hard-drinking, skirt-chasing, old white guys. And now, there's still a lot of hard-drinking white guys, but the scrutiny by the press has helped clean up the place. "Back room" deals are much less frequent. The press and the public know more about their government than they ever have before.

Suzanne: But the original House districts were quite small, compared to the half a million people you have to try and represent. Do you think the founders might want smaller House districts, even if that meant more of them?

Diana DeGette: I would not want to increase the size of the House. The lack of civility in the House—people being angry and rude—arises out of the fact that we have 435 members. We don't know each other, so the mutual trust and affection that can develop in a state legislature doesn't develop here. One thing I would do is find some way to change the rules of the House so that, more often, people were on the floor together during debates. That's a way to really get to know each other.

Dr. Bauer: I'd like to end by asking you what it's like to be a woman in Congress. There still aren't many women there.

Diana DeGette: That's right. In the House it's still only fifteen percent. I have found that even with only fifteen percent women, I haven't had too much trouble personally making my mark. I don't fit the stereotype—white male—of what a member of Congress should look like, so every now and then someone thinks I'm a staffer or someone's aide. In my first term, a senior Democrat mistook me for an intern. I decided to take that as a compliment. I often get mistaken for a spouse, and they ask me how my husband likes serving in Congress. But I was able to get on the Commerce Committee, and I've been able to pass a bill.

The other day on our little subway system, I got to talk to one of the most senior Democrats. The next day he came up to me and said, "I was talking to another member about you, and he said you were doing a good job, that you are a good legislator, so I'm very happy to get to know you." To be seen as a good legislator by this man who has been in Congress for decades, was a huge barrier for a young woman to overcome. John Dingell, who I talked about before, has been in Congress forty years. Since we have a seniority system, we all have member numbers, and his member number is one. He is the single most senior person in the House. And after I helped him with a complicated banking bill last year, he came up to me and said, "You're a good member, and I'm going to be using you for other projects from now on." So in the hard work of the legislative process, I find very little sexism, at least in my party.

My poor husband, he has a career; he's a lawyer. Most of the congress-women are not married, so there are very few congressional male spouses. He always gets invited to sit on congressional spouses charity committees for breast cancer research. He went to the Democratic spouses lunch; he was one of only two male spouses. And he won a prize—a set of embroidered tea towels. He called me up afterwards, and said, "Guess what! I won the door prize! A set of tea towels!" He's sort of the mascot now for the congressional spouses. They think he's sweet.

★ ★ ★

students

CHAT ROOM

Jesse
a conservative
Libertarian

Krystal
a liberal
Democrat

Suzanne
a moderate
Republican

Turi
a moderate
Democrat

Will
a moderate

A Nice Place to Visit, but Would You Want to Live There?
★ ★ ★

Dr. Bauer: Is there a stereotype of a typical member of Congress?

Krystal: We tend to think that members don't do anything on Capitol Hill. And all politicians are bad. They are immoral . . .

Suzanne: Insensitive and uncaring.

Dr. Bauer: Why do people run for Congress, according to the stereotype?

Suzanne: For power.

Jesse: Self-interest.

Suzanne: To be part of that elite . . . I always think of those political cartoons of the guy with a mustache and pocket watch, chomping on a cigar and strutting around.

Jesse: One hundred thirty thousand dollars a year doesn't hurt, either.

Krystal: But how much were they making before they went to Congress? Maybe they make a real sacrifice to serve in Congress?

Jesse: I'd be hard-pressed to call one hundred thirty thousand dollars a sacrifice under any definition!

Krystal: If you were making a million dollars, or half a million, then one hundred thirty thousand dollars is a sacrifice. To lose four hundred thousand dollars is a significant drop in income.

Dr. Bauer: Let me give you an example of someone who has made a financial sacrifice—Republican Senator Bill Frist—one of the top heart surgeons in the country. Give five minutes' thought to what he could be making and then compare it to the one hundred thirty thousand dollars he makes in Congress. Still, I think Jesse's point is well-taken. To the average person, a congressman's salary seems large.

How does O'Rourke's portrait of a member of Congress differ from the stereotypes?

Jesse: If anything, it's worse. He makes no attempt to paint the congressperson as a strong, upstanding member of the community who is actually interested in the work of the people. He portrays them as just a bunch of self-centered busybodies!

Krystal: They don't seem self-centered to me! He shows that they do a lot of things. They go all over the place!

Will: And he gives reasons why they can't act like superstars—reasons based on their constraints.

Dr. Bauer: What are some of the things that keep members of Congress from getting things done?

Will: Hundreds of different interest groups to meet. Many different issues to discuss and consider. Details of bills that they need to learn about. It's a major constraint to have to deal with so many different things.

Turi: Responsibilities. So many different responsibilities that members can't give a whole lot of attention to any one thing, let alone the hundreds of things they have to do.

Dr. Bauer: Yes, the sheer workload is a killer. As Diana DeGette says in her interview, the committee and subcommittee system helps members focus. She may have to vote hundreds of times on the floor, but she has a deep understanding only of the issues in her committee and subcommittee.

Krystal: And these issues may not be the same ones the members ran on. They probably ran for election on two or three different issues and told their constituents, "These are my goals." They get to the House and realize that they have to learn about and handle about twenty other issues on top of the ones they promised to address. And they have to meet with that many more people. And that many more interest groups.

Dr. Bauer: Yes. Let me give you a quote here from the O'Rourke article. He says, "We expect our congressmen to know more about each of these than we know about any of them. We expect him to make wiser decisions than we can about them all. And we expect that congressman to make those wise and knowledgeable decisions without regard for his political or financial self-interest. Then we wonder why it's hard to get first-rate people to run for Congress.

So here was the congressman I was following, a good and conscientious congressman desperately trying to master all 275 of these issues during the approximately two hours a day when he didn't absolutely have to be somewhere else." Now, does that sound like the stereotypical congressman? He calls him good and conscientious. Is that the stereotype?

Suzanne: Absolutely not! But when I think of what Congresswoman DeGette had to tell us about her life, I don't think I would want to live her life. I don't think I

	would want to have to come to Denver every weekend, meet with constituents, leave my family in Washington, and constantly be running back and forth.
Krystal:	That's a lot of time away from your family, and you don't really have much of a life outside of Washington, D.C.
Suzanne:	And it has got to cost. You have to have two houses to do that. If you have children, and she has two little girls, then it gets only harder. And she said her husband gave up his job here and took a new job in D.C. It just seems like a lot of strain on your personal life and finances.
Dr. Bauer:	Let's go back to the issue of power. Remember one of the stereotypes is members get into politics for power. How much power does any individual member of Congress really have? How much power does the representative O'Rourke is following have?
Jesse:	That particular guy didn't have much. A new congressperson, no matter what the party, is not going to have much power to get things done. But if you are the chair of the Armed Services Committee, or the Ways and Means Committee—
Krystal:	Or the Rules Committee—you can wield a lot of power.
Suzanne:	Sure, but there are 435 members of the House of Representatives, and only a few can be powerful committee chairs.
Dr. Bauer:	So, most of the power in the Congress is held in the hands of a few people. Most of the members, particularly in the House, are just like this guy that O'Rourke is following around. He's scrambling, isn't he? He reminds me of a broken field runner in football: He goes this way and then he goes that way. He's not sitting in his office and receiving different members who come to him for favors. He's low on the totem pole. So, how do you get to be a committee chair?
Krystal:	After years of long hours and hard work. You get power, especially in the House, through the seniority system.
Dr. Bauer:	So, the stereotype is that everyone in Congress wants power. But, do they have tremendous power?
Jesse:	Only a few.
Suzanne:	And the desire for power may come from a desire to do work for the public good—as opposed to personal gain.
Dr. Bauer:	Let's talk about likelihood of getting power. What is your career choice if you really want to gain power quickly? Is it Congress?
Turi:	No, probably business. Bill Gates is more powerful than any fifty members of Congress put together!
Dr. Bauer:	I talked to Diana DeGette throughout her freshman year, and she was lucky to get some of her own ideas attached to somebody else's bill. Now, in her sophomore term, she has a wilderness bill of her own. It is dead, but it's a bill.

Turi:	She's on some committees, though.
Krystal:	Everyone gets appointed to committees. The House Democratic Caucus has a Steering Committee, and when you're new, you lobby them to get a good committee. DeGette's one of the few freshman to get on the exclusive Commerce Committee.
Jesse:	But it's likely she is doing the scut work of those committees. Whoever is the most junior member ends up—you see them late night on C-SPAN—sitting in the House chamber and listening to everybody give a speech. That's a lot of what she is doing.
Dr. Bauer:	Actually, those people you see introducing the speakers are the floor managers of the particular bill. Each party appoints a manager who works with the whips to get the speaker's list heard and the support organized. Those are the more senior members. Diana DeGette got to manage a bill on the floor for about twenty minutes this last year, because Congressman John Conyers (D-NY), one of the most senior members of the House, had to go to the restroom! She did such a good job, they'll probably let her manage a bill sometime soon. What she did say in her interview is that she got the notice of some senior people, such as John Dingell (D-MI), who is the most senior member of any party in the House.
Will:	And that was a big deal. It had a strong impact on her. If she can make a name for herself, she can gain a little bit of power—meaning, the capacity to do a little bit more of what you want to do. It helps tremendously.
Dr. Bauer:	Sure. One type of political power is influence. And right now, by gaining the attention of some of the senior people, and working as a whip, Diana DeGette is on the way to building a congressional career.
Suzanne:	Does she get any power because of who she replaced?
Dr. Bauer:	Good question, Suzanne. And the answer is, no! None whatsoever! In fact, when a new member wins an open seat due to retirement, he or she has to prove herself from day one. No one assumes that just because Pat Schroeder used to be in Representative DeGette's seat that DeGette will have Pat's national standing and influence.
Suzanne:	Okay, that's the way it works in Congress. How does it work in her congressional district, in Denver? She doesn't inherit any of Pat Schroeder's power or seniority, but she has Pat Schroeder's golden image to live up to.
Dr. Bauer:	Yes, and that's difficult. Constituents really don't understand how long it takes a new member of Congress to gain recognition and influence. It's one of the dangers of replacing someone as nationally well known as Pat Schroeder. The ordinary voters thinks, "Gee, Pat Schroeder was on the national news all the time, how come Diana DeGette isn't on the national news all the time?" Well, the *Denver Rocky Mountain News* doesn't even spell her name right all of the

time! New members build a record of accomplishments as fast as they can, which Diana has been very busy trying to do.

It is going to take a while for her to establish her identity. And in the meantime, as Jesse said, she is doing scut work. New members of the House and Senate are really like fraternity pledges: They have to earn their way into the inner circle. So, the stereotype of the powerful member of Congress is often inaccurate.

P. J. O'Rourke—very conservative and antigovernment—said something that surprised me: "The congressman is genuinely likable—as most politicians are." And later, when he's describing a meeting with the local firefighters, one of many meetings with constituents, he says, "Politicians are interested in people. . . . The congressman was interested in the volunteer firemen."

Turi:	Does a senator have to spend time with the local firemen when they come to Washington?
All:	No.
Suzanne:	Senators are there for six years; they don't have to spend all of their time campaigning, which is what happens to people in the House.
Dr. Bauer:	That's right. There are many differences between members of the House and Senate, and when people think of Congress, when they think of the big, powerful, rich person who has lots of influence, I think they are thinking of senators. Individual senators have far more influence. How come? Why is it we hear more from senators in the press and on TV?
Krystal:	There are a whole lot fewer of them.
Suzanne:	And they represent the whole state. A senator's views on a news show broadcast to the whole state holds more interest to more people than the person from the First Congressional District in the House.
Dr. Bauer:	So, what is the lesson here? What parts of the stereotype are true?
Krystal:	That they don't get anything done. But it's subtle. If constituents mean that a member doesn't do anything, that's not true—the representative is reading, learning about, and voting on every single resolution, every single bill that comes before the House. If constituents mean that the member can't effect change—"get something done about the water supply"—that's true. A member has a little bit of influence on a lot of issues.
Dr. Bauer:	Right. And only has a lot of influence on issues in their committees, especially in the House.
Jesse:	O'Rourke also talks about conflicting goals—it's hard to get something done if one day the party opposes China on human rights, and the next day considers trading with China.
Dr. Bauer:	What are some of the reasons for that?

Jesse:	I think, especially in the House, things are done for the immediate political purpose, rather than for any long-term, broad goal.
Dr. Bauer:	Right, and that is one of the stereotypes of the House that appears to be true.
Krystal:	The members are always looking for immediate gains that will affect reelection.
Dr. Bauer:	Each member is looking out for his or her own little district, and nobody is looking out for the whole. Therefore, we see overspending and contradictory spending bills.
Krystal:	They get criticized for that, but isn't that why they were elected? To bring jobs and contracts back to the community who sent them to Washington?
Jesse:	Bring back the pork barrel spending!
Dr. Bauer:	Does any member of Congress care if the extra spending is done in their district?
Jesse:	Yes! Absolutely! They want it done; it has got to be done in their districts. Ron Dellums, congressman from, I think, the Bay Area of California strongly opposed defense spending, was always looking for ways to decrease defense spending. But when the Base Closing Commission targeted two or three bases in his district for closure, you couldn't have found a more pro-defense guy the next day! Because the cuts were coming out of his district that stood to lose military spending, civilian support jobs, and defense jobs!
Dr. Bauer:	And again, that part of the stereotype is true. But it is also by design, isn't it? Isn't this why we have a House of Representatives, to represent smaller constituencies? If this is a problem, it's a problem we have set up for ourselves.
Suzanne:	Of course. Originally, only representatives were elected directly by the people; senators were chosen by their state legislators. Senators didn't represent the guy that owned the livery shop, or the tavern, or the farm. They represented the state as a whole. I think that makes a difference. The House of Representatives is supposed to be the local voice in Washington.
Turi:	State interests versus cities and towns.
Suzanne:	Right.
Dr. Bauer:	There is a structural difference between the House and the Senate, set up in the Connecticut Compromise that created this bicameral national legislature. And unless we change the Constitution, we are going to continue to get members of the House of Representatives who are going to protect the one or two industries in their district and bring in more.
Suzanne:	But, that is what we want, isn't it? The knowledge that someone is interested in and will speak for the hog farmers or whatever—the local interests.
Will:	Yes, we want pluralism, a government listening to multiple interest groups who are jockeying for position.

Dr. Bauer:	What did Congresswoman DeGette say about raising funds from interest groups?
Jesse:	On the morning after the election, fund-raising starts for the next election two years away. At least for the House.
Will:	Not only that, but it's a process that, if I recall, she really didn't like, but it's a necessity.
Krystal:	Especially being a freshman. To maintain that seat, you really do have to spend your first term fund-raising.
Dr. Bauer:	You are most vulnerable in what they call your sophomore reelection. And after that, the odds of being defeated go down steeply. And yet I have never met a member of Congress, no matter how safe their seat, who would admit to having a truly safe seat. Over ninety percent of the members of the House routinely get reelected with over sixty percent of the vote, which is considered a landslide. And yet, they continue to raise massive amounts of money. Why would they continue to raise money?
Jesse:	Well, they don't know who their opponent is going to be.
Suzanne:	It's better to have the money and not need it, than to need it and not have it.
Dr. Bauer:	That is something they all live by!
Suzanne:	Fund-raising doesn't have to be all bad. I think fund-raising is also a good way to keep in touch with what's going on in the district.
Turi:	And in touch with the people in their districts.
Suzanne:	Right. I know the O'Rourke article makes a point of how many constituents get in touch with their congressman every year. But you might never hear from a banker, unless you contacted him for a donation. And he might be important to your reelection, over and above money.
Dr. Bauer:	Fund-raising can be a real measure of support. You find out very quickly if people in your district support you or not by the way that they support financially. And a large war chest scares off the opposition. All the members amass giant war chests of money, even though they don't know if they'll need it. Increasingly unopposed congressional elections are the trend. In Florida, I believe, in 1998, out of a congressional delegation of eighteen, only four or five members had opposition on the ballot.
Jesse:	If the member already has name recognition and is a member of the party in the majority in that district, that incumbent has an advantage.
Dr. Bauer:	A huge advantage. So we have a system in which fund-raising is constant, especially for members of the House of Representatives. But senators also raise money all the time, even though they run once every six years. Does anybody know what the average Senate race costs?

Turi:	Five hundred thousand dollars?
Jesse:	More. It's well into the seven figures. In states like New York, Texas, California, the Senate races of the major candidates combined, cost thirty to forty million dollars.
Jesse:	But, even in the smaller population states like Colorado, last year I think Senator Campbell spent a couple of million on his reelection campaign.
Turi:	What was I thinking of, then?
Dr. Bauer:	House members. House members are closer to that half-a-million-dollar spending range. A hard-fought House race now costs one million dollars. That's what Diana DeGette spent to win her first election to the House. When I ran in 1984, the average House winner spent two hundred fifty thousand dollars.
Turi:	When I was working on a campaign, I was dumbfounded by all of those figures. We started looking at what our opponent had and what we had and thought, "Wow! What good we could do in this society if we just took all this money and spent it to help people."

★ ★ ★

For Additional Reading

Go to InfoTrac College Edition, your online research library at

http://web1.infotrac-college.com

Enter the following search terms using the Subject Guide or Key Terms.

casework   constituencies   constituency service

12

The Executive Branch

A PERSONAL PERSPECTIVE ON **the Presidency**

MONICA BAUER

EVERYONE HAS A SPECIFIC IMAGE OF THE PRESIDENCY, whether we know it or not. We are shaped by the political experiences we have, especially those experiences when we are too young to understand what politics is. People who study the learning process in young children often note that the president is the first political figure children know. They form an opinion on the president as a type of protecting father figure. It is comforting to imagine the country is being cared for by a wise and trustworthy person who won't let anything bad happen to it.

That is not unique to American government. All children everywhere are taught a form of patriotism as they grow, beginning with a simple idea: Their government is a good government. Egyptian students have told me that as young children they always started their schooldays by reciting the Egyptian equivalent to the American Pledge of Allegiance. It was painful for them to discover as college students that their government, in particular their president, was widely believed to be corrupt.

During President Clinton's impeachment and trial, one of the many problems that arose was what to tell children about impeachment. That was a problem not just because of the sexual nature of the charges, but also because children are taught to believe that authority figures are good people. Notice they are not taught that authority figures are merely competent at their jobs as presidents, principals, priests, rabbis, ministers, mayors, and so on. For a child, it is important that an authority figure is worthy of trust, and that translates into more than being good at a day job—far more.

Yet, anyone who studies politics as a college student comes quickly to understand that the presidency is an office that has been filled by a wide variety of people. Some of those occupants of the Oval Office have been worthy of a child's trust in their personal character; many have not. For a good number of people who now teach political science, the first president they can really remember from their youth is Richard Nixon.

Nixon was a brilliant and complex man who had overcome poverty and risen from a working-class background. He inherited a war he pledged to end but didn't end until midway through his second term, leading to charges that he had lied to the American people about his plans. He used the power of his office to harass his enemies, ending in the infamous Watergate investigation, in which the Founding Fathers' nightmare of an unchecked president seemed nearly to come true.

It makes sense that those of us who grew up politically in Nixon's shadow would come to be suspicious of any and all presidents. That includes members of the media and the press, as well as political science textbook authors. In a real sense, Nixon lives on every time "gate" is attached to a scandal. That the media immediately began calling Clinton's sex scandal "Monica-gate" is proof enough of this continuing influence.

I remember watching every single moment of the Senate and House Judiciary Committee hearings on Watergate. I was nineteen years old, the age of most college freshmen. There was high drama: good guys and bad guys, bombshell revelations of secret tapes, and a fight over releasing those tapes. When the tapes were finally delivered to the committee by order of the Supreme Court, eighteen and one-half minutes of a pivotal conversation between Nixon and others had been mysteriously erased. There was more excitement in the Watergate story than any movie that came out that year, and the nation was holding its collective breath, waiting to see if Nixon would be impeached, convicted, and removed from office.

One of the things most shocking about the tapes was not the content, which included blatant references to bribing witnesses, but the Richard Nixon who was revealed on those "secret" recordings, which Nixon himself had authorized. That Nixon swore and cursed his political enemies, using so much foul language that, when the transcripts were released in printed form, it seemed as if every other word had to be left out. Nixon's public persona was that of a careful and intellectual person who might be a little insecure but certainly not angry and vengeful. That was not the Nixon the public knew—and obviously no role model for children.

It is with that context in mind that I spent the year of Clinton's impeachment, trial, and acquittal, trying to explain the presidency to my American Government students. Some were angry and confused; some had come to expect such behavior from politicians—they didn't seem to think less of Clinton, the president, because of the mistakes made by Clinton, the man.

At the end of this chapter, you will read an interview with Federico Peña, former secretary of both Transportation and Energy in the Clinton cabinet. He describes his own feelings of frustration and disappointment when the Clinton he thought he knew turned out to be someone different. Peña had trusted Clinton when he told his cabinet the charges about the affair with the intern were completely false. He had publicly and privately defended the president, trusting Clinton's face-to-face assurance of his innocence. And in the end, he saw the other Clinton, the one who not only engaged in juvenile sexual behavior, but could and would lie to keep his behavior from hurting his family, his presidency, and his country.

I, too, felt a sense of betrayal. I had publicly supported him after he became the Democratic nominee, even though he was not my first choice for president in 1992. When he told the whole world, on television, "I did not have sex with that woman, Miss Lewinsky," I wanted to believe him. But my friends in Washington told me that the whole town was ready to believe the story about the affair with the intern, because Washington had decided years ago that Clinton was a man ready to lie, especially about his sex-capades.

During the spring of 1999, I was teaching the upper-level course about the presidency when former Clinton aide George Stephanopoulos published his memoir, *All Too Human: A Political Education.* I read portions of it to my students. Their reactions were interesting. A few students, mostly Republicans, took the damning Stephanopoulos book as evidence that Clinton was the worst person to ever disgrace the office. The majority of my students, Democrats and independents but including some Republicans, found the whole thing trivial. Their position was "If we're going to discuss Clinton's problems, let's discuss why he couldn't get health care passed, or why he can't lead in Kosovo. But this sex scandal was something that should never have been in public view."

In this section, I have chosen readings about how flawed humans have performed the complex job and mythic role of president. How would you rank President Clinton among his peers? Will he be remembered as a great president for his handling of the economy, or a failed president because of the stain of scandal? I have my own opinion on the matter. What do *you* think?

Mediocrity at the Helm: Evaluations of the President in Political Science Textbooks

J. M. Sanchez

Citizenship training or the study of civics has been a task traditionally assigned to secondary schools. However, the recent decline in the overall quality of American public education is reflected in government or civic courses which are described as "vapid, over-simplified, excessively patriotic and contentless." The current civic education of young Americans now seems to take place in the introductory American government course at colleges and universities; it is there that many undergraduates experience their first analytical exposure to the political system. In the context of an introductory course, a core textbook can be extremely influential, particularly when it has been selected by the instructor. Such a text then becomes the central authoritative source of information for students who are politically unaware.

Historians and political scientists who specialize in the study of the American presidency have through the years attempted to evaluate the relative performance of the forty men who have occupied the office. The "ratings" which emerge from case studies by individual scholars, or, more commonly, from the polling of presidential experts have provided a fairly standard list of the "great," and "near great" presidents as well as of those who have been judged "failures." College textbooks describing the American political system include similar evaluations of the individuals who have served as chief executives.

Previous analyses of how such textbooks measured presidential performance have focused on the theoretical definitions of the office. A compilation by Thomas Cronin showed that the texts' descriptions of the president were unreasonably ambitious. The authors ascribed so

Reprinted with permission of Elsevier Science from *The Social Science Journal*, 33, no. 22 (1996). © 1996 by Elsevier Science.

many powers to the chief executive that Cronin, anticipating that the reality could never live up to the expectations created by the books, called on authors to "demythologize" the presidency. Writing several years after Cronin, Hoekstra found that the textbooks had indeed "tempered the exaggerated expectations for the presidency" by emphasizing the activities of other institutions (pressure groups, Congress, political parties) which could curb presidential power. However, Hoekstra noted that the texts retained "unduly schematic analyses" featuring the traditional roles or "hats" of the president. These extensive checklists still tended to create unrealistic expectations; as the author of an introductory text concedes:

> To accomplish all the different things expected of him, a president would have to possess a truly amazing collection of skills. He would have to be a great communicator and campaigner, an adroit politician among politicians, a consummate administrator, a great conceptualizer of policy and a great democratic leader.

In contrast with the Cronin and Hoekstra studies, I have sought evaluations of individual presidents in introductory political science textbooks. After reviewing 36 texts, references to each president were tabulated according to the qualitative assessment, if any, made of all 40 individuals. The comments were then sub-divided among three broad categories:

1. Personal background factors (characteristics attributed to the president and references to events prior to his election to office);
2. Domestic developments (incidents, policies or trends which transpired in the United States during his administration); and
3. Foreign developments (international situations involving American interests).

GENERAL FINDINGS

Most Presidents Are Described in Negative Terms

The specific reviews of presidential conduct are far more critical than one would anticipate from the Cronin and Hoekstra studies. Whether mentioned frequently or not, presidents do not receive very favorable ratings from the political science profession. Of 5,322 evaluative references made in the 36 texts, only 2,017 (38 percent) are positive. Undergraduate students are unmistakably given the impression that most of the men who have occupied the White House have fallen far short of the competence level expected by scholars in the field. Two factors may help to explain the harshness with which presidents are treated.

First, secondary schools are well known as promoters of a highly positive view of the political system. Since "no political culture deliberately socializes its young to view its leadership negatively," public education is expected to inculcate students with patriotic values as well as pride in a nation's history. Myths about great men who have served as presidents furnish American children with heroic figures, a sense of common identity and respect for the values upheld in largely apocryphal stories. Such unquestionable endorsement of the status quo may also be very appealing to high school instructors fearful of controversy and the parental complaints which may follow negative assessments of specific chief executives. The publishers of high school textbooks, hoping to appeal to as wide a market as possible, are also known to seek a safe middle ground less likely to antagonize any particular group. The ensuing results are usually detailed descriptive accounts of presidential activity with few evaluative comments. Authors of college texts, presumably freer from such constraints, may want to "balance" the blanket endorsements of the public school

system with a strong dose of realism, therefore producing a much more demanding assessment of office-holders.

Secondly, the critical notices could be accurate in their low regard for past presidents. As far back as 1889 (when Lord Bryce was already claiming that the American political system was not likely to promote "great men" to the White House) and as recently as the 1992 presidential primaries (when "none of the above" was more popular with many voters than the candidates put forth by each party), aspirants to the presidency have been found wanting. Without delving into the political factors which work against the selection of an outstanding individual to represent one of the major political parties, it would still strain credulity that only a handful of the nation's forty leaders had successfully carried out their constitutional duties and responsibilities.

Nevertheless, students relying on their introductory American Government texts are likely to conclude that most presidents did not do a good job. While the books reserve the specific term "failure" only for the likes of Warren Harding, Ulysses Grant or Andrew Johnson, their remarks about four of the last five presidents (excluding the incomplete presidency of Bill Clinton) are at least three times more negative than positive. Such calamitous assessments may be creating a new American political myth. "The historical reading of America as a land particularly favored by providence," point out Ellis and Wildavsky may be replaced with a portrait of Americans "as an unlucky people done in by unworthy presidents."

No Objective Standards of Measuring Presidential Performance Are Articulated

The mere fact that presidential greatness has often been determined by polls of professional students of the office suggests the dearth of objective criteria by which to evaluate performance. After all, no other comparable observation about the political system is validated by conducting surveys among scholars. The absence of "established yardsticks" has led some political scientists to dismiss such ratings. "All evaluations of presidents and their power . . . are merely value judgments rooted in idiosyncratic preferences." Others indicate that "the grounds for evaluations and the relative importance of the criteria can be inferred from context, but they are rarely the focus of systematic, conscious inquiry."

Just as with most lists of presidential rankings, the textbooks offer students very little guidance as to how to gauge a president's record. Events or initiatives described as "successful" are mentioned in connection with a particular president, but seldom does an author then go on to discuss additional information which would furnish a better understanding of the powers and constraints of the office. Likewise, descriptive terms or phrases are applied to certain presidents, with little supportive factual information that would allow readers to grasp the wisdom or the folly attributed to the president in a specific situation. . . .

Modern Presidents Are Generally Rated Below Their 19th Century Counterparts

The last ten men to have reached the White House are the recipients of positive assessments in only 35 percent of the comments. By contrast, the favorable remarks about the eight presidents in Group Two reach an average of 60 percent. The difference is even more striking if two presidents (Woodrow Wilson, sharply criticized for what is depicted as his mishandling of the Treaty of Versailles, and Andrew Johnson, habitually cited only in the context of explaining the impeachment process) are removed from Group Two. The remaining six presidents would then average an extremely high 70 percent. By comparison, a similar removal of the two post-war presidents with the lowest ratings (Jimmy Carter and Richard Nixon) would only improve Group One's average from 35 to 43 percent.

Political scientists may well be projecting the same nostalgic attitude toward the past which is encouraged by national myths about heroic historical figures and underlies the country's futile search for individuals worthy of collective admiration. The great presidents of the past may have been truly unique individuals or their reputations may have endured only because they did not have to withstand the probing examinations of tabloid journalism. In either case, both professional students of the presidency and the public have concluded that modern occupants of the White House are not comparable to their predecessors.

Could They Be Elected Today? Too Human to Be Heroes?

Ken Burns

"The cheek of every American must tingle with shame," wrote the indignant *Chicago Times*, "as he reads the silly, flat, dish-watery utterances of the man who has to be pointed out to intelligent foreigners as the President of the United States."

What foul speech of what poor misinformed president could have produced this particularly virulent attack from a reputable and highly read newspaper from the shores of Lake Michigan? This diatribe, although it could have come from nearly any era in American history, actually was published in November 1863. The president then was Abraham Lincoln, and the speech was, incredibly, the Gettysburg Address.

Fortunately, other positive voices from the press rose up and joined a swelling chorus that has, over the years, come to see those "dish-watery utterances" as the finest speech ever given in America.

As our nation matured and the relationship between the presidency and the press evolved, the expectation of general impartiality among our major newspapers and magazines (and later radio and television) became the norm. The history of journalism with regard to the presidency in particular and our political life in general became one of fair-minded confrontation and questioning, mingled with a mutual sense that each side needed the other.

Presidents and politicians found ways to use the press to amplify their agendas; the press found in the rich and not always pure stories of how government is conducted the major on-going drama of the republic, a fascinating operatic narrative that has never gone out of fashion and, most important, never lacked for paying customers.

But since Watergate, when the press forced the resignation of President Nixon, the balance has tilted again. No president has been immune,

Reprinted by permission of the author. From *USA Weekend*, August 2, 1998. © 1998 by Ken Burns.

with the possible exception of Ronald Reagan, to the relentless exposing of flaws, major and minor, in their presidencies and character. With Nixon gone, Presidents Ford, Carter, Bush and Clinton especially have felt the never-ending sting of intense scrutiny.

With President Clinton the focus of an independent counsel, a grand jury investigation and a barrage of sex- and scandal-tinged coverage, I wondered who from our pantheon of past presidents could get elected today.

THE ENDLESS WHAT-IFS OF HISTORY

Now, history is always full of what-ifs. People, usually at their peril, like to imagine what things would be like if the past hadn't happened the way we all know it did. What if Robert E. Lee had triumphed at Gettysburg and the South had won the Civil War? What if John Kennedy hadn't been shot? Or what if the Germans had gotten the bomb first?

The speculation and arguments produced by these questions often make good dinner conversation, but usually nothing else, more heat than light. Still, we sometimes can't resist the urge, and when you think how different our late 20th-century media-dominated culture is from the rest of the great pageant we call American history, well . . .

WASHINGTON VS. JEFFERSON: NO CONTEST

It is satisfying to realize George Washington could get elected any time. Like our 40th president, Ronald Reagan (and, I'm sorry to say, 29th president Warren G. Harding), he looked like a president.

All the Founding Fathers, of course, have this advantage, but Washington is above the rest. He was tall, dominating, fair and brilliant; he had an ability to command the attention of any room he entered; and he so loved his fledgling country that he was willing to give up power, near absolute power, twice to see it survive.

The fact that he may have fudged his Revolutionary War expenses would undoubtedly bring a special prosecutor and constant press attention, but one senses he might have survived and not been forced to resign.

Thomas Jefferson—with his problematic (so polling and focus groups suggest) red hair—I'm afraid would not fare as well. He hated being out in the public eye and had a weak, unimpressive speaking voice. His constant personal debts would have made launching campaigns difficult, and he was known to be an aesthete, a lover of fine wines, the French and all things intellectual and scientific.

If he, by chance, made it to the presidency today, his administration would be in perpetual turmoil and scandal, as the Sally Hemmings affair, his purported but still unproven liaison with one of his slaves, would go on and on and on.

Abraham Lincoln, arguably our greatest president, though elected the first time with only 40 percent of the vote (less than Bill Clinton's much-maligned 1992 percentage), would, I fear, run into many of the same problems of perception.

First, he was not to many people photogenic, and certainly not telegenic—"so awful-ugly" a contemporary wrote of the rough-hewn man from the backwoods of what was then the frontier. He also was quite melancholy at times, subject to depression, which might find, in our day and age, relief in the form of psychotherapy or even medication.

That would, of course, like an "Eagleton Factor" (Thomas Eagleton was forced to withdraw as George McGovern's 1972 vice presidential candidate after acknowledging he'd had electroshock therapy), prevent his ascension to the highest and most important office of the land. I suppose the press would say it was only doing its duty by reporting this condition.

LINCOLN'S OFF-COLOR HUMOR

And if his depression didn't end his career, perhaps his unusual sense of humor and fondness at times for off-color jokes might derail him in an era where every word spoken offstage by a president seems to be recorded by some microphone.

Or his loose cannon of a wife. Surely, Mary Lincoln, eventually institutionalized by her own son, would be a liability today. And there must be something compromising, like Whitewater, in his dealings all those years as a lawyer for the big railroads. Never mind that he, more than any other president, did more to curtail individual liberties once he became president by suspending habeas corpus for a time. And he launched and maintained a war, often unpopular and seemingly unwinnable, that produced more American deaths than all other American wars combined. Perhaps we could have done without Mr. Lincoln, after all.

TEDDY ROOSEVELT, THE ROSS PEROT OF HIS DAY

I'm also worried that the loud, pugnacious, blunt, irrepressible Teddy Roosevelt would have trouble today. He seems, like a Ross Perot, just a little too hot for the cool medium of television, and though robust and energetic, not the aloof patrician favored in our films and novels of what a president should look like.

AND WOODROW WILSON? WELL, HE'S A COLLEGE PROFESSOR. NEED I SAY MORE?

Or what about the man who, it turns out, had an affair with his wife's social secretary? And, when his wife found out, promised never to see the other woman again, but was actually with her many times, including when he died?

This man, by the way, would launch the greatest assault on the Constitution a politician has made in the 20th century, where he hoped, before he was stopped, to completely remodel to his own design an entire branch of our government. This is a man so manipulative and controlling that few ever really felt they knew the whole of him, a man with almost no truly close friends.

On top of it all, this was a man so infirm that he was physically unable to stand on his own, was in a wheelchair most of his adult life and was, by today's standards of scrutiny and "concern," undoubtedly unable to lead us out of a huge economic depression, let alone a world war. I refer, of course, to Franklin Delano Roosevelt. But perhaps we could have done without him, too.

What's to be done? Obviously, we could not have survived as the great country we are without these great, but clearly flawed, individuals. But it's not clear these great individuals could have survived our current scandal-addicted media. Like the sanctimonious village elders of Colonial America, we love to stitch a scarlet "A" on all the less-than-perfect among us, and seem to have forgotten that heroes and presidents are not pure, but flawed human beings struggling, negotiating, warring in a much more interesting drama with these conflicting and complicated sides of themselves.

What is needed is restraint. Not every flaw is character-defining, not every mistake a crime. Sometimes personal attributes have no bearing on public performance. Sometimes entertainment or knee-jerk criticism is not news. Sometimes, even now, our politicians—yes, even our presidents—are heroes. History will bear this out.

But what would happen if Lincoln gave his Gettysburg Address today? Unfortunately, the TV reporter sent to cover the trip would do his stand-up while the president was delivering his speech in the background and whisper, "The president came to Gettysburg today to try to distract attention from his disastrous military campaign out west in Tennessee." And that spin would prevent us from even hearing the greatest speech ever given in America. Even the *Chicago Times*, which was so critical of it, reported the speech.

And so, sadly, the question of today must be: How many other Gettysburg Addresses have we not heard?

Student Interview with
Federico Peña
Former Secretary of Transportation
and Energy

Krystal
a liberal
Democrat

Suzanne
a moderate
Republican

Will
a moderate

What's It Like to Be a Member of the Cabinet?
★ ★ ★

Federico Peña served as Secretary of Transportation and, later, as Secretary of Energy in the Clinton cabinet before retiring from public service. Before those high offices, Mr. Peña was the mayor of Denver and a member of the Colorado legislature.

Will: Mr. Secretary, a good place to start might be to ask what kind of impact you think you were able to have as an individual cabinet member?

Federico Peña: To run a major federal department is an enormous undertaking. When I headed the Department of Transportation, we had one hundred ten thousand employees and a budget of about thirty-eight billion dollars. And *it* had a number of subsidiaries: the FAA, Coast Guard, the Federal Highway Administration, the Federal Transit Administration that runs light rail and buses, the Federal Maritime Administration that deals with shipping, the National Highway Traffic Safety Administration, responsible for setting safety standards for cars and setting fuel-efficiency standards.

The general advice to new cabinet secretaries is to focus on two or three things—because you're not going to be there very long. The typical cabinet secretary lasts for eighteen months! I lasted for four years at Transportation, then I went to Energy for a year and a half. I'm one of the few cabinet secretaries in history to have headed two departments. Needless to say, I ignored that early advice. My approach was to work on improving the department in as many ways that I could and still be nimble enough to respond to crises. And we had plenty of crises—no matter what priorities you think you set, you've got to be prepared for emergencies.

I'm proud that we signed forty international air safety agreements with other countries. I'm proud of our response to domestic crashes. We had had a record number of deaths. It was shocking. People were afraid to fly, and we had to do something about that. We brought in the CEOs of the major airlines and representatives from consumer groups to find a way to fly more safely—and we succeeded. When you think that on any given day there are more than one million people in the skies, safety has to be the number-one concern.

I'm proud of trying to make the department more human. A lot of people who go to Washington and serve as cabinet members keep their distance. But as a community activist, then state legislator, and then mayor, I had always been close to the people. I wanted to bring a humanizing connection between what we did in the department and the people. For example, I went to schools all over the country to talk to kids about wearing bicycle helmets, buckling their seat belts, drinking and driving—being safe. People were surprised. They said, "Aren't you too busy to go into elementary and high schools?" And the answer was, "No, not as long as we lose forty thousand people every year in highway crashes in our country." That's an astronomical number. By comparison, around sixty thousand Americans died in the Vietnam War. The leading cause of death for people between ages five and twenty-one is automobile accidents.

Some people said I shouldn't have gone to airline crash sites, that I should have delegated those trips to my FAA director, but I disagreed. I think it's very important for the head of a department to see things first hand in order to fully appreciate the magnitude of the crisis. Furthermore, when you go and see the disaster, you make solutions a priority.

When the earthquake hit LA and shut down three major highways, I went out to meet with the mayor and the governor, and we rebuilt those highways in record time. We did a lot of good work accelerating construction.

So when I asked myself, as you asked me, "As secretary of transportation, how can I make an impact?" my response was, "I can help save lives." I can put a human face on the government that is there to help when disaster hits. These are the things I feel good about as secretary of transportation.

In the Department of Energy, I feel good about the work we did in Russia. One of our highest priorities was working with my counterparts in Russia to do two things: one, to ensure that facilities in the former Soviet Union would develop the proper security measures to protect plutonium and other nuclear materials, and two, to convince the Russians to take the surplus plutonium

	they had and commit to disposing it in such a way that it could never be used for nuclear weapons.
Suzanne:	How does the cabinet work? I got curious when we were reading *Locked in the Cabinet,* Secretary of Labor Robert Reich's book.
Federico Peña:	It seems to me he mentioned me in there. I think he said the secretary of transportation became the secretary of disastrous crashes. It seemed that way for a while. But to your question:

Theoretically, the cabinet should meet frequently with the president and bring the resources of their departments to the White House. And by the *White House,* I don't just mean the president, but also the chief of staff and other members of the president's staff. I don't think people understand that the real resources of government are not in the White House, they are in the departments.

The cabinet should be sure they know exactly what the president's priorities are. And this president's priorities were rebuilding the economy, improving education, and trying to give people an opportunity to succeed in life. Once the president lays out the agenda—the five or six things that are the most important things to do—then cabinet members should look at their departments and ask, What resources do I have that can support the president's agenda?

In the area of the economy, for example, I had a huge budget at Transportation that we could use to bring more jobs to people—do such things as build more airports, highways, transit systems. Spending on that kind of infrastructure creates a ripple effect that can rebuild a whole city's economy. I knew that from my experience as mayor of Denver. The real task of a cabinet member is to use those resources to support the president's agenda. I think that worked relatively well in our administration.

The cabinet works together to solve national problems. And you can best do that when you have very good communication with other cabinet members. The other reference to me in Reich's book was about the time I heard there were going to be major changes in my department, but no one had contacted me from the White House. So I called Bob Reich and said, "Bob, are you having this problem?" As it turned out, a number of cabinet members were having the same problem! The joke became, "Are you in the loop to get information?" And Bob Reich said, "The first question should be, *Is* there a loop!" And in many cases, there was no "loop," no communication between the White House and the cabinet. I think that Bill Clinton, as a new president with a new team, had to learn that communication needed to flow up and down the organizational chart. After Leon Panetta became White House chief of staff, communication got a lot better. He was very good at getting the departments to work together—the way it should work.

The cabinet should be a place for the interchange of ideas and debate. I think, at times, there was a sense that the cabinet meetings were not as lively as they should have been. I think they improved over time and became more efficient.

Krystal: Should the president make sure that he assists his cabinet and keeps them "in the loop"?

Federico Peña: There's an indirect effect that presidents can have on departments, but the real relationship should be the cabinet members responding to the president. If you disagree with the president's priorities, you shouldn't join the administration. I think the first level of accountability is the cabinet being accountable to the president. The president is accountable to the American people.

Now, every once in awhile an issue would arise that the president had not set as a priority, but that we thought was important to the American people. In that case, if I felt that the OMB, or the Treasury Department, was blocking something my department felt was necessary, I would go to the president and say, "This is really important. Other parts of the executive branch don't seem to see the importance of this. Let me tell you why it's important." Nine out of ten times, the president would say to me, "You're right. Let's fix it." And he would direct the rest of the executive branch to help me out.

Let's recall who the people are who join the cabinet. These are people such as Bruce Babbitt, a former governor and presidential candidate; Henry Cisneros, former mayor of San Antonio. Many of us were used to being accountable to the voters, and I think we brought that to the cabinet. We had a sense that we weren't just accountable to the president, but that we had a responsibility to the American people.

Krystal: I wondered about your experience with President Clinton. He has a reputation for a management style that puts him at the center of spokes in a wheel, so that people can come to him, and he listens to everybody. Was that your experience?

Federico Peña: Absolutely. People have passed judgment on Bill Clinton for a number of things, but if you ask the question, "Can you find a person to be president who is, first of all, extremely gifted intellectually, who can connect to the everyday concerns of the American people, who comes with the right motivation to do the right things and not just the politically easy things?" Bill Clinton satisfies all those criteria. And the wonderful thing about Clinton was, if you were sitting around a table with Bill Clinton, and you wanted to discuss an issue you didn't think he knew much about, he would listen. And he would ask for, and get, the best advice of everyone sitting around that table. Then, at the end of the meeting, Clinton could summarize exactly what everyone else had said. It was as if he said, "You all are concerned about A, B, and C, because it affects X, Y, and Z. Now here is how we are going to deal with it." It was a pleasure to have a meeting with Bill Clinton, because he would get things done. And that's pretty unusual in someone who has to listen to a wide variety of problems. From the environment to international trade, to transportation, to crime, the presidency bears an extraordinary burden of issues, and for Clinton to be able to handle all of them, every day, and make decisions about them, every day, was pretty remarkable.

Dr. Bauer: When we teach about the presidency, we talk about the influence of the chief of staff in organizing the White House. In other words, the way the White

House is organized, or unorganized, can make the president seem decisive or weak. You served under two very different chiefs of staff. Can you describe the differences in style between these two men and how their styles affected the way the executive office of the president worked?

Federico Peña: These were two very different people, Mack McClarty, the first chief of staff, and the second, Leon Panetta. Mack is a friend of mine, and he's a business person. Businesspeople take some time to understand the mechanisms of government. Government does not, and really can't, work the same way as a business. Mack ran a corporation, and when he had to make a decision for the corporation, he didn't have to ask his treasurer how to effect the decision. He just went and did it. The government is very different. In the government, you've got to work with a variety of forces within the White House, then you have to work with a variety of forces in the Congress, including representatives from interest groups, which may or may not like what you're proposing. And then you've got to work with governors and mayors, so I think it took Mack awhile to get used to that kind of atmosphere.

Now Leon Panetta came from government. He served a district in California and chaired the Budget Committee in the House of Representatives. Then he became director of OMB when Mack was chief of staff. Then the president asked him to become chief of staff. So Leon had all the training, and all the experience, to understand how to deal with the Congress. He could go down to the Hill and talk with the leadership and tell them exactly how he felt. Leon came from the Congress, and the Congress had great respect for him. Then he could turn around and tell the Office of Management and Budget what to do, because he used to be the director over there. And Leon had a way of dealing with the cabinet departments. After years of experience, he was good at oversight.

Mack worked very hard. He's intelligent and obviously very devoted to the president. They had been friends, I think, since kindergarten. After he stepped down as chief of staff, the president asked him to be an adviser working on trade issues in Mexico, [and] Central and Latin America. He did an absolutely great job working with CEOs from all over the hemisphere to increase trade. This was a job that matched his talents perfectly.

Krystal: So how did you communicate with Congress?

Federico Peña: There is nothing more important in politics than personal relationships. That can be even more important than party affiliation. If you have relationships with members of Congress, sixty to seventy percent of the time they are going to treat you fairly. There will always be times when, because of partisanship, even a good friend is going to let you down. Sometimes the Congress really wanted to criticize the president, and I just happened to be the person who got the heat. That happens more frequently than not in Washington, and I don't find that a very pleasant experience.

But I think I had good relationships with people on the Hill. When I was mayor of Denver, I spent a lot of time in Congress, lobbying on behalf of the city, looking for airport funding for the new Denver International Airport. That helped me get to know a lot of members. Then, when I became part of the cabinet, I made time to spend with members of Congress and got to know more of the leadership. I'd say that the substance of political issues comes in second to relationships. That's the nature of politics.

Will: How do you feel about the role of the media in terms of your political life?

Federico Peña: Obviously we need a strong media. They have a legitimate watchdog role to play: to ensure that there is no corruption in government and to make sure the government is responding to the people in a straightforward fashion. I think that is absolutely critical. That's what makes our democracy the strongest in the world. But I think the media makes mistakes in attempting to create stories that are not factual. They blur the line between reporting and editorializing, and that's inappropriate. I think the media, especially the print media, need to go back and embrace the fundamentals of objective journalism.

Pick up articles, look at the adjectives that are used, and ask yourself if the writer, with the same set of facts, could have slanted the story differently just by using different adjectives. Then look at the headlines. Ask yourself if the headline reflects what is really being said in the story—often it doesn't. What truly amazed me was that after I held a press conference or testified before a congressional committee hearing, and several different newspapers had covered it, the stories would all be very different. And my staff and I would sit around the table and say, "Were we at the same hearing?" [Laughter.] We'd give exactly the same information to different reporters, and they'd all take a different slant. That is very confusing to the people in government doing the talking, and probably even more confusing to the reader, who has no idea what actually was said.

Suzanne: You were in the middle of several classic media feeding frenzies. I wanted to ask you how that felt, to be in the middle of all that?

Federico Peña: It's the nature of the job, and it goes with the territory. I don't think that will ever change. So if you're uncomfortable in that situation, then you shouldn't be part of the government at that level. Unfortunately, the result is that some good people—talented people—will not serve at a high level in government because they can't put up with the press.

Furthermore, the media plays "the blame game." When something goes wrong, the media has to blame someone. There is less interest in how to fix the problem than in finding someone to blame—and then setting out to destroy that person personally and professionally. There is too much of that going on in Washington, frankly. And that is another reason why people leave the government—they get tired of that.

We ought to examine how we deal with mistakes in the government. The media inclines too strongly toward an assumption of conspiracy or dirty dealing. Sometimes it's just a simple mistake! But media people will dig around, craft an interesting theory, see connections where there aren't any, come to you, and actually say, "This is why I think you made that decision." And you'll sit there asking yourself how they ever came up with that screwball idea. But the media believe it. So then you have to go back and explain very carefully, "No, you're wrong, that issue never even entered into my mind." Every single time you make a decision, there are people around you accusing you of ulterior, hidden motives. It can't be true that you simply mean what you say! That has got to stop, that kind of continuous, negative, second-guessing of public officials. It turns into a chess game, instead of a straightforward exchange where I say what I mean and the media reports it.

Krystal: *Newsweek* has a feature that plays the blame game every week. They call it "Winners and Losers." That oversimplifies politics so much, I can't stand to read it. What do you think of that kind of reporting?

Federico Peña: Oh, it's really bad, so arbitrary. The media will build you up as a winner for awhile, then when they feel like it, you become one of their losers. This happened to Madeleine Albright, our secretary of state. At first the media thought she was just wonderful, which she is, by the way. And now she's being criticized by the media all the time. That happens to everyone in Washington. Your star rises and falls, frequently for no discernible reason either way.

Dr. Bauer: You were in the Clinton White House when Vince Foster, the president's friend and adviser, committed suicide. In the George Stephanopoulos book, *All Too Human,* he describes how this episode eventually led him into therapy as a way of coping with the enormous stress that exists in the White House. How did you cope with the pressure?

Federico Peña: First, I had a strong family. If you have "troubles at home," you will not survive. You've got to have a family that understands that you won't be around very much. I traveled to over thirty-five countries as a cabinet member; traveled all over the United States on a moment's notice. I'll never forget that I tried to take my wife on a vacation down to Florida, and we were there all of five hours when I got a call that I needed to get back to Washington right away, and the Coast Guard sent a plane for me.

Second, you have to know what you believe in. You can't have a lot of doubt about your own principles. Doubts will send you bouncing back and forth when people criticize you.

Third, you need to find a way to decompress. I used to run every day. I would put it on my schedule and do it—release some of the pressure and tension I was carrying inside. It's very easy to work in these jobs twenty-four seven, but you will run yourself into the ground and end up in the hospital. So you've got to find a way to balance things and understand that you *must* delegate decisions to others, pick your priorities, and focus only on the most important things.

Suzanne: If you could add two positions to the cabinet, what would they be?

Federico Peña: I wouldn't add, I would reorganize. I would take things out of transportation and send them to commerce and take things out of commerce and send them over to treasury. Why did I have the Coast Guard as part of my duties as secretary of transportation? If I had the power, I would reorganize more logically the cabinet responsibilities that just grew over time. But it's almost impossible to do that kind of work as a cabinet secretary. First of all, the people in your department have all been there for years, and they see you as temporary. Imagine what would happen in corporations if everyone treated the CEO like temporary help! It's very hard to do major surgery on the government, but I think it needs it. We could be much more efficient, if we reorganized.

Suzanne: By the time cabinet secretaries get confirmed by the Senate, kicked around by the press, and moved into their new jobs, the term is almost up. It's a wonder that anything gets done!

Federico Peña: I think you're right—it's amazing that anything gets done, and yet it does. The nominating process can take months, and a single senator who is angry at the president can hold up your appointment indefinitely. Think of that: A single senator can block a nomination! In fact, that happened to me when I was waiting to be confirmed as secretary of energy. It took three months for me to get confirmed, because one senator was unhappy with the president over nuclear waste disposal that I had nothing to do with. He wanted to get the president to change his mind, and in exchange, he'd allow me to be confirmed. The president didn't change his position, but minor adjustments were made. That's another reason why some good people will not serve in government—they just won't put themselves through that confirmation process.

If confirmations take too much time, then the president is really stuck. People expect a president to hit the ground running, with the whole team in place, and get a good part of his agenda going in the first hundred days of the presidency.

Krystal: Do you think that Clinton got a good percentage of his agenda accomplished in his two terms?

Federico Peña: I think that when historians look back at the Clinton presidency, they are going to see that about seventy percent of his agenda was accomplished. He balanced the budget with a record surplus. He got the economy going again. He's tried to work on education; developed the AmeriCorps program. The one obvious failure was health care reform, but that was just too big, and he couldn't get it through Congress. Looking back on it, it would have been better to make a series of small reforms over a number of years, rather than try to do a massive overhaul. He certainly has been committed to the environment. When you look at his record objectively, I think he will be rated very highly.

Will: Setting the scandal aside.

Federico Peña: Yes, setting that aside and just looking at the results of Clinton's policies. Compare his goals to what he accomplished, and I think the record is pretty remarkable. Given the fact that he got a Republican Congress in 1994, he got a lot done.

Will:	How often did you get to meet with the president?

Federico Peña: It depended on what was going on. Sometimes, if there were important issues coming up, I'd see him three or four times a month. At other times, only once a month. I was always very careful not to bother him with things that could be settled by someone else—the chief of staff, or the vice president, or the head of another department. You have to be very thoughtful about how you use your relationship with the president. You don't want to discuss an aviation agreement with Canada when he's in the middle of dealing with a government shutdown or a foreign policy crisis. I only went to him when I had something extremely important to talk about.

Dr. Bauer: I want to ask about the impeachment crisis. You know the major players personally. Early in the Lewinsky scandal, before the president admitted that he had lied, I saw on TV Madeleine Albright, backed by other cabinet members, defending the president.

Federico Peña: I was at that cabinet meeting. The White House staff asked for certain cabinet members to come out and speak on behalf of the president. They didn't ask for volunteers, they told us who they wanted to speak. That happened regularly when problems came up. Certain members would be asked to speak.

Dr. Bauer: So you were at the meeting where the cabinet sat around a table and heard the president personally explain that he was completely innocent. How did you feel when the big confession came out a few months later?

Federico Peña: Very disappointed. I think all of us felt that he let us down. People felt angry and hurt. But in the end, after all those feelings and emotions surfaced, I think people were very forgiving. And as you saw, very few people left the administration. In fact, no one left, with the exception of the press secretary, Mike McCurry. In the end, I think people on the inside of the administration were able to forgive and say, "Let's get on with the people's business."

And, too, President Clinton is a very likable person. He's the kind of person you would love to have here right now. He's very warm and very personable, and he loves to be with people. There are some people in politics that really don't like to be around other people, but Clinton gets depressed if he can't be around people. And he's very entertaining, and he's bright and invigorating. The experience created a real duality. We genuinely liked the guy. And then we'd think, "But how could he let this happen?"

Dr. Bauer: How do you repair the level of trust?

Federico Peña: You have to earn people's trust, I think. Let's take an example. Whenever people are hurting, after an earthquake, or the recent tornado that devastated Oklahoma, Clinton gets out there and connects with the people. But more importantly, the administration delivers. In the Bush administration, FEMA was criticized as an agency that couldn't deliver. The Clinton administration reformed FEMA and got it to work. That's how you rebuild trust. You keep on delivering the things you promised. Every day. That's why Clinton's job approval ratings remain high. He delivers what he promised, whether it's a balanced budget, welfare reform, or disaster relief. If it is within his power, you know he will deliver.

People struggle to evaluate Bill Clinton. Do you concentrate on his personal failings, or do you concentrate on his sizable policy accomplishments? I think this administration will end with Clinton still getting high job approval ratings. Those personal issues will always be there for historians to consider. But it's been fascinating to see how the American people responded. The political pundits in the media all thought this president was finished. They have consistently underestimated his energy, his commitment, his willingness to fight back and to continue to do his job. And he does it very well.

But it frustrates his critics. It drives them up a wall. He keeps coming back, time after time, and does the right thing for the American people. And for that, the American people have said, "We still want this guy."

★ ★ ★

CHAT ROOM

Jesse
a conservative
Libertarian

Krystal
a liberal
Democrat

Suzanne
a moderate
Republican

Turi
a moderate
Democrat

Will
a moderate

Ideals, Role Models, and Real Presidents
★ ★ ★

Dr. Bauer:	We're going to begin our discussion of the presidency with the question, Why is it that so many political science textbooks give such a negative view of American presidents?
Suzanne:	The Sanchez reading refers to the way introductory American government texts describe the presidency. It is such a big job, we expect so much of our presidents that inevitably we see most presidents as failing to measure up.
Dr. Bauer:	So it's almost impossible for a president to be great?
Suzanne:	That's right.
Dr. Bauer:	What do you all think about that?
Will:	Well, to do the job described in college texts is tough: The president has to possess an "amazing collection of skills." He has to be a communicator, a campaigner, a great politician, "a consummate administrator."
Suzanne:	Presidents come into the office with no experience because there isn't another job anywhere quite like it. I think the college textbooks have it right! It is almost impossible! They not only have to know about running for office, they also have to know about hiring good advisers and setting up the White House once they win. Then the president has to know about domestic policy and foreign policy. Here in college, when we major in political science, we have to concentrate in either U.S. or foreign affairs. But a president has to be equally good at all of it to be considered a success, and who can do all that equally well?
Krystal:	It seems to me that there are some ways to gain experience. For instance, a senator has to deal with both foreign policy and domestic policy. So I think there are ways to get preparation for the job.
Turi:	But nothing trains you for the presidency, for all the roles you have to play. Presidents are expected to be "up to speed" in a very short time. They're thrown into all sorts of emergency situations that they couldn't possibly have

	prepared for. They don't begin to have the experience they need until they're halfway through their term and need to think about reelection so they can complete what they've started.
Suzanne:	We all have this nostalgic attitude that previous presidents were so much greater, but being president today may be harder than ever.
Will:	That's another point Sanchez is trying to make. Authors write introductory political science texts to dispel myths that students bring to college from high school: that George Washington and Thomas Jefferson were great, that all the presidents were great. Textbook authors write to show another side.
Dr. Bauer:	Let's focus on what you said about the myth of great presidents.
Krystal:	When we talk about high school versus college, we need to remember that these two types of schools do very different things. The job of the secondary school is to socialize us—give us that positive attitude so we stand up and say the Pledge of Allegiance with pride. Later, when we move on to college, we have the academic freedom to question the authority of others.
Will:	I agree with that, but the article takes it a step further and suggests that the publishers of the high-school textbooks are actually trying to stay in this middle ground and not antagonize any group. So they have to take a little bit different slant, because they are worried about making the parents of the students angry, as well.
Dr. Bauer:	High-school textbooks steer clear of ideology. They don't want the Republican parents screaming because Reagan's not rated as a great president, and they don't want the Democratic parents screaming because JFK isn't rated as a great president. Looking at presidential flaws can be an ideological football, so high-school texts whitewash comparisons of presidents and say they were all swell. If the high-school texts mythologize the presidency, what do the college texts do?
Krystal:	Thinking back on my 101 classes, I don't remember the textbooks discussing ideology in any depth. We sort of skimmed through the presidents with an emphasis on a few achievements. It's not like big discussions were held over whether George Washington was better than Thomas Jefferson.
Dr. Bauer:	But Sanchez found that most introductory American government texts provide some sort of ranking of the presidents. Sanchez compared thirty-six different texts. You would imagine that thirty-six different texts would vary in ideological points of view.
Turi:	But most of those thirty-six texts don't vary when it comes to rating presidents! They all agree: Modern presidents, with the exception of one or two, aren't very good!
Dr. Bauer:	That's consistent over thirty-six texts. And you're right, Krystal, there's very little discussion about the presidents. When discussion does appear, it is negative almost seventy percent of the time. Is it good or bad for students if in high school, all the American presidents are great, and suddenly in college, the pres-

idents all stink? That's the key issue: Does a negative view of American presidents in college textbooks affect students?

Jesse: I think it has an effect. I think the student feels a tremendous disillusionment. It's hard to recover a faith in the presidency. If you take an upper-level course on the presidency, they eventually tell you about the limitations of the office, what presidents have done in crises, which presidents never had a crisis so we don't know if they were good or not. And you end up with more respect for presidents.

Dr. Bauer: But most people who take Introduction to American Government don't continue in political science!

Suzanne: If there is an effect, I don't think it's so bad. If the ultimate goal is not to teach about the presidency itself, but to teach people to question myths, to research the truth, to look more closely at government, then the negativity in college textbooks might be an effective wake-up call.

Dr. Bauer: So far we have looked at the myth of the perfect presidents of the past versus the reality of recent presidents. When we turn to Ken Burns's article, "Could They Be Elected Today? Too Human to Be Heroes?" we get an interesting spin on both problems, don't we?

Will: Burns picks up on the point that our so-called "great Presidents" might not have been so hot by today's modern standards. Not only has the office of the president changed and gotten more complex, as Suzanne said, but the press is much more of a problem today.

Krystal: Look at what Burns says about Lincoln! He's the president most of us think of as truly heroic, but Burns says Lincoln could not get elected today.

Dr. Bauer: It's only after his death that Lincoln was judged a great president. You should read the stuff that was written about Lincoln during his presidency! And Burns says if our modern press had been around then, presidents most of us consider great or heroic could never have been elected. As tough as the press was in Lincoln's day, since Watergate, Burns calls them "scandal-addicted." What would today's press have done to these historic figures?

Suzanne: Thomas Jefferson's red hair would not have looked good on television.

Dr. Bauer: Yes, but what factor would have prevented Jefferson from being elected president, according to this article?

Krystal: His debts.

Turi: His affair with Sally Hemmings!

Dr. Bauer: Yes. Sally Hemmings was his slave, and it was rumored that he fathered her children. It was a scandal at the time. It was used against him by his opponents in the newspapers of the day. If he were running now, the Jefferson–Hemmings affair would be on "Hardball," "Crossfire," and "Larry King"—it would be all over. The media would love that story. They'd hunt down Sally Hemmings and force her to go on the record. What does Ken Burns say about Abraham Lincoln?

Turi:	His wife would be a big problem if he were running for president today.
Dr. Bauer:	His wife was sometimes quite depressed.
Krystal:	And so was he.
Turi:	This surprised me. I didn't know Lincoln was so frequently depressed.
Dr. Bauer:	Yes, most historians think he suffered from depression, but Americans don't like to think of their presidents as having psychological flaws. Maybe past presidents appear great because they didn't have the modern, relentless press peering at their flaws. We're not as aware of their weaknesses as we are of every weakness in the modern president. For example, who is another historically great president whose flaws we have forgiven and forgotten? Which president had an affair with his wife's social secretary?
Will:	FDR.
Suzanne:	Franklin Delano Roosevelt.
Dr. Bauer:	Franklin Roosevelt was a deeply flawed human being, Abraham Lincoln was a deeply flawed human being, Thomas Jefferson was a deeply flawed human being. But when they were elected, did these deeply flawed individuals do some great things despite their flaws?
Turi:	Yes.
Krystal:	Apparently, people at that time recognized that they had flaws and voted for them anyway.
Jesse:	Somebody has to get elected. Regardless of the flaws people saw in Lincoln, they saw more flaws in the people who were running against him.
Will:	Yes we are all flawed, but Burns makes a distinction that I think is important. Not every flaw is character defining.
Jesse:	I agree. The question becomes, Do some flaws even matter? Does it matter, or did it matter at the time, that Thomas Jefferson was having an affair? Did the people of the time think that was going to affect the way that he conducted himself in office? Clearly, that's a question we're still asking today after the impeachment trial has concluded. If you think that these flaws necessarily will affect his performance in office then, yes, maybe we need to know about them. But if don't think they will, why bring them up? It doesn't matter.
Dr. Bauer:	Many voters at the time knew these past presidents had personal lives that were not suitable role models for children. There's a famous story about Grover Cleveland who had a child born out of wedlock. After Cleveland won the presidency, the scandal became very public with a child's nursery rhyme: "Ma, Ma, where's my pa? Gone to the White House, ha, ha, ha." These presidents were elected anyway, despite their personal problems. Would they have been elected today? That's the question Burns is asking.
Turi:	Burns is saying, if you want to look to a past when all the presidents were heroes and great role models, it doesn't exist.

Will:	And if we wanted presidents to be perfect, not even the so-called great presidents would have been elected.
Dr. Bauer:	As "Mediocrity at the Helm" points out, we've never had perfect presidents, but we've managed anyway. We seem to veer between a myth of great presidents and a myth of presidential inadequacy.
Krystal:	Essentially we're hiring a person to do a job, and we don't know if the person's going to work out. It's the chance we take. We may have to fire them, or their term may end, and they may not get a second chance.
Will:	Yes, but to Americans, the presidency is seen somehow as something much more special than just a job. The president fills such a symbolic leadership role for the whole country that we get caught up in trying to elect perfect people. No other part of the government gets that much psychological weight. For example, how come there are no rating systems for great Speakers of the House?
Turi:	It's easier to pinpoint and judge one person than deal with Congress!
Dr. Bauer:	Right, and it's easier for one person to grow to mythic proportions rather than a body of 535 members!
Suzanne:	And not just in this country, but worldwide. A large portion of the world's population would recognize Bill Clinton before they'd recognize the Speaker of the House.
Dr. Bauer:	How many of you know who the Speaker of the House is right now? He keeps a very low profile.
Turi:	Can't cough up the name.
Krystal:	Nope.
Jesse:	The only one rolling around in my head is the speaker of the Colorado house.
Dr. Bauer:	Dennis Hastert is the Speaker. And even you, my top students, didn't know his name. We used to have a system that was described in the 1890s as *congressional government,* when the Speaker was extremely powerful and very well known. But the twentieth century has been one long story of increased presidential power. And that means the president has the highest profile of anybody.
Turi:	So, here's how things are different for presidents: If we hire a person for just a job, we don't care about their personal lives. But because we only have one president whom we look up to as a mythic figure, we hold him to a higher standard.
Will:	And that's how we ended up impeaching Bill Clinton!
Jesse:	I've seen this in a lot of campaigns. Once a candidate comes along who doesn't seem to have any flaws, then the press seems to double its efforts to find something, because nobody is that perfect!
Turi:	We want to find the negative.

Krystal:	Because I think we want to destroy this myth. I don't think that's so bad. We should know they couldn't possibly be perfect people.
Dr. Bauer:	Well, let me throw this out, because I think you've just touched on an important point. If we demythologize the presidency, we take the myth away, we show the people warts and all. This is what the post-Watergate media wants to do, don't they? Do you think that Krystal is right? In tug of war between the wart-exposing media and the perfect candidate in the campaign ad, will we come to have a balanced view of the president? Or do we need the myth in order to trust our presidents?
Jesse:	Burns brings up a good example: Ronald Reagan was the first divorced president. Twenty years earlier, that would have been fatal. But by 1980, we accepted that kind of flaw. Maybe we are all getting more mature.
Krystal:	And perhaps we're happy with the Constitution, and that's all that really matters. The president may be a symbolic leader, but he doesn't run the country all by himself, and if he's less than perfect, why should we care?
Will:	Maybe we are in the middle of a demythologizing process; maybe we are growing up as a nation, because after all, Bill Clinton is certainly flawed. And yet what's Bill Clinton's job approval rating?
Turi:	It's high.
Krystal:	Yes, and it stayed high for an extremely long time, surprising to most people.
Dr. Bauer:	And this was true despite what Burns calls "our current scandal-addicted media" going into great detail about Clinton's sex life.
Jesse:	The American election process makes a big deal about character. In negative ads, in the media, candidate so-and-so smoked dope when he was younger and candidate so-and-so had an affair. It's the candidates' own fault because they raise the issue. You can't bring up character and not expect it to be used against you.
Dr. Bauer:	They bring it up because the press is going to bring it up. George W. Bush is now talking about his flaws because he knows the press is going to go after him, so he'd better bring it up himself. It's self-defense. Burns focuses on a "scandal-addicted media" but doesn't say anything about scandal-addicted negative campaigns.
Krystal:	I still think it's progress to be honest about our leaders instead of trying to hang onto these myths! Let's admit that we, including our presidents, are flawed and stop trying to present ourselves as perfect people.
Dr. Bauer:	It's also much more exciting for the media to talk about a character flaw than it is to talk about the actual issue positions of presidents or presidential candidates.
Suzanne:	It is easier to discuss those character flaws than it is to make persuasive arguments about policy decisions or legislative achievements. If you start discussing what Bill Clinton did or didn't do about education in Arkansas, what

	do you have to do? Define his policies, analyze them, compare them to his opponents'. It's so much easier to ask if he's been faithful to his wife.
Jesse:	Makes the ten o'clock news sound bite, where policy discussion doesn't.
Dr. Bauer:	Ken Burns asks two things: "Could they be elected today?" and were past presidents "too human to be heroes?" Does the modern press allow anybody to be a hero?
Turi:	No.
Krystal:	The appeal of demystification is that it allows a person to be heroic in special areas, not an all-around perfect person.
Dr. Bauer:	That's an interesting point. Here's an example. In the presidential primaries, people talked about the heroism of John McCain. Now Senator McCain is a true hero in an old-fashioned sense. He was a POW during Vietnam, and he acted heroically when he was a POW, but when he came back from Vietnam, he had a terrible time with his wife. The marriage blew up, he had several affairs, and his campaign is now busy trying to make sure that the press doesn't make his marriage problems the big deal about John McCain. So I think that's an interesting point, Krystal. We can still have heroes, but they're heroes in one part of their lives.
Will:	Let's not expect them to be heroes in every way.
Dr. Bauer:	So maybe we can have a president that is heroic in making economic policy even though he has problems with his sex life. That's a very different view of heroes, and after the Clinton impeachment, it is certainly Ken Burns's view.
Suzanne:	Then, it's good for students to make distinctions and see presidents with more discerning, less star-spangled eyes. We live in a democracy that is supposed to involve people in the process. We need to start looking at candidates for office in a different, more thoughtful way, accepting flaws, and leaving room for the heroic. If we're saying we haven't had good presidents in the recent past, but we want to do better, this is one way to go about it.

★ ★ ★

For Additional Reading

Go to InfoTrac College Edition, your online research library at

http://web1.infotrac-college.com

Enter the following search terms using the Subject Guide or Key Terms.

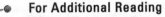

cabinet	feeding frenzy	scandals
chief of staff	impeachment	spokes-in-a-wheel management
divided government	presidency	style

13 The Judicial Branch

MONICA BAUER

A PERSONAL PERSPECTIVE ON the Supreme Court and *Roe* v. *Wade*

ONE OF THE MOST CONTROVERSIAL CASES ON WHICH THE Supreme Court has ruled is *Roe* v. *Wade.* Before *Roe,* most citizens expressed no great concern over who was appointed to the Supreme Court, or what kind of philosophy the justices followed when they got there. The readings in this section focus on the controversies over appointments and judicial philosophy. These topics reveal that court decisions can and do change people's lives. And no case illustrates that better than *Roe.*

The Supreme Court relies on precedents set by past cases when they decide a current case, but *Roe* had few precedents. The Supreme Court argues over what the framers intended when they wrote the Constitution and the Bill of Rights, but there was little in the historical record about the framers' views on abortion. That left the Court to find an opinion using a combination of tools—including simply constructing the most reasonable argument that seemed to fit a broad interpretation of certain words in the Constitution. What the Supreme Court is not supposed to do is make a decision based on religious beliefs or their own personal philosophies. These are, however, the tools ordinary people use to decide their opinions about abortion.

For the public, abortion is an issue colored by religious belief. Very few scientists are attempting to define exactly when human life begins; science, after all, deals in what can be proved or disproved. How can one prove or disprove the exact moment human life begins? That is a question for theologians and philosophers. But it is the key question in the abortion debate. If abortion kills a person, it is murder. If the fetus is not a person, then the woman who aborts is exercising control over her own body.

When I was an undergraduate, I spent a semester taking a philosophy course that focused on the topic of abortion. It was just three years after the *Roe* v. *Wade* decision, and the idea of abortion rights was still relatively new. In this philosophy class, we studied some arguments that have now become classics in the abortion debate. One argument defined the difference between a fetus, which had no right to life, and a baby, which would have such a right, hinging on whether or not the fetus had a particular hallmark of personhood: a personality. In other words, to be human requires a sense of individuality—singular experiences that you feel and understand to be your own.

A baby, even a one-minute-old baby, has a sense of personhood, a sense of self. Babies know when they are being held, or hit, or fed. They communicate out of personal needs and desires. I didn't realize just how individual a newborn baby could be, until I became a mother. The first moments after my daughter's birth convinced me that a new individual had entered the world. Some babies cry at birth, but my daughter looked at the world, took it in, and showed all of us what kind of personality she had. She was calm and contented, but aware and very interested in everything that happened to her. She was a person right away, a person different from me, even though only a few minutes earlier she had been part of me.

That sense of personhood can only come from a highly developed brain. A fetus at six weeks, which is the age when more than ninety-five percent of abortions take place, has a brain the size of a small thumb. Scientists tell us a brain that size can't even feel pain. A brain that size is completely without awareness, especially self-awareness. For some philosophers, killing a fetus that size is the moral equivalent of killing a fish.

Other philosophers say that that analysis misses the point. A fetus at six weeks is uniquely human because it has the possibility of becoming a self-aware person later in its development. A fish will never grow a brain large enough to understand love and loss, Shakespeare and calculus, but the human fetus will. That is the argument from potential.

Still another philosophical argument looked at abortion from the woman's point of view and viewed abortion rights as an individual liberty. The analogy was made between government forcing a woman to remain pregnant and government ordering a man to remain attached to another person for nine months. Imagine a healthy, adult male tethered to a less-healthy person by an IV that delivered blood continuously from his heart to the other's.

A woman who is pregnant is tethered to her fetus in the same way. Her body becomes something less than her own. She may react easily to pregnancy, or she may experience any number of symptoms, from nausea and vomiting to gestational diabetes, a type of diabetes specific to pregnant women. Late in the pregnancy, her mobility will become limited, and she will find herself exhausted doing the simplest tasks. If the fetus becomes diseased, she runs the risk of dying herself.

If she is pregnant by choice, then she accepts these risks. But if she is not pregnant by intention, then a government that would outlaw abortions is a government forcing her to give up her own body and health for the well-being of another. If we think it immoral for a government to force a healthy male to give up nine months of mobility to medically treat another person, then it logically follows that we must also find it immoral for government to force a woman to remain pregnant. The interesting thing about this argument is that it doesn't depend on the definition of when a fetus becomes a human life. The emphasis is on the liberty of individuals: Can government force us to help other people, even to performing life-giving tasks?

I thought about these arguments when I was pregnant with my daughter. Because she was wanted, and planned, the inconveniences of pregnancy were not that hard to bear. Then, when I developed life-threatening complications after giving birth, I thought about it again. I nearly died having this baby. But this was a baby I wanted and adored. How would I feel if this were my fifth baby instead of my first, or a baby I could not afford to raise on my own as a single mother? How would I feel if this baby were the result of date rape at a young age?

Just last month, as I was working on this book, one of my older, nontraditional students told me about her recent experience with her own seventeen-year-old daughter, who had confided that she had become pregnant. "We have always been strongly pro-choice in our house; in fact, my daughter had volunteered for Planned Parenthood the previous summer. Our church is a pro-choice church, and there is no sense that having an abortion would betray religious values. So as soon as possible, she and I went together and had her pregnancy ended. But, Dr. Bauer, no matter what you hear on the anti-abortion side of the debate, I want you to know that the abortion was neither simple nor easy," she said, with a mixture of tears, anger, and sadness.

"My daughter continues to struggle with feelings of sadness and mourning for a potential life. Even I felt the loss of what might have been: a first grandchild. Yet both of us remain clear that this was the right decision for her—that this was the wrong time for her life as an independent young woman to end with the twenty-four-hour-a-day, eighteen-year obligation to care for a child.

"Dr. Bauer, I wanted to say this in class the other day, when somebody said abortion was too easy under the law today. I wanted to say that my daughter's abortion was painful and difficult. It was hardly the type of thing a young woman could or would do without thinking."

In an ideal world, no woman would become pregnant without intention. But one of the challenges of political science is coming to grips with human nature. If we believe human nature can and should be controlled, then perhaps pregnant women "get what they deserve." After all, most terminated pregnancies are the result of consensual sex. But if we believe that human nature leads people to make mistakes, then our attitude toward unplanned pregnancy may be more forgiving. (What I would term "forgiving," conservatives such as George Will might call "permissive.")

In the opinion written by Justice Blackmun in *Roe* v. *Wade,* we find a view of abortion that centers on personal liberty for the woman. Justice Blackmun could not have placed the liberty of the woman ahead of the liberty of the fetus, if he thought they were equal. Blackmun believed the fetus gained more rights as it grew closer to what some philosophers would term "true personhood." Obviously,

Blackmun could not have written his opinion if he believed that the fetus were a human being from the moment of conception, rather than a creature that held the potential to become human. Because of this opinion, Blackmun is reviled by some, including the columnist Vince Page in his column printed in this section, "They Called Him 'Author'." In large part because of Blackmun's opinion in *Roe* that even a court with a majority appointed by Republicans has refused to overturn, John Leo wrote "In the Matter of the Court v. Us," also one of the readings in this section.

That leads us back to the beginning of this essay. Some people are sure they know that the fetus is a human being deserving of full constitutional rights from the moment of conception. They are sure, because they hold deeply felt religious beliefs that proclaim this to be true. William James, a philosopher of religious experience, once wrote that "faith means belief in something concerning which doubt is theoretically possible." Justice Blackmun understood that the definition of when human life begins may always be beyond proving.

Here was Justice Blackmun's dilemma: If abortion remained a criminal offense, what would be the justification? Abortion conducted under safe and sanitary conditions no longer threatened a woman's health. The only remaining justification would hinge on accepting one religion's definition of human life: that it began at conception. But that belief was not shared by other religious groups, and certainly was not shared by those who followed no religion.

Now, I am not a huge fan of *Roe* v. *Wade* as constitutional law. Along with the Clinton-appointed Justice Ruth Bader Ginsburg, I believe the arguments are sometimes vague and hard to follow. Given the scientific difficulty of deciding when human life begins, however, I think Justice Blackmun had no choice but to rule that in the first two trimesters of pregnancy—during which there was vast disagreement and doubt about what rights could or should be given to the fetus—the choice should be left to the woman carrying the fetus. Justice Blackmun retained the right of the government to protect the life of a third-trimester fetus.

This allows those whose religious teachings forbid abortion to refrain from having abortions. And it allows those whose religions do not oppose abortion to exercise their own judgments over their own bodies. And, of course, it allows those who follow no religion at all to follow the dictates of their own consciences.

Because of *Roe* v. *Wade,* and other controversial decisions by the Supreme Court from the 1950s to the 1990s, nominations to the Supreme Court have become pitched battles. So much is at stake that special interest groups turn nominations into minicampaigns that mock and distort the Senate's constitutional duty to offer "advice and consent" to judicial appointments. It is tempting for a president to appoint the least offensive nominee: A judge's potentially mediocre or outstanding contribution to our interpretations of the Constitution now runs a clear second to easy confirmation. Some people are so angered by the decisions of the Court that they want to put a check on the Supreme Court itself.

What do you think?

Excerpt from "Robert Bork and Civil War"

Edward Lazarus

Announcing Powell's departure, Chief Justice Rehnquist knew he was "dropping a bombshell." Powell's retirement promised a major upheaval in the politics of the Court and threatened to shatter already fragile bonds of civility. There is a tradition at the Court that when a Justice retires, the other Justices purchase for him the chair he has used on the bench. The price is cheap, roughly five dollars per Justice, but in this case the act was especially dear. The loss of Powell inspired profound sadness and also, especially among the liberals, no small amount of dread.

The reaction at the White House, by contrast, was pure jubilation. From the outset of his presidency, Reagan had hoped for the chance to shift dramatically the balance of the Supreme Court. Already he could account for two of the Court's nine members. Yet his substitution of O'Connor and Scalia for Stewart and Burger, while shoring up the Court's conservative wing, had not materially affected the outcome of key cases. With Powell's departure, the prospect of a solid conservative majority was finally at hand.

So, too, was the ideal nominee: Judge Robert Bork, the sixty-year-old intellectual dean of the conservative legal world. In terms of experience and qualifications, a more perfect legal résumé would have been hard to imagine. Bork had been a tenured professor at Yale Law School, solicitor general of the United States (in the Nixon administration), a successful corporate lawyer, and, as of 1981, one of twelve judges on the D.C. Circuit (the nation's second most prestigious court).

Philosophically, Bork was perfectly in tune with the administration, in some ways even its bandleader. For more than thirty years, he had been in the forefront of conservative academics

who savaged the post-*Brown* Court as an out of control "Imperial Judiciary" usurping authority from the democratically elected branches of government. More technically, Bork was the nation's premier advocate for interpreting the Constitution according to the "original intent" of the Framers, a controversial jurisprudence, which Attorney General Meese had adopted as the intellectual centerpiece of the administration's attack on liberal legal precedents.

In Bork's view, the most significant rulings of the Warren era (as well as like-minded ones of the Burger Court) were products not only of poor reasoning but of what he described as totally "indefensible" and "illegitimate" methods for interpreting the Constitution. Among the opinions he considered utterly without constitutional foundation were the Court's reapportionment cases establishing the principle of "one-person, one-vote," cases striking down poll taxes and prohibiting the enforcement of racially restrictive real estate covenants, all decisions upholding affirmative action, or those based on a generalized "right to privacy," including *Roe* v. *Wade* and its precursor, *Griswold* v. *Connecticut,* establishing a right to use birth control.

Not surprisingly, the Democrats, who had regained control of the Senate in 1986, tried to head off Bork's selection. Senator Joseph Biden, the chairman of the Senate Judiciary Committee, warned the White House that choosing Bork, regardless of his credentials, would provoke an intense confirmation fight. When he was paid no heed, liberals on and off Capitol Hill started girding for battle.

Within hours of Reagan's selection of Bork, Sen. Edward Kennedy, on behalf of the entire civil rights and civil liberties establishment, sounded the war cry. "Robert Bork's America," Kennedy warned with calculated hyperbole, "is a land in which women would be forced into back-alley abortions, blacks would sit at segregated lunch counters, rogue police could break down citizens' doors in midnight raids, school children could not be taught about evolution, writers and artists could be censored at the whim of government, and the doors of the Federal courts would be shut on the fingers of millions of citizens for whom the judiciary is—and is often the only—protector of the individual rights that are at the heart of our democracy." So began a nomination battle of unprecedented rancor and ferocity, which ended when a man whom the Senate had approved unanimously to sit on the court of appeals was soundly rejected by the same body (58–42) for a seat on the Supreme Court.

I had just graduated from Yale Law School and was beginning a clerkship with Judge William Norris (a leading liberal on the Ninth Circuit) when Bork was chosen. To everyone I knew in the close-quartered world of legal academia, clerking, and judging, to everyone I knew with a serious interest or stake in legal policy, nothing was more important in that summer of 1987 than what happened in and around the Senate Caucus Room where the Bork hearings unfolded and Judge Bork himself jousted for more than thirty hours with Senator Biden's committee. I took sides; all of us took sides, passionately and irrevocably, as others before us had divided over the Rosenbergs' guilt or whether Nixon should be impeached.

The nomination, of course, was important on its own terms. Everyone understood that Bork's elevation to the Court would in all likelihood substantially alter the course of constitutional law. But the fears and allegiances that caused us so aggressively to choose up sides transcended even such considerable consequences. For liberals, the Bork hearings were more than a defense of hard-won victories regarding civil rights and civil liberties. They were a test of where the nation was headed, with one road leading toward a more just society and the other toward political recidivism and the moral straitjacket of the religious right.

For conservatives, the fight was no less fundamental. Bork's nomination was a chance to curb a rights-happy Court that had overstepped its authority and undermined the social order. More broadly, his nomination stood for a philosophical commitment to the value of limits, rules, and standards as opposed to the "anything goes" relativism that since the 1960s had come to prevail in everything from morality to legal interpretation. As *Time* magazine assessed the takes, "All at once the political passions of three decades seemed to converge on a single empty chair."

From the liberal perspective, the long fuse to the Bork hearings was the moment Ronald Reagan took office and began a concerted campaign to put his distinctive conservative stamp on both federal law and the entire federal judiciary. In that sense, the fury liberals unleashed on Bork was not personal to him but the culmination of more than six years of anger and frustration as they watched Reagan's revolutionaries swing wrecking balls at the edifice of legal rights they had been building for a generation.

The most obvious (but by no means the only) method for bringing the Reagan Revolution to the federal legal system was the judicial appointment process. Many presidents, Franklin Roosevelt quite effectively, have sought to appoint like-minded judges to the bench. Careful judicial selection is an obvious and natural way for any administration to perpetuate its political legacy through the long-term work of hand-picked, life-tenured judges. The Reagan administration, however, aiming in Ed Meese's words to "institutionalize the Reagan Revolution," raised this previously rather informal practice to something closer to fine art.

Under Attorney General William French Smith, the Justice Department had established an Office of Legal Policy to oversee a screening process that deliberately and substantially increased executive branch control over nominations. In a sharp break with tradition, the administration curtailed the role of senators in the choice of lower court appointees for their respective home states. (In the less partisan past, even senators of the opposing party had participated in the selection process.) Also, for the first time

White House and Justice Department officials conducted detailed interviews with leading judicial candidates about their legal philosophies. Staffers at OLP minutely scrutinized candidates' written works for hints of political or legal apostasy. One leading contender for an opening on the D.C. Circuit was scrubbed because, despite superb credentials and an otherwise strong conservative background, he'd given small donations to a gun control group and to Planned Parenthood. Another candidate lost out because of ties to a legal aid society.

After winning reelection in 1984, President Reagan was on track to appoint more than half the federal judiciary before leaving office, and this fact loomed ominously over every group, legal and political, whose power derived from the rights explosion of the Warren era. Liberal interest groups geared up for a counteroffensive in the Senate, the body charged by the Constitution with advising in and consenting to the president's nominations. With Ted Kennedy as their champion, the civil rights and abortion rights communities—accusing Reagan of trying to "pack" the courts with right-wing extremists—worked furiously to head off the most reactionary judicial candidates and to torpedo those nominees who appeared most vulnerable.*

Starting in 1985, these efforts succeeded in a few highly publicized cases. Jefferson Sessions III became the first victim of confirmation scrutiny when the NAACP revealed his history of making oddball and offensive racist remarks.** A few other names were withdrawn before public hearings.

In general, though, despite a few close votes, Reagan succeeded in naming a cadre of unusually young, often enormously gifted ideologues to fill his large reservoir of judicial vacancies. Leading academics such as Richard Posner and Frank Easterbrook as well as rising conservative stars such as J. Harvie Wilkinson III and Alex Kozinski (both former Supreme Court clerks), invaded the courts of appeals with sparkling intelligence combined with a conscious desire to undo the liberal status quo. Other less sterling appointees understood well enough whom and how to follow. To liberals, the better appointees were evil geniuses, the lesser ones just evil. . . .

Naturally, conservatives thought that the roles were reversed, that they were crusading to rebuild a world liberals and leftists had shattered and defiled in the 1960s. Almost everything the left cherished—from welfare entitlements to the sexual revolution—was born in the social, political, and legal upheaval of this decade. For Bork and his supporters, it had been a time of moral abdication, disorder, and decline.

From his base at Yale Law School, Bork had sallied occasionally into politics. He took to the pages of *The New Republic* to denounced the Civil Rights Bill of 1964 desegregating private hotels and restaurants as an unwarranted intrusion on the right of individuals to chose with whom to associate. He wrote position papers for Barry Goldwater in the 1964 presidential campaign and, four years later, organized academic support for Richard Nixon. When Congress challenged Nixon's legal authority to extend the Vietnam War to Cambodia, Bork provided a legal refutation. In the same vein, he offered theoretical grounding for prohibiting court-ordered housing.

The formative environment for Bork's views, however, was not the public arena of politics but the cloistered halls of academia, in particular

*Many liberals have harped on the Reagan administration's systematic effort to "pack" federal courts with like-minded judges. It is difficult to pinpoint a sound basis for objecting, however. Reagan was elected in part because of an expectation that he would use the presidency's appointment power to further his ideological agenda. That he did so, even with unprecedented zeal, was part of his mandate. By the same token, the Democrats who controlled the Senate had every right not to confirm his nominees because of their ideology or from a belief that ideologically motivated nominees (of whatever stripe) often make poor judges.

**Ironically, Sessions is now a U.S. senator from Alabama with a seat on the Judiciary Committee. In that position, he has played a significant role in holding up the confirmation of President Clinton's judicial nominees.

Yale University and its preeminent law school. It is difficult to describe for anyone unfamiliar with this world the intensely personal nature of its philosophical disputes or the depth of the schisms that divided faculties and students in the late 1960s and the 1970s. Faculties broke apart, old friends stopped speaking, colleagues came to despise each other over the Vietnam War and how to deal with student sit-ins, strikes, and other acts of civil disobedience. One's stands on the war, on matters of race, and on student protest were tests of character as well as politics. Opponents were not merely wrong, they were evil or complicit in evil.

In Bork's own thinking, events at Yale in 1970 appear to have been decisive. In April of that year, Yale was brought to a standstill when Black Panther Bobby Seale was charged with murder in a New Haven criminal court. Campus radicals whipped up frenzy and called for a student strike to publicize their claim that Seale could not get a fair trial in New Haven or anywhere else in America. Outside groups threatened "to bring Yale to its knees" through a campaign of on-campus violence. On April 23, at a feverish faculty meeting convened on a campus criss-crossed with roving bands of protesters, Yale President Kingman Brewster voiced sympathy with the students' appraisal of the American justice system and the professors voted en masse to countenance the unprecedented student strike. Despite this act of solidarity (or abject surrender, depending on one's perspective), four days later a suspicious fire struck the Yale Law Library, charring a wall of books. (A newspaper photo published the next day shows a stunned Bork observing the damage to his intellectual sanctuary. And, notably, Bork chose the memory of smoldering books as the starting point for his most recent attack on "modern liberalism.")

To academics who spent their lives contemplating the meaning and consequences of freedom or its absence, who cherished the ideal of a university as a seat of learning and rational discourse, the disruption of domestic order and the complicity of some teachers and administrators

in that attack were beyond forbearance. Bork's closest friend and mentor, the law professor Alexander Bickel, though opposed to the war, saw the campus and the country disintegrating into a "dictatorship of the self-righteous." The campus radicals, he declared, were engaging not in meaningful dissent but rather in intimidation, a kind of "vandalism . . . a series of curses which do not pretend any attempt at persuasion."

That fall, having seen Bickel hung in effigy in the law school courtyard on alumni weekend, Bork started work on his first major article in constitutional law. It was a rumination on the First Amendment that, not coincidentally, placed especially radical forms of political dissent outside the realm of constitutional protection.

When the Vietnam War ended and campus agitation subsided, the civil strife in academia did not. Whether the issue was affirmative action, multiculturalism, women's studies, or hate speech, the two sides perpetually replayed old themes and kept campus animosities fresh. What commentators now call the culture war was an everyday truth with an enormous power to divide and alienate. . . .

To Bork, the Warren Court was guilty of sins analogous to those he observed among his colleagues. Just as leftist law professors wielded scholarship as a weapon to further their political aims, the liberal Justices of the Warren Court abandoned traditional legal reasoning in favor of a "results-first, premises to follow" approach. Rather than interpret the Constitution according to its original meaning and purposes, Justices Brennan, Douglas, Goldberg, Fortas, and some of their successors had updated the document to conform with their own fashionable ideas. Rather than carry out their limited mandate of enforcing the specific commands of the Constitution within the Court's sphere of special competence, these Justices had set themselves up as an all-powerful liberal elite imposing on the country their own notions of right and wrong, fair and unfair. What CLS preached in theory, liberal Justices had put into practice: for both, there were "no rules, only passions."

Bork's own jurisprudence was a furious rejoinder to both his academic and his judicial foes. He proposed a much more circumscribed judicial role. In a representative democracy, Bork asserted, political judgments are to be made by the democratic branches of government and may be overridden by the unelected judiciary only if in violation of some explicit constitutional command. The meaning of the Constitution, he argued, must be determined according to the intention of its "framers"—"those who drafted, proposed, and ratified its provisions and various amendments." All that counted, according to Bork, was "how the words used in the Constitution would have been understood at the time." And "the judge's responsibility is to discern how the framers' values, defined in the context of the world they knew, apply in the world we know." . . .

Liberals rejoiced when the Senate rejected Robert Bork. I counted myself among them. During the hearings, my co-clerks and I had spent more than a few off-hours thinking up and funneling to friends on the Senate committee staff questions that would expose the weaknesses and contradictions in Bork's positions. Years later, I'm still glad Bork lost. His subsequent writings—including his recent proposal that Congress be given the power to override Supreme Court decisions—have only reinforced the conclusion that Bork would have been an intemperate and partisan Justice, arrogant about a judicial philosophy he only selectively practiced and could not effectively defend.

But, that said, I have come to appreciate, as I did not even consider at the time, the deep and lasting damage that the liberals' approach to the Bork hearings visited upon the Court. Skewering Bork on the issue of privacy ushered in the era of "stealth" nominees, during which a chief qualification for the Court became a lack of public comment coupled with a denial of private comment on *Roe v. Wade*, the most disputed case of the modern era. The Bork experience also established intense political campaigning and special interest lobbying as a fixed part of the nomina-

tion process. Such truth-twisting campaigning made a casualty of candor in the selection of life-tenured appointees to our highest court. The lobbying ate away the thin but crucial divide between law and politics—the public belief that the Supreme Court is not merely another political institution and that judges can and should stand above the expedient trade-offs of the day.

But the problem that the Bork hearings created for the Court penetrated far deeper than the institution's image and was more serious and immediate than such an almost quaint concern with keeping law and politics separate. The development of law, especially constitutional law, involves a delicate alchemy. If history is any judge, there is no single "right" approach to interpreting the Constitution. Certainly, neither the Justices nor the academics who dissect their work have ever agreed on one. Just as Bork's jurisprudence of original intent suffered from the inherent weakness of too closely linking the law to an unknowable past, other modes of interpretation potentially cast he law adrift without reference to the text, history, and structure of the document that is the charter of both our government and our liberties.

The most we can expect and what we must demand from the Court as it expounds the law is an integrity born of consistency and sincerity. Legitimate constitutional arguments are not limitless; they may take several forms familiar to law. They may be based on history, on precedent, on the text, on inferences from the way our government is structured, on appeals to ethics, or on prudential considerations about the consequences of a decision. Often, these modes of argument are used in combination, melded into a convincing whole. And none is perfect for every circumstance. Deciding which modes of argument best suit the facts and circumstances of a given case is both an inevitable moral choice and the essence of judging.

To undertake this process as a body of nine independent, opinionated judges, whose views in hard cases often prove irreconcilable, depends on a decency of process. For the system to work, for

Justices in disagreement to achieve an exchange of ideas, undertake a search for common ground, or even reach an agreement respectfully to disagree, there must first be trust and belief in mutual good faith. There must be a sense that both sides are advancing legal arguments because they believe in them deeply and not as a stratagem for imposing their will on the law. There must be a sense that reasons matter more than results. The power to interpret carries the responsibility of good faith and self-denial. When these are destroyed, nothing remains but counting votes and the exercise of raw power.

Bork's mentor, Alex Bickel, had written shortly before his death in 1975 that our system "cannot survive a politics of moral attack." Whether or not that is true as a general matter, the delicate process of collective judicial decision breaks under the weight of unrelenting ideology and the arrogance of certainty. That was the highest cost of the Bork nomination. Before the hearings ended, the possibility of trust, good faith, and self-doubt had been vanquished. Each side was convinced of its own virtue while, at the same time, believing that no tactic, no hypocrisy, no lie was too low or base or simply wrong for the other side to forgo. Both sides concluded that the best recourse in the future would be to fight fire with fire.

The final vote on Robert Bork's nomination (he refused to withdraw even when defeat was inevitable) was a beginning, not an end. Conservative political commentators, blaming liberal "dirty tricks" for their setback, exhorted followers to carry on Bork's war against the imperial liberal judiciary. Meanwhile, Reagan's attorney general urged top Justice Department officials to avoid seeking consensus and to "polarize the debate" on prominent legal issues. Liberals deluded themselves into thinking that, a bit of mendacity aside, they had found a true mission in upholding "the rule of law" against the forces of darkness.

The Justices, split 4–4 and waiting, had their own allegiances, of course, as well as friend and protégés in the thick of the fight. Watching the hearings from their respective Chambers, they were one step removed from the full emotional force of the conflagration. But that was inescapably a short-term isolation.

By the time of Bork's nomination, the ligatures of trust within the Court were already strained to the breaking point. Weekly confrontations over the death penalty and sharp divisions over race, abortion, and religion had seen to that. By the end of the hearings, the storm of civil war was hard against the Court's front door. Every month, the backlog of controversial cases grew as the Justices anxiously delayed decisions until joined by a tiebreaking ninth.

Regardless of Bork's defeat, it was only a matter of time until Reagan succeeded in putting a new conservative on the Court. And when he did, the battle would shift with all its ferocity from the Senate Caucus Room to the Court's inner chamber—and some of us, still tracking blood, spoiling for the next round, would shift with it.

They Called Him "Author"

Vince Page

It is a sad fact of modern history that the only Supreme Court nominations which have faced a tough confirmation battle in the Senate have been those of the more conservative justices. It is telling, therefore, that the nomination of Justice Harry Blackmun sailed through the Senate in 1970 with a unanimous 94–0 vote. There is much less to cheer about in his legacy.

It was Dwight Eisenhower who, when asked if he had made any mistakes during his presidency, replied, "Yes, two, and they are both sitting on the Supreme Court." By at least one estimate, one-quarter of the justices appointed to the Supreme Court have deviated from the expectations of those who appointed them. At the top of this list is Harry Blackmun, a Nixon appointee. When he came to the high Court, Blackmun aligned himself with the other conservative justices of the day, as was evidenced by his votes. In the 1973 term, Blackmun agreed with Chief Justice Warren Burger, also a Nixon appointee, 84 percent of the time and with the more liberal William Brennan—one of the Eisenhower appointees who gave him pause—only 49 percent of the time. By 1985, though, a "red-shift" had occurred to the left. Blackmun was agreeing with Brennan much more than with Burger, 30 percent more to be exact. When questioned about this, Blackmun parroted the oft-repeated liberal mantra about "maturing" with the job.

This maturation led a lawyer skilled only in taxes and wills before his 1959 appointment to the U.S. Court of Appeals to become the architect of the *Roe v. Wade* decision, which legalized infanticide in America. On the day he died— March 4th, 1999—Harry Blackmun was remembered almost universally by those in the news industry as the "author" of the *Roe v. Wade*

decision, which struck down the laws of 48 states prohibiting the gruesome practice of abortion in America.

It is altogether fitting and proper that Justice Blackmun should be dissed by referring to him as an author. The term "author" should be worn like a badge of shame by any Supreme Court Justice. Their job is to uphold the original intent of the Constitution—period. Listen to the twisted words of Justice Blackmun as he tries to rationalize his dereliction of duty in the *Roe v. Wade* decision:

> The Constitution does not explicitly mention any right of privacy. In a line of decisions, however, . . . the Court has recognized that a right of personal privacy, or a guarantee of certain areas or zones of privacy, does exist under the Constitution. . . . This right of privacy, whether it be founded on the Fourteenth Amendment's concept of personal liberty and restrictions upon state action, as we feel it is, or, as the District Court determined, in the Ninth Amendment's reservation of rights to the people, is broad enough to encompass a woman's decision whether or not to terminate her pregnancy.

Oh really!? These are the very weasel words used by Justice Blackmun to say that the Founding Fathers explicitly intended to give all women the right to kill their babies. It's enough to make anyone upchuck, with visions of aborted baby parts dancing in their head. You will note too, I hope, the complete and total absence of any quotes in support of abortion from the Founding Fathers.

Nor will you find any references to abortion in the Declaration of Independence or the Constitution. After all, if the colonists were really concerned about their right to butcher babies, shouldn't we find references there? But there is no such mention of abortion in either document.

Reprinted with permission of Vince Page from his weekly political column, March 8, 1999; available from <http://rampages.onramp.net/~rampage/p030899.htm>.

No, Blackmun just made it all up, as if from out of the ether. He legislated from the bench. He engaged in Socialist sophistry. He decreed by judicial fiat that which he knew could never be achieved by political means. He cheated so that the liberal cause might endure.

Shortly after his death and long before today Justice Harry Blackmun received his reward. With the blood of 38 million infants on his hands, his heart stopped beating in a lonely hospital room at the age of 90, after experiencing complications from a hip replacement. It was time for Harry Blackmun to meet the Great Lawgiver himself, the Judge of Judges.

I am quite certain that, given Mr. Blackmun's eminent status, Jesus Christ himself decided to meet him at the pearly gates. Then, with a host of aborted but angelic babies floating around the Lord's head as if to form a halo, the Master of the Universe posed the ultimate question: "You want to go where?"

The Lord undoubtedly said good-bye to Mr. Blackmun as he screamed into the bowels of Hades. As for myself, I simply say good riddance.

Jesse
a conservative
Libertarian

Krystal
a liberal
Democrat

Suzanne
a moderate
Republican

Turi
a moderate
Democrat

Will
a moderate

Nominations and Judicial Ideologies
★ ★ ★

Dr. Bauer: Let's begin with the famous confirmation battle over Robert Bork, Reagan's nominee to the Supreme Court. What should the Senate's role be? Should it allow the president his choice? Why was there a battle over this guy?

Jesse: It's in the Constitution.

Dr. Bauer: What's in the Constitution? That there should be a battle over a Senate confirmation?

Jesse: That the president nominates, and that the Senate confirms. It doesn't have to be a battle—at least not the pitched ideological battles of the last twenty years.

Will: I think the framers intended to provide for the possibility that some presidential appointments might not be in the people's interests. In that view, the fact that Senate opposition is possible, Senate opposition as the public's watchdog is good and fits with the system of checks and balances. Senate confirmation may not always be a battle, but it shouldn't be a rubber stamp either.

Dr. Bauer: But here we had a classic battle of divided government: the president of one party, a Senate majority of the opposite party. That's pretty new, in the last fifty years. What goes on in this battle? Is there an honest discussion of this man's qualifications?

Krystal: Liberal groups, especially feminist groups led by NOW, banded together in a media campaign to oppose the Bork nomination. Feminist groups were especially worried that Bork would vote to overturn *Roe* v. *Wade*. The picture they painted of Bork resulted in what Edward Lazarus calls "the half-truth in advertising" about who Bork was. Then the White House fought back by labeling Bork a moderate, which wasn't true either—he's very conservative.

Suzanne: Don't you think it was pretty amazing that there were ads about a Supreme Court nominee at all?

Dr. Bauer:	Groundbreaking. It hadn't even happened when the first African American was appointed to the Court—Thurgood Marshall—right in the middle of the civil rights controversy. What were the ad campaigns like, run by those interest groups that wanted to stop Bork?
Jesse:	I remember seeing those. They couldn't have been more graphic if they had portrayed Bork with a pitchfork and wearing a Ku Klux Klan uniform. He looked satanic in those ads.
Will:	They started a style of turning a nomination into a political campaign, complete with polls and advertising.
Dr. Bauer:	But the Supreme Court is not supposed to represent sides in any political fight. The Court's job is to interpret the Constitution. For most of our history, confirmation to the Court was a one- or two-day affair that centered on qualifications. Was Bork qualified to be a Supreme Court justice?
All:	Yes.
Turi:	But Bork would have seriously upset the balance on the Court. Isn't that why Democrats and Republicans fought so hard over his nomination? There are nine justices on the Supreme Court, so it takes five votes to reach a majority decision, and the Court had just lost a liberal justice. Any new appointee could affect the Court's rulings—particularly on abortion.
Jesse:	But the framers anticipated that the finest legal minds would be appointed to the Court: to the best of their abilities they would arrive at their decisions to do justice to the Constitution. There wasn't thought to be a need for balance because there wouldn't be such a wide division in how to interpret the Constitution.
Suzanne:	And before John Marshall made the Supreme Court an important institution, with the decision in *Marbury* v. *Madison,* nobody wanted to be on it because they didn't consider it an important part of the government. John Jay said he'd rather be governor of New York than serve on the Supreme Court. But presidents see Supreme Court appointments as living legacies. Long after a president has left office, their appointees will still be defining the law.
Turi:	Their legacies means the presidents' stands, their viewpoints, their ideas live on?
Dr. Bauer:	Yes. Some have argued that a Supreme Court appointment is the single most important power a president has because of its far-reaching consequences.
Krystal:	A Supreme Court appointment is a lifetime appointment.
Dr. Bauer:	But as Suzanne said, before the 1930s, a Supreme Court appointment wasn't thought of as that important. The Court was seen as impartial justices who agreed to take cases on appeal under the doctrine of judicial review and strictly applied the Constitution to laws passed by the state and Congress. Then, especially in the last fifty years, the Court acquired new power from a new phi-

losophy of interpretation, a philosophy that abandoned the idea of strict interpretation of the Constitution in favor of looking at broader principles behind the words. With this new power, it suddenly became very important who sat on the Court. Now, why wasn't Bork a good candidate for the Court, according to the liberals?

Jesse: He wants to go back to the older role and older philosophy of the Supreme Court. He's a proponent of the original intent doctrine: to look at what the original framers of the Constitution meant when they wrote it. But he also casts all of his interpretations in the most politically conservative light. For example, Lazarus talks about Bork's dislike for civil rights laws.

Dr. Bauer: What part of the Constitution is the Court interpreting when it looks at most of its civil rights cases?

Suzanne: The Fourteenth Amendment, because it applies the protections of the Bill of Rights to citizens of the states and overrules state laws through the supremacy clause.

Dr. Bauer: Edward Lazarus talks about the intentions of those who wrote the Fourteenth Amendment in 1868. If you as a justice were to follow the original intent of the Fourteenth Amendment, can you interpret the Fourteenth Amendment to mean that schools may not be segregated by law?

Jesse: No, not if I followed Bork's philosophy of original intent. At the time the Fourteenth Amendment was written, schools were segregated by law. And it wasn't too long after that, in the case of *Plessy* v. *Ferguson* in 1898, that the Supreme Court reaffirmed that the Fourteenth Amendment allowed segregation.

Krystal: The separate but equal doctrine.

Dr. Bauer: So if we use Bork's philosophy of original intent and strict construction, which says that justices should interpret the Constitution from the plain words as they were written, how do we get from *Plessy* v. *Ferguson* to *Brown* v. *Board of Education?*

Will: I'm not sure you can. Bork argues that justices should use original intent and strict construction as a way to avoid inserting their personal opinions into their interpretations of the Constitution. But as the article points out, even if you do look at the original intent, you still place your personal interpretation on what that group of framers really meant.

Krystal: I don't think you can get to *Brown* v. *Board of Education* using original intent and strict construction. I can agree that original intent should be the primary tool, but I don't agree that it should be the sole source of understanding how we should apply the Constitution today.

Dr. Bauer: What did you think of Justice Brennan's description of original intent: "arrogance cloaked as humility"?

Krystal: That's because you can play all sort of games with original intent.

Suzanne:	Whose original intent? The people who wrote the Constitution? Those who ratified it? Those who debated it in the *Federalist Papers?*
Dr. Bauer:	But this is Bork's judicial philosophy, and you have to give him credit for being consistent with it over the course of his legal career.
Jesse:	Regardless of what the issue was, and regardless of the potential opposition, he stuck to his principles. You always knew what his position was.
Dr. Bauer:	One of the reasons Robert Bork recommends that the Court use original intent is to counteract what he sees as a liberal bias on the Supreme Court. Let's look at this for a second. One of the biggest problems college freshmen have with the Supreme Court dilemma is the question, "Can you be unbiased when making a judgment?" Are there ways to be less biased?
	Bork sees a liberal bias, not just in the Court, but in a lot of places, resulting from the sixties. According to Lazarus, the sixties were a particularly formative time for Bork. Why?
Will:	He was a law professor at Yale in the sixties.
Dr. Bauer:	What was going on at Yale during the sixties?
Jesse:	The antiwar movement and the beginnings of the very liberal critical legal studies movement, which essentially said that the original intent behind most law is to oppress the poor. In Bork's mind, the sixties was an explosion that pushed the country far to the left.
Dr. Bauer:	In fact, some people said there was only one place in the whole country further left wing during the sixties, and that was Berkeley. So the changes to Bork's beloved Yale Law School during the sixties had an impact on his thinking.
Turi:	Radical students go so far as to burn books.
Krystal:	The law library gets set on fire as a protest.
Suzanne:	But Bork makes the same mistake many of us make, by thinking that just because something is going on in your own little corner of the world, it is happening all over the country. In Bork's little corner of the world, America does seem as if it is falling apart.
Krystal:	On the Yale Law School faculty, there is a war going on between liberals and conservatives, and Bork knows he is in the minority.
Jesse:	He feels under attack.
Dr. Bauer:	And to be fair to Bork, some of the radical positions taken at Yale in the sixties were extreme and openly Marxist. The people on the far left had no interest at all in compromise; the atmosphere at Yale was confrontational and nasty. What does Bork think of the Warren Court that was deciding cases in the sixties?

Will: The reading says Bork saw the Warren Court as "guilty of sins just like those he observed in his colleagues. Just as liberal scholars used their scholarship to further their own aims, the liberal Warren Court abandoned traditional legal reasoning in favor of a results-first approach."

Dr. Bauer: Part of traditional legal reasoning is judicial restraint. Is it fair to say that Bork wanted the Warren Court to use more judicial restraint? What is judicial restraint?

Jesse: That's the idea that when Congress or a state legislature passes a law, the Court assumes it be constitutional and restrains itself from overturning laws. And, yes, I think Bork wanted more judicial restraint in the Warren Court.

Dr. Bauer: Bork thinks that, in a democracy, the Supreme Court shouldn't have much power. Decisions about capital punishment, abortion, even about civil rights, are best decided at the local level. Bork doesn't think that the federal government should force the states to legalize abortions, for example. In Bork's view, the Constitution leaves that up to the states. The proper role of the Court is to restrain itself from taking over a role the Constitution gave to the states. It's a state's rights argument as well. Bork has more faith in local democracy than those who see the Supreme Court as a defense against local prejudice. This brings up another debate in every freshman American government course: Is it a good idea for a branch of the federal government—the judicial branch, which is not democratically elected and can't be democratically removed—to have so much power?

Jesse: If their power rests on the Constitution, yes. Democracies, unchecked, can do bad things under the "tyranny of the majority." A democracy, meaning a majority of voters, kept civil rights out of the hands of people of color in this country for hundreds of years. I forget which Supreme Court justice said, "An individual's rights cannot be waived simply because a majority chooses that they be." In our democracy the Constitution and the Supreme Court protect the individual voice.

Krystal: I've always looked at the courts as an institution that supported the rights of minorities, the court of last resort for justice.

Jesse: Recently that's been true. But look at the history of the Court up to the 1930s—they were not for the minority.

Krystal: I'm not saying the minority always gets the protection of the Court. I am saying it's where the minority can go to try and get justice.

Dr. Bauer: What happened when the senators asked Bork about the *Brown* v. *Board* decision?

Jesse: "He embraced Brown as not only consistent with original intent, but compelled it." Lazarus says that contradicts all of Bork's opinions up to that time. In the next paragraph, the author says that, "Despite evidence of his original intent philosophy, with Houdini-like deftness Bork escaped the conclusion that it *(Brown)* was wrongly decided, and found a general principle of racial equality in the Constitution." But the author's point is, up to that time, there had been no general principle of racial equality in Bork's reading of the Constitution.

Suzanne:	We think of Bork as being so consistent, but when he saw his nomination about to go down the drain, he said what he had to say.
Krystal:	Sure, if he had come out and said *Brown* was not rightly decided, it would have made the liberal campaign against him seem right on the money.
Dr. Bauer:	Almost every American government text talks about this nomination fight. What did you find to be the most interesting thing in this selection? Is there anything here that made you look at it a little differently?
Krystal:	I like the author's argument that there is no single correct approach to interpreting the Constitution. I think interpreting the Constitution is a human process and no single tool is going to eliminate human bias. But this two-hundred-year-old document has to grow with us.
Suzanne:	It fascinated me that Bork thought he could discover the original intent of the framers. I'm not sure that *they* knew exactly what their intent was. And even if certain individuals knew, I don't think there was ever any exact collective sense of intent when the Constitutional Convention voted on it. The Constitution itself is full of compromises that brought together opposing ideas. That's why we had to have the *Bill of Rights* to begin with. What the framers thought were clearly understood, implied rights, weren't clear to the populace who wanted written assurances of individual rights. That was a compromise. Then we have the Ninth Amendment, which says in effect, "Just because it isn't in the Constitution, doesn't mean that it is not a right that the people can claim." And if that was true over two hundred years ago, and our society is so much larger and more complex, it still must be true today.
Dr. Bauer:	That's a very interesting argument Suzanne. That if the framers had not wanted the Constitution to grow and change with the times, they would not have written the Ninth and Tenth Amendments, which are there to spell out that there are other rights not mentioned.
	Bork argues that if you want to have a Constitution change with the times, create an amendment and send it to the states for ratification. Don't amend it by judicial interpretation. What do you think about that?
Jesse:	I might agree with that.
Suzanne:	But that doesn't give us enough flexibility, Jesse.
Jesse:	Amendments are more clear than judicial interpretation.
Turi:	But don't you think that's a little unrealistic? In the entire history of our country, fewer than thirty amendments have passed, and that includes the first ten,

	the Bill of Rights, that were all passed together right away. It's too hard to amend the constitution, especially for a country where there is so much rapid change.
Dr. Bauer:	Let me give you a piece of concrete evidence about amending the Constitution. There's been a proposed amendment to the Constitution to make burning the flag illegal, and that has been bouncing around the Congress for four or five years now and hasn't even gotten to the point where it can be sent to the states for ratification. If we can believe the polls, that amendment has the support of about ninety percent of the voters. Now if it takes that long to amend the Constitution to outlaw burning the flag, I rest my case.
Suzanne:	Even if you do pass an amendment, cases will still go to the Supreme Court to interpret that amendment! And as generations on the Court change, past decisions will get overturned. So either way, the Supreme Court will continue to interpret the Constitution.
Dr. Bauer:	I'd like to go back and finish up with Bork's confirmation fight. At the end of his discussion, Edward Lazarus writes, "Liberals rejoiced when Bork was rejected. I counted myself among them." But then he talks about what this battle did to this Court as an institution.
Jesse:	It changed the way nominations were handled; he calls the next few nominees "stealth nominees." We didn't hear much about them, except that they were either for *Roe* v. *Wade,* or had no comment.
Will:	The bad feelings arising out of the Bork fight broke any sense of community inside the Court that had been holding the different factions together. Lazarus says the "search for common ground" became totally lost as the Court got pulled into the culture of winners and losers.
Dr. Bauer:	Lazarus says "the lobbying ate away the thin but crucial divide between law and politics—the public believes that the Supreme Court is not merely another political institution and that judges can and should stand above the expedient trade-offs of the day." What do you think about this "thin but crucial divide between law and politics"?
Jesse:	I think it's important to the Court that they be seen as more than political, and I think that was one of the reasons why justice after justice, and chief after chief, tried so hard, on the big, historical cases, to get unanimous decisions. Now we are getting decisions of huge importance handed down five to four.
Dr. Bauer:	*Brown* v. *Board* was decided unanimously. *Roe* v. *Wade* was seven to two. I think citizens need to believe that an institution as powerful as the Supreme Court, whose power cannot be checked or balanced by anything short of amendment, is united on important cases. Otherwise, the Court loses legitimacy in the eyes of the people, and begins to look more and more like ideologically rigid politicians. The court of last resort in our constitutional system cannot simply represent the dominant political party.

Suzanne: A divided court doesn't have to mean a political court. It could just mean honest differences of opinion. They are appointed for life in order to pull them out of politics. And I think that works most of the time. The best evidence I have for that is Earl Warren. When Eisenhower appointed him chief justice in 1953, he thought he was appointing a true conservative. It didn't turn out that way at all!

Dr. Bauer: But Vince Page particularly doesn't like the fact that, once on the Court for life, a justice is not compelled to keep the ideology of the president who appointed him. He thinks these justices who change their minds are traitors. Who is his number-one example in the reading "They Called Him 'Author'"?

Turi: Blackmun.

Dr. Bauer: And what was Blackmun's confirmation vote in the Senate?

Turi: Ninety-four to zero.

Dr. Bauer: And which president does Blackmun, according to Page, betray? Who appointed Blackmun to the Court?

Jesse: Nixon.

Dr. Bauer: Nixon wanted to appoint conservatives to the Court, and he thought he had one in Blackmun. What made Nixon so sure? What was Blackmun's experience before going to the Supreme Court?

Jesse: The U.S. Court of Appeals.

Dr. Bauer: The U.S. Court of Appeals is sort of the farm team for the Supreme Court, and who appointed him to this farm team?

Suzanne: Eisenhower. So if Eisenhower, a Republican president, appointed Blackmun, then Nixon felt comfortable submitting his name for the Supreme Court.

Dr. Bauer: Nixon had had a couple of really bad nominees to the Supreme Court, two that were almost laughed out of Washington as incompetents. That's extremely rare. From 1894 to 1969, only one nominee to the Supreme Court had been rejected by Congress. But Nixon's first two nominees were rejected in 1969 and 1970. Later in 1970, Blackmun was confirmed by the ninety-four to zero vote in the Senate.

One of the people Nixon tried to get on the Court was named Harold Carswell, who was considered really mediocre. A senator from my home state of Nebraska, Roman Hruska, was famous for his defense of Carswell, something like, "even mediocre people deserve representation on the Supreme Court."

Blackmun died recently, after having retired in 1994. This article was written *after* Blackmun died and five years after Blackmun left the Court. Why does Vince Page hate Blackmun so much?

Turi: Because he was the author of the opinion in *Roe* v. *Wade*.

Dr. Bauer:	What's Vince Page's point about judicial activism?
Jesse:	He says Blackmun was a champion of judicial activism. That Blackmun wanted to find abortions legal, so he twisted the Constitution into a knot to get there. Instead of upholding the original intent of the framers of the Constitution, Blackmun twisted and rationalized from the right to privacy in the Ninth Amendment, then applied it to states under the Fourteenth Amendment.
Will:	Page sounds very much like Bork. He accuses Blackmun of legislating from the bench. He thinks Blackmun achieved by interpretation a new law that Page thinks should have come from a legislature.
Dr. Bauer:	Why do you think I included this in our set of readings on the Supreme Court?
Krystal:	So we could see the sheer depth of emotion—the hatred—that a single justice, or the Supreme Court as an institution, can inspire.
Dr. Bauer:	After Justice Blackmun died, stories came out about death threats. At one point, Justice Blackmun had been shot at. He asked the FBI to go through his mail for death threats and had security around his house at all times.
Turi:	Because he wrote *Roe* v. *Wade?*
Dr. Bauer:	Yes. The FBI was trying to make sure that a Supreme Court justice would not be assassinated. This is the level of hatred and anger that can exist when people discuss the Supreme Court.
	It's ironic: Robert Bork formed his views partly in reaction to extremists who scared him because they could be violent. But the movement based on Bork's philosophy of judicial restraint, combined with the high emotions of the abortion debate, inspired a small number of people to bomb abortion clinics and kill staff. Of course, Bork would be very upset to think that his views were used to support death threats.
Suzanne:	And that's amazing to me, because it's not as if killing Blackmun would have changed the decision. It was a seven to two decision.
Dr. Bauer:	I want all my students to understand that some people are whipped into an absolute frenzy of hate at the mention of the Supreme Court. Pro-life conservatives would say the Court brought it on itself by sticking its nose into issues like abortion and "legislating from the bench." But when mainstream conservatives such as George Will write about abortion, they do it in a much more thoughtful manner. I found Vince Page on the Internet—and I especially want my students to understand that the Internet may not always be their best source for material that makes them *think,* but it can be a very potent source for material designed to make them *feel.*
Suzanne:	I think I know why you put this in with the Bork nomination. People's emotions were at a fever pitch there, too—a lot more feeling than thinking on both sides.

Jesse: So much of this anger at the Court as an institution is centered around that one decision.

Will: What I find interesting is that the Court didn't back down on *Roe*. Even when there was so much public anger from this group of dedicated people, the Court majority didn't back down. Even with death threats, the Court didn't back down. Even with a majority of Republican appointees on the Court, *Roe* has not been overturned. I think that, whether or not you agree with the *Roe* decision, you have to respect the Court. They are doing more than just reflecting their political party ideology, or *Roe* would have been overturned when the Court gained a majority of Republican appointees. I think the Supreme Court has done what the framers intended in one important way: It does not fear any organized political groups, no matter how angry. Maybe that "thin but crucial divide between law and politics" is still there.

★ ★ ★

In the Matter of the Court v. Us

John Leo

Robert Bork's new book, *Slouching Towards Gomorrah,* contains a surprising suggestion: a constitutional amendment allowing Congress to override any Supreme Court decision by a simple majority vote of both houses.

Bork is brilliant, conservative, pessimistic and angry. He calls the court "despotic," which is too strong a word for the giant shadow the court now casts over normal democratic politics. Much of his language is so rough that he sometimes seems to be preaching only to the converted.

Yet his idea is not a wacky one. Canada's Constitution allows legislative overrides of the judiciary in some cases. Britain, with no written constitution, has the same principle built right in. Any democracy can do it. The chances of an override amendment passing here are currently around zero. But Bork believes frustration is building steadily, so he's putting the idea on the table now.

Bork thinks the court is basically an instrument of the intellectual class: the law schools, the academy, the foundations, the media, the arts community, activists on the left. Judges come and go. Sometimes mavericks, such as Antonin Scalia, squeeze through and resist pressures to "grow" on the bench. Sometimes the Supreme Court strays from the script, as in the current waffling over affirmative action and racial gerrymandering. But in general, the court can be relied on to enact the agenda of its class, finding whatever principles it wishes to in the Constitution, imposing its own cultural and political values on large and unwilling majorities. "What matters," Bork writes, "is that the result be consonant with the modern liberal mood."

Crisis of legitimacy. He is hardly the only important social or legal critic who thinks this way. Mary Ann Glendon, who teaches at Har-

vard Law School, refers to the intellectual elite as "the semiskilled knowledge class," and has this to say about it in her book *Rights Talk:* Its "common attitude that the educated are better equipped to govern the masses finds its institutional expression in a disdain for ordinary politics and the legislative process and a preference for extending the authority of the courts, the branch of government to which they have the easiest access."

The elements that Glendon sees at work—elitism, corner cutting, righteousness, love of the quick fix, contempt for democratic politics—are a combustible mix. And as the country has grown more conservative, the elite has relied more heavily on the courts. It doesn't organize or seek consensus by going to the American people; it litigates and goes around them. Major social policies don't arise from democratic consensus making in the political arena. They appear out of the blue, unsupported by any semblance of social consensus. The result is a growing crisis of legitimacy.

This system works so well for the class that runs it that Bork thinks the British have learned the lesson. In Britain, the primary advocates of a U.S.-style constitution with judicial review are the Labor Party and intellectuals. That development, Bork writes, "would shift a great deal of power from the British electorate to judges who would better reflect the leftist agenda."

The elite pressure on justices who vote the wrong way is enormous. Opinion at the law schools, which are increasingly devoted to free-wheeling judicial activism, matters a lot to the court. Lino Graglia, law professor at the University of Texas, says: "The approval of the law schools means as much to a justice as a *New York Times* review of a new play means to a playwright."

Some of this pressure helps account for the fact that nine straight Republican appointees made such a small dent in the court's ideology. The system is set up to produce converts. Justice

Reprinted, with permission, from *U.S. News & World Report,* 121, no. 14 (1996). © 1996 by U.S. News & World Report, Inc.

Harry Blackmun, widely derided as a lightweight and as former Chief Justice Warren Burger's "Minnesota twin," transformed himself into a famous, wildly applauded figure by conjuring the right to abortion from penumbras in *Roe v. Wade.* Similarly, David Souter, mocked as a tongue-tied, talentless nerd, unexpectedly voted for abortion rights in *Planned Parenthood v. Casey,* and now is hailed as "a brilliant conversationalist" and "the conscience of the court," to cite two of the compliments the *Christian Science Monitor* recently heaved at him. The same miracle transformation presumably awaits Clarence Thomas, should he wish to reinvent himself by embracing the expected values.

"They know they have the power," says Graglia. "Are they going to use it and become famous for some breakthrough decision, or are they going to just trudge along applying the Constitution?"

The court has developed the sad habit of creating linguistic sinkholes in its decisions that later can be cited to justify rulings that are even further out. This amazingly gassy sentence appeared in *Casey:* "At the heart of liberty is the right to define one's own concept of existence, of meaning, of the universe, and the mystery of human life."

This "mystery passage" can be cited easily the next time to justify suicide clinics, gay marriage, polygamy, inter-species marriage or whatever new individual right the court feels like inventing. We are moving firmly into the court's post-constitutional phase. The more you think about this, the less radical Bork's idea seems.

Jesse
a conservative
Libertarian

Krystal
a liberal
Democrat

Suzanne
a moderate
Republican

Turi
a moderate
Democrat

Will
a moderate

CHAT
ROOM

Should the People Rule?
★ ★ ★

Jesse: I've been looking forward to discussing this reading by John Leo, "In the Matter of the Court v. Us," because I had a class on free speech, and one of the things we had to read was written by Mary Ann Glendon, who's mentioned in this article. A whole bunch of stuff has been written lately that's critical of the Supreme Court.

Dr. Bauer: Let's look at this. John Leo is a conservative columnist who writes regularly for the magazine *U.S. News & World Report*. Leo writes that "Bork is brilliant, conservative, pessimistic and angry." Why is he so angry? What is the thesis in this particular article?

Suzanne: He wants congressional overrides of Supreme Court decisions.

Jesse: To counteract the judicial activism of the Supreme Court. When the Supreme Court overturns laws passed by elected representatives in state legislatures or Congress, the Congress should respond by making sure the people get what they wanted.

Dr. Bauer: Is this an attractive idea to you?

Krystal: No, not at all. Primarily because if you think the Court is in a crisis of legitimacy now and appears politicized, just wait until the Congress can overturn their decisions. Then there will be a real political crisis on the Court, and it won't ever stop.

Suzanne: I'll go even further than that. If you adopt a policy like the one John Leo and Bork are advocating, you might as well do away with the Court. Congress could just do . . . whatever! I mean, why have a Court?

Jesse: Well, it depends on how it is enacted. Suppose that in the same way Congress has to get to a two-thirds vote to override a presidential veto, they need two-thirds to override a Supreme Court decision. That's a high barrier.

Dr. Bauer:	Why is it that Bork and Leo want this radical change?
Krystal:	They say the justices come from a particular intellectual class that is going to be liberal, no matter what.
Dr. Bauer:	But let's name who is on the Court today. Republican appointees Rehnquist, Scalia, Thomas, O'Connor, Kennedy, Souter, Stevens; Democratic appointees Ginsburg and Breyer.
Jesse:	I think they are responding to the Court of twenty years ago, not the Court today.
Suzanne:	But the Republican appointees don't all think alike. But if they did vote as a group, and as conservatively as Bork, do you think this article would have been written?
Krystal:	No, they wouldn't have been upset with that Court.
Dr. Bauer:	What does the article say is the reason why these seven Republicans *don't* vote together with a Bork philosophy? What's pushing them away from strong conservatism?
Turi:	A system that is "set up to produce converts." They have the right to change their minds, change their ideology over time, or even set aside their ideology and look at issues.
Jesse:	There's a quote here from Lino Graglia: "The approval of the law schools means as much to a justice as a *New York Times* review of a new play means to a playwright."
Turi:	So, is there pressure coming from the major law schools against justices voting the "wrong way"?
Dr. Bauer:	That's what Leo says.
Krystal:	The assumption here is that the important elites who run the law schools are ultraliberal, and I'm not sure that's true. Bork was at Yale Law, and Glendon teaches at Harvard Law.
Dr. Bauer:	Leo's point is that a transformation takes place, one that turns good conservatives into born-again liberals, and they blame elite pressure. What's their evidence for this?
Jesse:	Justice Blackmun, whom they don't like because of his opinion in *Roe* v. *Wade,* and David Souter, whom they describe as a "talentless nerd" but is now being "hailed as 'a brilliant conversationalist'" because he became less conservative. And Leo says the same transformation awaits Thomas, "should he [wish to] reinvent himself by embracing [the] expected values."
	I will say that there is one part of this article I really like. John Leo says the Court is moving into a "post-constitutional phase." Opinions are not particularly well reasoned. I agree—the biggest offender being the decision in *Roe* v. *Wade.*

Dr. Bauer:	So does Justice Ruth Bader Ginsburg, who gave a speech that really lit into the *Roe* decision for its hazy logic. This is a legitimate criticism, but is it good evidence for an inevitable process that will transform all the justices? Do these examples make Leo's case, that we need a drastic change affecting the Supreme Court, because the system itself is self-corrupting?
Will:	There should be better reasons than these. If you look at the collective whole, I don't see that conservatives will all become more liberal, just because a few have in the past.
Jesse:	And you have to remember, that if Leo shares Bork's perspective, then even Clarence Thomas can look like a liberal. I think Leo's real complaint is that there aren't enough people on the Court that are conservative in the way he would like them to be. And he's frustrated that after twenty years of Republican appointments, this is the Court we have.
Dr. Bauer:	But one of the things that bothers me about this article is, aren't the people advocating radical change the same people whose judicial philosophy rests on *original intent?* First, Bork says that we should leave the Constitution as it was written and only interpret it as the original framers intended. Then he says we should *change* the Constitution. How would the framers feel about Bork's proposal?
Will:	They wouldn't want one branch—the legislative—to be able to undermine another—the judicial. The framers set up three branches of government for a reason. For Bork and others who agree with an original intent philosophy and then decide that the original constitutional design isn't good enough is a contradiction that appears to serve political ends.
Jesse:	When the framers set up the Constitution, they allowed only one branch of government to be directly influenced by the popular vote, and that was only really half a branch, since it was only the House of Representatives. The framers didn't seem to think very highly of the opinions of ordinary people.
Dr. Bauer:	When you find a contradiction in an argument, such as an original intent proponent suddenly backing a drastic change in the design of the Constitution, it should make you think twice about the argument.
Will:	Usually, I think, a contradictory argument is put forward when the real, straightforward argument is not as persuasive. What they really want to argue for is more true conservatives on the Court. Now they want Congress to have a say, because Congress is controlled by the Republicans. But should the Democrats take control of Congress in the 2000 elections, I predict this argument will go away, fast.

★ ★ ★

For Additional Reading

Go to InfoTrac College Edition, your online research library at

http://web1.infotrac-college.com

Enter the following search terms using the Subject Guide or Key Terms.

case law	Robert Bork	structure of the courts
judicial review	*Roe* v. *Wade*	Supreme Court
legal realism	stealth justice	Supreme Court nominations
precedent	strict construction	

14 Domestic Policy

A PERSONAL

PERSPECTIVE ON

Welfare

MONICA BAUER

FOR MOST OF MY LIFE, WELFARE WAS AN ISSUE THAT SHARPLY divided the two parties. The Democrats were always in favor of increased benefits and increased eligibility, or so it seemed. The Republicans were the mirror opposites, calling for an end to a social welfare safety net and gaining a good deal of support from angry taxpayers by focusing on welfare cheats.

Since 1996, when President Clinton agreed with a Republican Congress on a plan to "end welfare as we know it," welfare and welfare reform haven't been in the news much; when they have, the news has been mostly good. Welfare rolls have been cut dramatically in most states, with steep declines of as much as fifty percent or more in many places. That may be as much because of an amazing economic boom as any deliberate change in welfare policy. Two big questions remain: What happens if the economy slides back into a recession, eliminating instead of creating jobs? And what happens to the least-prepared of the poor when they reach their limits for benefits (between two and five years in most states)?

Neither party seems anxious to deal with these questions. But during your lifetime, those questions must be answered. How you answer them depends on how you think about the larger issue of the government's role. Should government use the tax money of the better off to help the worse off?

One way I ask my students to think about welfare is to imagine what the country would be like if all welfare spending stopped tomorrow. No more food stamps or welfare checks; perhaps even an end to Medicare for the poor. Would the poor find a new strength and self-reliance, as some of our readings suggest, or would they and their children struggle at the bottom of society?

It may be hard to imagine a nation without any help for the poor, but I have lived in a Third World nation without a safety net for its poor. Let me tell you what it was like.

In Egypt, there are beggars on the street, even though begging is condemned in the Koran. The worst part about the begging is the stories you hear of children whose limbs are deliberately broken so they may appear more pathetic and earn more money for the family. In fact, I was warned by our family friend and maid, Wahida, not to give any money to beggars, as it only encourages parents to use their children that way. Although in Egypt, children are supposed to be in school until the sixth grade, children make the best beggars, so some families will keep their children out of school to beg.

The children I saw during the school day who weren't begging were part of a group of outcast families who lived in the garbage dumps of Cairo. Because Egypt doesn't spend much money on garbage collection, children come along on their donkey carts to pick up the trash. They take the trash home, pick through it for materials they can sell or use, and dump the rest just outside their front doors. You can imagine the kind of germs that thrive in such an environment. These families are living in filth, and they pay the price with a high infant mortality rate and a whole host of diseases that we never see in the more economically developed world.

When I took the typical tourist trip to the countryside, to view the magnificent tombs and temples that date back to the Pharaohs, I met a whole different class of beggars. Beggars in Cairo aren't very aggressive. They tend to be alone or with a small family group on a particular corner. Beggars in the countryside swarm over a tourist because of their sheer number. Our Egyptian guide warned us about this. She also said that if we wished to give, we should give pencils, because the children needed them for school and the families could not afford to buy them.

Soon I ran out of pencils, but the little hands kept grasping for more, and children appeared as if out of nowhere. I began handing out Egyptian coins, and yelled for help. Fortunately, my husband waded through the little bodies, grabbed my arm, and pulled me out of there. It was a terrible feeling, looking back at all those sad, small faces, each crying out, "Madame, please."

After that episode, I channeled my charity through my local church and started sponsoring a Sudanese refugee family. That allowed me to feel a little less guilty, aware every day that I lived a life of incredible privilege in the midst of poverty. I got used to looking away when the beggars in Cairo raised their hands to me and cried out, "Please, Madame." But on Mother's Day, 1993, I ended up emptying my purse into the lap of a woman selling flowers on the street. She looked as if she weighed fifty pounds, and she was trying to nurse an infant, who was obviously unable to get any nourishment from this poor woman. By her side was a two-year-old, too tired to do anything but look up and hold his hand out in a way that spoke volumes. Very likely, this child would not live to be three—and he seemed to know it.

This mother and her children did not know that it was Mother's Day in the United States, but I did. As tears ran down my cheeks, I gave her just about everything I had on me at the time. She smiled and had her two-year-old hand me a rose.

I remember contrasting that experience with an incident at a national church event called "Economic Justice for Women Who Are Poor," held by my United Church of Christ in 1983, just after I was ordained. At this conference, I met many women on welfare. They were militant and angry. The governor of Massachusetts was trying to start something new—"workfare," under which welfare recipients would have to do something to earn their benefits. These welfare rights activists believed workfare was the same as slavery. They gave speeches saying they had a right to stay home with their children instead of working at a low-wage or workfare job. They believed welfare was something they were entitled to because they were poor.

How thrilled that Egyptian woman would have been with government workfare! I'm sure she would have showed up early every day and done proudly whatever was asked of her, for the privilege of earning her way in a country that would not let her children starve. I think it was the militancy of the welfare rights activists, who insisted they were entitled to a check, that finally sent many Democrats over to the side of the moderates, eventually represented by Clinton.

When the Aid to Families with Dependent Children program (AFDC) was created during the Depression, it was supposed to help widows with children. At that time, FDR and the whole country knew that women were unlikely to get a job that could provide for a family. Women were paid less than men for the same work, and most weren't even considered for the kind of job that could support a family. (Neither Sandra Day O'Connor nor Ruth Bader Ginsburg was able to land even an interview at a law firm after they graduated from law school, as recently as the 1950s. Today each sits on the Supreme Court.) By the 1980s, however, most recipients of AFDC were unwed mothers who had dropped out of high school, secure in the knowledge that they could move away from their families and get places of their own, courtesy of the U.S. government. That was not the program FDR had in mind.

Even when FDR proposed government jobs for the poor, they were supposed to be temporary measures. The government provided a safety net so people would not starve during a depression, but the government expected people to get real jobs as soon as they could. Welfare was always meant to be temporary, but by the 1980s, there were some families that had raised two or three generations on welfare. Although the average stay on welfare was about two years, welfare had become a way of life for some families.

When I went to that church conference in 1983, I was prepared to support the poor; my church had taught me to do that. And if welfare rights activists hated workfare, I was supposed to follow their lead. But I couldn't help thinking of all the young women I knew back in my own congregation who were struggling to combine jobs and motherhood. They paid a huge percentage of their salaries for day care. Many were sad and angry that they couldn't be full-time mothers. But they couldn't afford to stay home with their children. It began to seem less than fair for the government to take money from the checks of these hard-working mothers to give other mothers the chance to stay home with their kids. I think that is what really killed welfare; that is, welfare mothers were getting something working mothers very much wanted but could not afford.

On the other hand, I knew from personal experience that a little government help could go a long way. When I dropped out of high school at seventeen, got married at eighteen, and moved to another city to look for fame and fortune in the world of music and theater, I needed help. It was 1972, and there weren't a lot of jobs available. My then-husband was a high-school graduate with some college education and no marketable skills. We ended up in Minneapolis living in a slum hotel, one room and a shared bath. I saw a man stabbed at our bus stop and people shoot up in our alley.

Both of us had grown up in a working-class neighborhood where people struggled to make ends meet, but no one was getting stabbed or shooting heroin. We were young, scared, and clueless about making our way in this world. Every day we were married was a struggle to survive economically, a struggle we were in no position to win.

In Minneapolis, we worked at day labor jobs, meaning you work every day wherever they send you and get less than minimum wage after the day labor company deducts its commission. I worked at factories, hotels, and commercial laundries while my husband did mostly factory or yard work. Eventually we had enough money for a real apartment with a real kitchen. That was important, because without a kitchen, we wouldn't be eligible for food stamps.

Someone on the day labor bus told us about food stamps, and from that moment on, getting food stamps became a goal. Until we got our food stamps, we were hungry on a regular basis. It wasn't terrible, because we were both young and healthy and didn't have a child to feed. But it was an experience I would not like to repeat.

Once I got so hungry that I went down to the local fast-food fish place and asked if they had any scraps for my cat. It worked. We ate their scraps every day for two weeks. I found out at the food stamp office about churches that gave sacks of groceries to the poor. We would go down, line up, and take whatever we were handed. That's when I discovered that some people had a bizarre idea of what poor people liked to eat. One month we got a lot of flour, but didn't have any way to use it. Another month, we got a lot of rice and beans, which I also didn't know how to cook.

Like many such couples, the strain of trying to get by eventually took its toll, and we divorced. A few years later, almost a college graduate, I was a staff member on a YWCA project to lift women out of welfare. I spent hours with women who were going through a training program, and I got an earful about what it was like to live on welfare, year after year. In a word: miserable. The rules were so strict at that time (1978) that you lost benefits for trying to work. If you took the only jobs you were qualified for, they kicked you off welfare and took away the medical benefits that kept your kids healthy. In short, the government had devised a no-win situation for single mothers. If you married the father of your kids, you lost all your benefits. If you worked, you lost. No wonder a whole group of single mothers just gave up and decided to live the way the system had designed for them to live.

As a political scientist, I am encouraged to see the system reformed: It now helps women get jobs while keeping their medical and day care benefits. As a woman, I sympathize with the fact that welfare is largely a woman's experience, and that women with children will do whatever they have to do to make sure their kids are okay. I see both sides of the welfare argument. As usual in American politics, the truth I find is never at the extremes, but almost always in the middle.

The two readings in this chapter detail common descriptions of the evils of government-sponsored welfare and the plans the government is developing to make welfare help people as it was intended to do. There will always be poverty. But there need not always be welfare. After reading the articles, ask yourself if the government should help the poor, and if it can do it well. What do you think?

Put Welfare Out of Its Misery

Ken Hamblin

Like the unfolding of an air-tight murder case, evidence continues to mount against the policies of the liberal socialists.

Despite the repeated failures of the welfare state they promoted in the name of lofty notions, these liberals are unwavering in their insistence that the quality of people's lives is enriched when the government assumes responsibility for their existence.

But case after case shows otherwise.

A pathetic case in point is embodied in the results of a study recently reported by *The New York Times,* concerning the impact of public assistance on 790 Atlanta-area welfare families. The study was conducted by Child Trends a non-profit research group working for the U.S. Department of Health and Human Services.

The children in the study group were between 3 and 5 years old, and almost all of them were black.

By testing these children, the study concluded that they were likely to have trouble when they started school.

According to *The Times,* the study revealed that: "On average, the children . . . correctly answered only slightly more than half the questions in a test of concepts and skills—such as shapes, colors and understanding such relationships as under or 'behind'—needed for school readiness."

As I would have predicted, the article also reported that the welfare babies of these ghetto mothers scored lower on vocabulary tests than did a national sample of black children.

Even though the study indicated that the longer a family stayed on welfare, the lower the children tested, some liberal-minded pundits, such as a spokesperson for the Children's

Defense Fund, refused to address the obvious effects of welfare itself as were clearly revealed in this study.

Instead, senior staff lawyer Nancy Ebb used the test results as ammunition to argue that higher-quality child care be made available to welfare families. In essence, calling for more welfare, more of the same.

I grew up on the dole. And I contend, from firsthand experience, that it is impossible to live on welfare for years at a time without losing your drive and your ambition. It's impossible to provide cognitive stimulation and emotional support to your children—support the study showed was lacking among these welfare families. Even when I was growing up under welfare 40 to 50 years ago in New York, there were poor people around me conditioned by welfare who gave me a lot of reasons for it to seem irrational for me to even think about trying to compete outside the boundaries of the ghetto.

Our brains were designed to accommodate an endless thirst for knowledge, experience and information.

But we deaden that brain activity when we substitute the dreams and ambitions that are fostered in active brains with a guarantee of survival tied to a regular welfare check.

The people subject to today's liberal folly of welfare are robots—living a mechanical existence, lost souls decreed by their liberal lords to dwell eternally in ignorance brought about in large part by lack of stimulation and, thus, drive.

Today, I see American ghettos abounding with people who are languishing in the shadow of society, never daring to reach for the fruits of success available to everyone in America.

By continuing to offer up promises of additional government assistance in the way of more conveniently delivered welfare checks, and broader and better social programs, the liberals have managed effectively to all but snuff out the basic survival devices in poor people.

They have deadened the very survival devices families need to pass on to their children.

Despite all the visible shortcomings clearly attributable to the development and ongoing expansion of the welfare state, these liberal socialists continue shamelessly to ignore the facts and to idealize and promote the supposed benefits.

The only compassionate way to save the poor children in the U.S.—whether they are black, Hispanic or white—is to kill the American welfare system as we know it. Shoot it squarely between the eyes.

CHAT ROOM

Aussie
a liberal
Jewish Palestinian

Gino
a moderate
Democrat

Jesse
a conservative
Libertarian

John
a liberal
Democrat

Shane
an African American,
liberal Democrat

Some of Us Have Been There, Done That
★ ★ ★

Dr. Bauer:	Let's begin our discussion of welfare, welfare reform, and public policy with an article by an African American conservative, Ken Hamblin. What's Ken Hamblin's argument?
Gino:	That he grew up on welfare, and it's a horrible system. It breeds laziness and doesn't help anybody learn how to compete outside the ghetto, and it should be killed off—"Shoot it squarely between the eyes." Not too subtle.
Dr. Bauer:	He's an opinion writer. He wants to arouse and persuade by his language. So, what did you think?
Aussie:	Well, I think first, he needed to define what welfare is, because welfare can be broken into different programs. If he were sitting in front of me, I would ask him if he's talking about the SSDI, or the AFDC, or . . . ?
Dr. Bauer:	When people say "welfare," what do you think they mean?
Gino:	Public assistance.
Dr. Bauer:	Public assistance. But which of those programs?
Gino:	Food stamps, a monthly stipend—the check—and government-subsidized housing.
Dr. Bauer:	Those are a lot of benefits, aren't they? When people talk about the most controversial parts of welfare, what do you think they are talking about?
Shane:	AFDC.
Dr. Bauer:	AFDC: Aid to Families with Dependent Children. We can assume that's what he's talking about.

Gino:	Well, there's a large inaccuracy in his article. He talked about inner-city ghetto African Americans, when the majority of people on welfare are *not* inner-city African Americans. The majority are actually whites. He bases his case on an inaccurate description of who gets welfare benefits.
Dr. Bauer:	Still, he says he grew up on welfare.
John:	He criticizes the liberals who have "used the test results as ammunition to argue that high[er]-quality child care be made available to welfare families." I don't know . . . I think that's a pretty obvious conclusion to draw from this study. But Hamblin draws the opposite conclusion: eliminate child care provided by welfare.
Dr. Bauer:	So, like most newspaper columnists, he's not a social scientist, but he uses social science, doesn't he?
Aussie:	Yes, he does.
Dr. Bauer:	We find that a lot in commentary writers who are trying to persuade us and change our opinions. And that's not necessarily a bad thing. But you need to ask yourself, Is the writer using social science in a valid way? Is he using this study well?

He says, "Even though the study indicated that the longer a family stayed on welfare, the lower the children tested, some liberal-minded pundits, such as a spokesperson for the Children's Defense Fund, refused to address the obvious effects of welfare itself as were clearly revealed in this study." His claim is simple: Welfare leads to lower test scores. Eliminate welfare, and scores will rise. Can we blame welfare itself for lower test scores? Can he make that claim from the study? |
| John: | It depends on your point of view. If you're coming from his point of view and want to make a point against welfare, it's an obvious connection to make. But if you're looking at it from an objective view, or even from the other side, his claim is the opposite of what the study concluded! |
| Dr. Bauer: | Let me try to give you a tool of analysis you can use, no matter what your opinion is. This is a tool called "analyzing the variables."

Variables are things that change, or "vary," over time: We try to evaluate claims and arguments about real life by picking out which variables make a difference and which variables don't. For example, if we change the variable "how much child care we give people," that should affect how long a person stays on welfare. If we change the variable "how much job training we give people," that should affect how long a person stays on welfare. But if we change the variable, "how much junk food people eat," that should not affect how long people stay on welfare. If you're trying to fix welfare policy, you look for the variable factors, things government can change, that can have a direct effect on how long people stay on welfare. |

Using this study, Hamblin sees a direct relationship between staying on welfare and lower test scores, and therefore his conclusion is, "staying on welfare causes lower test scores." Is there a different variable—that has nothing to do with people staying or not staying on welfare—that might explain why the test results of children on welfare are getting worse?

Gino: The education systems are a variable, some schools are better than others. I mean, what if the schools for these children don't have as much money as suburban schools? If they don't have as much money to pay a certain number of teachers, the class sizes are larger, and the students don't learn as well. They don't get the preschooling a middle-class or upper-class child gets. These are variables that affect test scores. That's something Ken Hamblin doesn't say in his article.

Jesse: Well, these are preschool children, so they haven't been exposed to public schools. But there are other variables you could look at, such as the educational levels of the parents. I don't like jumping on Hamblin any more than I have to, but this article is an example of the way you can use statistics to support just about anything you want.

If you see a newspaper article that includes statistics, you have to question the statistics, because whoever is using the statistics is using them for a purpose. And any statistics that would run against their argument, they either downplay or skip altogether. I agree with Hamblin's point overall, but I think anytime we see statistics, we should take them with a grain of salt.

Dr. Bauer: Right. When we train social scientists, we try to teach them how to use statistics. One of the points we emphasize is, "Can you draw *these* conclusions from *those* data? Or is there another explanation for the data?" Let me offer an alternative explanation for the data Hamblin cites. The average stay on welfare is just a couple of years—did you all know that? I know from my own work with welfare women that if a family is on welfare longer than that, chances are there are multiple dysfunctions in the family: drug abuse, alcoholism, mental illness, physical problems, severe dysfunction. So, if you put those variables in the mix, it does not surprise me that kids who are on welfare longer seem to lose ground compared to kids who are on welfare a short period of time.

Does that make sense? I don't think that's ideologically loaded. I hope it's not; I hope it's just a commonsense analysis. It could also be that welfare makes people less intelligent, but if that's true, then I have to ask Mr. Hamblin, how did he get so smart?

Mr. Hamblin says, "I grew up on the dole. And I contend, from firsthand experience, that it is impossible to live on welfare for years at a time without losing your drive and [your] ambition." Now, in social science, we try to stay away from words like *impossible, always, never, must*. Those are bad words for social science, but you often find them in the newspaper. Few things are actually impossible; few things always lead to disaster. Let's try a logic test on Mr. Hamblin's argument. Here are the first two premises:

Mr. Hamblin grew up on welfare.

Mr. Hamblin says it is impossible to live on welfare without losing drive and ambition—

Gino: But he has drive and ambition!

Dr. Bauer: Yes. Logically, the premises should lead to the conclusion that Mr. Hamblin does *not* have drive and ambition. But clearly he does. Notice you don't have to defend a lifetime on welfare to disagree with Ken Hamblin's analysis.

He also ignores a crucial part of the welfare reform bill passed by President Clinton and the Republican Congress in 1996. How long can people stay on welfare now?

Jesse: In most states, only a few years, and then they either have to find work in the private sector or be assigned a workfare-type job, where they work for their benefits. And I think that's a much better system than we had before. I still agree with Hamblin, even if his reasoning is a little sloppy.

★ ★ ★

Excerpt from Remarks at a National Press Club Luncheon, February 17, 1998

Alexis Herman, U.S. Secretary of Labor

Labor Secretary Herman had just returned from a fact-finding tour of welfare reform programs throughout the United States.

When I present my findings to the president, I will present six core challenges that emerged throughout this tour, along with the recommendations to meet them. Today I want to talk in plain terms about those challenges—what I heard, where I've been, and what I believe we need to do to make Welfare-to-Work a lasting success.

The first step, the first challenge, is to end the stigma of welfare. You know, people really do want to work. Their hearts and their hands literally ache for the dignity and respect that work brings. They want to show their children that they are achieving. And they want to be recognized for what they are—not old welfare recipients, but what I call "new workers."

Time and time again, in community after community, individuals told me about the stigma of being on welfare, and that it didn't end even after they began a job. They were labeled. They were stereotyped. They were boxed in by prejudice: "Can I really trust this person? Are they really up to the job?"

The fact is, people on welfare are just like you and me. They deserve the dignity, the respect, and the title of workers. And we must demand that these rights, and benefits, and protections of workers are, in fact, theirs. That includes a fair wage, equal opportunity on the job, safe and healthy workplaces, and every other labor safeguard that is theirs by right and theirs by law. When the president called for an increase in the minimum wage, he did so with a recognition that it is very important to make work pay, and thereby, improve the standard of living for millions of working families in this country.

Washington Transcript Service 02-17-1998.

The second challenge is to understand that success is not just about getting a job. Success also involves keeping a job. We need to focus on the "to" in Welfare-to-Work. And that means taking a very hard look at the barriers between a welfare recipient and a job.

In order to *get* work, you have to first get *to* work. And for many on welfare, that means getting up before sunrise, waiting for the bus, getting on the train, praying that the car will start on time this time. Sometimes it means a two-hour commute each way, because that's where the jobs are.

It means finding quality child care for the kids, a place that's affordable and safe. And even if you're lucky enough to find a place and to pay for it, the center may not be open when you leave for work, or it may be closed long before you get back.

These challenges aren't necessarily unique to new workers. The difference, my friends, is in the degree.

For many of us, a dead car battery is a hassle. It may mean taking a cab to work. But for those on welfare, it could mean losing a job because you don't have the cab fare to pay to get to work.

What can we do to help these new workers manage the change and clear some of the hurdles that are in their paths to success? One solution, clearly, is in after-hour child care. A facility that I heard about in Delaware actually provides child care services on a 24-hour basis. It seems to me that we're going to have to have more of those kinds of centers in the future, because child care is vital. And that is why the president has proposed the largest investment in child care in our nation's history. It includes after-school care, and that is something that parents across this country have told me that they need.

I have seen a number of other creative initiatives. In Milwaukee, Wisconsin, I saw the success of the Job Access Loan Program, which provides short-term, no interest loans for emergency needs, like car repairs, money to buy uniforms for the job, moving expenses to relocate where the job is. For a worker just starting out, this small help can mean the difference between success and failure. And the repayment rate, by the way, is 80 percent. Significantly higher, I believe, than most consumer loans.

The administration has also proposed $100 million for Welfare-to-Work plans to bridge new workers to jobs through flexible transportation alternatives, such as van services. Two-thirds of new jobs are in the suburbs today. But three out of four welfare recipients live in rural areas or in central cities.

The vice president has established a community-based Welfare-to-Work coalition to sustain success. And this effort is designed to address the broad sweep of issues related to helping welfare recipients hold on to their jobs.

If we're going to be successful in ensuring the long-term success of welfare reform, then strategies that help to build bridges over the barriers—when we talk about the "to" in Welfare-to-Work—are, in my view, essential, they are critical.

The third challenge is for employers to acknowledge that welfare reform is good business and that it is good for the economy. Just as we need a change in mindset about these new workers, we also need to have a change in mindset about a new inclusive work force. A strong economy depends on well-trained, educated workers, and I know that successful employers understand that. But how do employers incorporate these valuable new resources into their workplaces?

They do this by mentoring, by investing in training, providing health care, pensions, and a real stake in the company's future, because, after all, the success of a business depends on the success of its workers.

Perhaps no one understands that better than Michael Shaughnessy, who is the president of the Color Matrix Corporation, a small business in Cleveland, Ohio, that I visited on my tour. Mr. Shaughnessy, along with Lisa Pate, are here with us today. Lisa is a Color Matrix employee.

Now Color Matrix is a 24-hour manufacturing facility with over 150 employees. Most of the workers are from the inner city. Most have never worked in a plant before, and most have had numerous barriers to employment in the past.

But Mr. Shaughnessy has teamed up with Cleveland Works, a nonprofit employment initiative that helps to train and link new workers to local businesses. Once on board, these new workers start with on-the-job training. They get good salaries, health benefits, a 401(k) plan, and tuition reimbursement. These new workers also interact with senior management and have a real sense of ownership.

Over 90 percent of those hired through Cleveland Works are still on the job today. And that's why Michael Shaughnessy can take the day off and be with us today because he knows that his plant is in very good hands. And so, Mr. Shaughnessy, we thank you for being with us today, and we thank you also, Lisa, for being a role model for what is possible for all of us, if we take the time, as you have done at Color Matrix, to make that real investment.

During my tour I also visited the Cessna Aircraft Company in Wichita, Kansas, with President Clinton. Now Cessna established a state-of-the-art facility to train welfare recipients for production jobs. About 200 graduates of this program are now working there and earning an average wage of $12 an hour, and they are gaining the tools to keep flying higher.

I also spent time at the Culinary Training Center in Las Vegas, Nevada, which is a joint union agreement partnership between the hotel industry and the Culinary Workers Union. It provides both pre-employment training and advanced training so that workers can continue to climb higher. And the main training center is located in the heart of downtown Las Vegas, with easy access to public transportation. It's a common-sense idea that's making a real difference in the lives of people.

Now these three employers do very different things in different places. But they all understand that it's good for the bottom line to have a skilled and involved work force. And it's good business to help workers move from dead-end jobs to life-long careers. This isn't charity. This is enlightened, economic self-interest.

The fourth challenge is recognizing that the hardest work remains, because the hardest to serve remain. We know that the case loads are dropping, but we don't have precise data on where everyone is going. But we do know that as the case loads go down, the real challenge is coming into much sharper focus.

Many long-term welfare recipients remain on the rolls. And although the overall case loads are declining, we've seen a small increase in the fraction of those who have been on welfare for three years or longer. We've also seen a slight rise in the fraction of those who have been on welfare before.

It's no surprise that those who are leaving and those who are coming back are having the most trouble leaving the rolls permanently because they have the most barriers to employment—long-term cases; limited math and reading skills; poor work histories; those struggling to overcome problems with substance abuse.

These are the toughest cases, and we knew that they would be. But we also know that welfare reform, in fact, won't succeed unless the toughest cases do. The president recognized this also, and together with Congress, provided $3 billion in last year's balanced budget act to help address this. The Department of Labor is charged with investing those funds in local areas around the country, and we are serving the 20 to 30 percent of welfare recipients who face the most difficult barriers to employment. Our resources don't go to distant bureaucracies but instead to the local level.

If you want to see what an initiative that focuses on the hardest-to-serve can do, then take a trip to Harlem—that's what I did—and visit a program there called STRIVE. That stands for Support and Training Results in Valuable Employment.

It is a no-nonsense program that in fact prepares individuals for the culture of work. And it stresses support after you're on the job, such as frequent phone contacts and individual counseling sessions. They teach life skills that we take for granted—showing up to work on time, dressing appropriately, calling in when you're sick, displaying a good attitude. STRIVE is helping to instill core values. And the job retention rate for STRIVE graduates after two years is, in fact, 80 percent.

There are no quick fixes here. There are no silver-bullet solutions. We are in uncharted territory, and this is, in fact, pioneering work. There are successful ideas and initiatives out there that all of us can learn from.

The fifth challenge is to focus on fathers. The objective of welfare reform is to help parents raise their incomes so that they can raise their kids. But usually, that parent is a mother. Unfortunately, usually she is also alone. But mom and dad both have responsibility to be there for support, both emotionally and financially.

Now, we know that kids have the best chance to succeed when both parents are involved and in some way showing responsibility. That is why this administration is deeply committed to child-support enforcement. But you know, you also have to have a job in order to pay support. And so one of the ways to help kids increase *their* earnings potential through their family environments, is to make sure that we are focusing in on the earnings potential of fathers and their ability to meet their obligations.

Last week, I visited in Los Angeles, California, a program that's called Parents Fair Share, which is partially funded by the Ford Foundation and works in cooperation with the local district attorney's office there. Now this innovative initiative provides fathers with training for higher income and counseling for higher self-esteem. It promotes parenting skills and provides a very strong support network. I listen to fathers tell me that they want to support their families. They want to reconnect. They don't want to be dead-beat dads. They, in fact, want to be dedicated dads. They want to be good fathers and good role models. And that is exactly what this initiative is helping them to do.

One father told me that he was ashamed that he didn't earn enough money to pay for the support. He said that when he visited his children, he used to go in angry and in a rage and not understand why he was feeling that way. But now that he's working and he's earning and paying his own way, he said: "Now I go in smiling, and I come out smiling, and I have to believe that that's better for my kids; I know it's better for me." He said, "For the first time in my life, I know something now about what it means to give love and to receive love."

This is an aspect of welfare reform that hasn't received much attention, but it is fundamental to strengthening families and building a better future for our kids. And we at the Department of Labor are going to make it a priority for model programs to help these fathers help themselves so that they, in turn, can help their families.

My sixth and final challenge is to call for action at every level. We have gone from a single federal program to 50 separate experiments around the country. Our success will depend in large measure on our new partnerships with governors and local officials. State plans are at various stages of development, and as I've traveled the nation, I've seen first-hand how some are working better than others.

Some states, for example, will reduce cash benefits as soon as someone gets a job. I've also heard many personal stories of individuals who have lost their child-care subsidies when they started a job, but other states such as Delaware provide transitional assistance up to 18 months.

Some states may create unintentional barriers. New workers may have to go to one office to let their case worker know that they've actually landed a job. Then another day in the month, they may have to take time off to pick up a transportation voucher. Still another day, they have to come back just to get a child care stipend. Think about it—for some of us that's like going to the department of motor vehicles three times in one month just to have your car registered.

We have to connect the world of welfare to the world of work in every way. And that includes implementing practical common-sense strategies and taking practical steps to help these workers on the job.

I want to commend state and local officials for their creative ideas. But I challenge them to do more: to take a hard look at their programs and see where there is real room for improvement, and to sit down with those directly affected, because there's nothing like talking with the people that you're actually trying to serve. There's no substitute for that.

I want to commend businesses for getting involved, for providing jobs and creating opportunity. But I challenge them to do more—join creative initiatives, such as the Welfare-to-Work partnership, that is headed by Eli Segal and has taken a leadership role in linking businesses with new workers. It was little more than a year ago when our president asked Mr. Segal to take on this challenge. Today it is an alliance of over 3,000 companies, large and small, reaching out to local partners—like Goodwill Industries, the National Urban League and the U.S. Chamber of Commerce—to move people from lives of dependency to lives of independence.

I want to commend labor unions for their good efforts to help new workers, such as the efforts that I saw in Las Vegas, Nevada, and faith-based communities and other labor market intermediaries for working together and for making a difference. But I challenge all of them to do more.

And I would say this even if I were not speaking here today at the National Press Club, that I want to challenge those of you who are in the media to do more. You have to make sure that America hears the voices of the many people that I have met. Whether it's the Lisa Pates of the world or so many other shining examples, they are there. You have to help us shed light on this situation. You have to help us shatter the myths.

Successful Welfare-to-Work efforts are going to take work, and it's going to take all of us. No one has all of the answers, but clearly there is a lot more that we can learn from each other.

Aussie
a liberal
Jewish Palestinian

Gino
a moderate
Democrat

Jesse
a conservative
Libertarian

John
a liberal
Democrat

Shane
an African American,
liberal Democrat

Have We Finished Reforming Welfare?
★ ★ ★

Dr. Bauer: So, let's move to these remarks by the first African American Secretary of Labor, Alexis Herman. She is delivering a speech at the National Press Club. She begins to talk about the "six core challenges" that are left in this new world of welfare reform. This world is very different from the welfare system that Ken Hamblin grew up on.

The first challenge is to end the stigma of welfare. Ken Hamblin would argue that the stigma is a good idea; the stigma motivates people to get off welfare.

Gino: People like Ken Hamblin have created the stigma that people on welfare are just lazy and worthless, and that's not necessarily the truth.

Jesse: I think the stigma's been around for a long time. The shame in the accounts of people, particularly in rural areas during the Depression, when they had to go on government relief payments or live off the county, makes their acceptance of help seem worse than death. They were proud and used to being able to provide for themselves—ashamed to take a government handout. And that made them work that much harder to get off it.

Gino: Part of the stigma of welfare is the perception that the poor are taking money from all of us. But in reality, welfare takes about one percent of the federal budget, and that's a very small portion for people to be up in arms about.

Dr. Bauer: We do get excited about it, don't we?

Shane: It's always viewed as shameful, not as something that anybody, at any time, might need. When people think of welfare, they still think of poor minorities—and that's a stigma in itself.

Gino: Most people imagine someone sitting home, watching TV, and waiting for the check to arrive. They don't imagine the person trying to find work or worrying about their children. Herman talks about the idea of family values, but when a woman on welfare wants to stay home and take care of her kids, it's a whole different story. That's not family values, it's like, "Oho, you're just trying to get welfare money! You're using your kid as an excuse to stay home and not work."

Dr. Bauer: This stigma thing is important, because it runs as a thread through a lot of social welfare policy. The liberal opinion has been to remove the stigma. The conservative opinion has been that shame (which is what we mean by a stigma, something that is publicly seen as shaming a person) motivates people to change. What do you think about that? Do you think that a stigma is always bad?

John: What the stigma does is place these people in a category, like the untouchables: This is the group that is lazy and shiftless and irresponsible. That's the kind of stigma Secretary Herman is talking about. And I don't see that as a positive thing. For example, if I'm going to look for a job, and I tell you I'm on welfare, the first thing you're going to think, "This person's lazy." So, how could that be a good thing? I don't think negative stigma is ever a good thing.

Gino: I think that the stigma also helps set up the roadblocks that a lot of these people hit every time they try to get off welfare. If you get off, you lose your health care, you lose child care. You get stuck in a minimum-wage job and can't afford your own health insurance. The benefits like health care for the kids are what these people are staying on welfare to keep.

Dr. Bauer: Jesse, do you want to defend the libertarian point of view here?

Jesse: The libertarian point of view says whom I choose to hire is between me and that individual. So, if they don't want to tell me on their job application or résumé that they've been on welfare, that's okay.

John: Do you think it motivates people for society to stigmatize welfare mothers?

Jesse: When I was in my first year of high school and we were getting food stamps, that stigma *did* help me. It helped me a lot, because I knew that it sucked a lot having to go and pull out the little meal card that gave me lunch for the reduced price. When we went food shopping, we went to the generic sections in the grocery store—three aisles of black and white boxes and cans that said "Beer" and "Potato Chips" and "Cereal" on them. That sucked. I don't know how it helped my family, but it made me determined that I would do whatever it took to ensure that I got out of that. I didn't go back. So, I would say, for me, the stigma worked. If I had to work eighty hours a week, at this point in my life, to stay off food stamps, I think I could and would.

John: You describe a really hard time in your life, and I hear what you're saying, and yet, why did the welfare system seem so harsh? How did a stigma shape you so that even as an adult, you still have this anger?

Jesse: Because money doesn't grow on trees. And when somebody's giving, another's taking. To give to me, you have to take from somebody else.

Dr. Bauer:	I think we've set out the parameters of the argument over stigma: One side says it's a stumbling block, the other side says it's a motivator. I don't think we're going to solve that argument. But at least we've set it out. So, that's my goal. We'll set out the different sides of these arguments.

The second challenge Alexis Herman talks about is more concrete and practical. It's one thing to say that welfare is bad, but it's another thing to help someone move from welfare to work. What does she say are the most important practical challenges? And are these things you had thought about before? |
| John: | Reliable transportation to your job. |
| Shane: | And that part brought up a side issue for me. Secretary Herman said two-thirds of the new jobs today are in the suburbs. If welfare recipients live in the city, why not invest in and build up their neighborhoods, give them a vested interest in what's going on? |
| Dr. Bauer: | Good idea. This is what Jesse Jackson does for a living in Operation Push. He's been trying for twenty years to get major corporations to invest in the inner cities.

But, until and unless we see that inner-city development, how do you get out to work if you are poor to start with? If your job is at the mall, and you live downtown, how do you get there? |
Shane:	Four buses.
John:	I've had real-world experience with this, because I used to work with a gentleman at Ninety-fourth and Wadsworth, which is on the northwest side of Denver, and he came from Havana and Colfax, every day. And the only reason he was able to get to work every day was because of a program called "Bridges to Work." This was created by the Regional Transportation District. But when the RTD couldn't give him the direct route home, he would have to take a cab, and his transportation costs were astronomical. I mean, I had to take him halfway home one day, and I ended up taking him from the extreme north end of town to Broadway and Colfax, and that was half-way. He got home an hour and a half later! This doesn't help family life or saving money!
Shane:	Or community involvement. If he's spending all his time trying to get back and forth to work, does he have time to go to the PTA meetings? Schools, education, business development?
Gino:	People involved in welfare reform don't realize that by cutting the dollars that are going to programs like the transportation program, we will keep people on welfare and spend more.
Dr. Bauer:	I think that's a good summary of what Secretary Herman is saying—that we don't often think of transportation as a welfare issue.
Gino:	I look at transportation as a key part of the bigger picture. Most middle-class people are not going to vote for public transportation that puts money into something that doesn't help them. I drive my car. I can get to my work on time.

	It's not a "we" issue, it's a "me" issue. It's a selfish view that I am not going to pay for transportation that helps everyone. I want transportation that helps me, and I've got a car, so fix the roads and build more.
Dr. Bauer:	This is really interesting. Americans are saying to people on welfare, "Work or else!" Yet we don't vote for or fund mass transit.
Gino:	We demand that you work, but we won't give you the means to do that.
Dr. Bauer:	Secretary Herman also mentions child care, which is a huge problem. Most people on welfare have young children. Speaking as a mom, if you can't find good child care, you're dead. And if you can't find child care that is open when you come home after a long day at work, after having taken three or four buses home from work, you are in some trouble. She mentions transportation and child care. She says making welfare reform a reality is not just about getting a job, it's about keeping a job. Americans say we want people on welfare to get off. We want them to get a job and keep a job. But we are not putting money into transportation and child care, so we want the impossible.
	Herman's third challenge is for employers to acknowledge that welfare reform is good business. In other words, it's not an act of charity. It helps the bottom line and improves profits.
John:	She said it's "enlightened, economic self-interest."
Dr. Bauer:	That's right. So, now we turn to our Libertarian and say, "What do you think? Is it enlightened, economic self-interest"? You're all for enlightened self-interest, aren't you?
Jesse:	I'm very much in favor of enlightened self-interest, but I'm not sure that my definition of it is the same as everybody else's. As a free-market capitalist, I need to have workers who are capable of doing what I want in a reasonably efficient, reasonably productive manner. It doesn't do me any good to run a Web-design business and hire former welfare people who can work for minimum wage, because they are not going to have the skills I want. Computer language and technology people are not likely to be people fresh off welfare.
Dr. Bauer:	Well, it sounds like this Color Matrix Corporation that Secretary Herman talks about is doing okay hiring people from welfare. They've trained their employees, and they're making money. Now, your particular business is not going to train minimum-wage workers, but this one is. So, do you have any problems with companies doing this?
Jesse:	No! And this is the thing that I like about it: What the company saves by not having to hire expensive workers, it spends on training costs.
Gino:	This is enlightened self-interest. When an employee comes to work and feels that the owner cares enough to train them, they are going to work twice as hard as someone who knows that the owner only cares about the bottom line.

Dr. Bauer:	Okay, so we all feel good about enlightened economic self-interest, with Jesse's caution that you want to be able to hire the people you need that are good for your particular business, right?
Jesse:	Oh yeah, I love it.
Dr. Bauer:	Then let's move on to the fourth challenge. Here we get into something that touches on several of the readings that we have in this section. The fourth challenge is recognizing that the hardest work remains, because the hardest to serve remain. Long-term cases, limited math and reading skills, poor work history, struggles with substance abuse—these are the hardest cases. And then she makes an interesting statement. Alexis Herman says, "These are the toughest cases, and we knew that they would be. But we also know that welfare reform, in fact, won't succeed unless the toughest cases do." Now, my question to you is: Is she being idealistic, or is this correct? Does welfare reform's success or failure hinge on the eighty percent that are already moving into work settings, or does the success or failure of welfare reform hinge on helping this last twenty percent?
John:	I think the current system—the two to five years maximum—will fail because we haven't set up a system to take care of the last twenty percent. Welfare is just going to end for them, and they are going to drop off into oblivion.
Jesse:	But, it's already taking care of eighty percent, helped people into jobs and on-the-job training. And that's what welfare reform is about. And if we've done that with eighty percent, we are looking at a success rate that is, for our country anyway, amazing.
Aussie:	Where do we draw the line and say *this* is success? Aren't we supposed to treat everyone equally? Isn't that what this country is about? Trying to give everyone equal opportunity? Why are these twenty percent unsuccessful compared to the eighty percent?
Dr. Bauer:	Well, who are in this twenty percent?
Gino:	Drug abusers, people who lack education, have low math and reading skills.
John:	I don't think we realize what the long-term repercussions are of not worrying about that twenty percent. Twenty percent of the current welfare rolls is still a lot of people. It's going to be beyond anything any of us has ever seen in this country, because we've had welfare for a long time now.
Dr. Bauer:	Up to now, we haven't had too many people begging in the streets. We have some.
John:	Right, we have some, but we'd have many more, I believe.
Aussie:	If we're talking about a twenty percent who lack education and use drugs and so on, we're also talking about that community multiplying in the future.
Dr. Bauer:	Because the twenty percent that we can't serve have children.

Aussie:	Sure.
Jesse:	Well, there's two things I look at with that. First, it assumes, as Hamblin said, that children of people who are welfare-dependent are going to definitely grow up to be welfare-dependent. I think that's a reprehensible assumption to make. We didn't have welfare, as we consider it, until the Depression era, so what happened in the 140 years of our history before that?
Dr. Bauer:	I think we can all agree that there was worse poverty in this country before the 1930s, and certainly during the 1930s poverty increased in this country to such an extent that the government thought it had to intervene. Many people think that had we not created the New Deal and a welfare system, we would have had political upheaval. Because it was not the case that only a small minority of people were hungry or poor. By one estimate, twenty-five percent of the population—not the welfare rolls, the population—was unable to feed themselves, and in a democratic political system, that cries out for response.

So, my question is, If we need to help the neediest twenty percent, how much are we willing to invest? The program the secretary holds up as one that's dealing with the hardest twenty percent to serve is this group in Harlem called STRIVE. And they do a lot of things. They have support after you're on the job. They have frequent phone contact and individual counseling sessions with clients. They teach life skills; they are helping to instill core values, and they do it well. The job retention rate for these graduates after two years is eighty percent. That's pretty good. But notice how many services you have to give to these cases in order to get them up and running. Do you think the American people have the will to spend the kind of money it would take to duplicate the STRIVE program all over the country? |
Aussie:	I think this country is based on results. If you show me the facts, then I'll pay for it. If you don't, then I don't want to invest in it.
John:	But which facts are members of Congress going to see? Which facts are the media going to show us? Are the media going to continually tell us that people on welfare can't succeed, like they have for the last thirty, forty-some-odd years? Or are they going to present facts that give us some optimism?
Shane:	Well, the politicians and the media never dealt with the facts on welfare, the percentage of the national budget, who benefited.
Dr. Bauer:	And what does she say about the media?
John:	"I want to challenge those of you who are in the media to do more." She wants them to fight the stigma and make sure that the American public sees what is happening with welfare, not what the media thinks will sell more papers, or get higher TV ratings.
Dr. Bauer:	Voters respond to what they see in the media. Is the media doing a good job in talking about programs that work with these hardest to serve? Have you read a story in the last year—a success story—about the hardcore unemployed?
Aussie:	No, I haven't seen anything like that.

Dr. Bauer:	Do you remember hearing stories about people who committed welfare fraud?
Aussie and Gino:	Yes!
Dr. Bauer:	Yes, you did. So, those stories have been on the air.
Jesse:	If I could interrupt. We seem to have decided that we want some big welfare program to pour money into this twenty percent still stuck on welfare. I don't want that. Do you really want to have a federal welfare policy that is nation-wide, or do you want one that is much more local, much more flexible, much more responsive to the individual conditions that are different in Denver and West Virginia?
Shane:	The problem is that the states have not been all that responsive. You keep thinking that if welfare is on the state level, then they will address the hardest twenty percent.
Jesse:	Actually, I don't have faith in either the state or the federal.
Shane:	Still, I'd rather get help for everybody at the federal level, and you see it at the state level.
Gino:	No, Jesse would rather see it at the personal level.
Jesse:	No, no. I'd rather see it at the STRIVE level. And at the church level. And at the level of other local charitable organizations.
Gino:	I know your political views, and you have this ideal that people are going to dig deep in their own pockets. No, you have to see the reality of our personal instincts as people; they think of "me" before they think of the community. I don't understand where you get this idea that in the past we did okay without government help. I'm a history major, and I've read about the Rockefellers and the Andrew Carnegies. These guys wouldn't pay their workers a living wage. So, I don't understand how we've changed so much that we can safely return to a system of help that came only from private charity.
Dr. Bauer:	Well, let me just bring this back to my discussion of Egypt, because Egypt is a society where the government doesn't do anything. Help comes from private charity or it doesn't come. During Ramadan, the Muslim holy month, the wealthy put on banquets for the poor. That's one month a year when the poor get to eat one good meal a day. The rest of the time, rich people are cruising the streets of Cairo in their Mercedes-Benz cars, past the people on the streets who are begging, past the children whose limbs are malformed, past people with birth defects who have no money to fix them; horrendous poverty that we don't see in this country. I didn't see Jesse's version of charity in Egypt. I saw great wealth, and I saw great poverty, and I saw occasional charity—occasional charity. Jesse, I think government has to assume some responsibility, or no one else will.

★ ★ ★

For Additional Reading

Go to InfoTrac College Edition, your online research library at

http://web1.infotrac-college.com

Enter the following search terms using the Subject Guide or Key Terms.

Aid to Families with Dependent
Children (AFDC)

food stamp program

means test

Medicaid

Medicare

Supplemental Security Income
(SSI)

welfare-to-work programs

15 Foreign Policy

MONICA BAUER

A Personal Perspective on War

WAR IS NOT A POLICY CHOICE LIKE WHETHER OR NOT TO TIE federal highway funds to an increase in the state's drinking age. I've visited the Vietnam Memorial Wall where those names are listed in black granite so starkly that you are reminded that war means dying. I've seen people break down in tears as they touch a name, leave behind a rose, a child's picture, a military service ribbon. War is the single most serious decision a nation can make, because it always means death.

Some peace activists in my generation shared a simple-minded view of the military as a bunch of pro-war thugs, an extension of the playground bullies who enjoyed taking lunch money from defenseless kids. But stereotypes are seldom true. I found out how wrong stereotypes can be when I ended up in the military. I served in the National Guard while I was an undergraduate, because it was the only way for me to make actual money as a musician. (I was a percussionist in the Forty-third Army Band.) I went to basic training at Fort McClelland, Alabama, under drill instructors who had seen combat in Vietnam. They didn't talk about it much, but I got the unmistakable impression that they had hated it. President Eisenhower, architect of one of the greatest blood-baths in history, the D-Day invasion, said no one hates war as much as a military man, because he knows best what war is like.

I thought a great deal about war and pacifism when I was an undergraduate and later in seminary at the Yale Divinity School, and I decided that I was a pacifist.

A pacifist can't pick and choose which wars he or she will support; a pacifist believes no war is ever justified. I would not fight a war, but that wasn't much of a challenge, because nobody was asking me to fight one at the time. The government was asking me for my money, however, to build weapons of mass destruction on a massive scale, in the greatest nuclear arms buildup in human history. I looked down on my newborn child, took a deep breath, and openly declared myself a war-tax resister.

By doing that, I felt I was part of an honorable Christian tradition. The early Christians were notorious for their refusal to fight in the Roman army. Then, in the fifth century C.E., the African Bishop Augustine wrote to explain that Christians could indeed join armies and fight for Rome as long as the war they were fighting was a "just war." Augustine's theory examined wars and found that not all wars were the same. A war defending your country against an invader is a "just war," whereas a war to invade your neighbor's territory out of sheer greed was an "unjust war." Still, I was a pacifist. There were no just wars.

After three years of study, I was ordained a minister in the United Church of Christ. Our denomination has its roots in the Congregational tradition of the Pilgrims. Over the years, my church has evolved into one of the most radical, politically active, left-wing churches. We don't have a centuries-long tradition of pacifism, but we were heavily involved in resistance to the war in Vietnam. By the time I was ordained in 1982, the Vietnam War was long over, but my church had not stopped protesting about war.

There was a great deal of talk in 1982 about the coming nuclear world war. Having grown up in Omaha, Nebraska—the world headquarters of the Strategic Air Command, the center of America's nuclear strike force, and the number-one target on every Russian battle plan for World War III—it didn't seem at all far-fetched that, inevitably, there would be a war that would wipe out life as we knew it. During the Cuban Missile Crisis, the closest we ever came to nuclear war with Russia, I was a third grader convinced I would never live to see grade four.

By the time I was ordained at age twenty-nine, I had heard all my life that nuclear war was likely in my lifetime. So when the national leadership of my church began to denounce the Reagan arms buildup as a prelude to nuclear war, I didn't question its logic. The slogans I saw a million times plastered on the cars in church parking lots read such things as, "It is impossible to prepare for war and peace at the same time," and "Every arms race ends in a war." I believed them. I had never studied political science. I didn't understand foreign policy. And the reason I'm telling you this is to help you understand why I became a war-tax resister.

That same year of my ordination, as I was taking up my first job as a youth minister at a church in a wealthy Connecticut town, I declared I would refuse to pay any income taxes until the Reagan administration ended its arms buildup. None of my money would go to prepare for World War III. Although my national church leadership was recommending that more members of the United Church of Christ do that, it was really the Quakers who were the most active. So I hooked up with the local Quaker peace activists, and we announced our tax protest together, hoping to ignite a nationwide movement to stop the Reagan administration.

The consequences of that action reverberate through my life to this day. Within a year, I lost that first job in the ministry and had to move my family back to Nebraska to take up a church in a small town so desperate for a pastor that they would take even me. Despite what the national leaders of my church said about tax resistance, there was no great movement within the United Church of Christ. In fact, to my knowledge, not a single member of the national leadership practiced what they preached. Within two years, I gave up my protest, which was never much of a protest to begin with because I made too little money to actually owe any taxes in those years. It mostly meant that my husband, who thought I was a little nuts, filed his taxes separately.

Two years later I quietly began paying my taxes and began looking for ways to make my voice heard in a more powerful way. Just a few months after I started filing tax returns again, I ran for Congress.

The real moral of this story is what happened after I lost the general election for the U.S. House of Representatives. I began graduate study in political science at the University of Nebraska, and while I was there I took a long, hard look at my beliefs. I read more political philosophy and decided that not all wars were wrong. Although I still believed a nuclear war could never be a just war, because the end result would be the end of everything worth fighting for, I began to believe that certain wars could be justified. Three years after I got my doctorate in political science, the Soviet Union fell. All those slogans about the inevitability of nuclear war turned out to be completely untrue. It turned out that you could engage in the biggest nuclear arms buildup in history and end with peace. I would wish for all my students that they never hold views as tightly as I did during the Cold War, when I didn't question authority.

When the United States went to war against Iraq in 1991, I put my new political science skills together with my ongoing religious objection to war and found myself greatly disturbed about a war that turned out to be the most popular war in American history.

The Gulf War seemed to fit Augustine's criteria for a just war. For me, his theory is most persuasive when it seems to be a case of practicing one evil to prevent a much larger evil. The Gulf War appeared to be a defensive war fought to contain an aggressor. One of the great what-ifs of World War II was that if Hitler's aggression had been stopped, contained by an opposing force before he took over most of Europe, perhaps World War II could have been prevented. The lesson of World War II is to stop aggressors early, to prevent a larger war.

In this chapter, we are going to focus on the Gulf War and the question of intervention, specifically in Kosovo. As a student, you may want to use this chapter as a spur to more reading and discovery of your own stance on war. If you are a pacifist, then war is always wrong. If you are not a pacifist, then you must decide whether the Iraq and Kosovo wars were just. And you must decide whether continued economic sanctions are war, and if they are, then you must decide whether such sanctions are a just war.

The Gulf War appears to be a model for the way wars may be fought by the United States in the twenty-first century. Many of my students are Gulf War veterans. Reasonable people have grave disagreements over this war. Arguments can be made for both sides. But both sides can't be completely right. And when it comes to war and peace, can we afford to be wrong?

I began to think about that topic from a religious point of view. Then I became a political scientist and looked at it from a political point of view. Now I try to combine them to remain a moral person. Does this essay have meaning for those of you who have no religious views on war? Shouldn't you have a moral point of view and a political point of view? After all, war is killing made possible with your tax dollars. And sometimes your country may ask you to participate in ways far more frightening than paying your taxes. What are you willing to die for? What are you willing to kill for? What are you willing to ask your children to die for or kill for? Those are the real questions in American foreign policy. I wish you luck on your journey toward developing your own point of view. And don't forget the most important lesson: Never be so sure you are right that you stop asking questions.

Wag the Doubt: The Debate Over Clinton's Iraq Attack Blazes New Frontiers in Cynicism
William Saletan

Did President Clinton "wag the dog" by bombing Iraq on the eve of the House impeachment debate? Politicians and pundits launched the rhetorical war over that question even before the first missiles fell in Baghdad. While the damage mounts in Iraq, the debate at home is dragging politics to new depths. Here's a glossary of the debaters' latest tactics, in morally descending order.

1. Overt cynicism. The politician accuses Clinton of wagging the dog. Example: "It is obvious that he is doing this for political reasons" (Rep. Gerald Solomon, R-N.Y.).

2. Cynicism by innuendo. The accuser phrases the dog-wagging charge obliquely so that he can deny having made it. Example: "We have had either hostilities or threatened hostilities at interesting times throughout the last year" (incoming House Speaker Bob Livingston).

3. Backhanded cynicism. The accuser implies dog-wagging by saying either a) he can't bring himself to believe Clinton would wag the dog; or b) the White House has assured him it's not so. Example: "While I have been assured by administration officials that there is no connection with the impeachment process . . . [b]oth the timing and the policy are subject to question" (Senate Majority Leader Trent Lott).

4. Cynicism about principle. The accuser argues that because Clinton is inherently unprincipled, any seemingly principled behavior on his part is fishy. Example: Clinton must have bombed Iraq to avoid impeachment, because "how else to explain the sudden appearance of a backbone that has been invisible up to now?" (Solomon).

5. Cynicism by association. The accuser doesn't allege a causal relationship between the impeachment process and the bombing, but he blames Clinton for the correlation anyway. Example: "President Clinton has indelibly associated a justified military response . . . with his own wrongdoing. . . . Clinton has now injected the impeachment process against him into foreign policy, and vice versa" (Jim Hoagland, *Washington Post*).

6. Vicarious cynicism. Rather than stand behind his cynicism, the accuser attributes it to others. Example: "It is dangerous for an American president to launch a military strike, however justified, at a time when many will conclude he acted only out of narrow self-interest to forestall or postpone his own impeachment" (*Wall Street Journal* editorial).

7. Fake idealism about cynicism. The accuser says other people's cynicism makes it impossible for Clinton to govern well. Example: "The point is not whether this president would [wag the dog] . . . [b]ut for some significant portion of the population . . . there must be that doubt. And that doubt is the crucial nexus. . . . A president must have credibility when he makes decisions about peace or war" (former Reagan lawyer Peter Wallison, *New York Times* op-ed).

8. Fake patriotism about cynicism. Democrats say Republicans who accuse Clinton of wagging the dog are *inadvertently* aiding and comforting the enemy. Example: "Shame on you [Republicans] for playing into the hands of Saddam" (Rep. Martin Meehan, D-Mass.).

9. McCarthyism about cynicism. Democrats say Republicans who accuse Clinton of wagging the dog are *deliberately* aiding and comforting the enemy. Example: The GOP's

remarks were "as close to a betrayal of the interests of the United States as I've ever witnessed in the United States Congress" (Sen. Robert Torricelli, D-N.J.).

10. Recidivist cynicism. Having accused Republicans of cynicism for suggesting that Clinton cynically used the Iraq conflict to delay the impeachment vote, Democrats use the conflict to delay the vote. Example: The House should "not take up impeachment until the hostilities have ended. It shouldn't come up as long as our troops are in harm's way" (House Minority Leader Richard Gephardt).

11. Cynicism about cynicism. While publicly accusing Republicans of tactics aimed at gaining political advantage, Democrats privately gloat that the tactics will give Democrats a political advantage. Example: "'The rules we've always had is that politics stop at the shore,'" one senior White House official said, speaking on the condition of anonymity. 'Somebody changed the rules and it wasn't us.' But Clinton advisers said that they expected Mr. Lott's comments to backfire" (New York Times).

12. Reverse cynicism. While accusing Clinton of invoking the Iraq conflict to delay the impeachment vote, Republicans invoke the Iraq conflict to expedite the impeachment vote. Example: "I don't see any reason to postpone the vote. That plays right into Saddam Hussein's hands. That's what terrorists want—disruption" (Rep. Bill McCollum, R-Fla.).

13. Cynical anti-cynicism. While accusing Democrats of cynicism for suggesting that impeachment would undermine the war effort, Republicans argue that impeachment is the best way to honor the war effort. Example: "As those troops are engaged now, even now, defending . . . the Constitution of this nation, they have a right to know that the work of the nation goes forward. And in consideration of this, it is our intention, Mr. Speaker, to begin consideration of [impeachment]" (House Majority Leader Dick Armey).

14. Circular vicarious cynicism. Unable to prove that Clinton wagged the dog, Republicans argue that the mere suspicion of dog-wagging is grounds for impeachment. Examples: "The suspicion some people have about the president's motives in this attack is itself a powerful argument for impeachment" (Armey). "Perceptions that the American president is less interested in the global consequences than in taking any action that will enable him to hold onto power [are] a further demonstration that he has dangerously compromised himself in conducting the nation's affairs, and should be impeached" (Wall Street Journal editorial).

"Economic" Sanctions Are Killing the Children of Iraq
Stephanie Salter

Late last month, Rep. Bob Inglis, R-S.C., posed a somber question to his congressional colleagues about the future of American values.

"Are we a nation based on truth or moral relativism?" he asked. "Does the truth matter?"

Inglis was talking about the only issue to which Congress has given its full attention for month now, not to mention its most impassioned moral rhetoric: Should the president of the United States be removed from office for lying under oath about whether, where and why he touched Monica Lewinsky?

Would that Inglis were talking about the truth in Iraq, where hundreds of thousands of children have died as a result of our morality-spewing nation's economic sanctions on their country.

Economic sanctions. Such a benign sounding term. It conjures up images of inconvenience: They can't export all the oil they want to or get their hands on any iMacs.

The truth is, eight years of economic sanctions has meant the slow, thoroughly preventable deaths of an estimated 5,500 Iraqi children each month. These estimates come, not from Saddam Hussein and his lunatic henchman, but from a host of international relief agencies.

Other than question some of the numbers—maybe only a million Iraqis have died since the end of the Gulf War instead of 1.5 million—no one in authority in the United States has bothered to deny the truth of the dead and dying Iraqi kids.

No one has to deny. The American people don't seem to care.

Despite the evidence, we refuse to take any responsibility for the genocide in the Persian Gulf. We refuse to acknowledge that no amount of "humanitarian aid" can sustain a once-developing country for eight years.

Instead, we are satisfied with the lame (and morally relative) platitudes of our stumbling, policy-poor president, Congress and the departments of Defense and State. We actually swallow the sort of rationalization that Defense Secretary William Cohen offered during the last round of bombing: "Our fight is not with the Iraqi people, it is with Saddam Hussein."

Thousands of Iraqi children have simply starved to death, thanks to a crippled national infrastructure and the toughest sanctions ever imposed on any nation. Most of the little Iraqi dead have succumbed, however, to the kinds of diseases and infections that parents in the modern world no longer fear: diarrhea, typhoid, pneumonia, whooping cough.

These maladies are nothing that antibiotics can't wipe out. Nothing that rehydration tablets can't cure. Nothing that chlorine can't purify.

Too bad antibiotics and other medicines are not getting through to Iraqi people in sufficient quantities. Tough luck that chlorine, the cheapest, most efficient means of purifying drinking water, cannot be imported into Iraq because of our sanctions; chlorine can be used to make biochemical weapons.

Based on official assessments of last month's bombing of Iraq by the United States and Britain, *New York Times* reporter Tim Weiner concluded: "Starving Iraq has not subverted Hussein. Striking at his army and his spies with cruise missiles has not toppled him. Sanctions have slowed but never stopped his drive to build nuclear, biological and chemical weapons. . . . He may be as close to building a nuclear weapon—perhaps closer—than he was in 1991, U.S. experts say."

Are we a nation based on truth or on moral relativism? Does the truth matter? The answer, good citizens, is on passionate display these days in the chamber of the U.S. Senate. Doesn't it make you proud?

Reprinted, with permission, from *San Francisco Examiner,* January 10, 1999. © by San Francisco Examiner.

CHAT ROOM

Aussie
a liberal
Jewish Palestinian

Gino
a moderate
Democrat

Jesse
a conservative
Libertarian

John
a liberal
Democrat

Shane
an African American,
liberal Democrat

The Gulf War We Don't See: Foreign Policy Continues after the Crisis Ends
★ ★ ★

Dr. Bauer: We've all just read "Wag the Doubt" by William Saletan. This refers to a movie, *Wag the Dog,* which was a satire about a presidential adviser who decided to invent a war against an overseas enemy to take away media attention from a presidential scandal. The title comes from dialogue in the movie, where a presidential adviser describes a political world where the advisers have more power and control than the president; thus the tail wags the dog. But the phrase has come to mean any attempt to divert attention from scandal by use of foreign policy. It opened in theaters very close to the Clinton impeachment hearings. Did President Clinton "wag the dog" when he bombed Iraq? When we finally did bomb Iraq in 1998, when is it that we began bombing?

John: Right before the impeachment vote in the House.

Dr. Bauer: Now, I must tell you, that when I first heard about Clinton bombing Iraq, "wag the dog" was the very first thing that went through my mind. Why?

Gino: Because the movie had just come out?

Jesse: But I hadn't even seen the movie, and I was suspicious. I could imagine Clinton doing it. It is not that it is likely or probable, but that I can believe it of this man.

Shane: The first thing that went through my head was Reagan did it too! I don't put these things beyond our presidents.

Dr. Bauer: I think you're referring to the time during the Reagan presidency when we had a short war right after the Beirut bombing killed 258 marines.

Jesse: We invaded Grenada. In fact, it was the same task force that was going to relieve the Marines in Lebanon, and they got diverted to Grenada. I thought then that it was pretty amazing that this country of ten square miles was suddenly a massive domino theory threat to us. They were going to fall to the

	Communists, and the next you know, Mexico would go communist—that whole ridiculous Cold War domino theory that consumed our foreign policy for forty years.
Dr. Bauer:	These are the sorts of foreign policy interventions that fuel cynicism when people look at our foreign adventures. President Reagan sent troops to Grenada within a day or two after marines were killed while they slept in a barracks in Lebanon. "Wag the dog" has to do with timing. Why did the U.S. have to invade Grenada right away? If there was no real emergency in Grenada, then does it look like "wag the dog"?
Gino:	Yes it did. Reagan wanted to kick out some Cuban advisers who were doing exactly what they said they were doing: helping the people of Grenada build an airfield. If the Grenada invasion had lasted more than a week, there would have been more of an uproar. We expect that if we're going to war, the president better darn well explain it to us.
John:	Especially after Vietnam, which heightened Americans' isolationist tendencies. Historically, Americans don't like to get into faraway conflicts. And if we do, we want to know the exact parameters, how long it's going to last, and what our goals are. Because those were never specified in the Vietnam War—it wasn't even a declared war—it was a "police action" like the Korean War in the 1950s.
Gino:	The American public's chief goal in foreign policy is to avoid another Vietnam. So we demand to know before we get in too deep in any overseas conflict, how and when we are getting out.
Dr. Bauer:	The policy term is *exit strategy*.
Shane:	I see it differently. I see foreign policy as an area where the government lies all the time. If we had known that the reason we went to war in the Gulf was to safeguard oil supplies, and not to defend the Kuwaitis, I don't think the American people would've gone for it. The government has to propagandize a conflict, spin it and sell it, so that the public will buy it.
Dr. Bauer:	That's an interesting point. Let me build on that for a minute. A lot of countries will follow what is called *realpolitik,* which is a German word for a realistic foreign policy based on power and force. Advocates of this theory of politics call themselves *realists*. Under the theory of *realpolitik*, the morality of a foreign policy is not a factor; it is only important that the policy be in our national interest.
	When countries base their foreign policy on *realpolitik,* they don't demonize their enemy to justify their aggression. Instead, they baldly announce that they are taking over a province because they want it—they want the territory, the resources, the oil. And they take it.
	But American foreign policy has always had a moralistic tone, because we are, in fact, still a religious people. We are moralistic. We want to believe that we are acting ethically and only want to engage in a "just" war. Against absolute evil. Advocates of a moralistic foreign policy are called *idealists*.

| | I think Shane is absolutely right. If George Bush had announced that we were invading Kuwait for oil, we wouldn't have gone. So the Bush administration demonized Saddam Hussein and the Iraqi army. |

John: Yeah, the killing babies thing—Iraqis were throwing premature babies out of hospital windows in Kuwait. And it turned out they were doing no such thing. That was just propaganda.

Dr. Bauer: Yes, sometimes Shane is right about propaganda. You know who the person was who gave that testimony before Congress? The Kuwait ambassador's daughter.

Jesse: One of the things that kind of intrigues me about the earlier discussion of exit strategy is that I don't think it has to be exact, we just want to know a definite goal and a realistic time frame.

We didn't know how long World War II would take, but we knew what our goals were: to defeat the Germans and the Japanese. We fought the good fight and eventually triumphed. In Korea, we didn't have that. In Vietnam, we didn't have that. But the Gulf War was popular because, as I think one of the articles says, we knew what we were going to do, we did it, and we got out.

Dr. Bauer: And there was very little loss of American life.

Jesse: That helps a lot. A TV-friendly war with few body bags.

Dr. Bauer: Yes, pictures are very important. If you saw *Saving Private Ryan*—and I highly recommend it—you saw what was reportedly an excruciatingly accurate re-creation of war. If we had seen those pictures on the nightly news during World War II, would the D-Day invasion have continued?

John: I'm not sure it would have. TV has changed foreign policy because the American public, not just the soldiers, have *seen* war. The newspaper report that this many GIs died was sad but essentially just a statistic. But Vietnam television footage totally shocked us and changed our perception of war—especially after sixty thousand Americans had died and we had seen some of their faces on TV.

Jesse: I think that's why the Iraq war went over so well with the public. It was a nice, clean, surgical war. All the bombs seemed to hit—or at least we weren't shown any that missed. At the end of the Gulf War, we shot up an entire armored column that was fleeing. I know people who were there. The massacre left evidence behind: literally more than one hundred vehicles were left unmanned after the shooting was over. Pilots who flew over the area during the shooting said it was like shooting fish in a barrel. But we didn't see that.

Shane: And if we don't get straight information, how can we react to foreign policy decisions?

John: The government always tries to control the press during war.

Dr. Bauer:	Let's go back to Vietnam. The tide of public opinion began to turn against the war when the television coverage changed. From 1965 to 1967 the press sat in the Hilton Hotel in Saigon and every day went down for the Pentagon briefing. But in 1967, a group of very courageous journalists went to where the fighting was.
Jesse:	They put packs on and they went out with combat patrols. Some of them got shot, and a few died. But they were the ones that sent stories back to the TV networks—stories that were completely different from earlier coverage.
Dr. Bauer:	So it's important to be able to see what's happening overseas. Which brings us to these two articles about what is going on in Iraq right now, where there are no TV pictures, just eyewitness accounts. Who is dying in Iraq?
Gino:	The children who aren't getting medicines and food. I think the American people see this, but they blame Saddam Hussein.
John:	I was walking down the Sixteenth Street mall, and I saw two guys with a petition in favor of Iraq humanitarian aid. I asked if I could sign it, and they said, "You know, we have a hard time getting even ten people to sign this." People look the other way when it's a foreign problem.
Gino:	There are other factors too. During the 1980s, we dehumanized the Arab people after the Iranian hostage crisis. Iran became an enemy nation, and Arabs everywhere were labeled anti-American. Americans believe all Arabs are fundamentalist, terrorist Muslims, so that by the early 1990s if I said the word *Islamic* ———— , how would you have filled in the blank?
Aussie:	Terrorist, of course. My father's family is a proud Arab family, and they really resent that attitude. It makes it convenient to ignore the fact that Arab children are dying. I believe that we are responsible for these children. And like John said, we would rather look the other way than take responsibility for what we have destroyed and created.
John:	I think the United Nations is a group that has no courage. They do not stand up to a major power. This humanitarian aid to Iraq, the oil-for-food program, involves not just the United States; all the other countries are part of it. We have so much economic power over so many countries. If we don't like something another country does, we just cut off economic aid. We bomb the Chinese embassy in Yugoslavia, and after two weeks of letting off steam, the Chinese government does pretty much what we want them to do about Kosovo. No wonder the rest of the world resents the power of the U.S.
Dr. Bauer:	Many think that we operate in the UN the way we operate in NATO: We use them when we want to use them, and we ignore them when we don't. The United States likes to go in with allies because it makes us look better, but, in fact, if we don't have the allies, we'll go in alone. And if it is convenient to ally ourselves with the UN, we will, but if it isn't, we'll take action without them.

We used NATO instead of the UN in Kosovo because it was easier; we didn't have to deal with a Russian veto in the Security Council. So we ended up with NATO and they were, and are, harder to manipulate.

The UN is far more important today than it was during the Cold War when the Soviet Union could be expected to veto whatever the U.S. wanted to do. How important the UN remains, is, in part, up to the United States.

★ ★ ★

U.S. Doesn't Belong in Kosovo

Ted Galen Carpenter

President Clinton's assault on Serbia is a flagrant, shameful act of aggression. U.S. forces are attacking a country that has not attacked the United States, a U.S. ally or even a neighbor. That's the very definition of an aggressor.

Belgrade is guilty of nothing except attempting to put down a secessionist rebellion. Nearly a dozen other countries have done the same thing in the decade alone, often with far greater bloodshed. Russia's war in Chechnya, Sri Lanka's conflict with Tamil rebels and Turkey's suppression of the Kurds are examples.

The administration's spinmeisters insist Serbia is the aggressor, but that twists language in a manner reminiscent of George Orwell. "Aggression" has a specific meaning: unprovoked cross-border warfare, an unwarranted attack by one state on another. A country cannot commit aggression in its own territory any more than a person can commit self-robbery.

The argument also sets an extremely dangerous precedent. The traditional standard that developments within a country, however tragic, do not justify military intervention by outside powers should not be cast aside lightly. Without that limitation, the floodgates are open to intervention by an assortment of countries for any number of reasons or pretexts.

Might Russia and its ally Belarus someday cite the Kosovo precedent for attacking Ukraine because of its alleged mistreatment of Russian-speaking inhabitants in the Crimea? Could China and Pakistan argue that India's suppression of secessionists in Kashmir is a humanitarian tragedy and a threat to the peace of the region, justifying joint military action?

The administration contends Kosovo is not really an internal Serbian affair because the conflict might spread to Albania, Macedonia and, potentially, NATO members Greece and Turkey. It is curious, if not nauseating, to see President Clinton, Deputy Secretary of State Strobe Talbott and other alumni of the anti-Vietnam War movement make that argument.

They ridiculed the domino theory when Lyndon Johnson and Richard Nixon invoked it in Southeast Asia. They were even more scornful when Ronald Reagan invoked it in Central America and the Caribbean. Suddenly, they believe it has indisputable validity. At the very least, they owe the U.S. public an explanation of their dramatic change of perspective.

And the administration's policy is making the spread of the conflict more rather than less likely. The Serbs are not the party with expansionist ambitions in the southern Balkans; the Albanians are. Kosovo Liberation Army commanders have stated that their ultimate goal is a Greater Albania, described on nationalist maps as embracing additional chunks of Serbia, Macedonia and Greece.

By facilitating Kosovo's secession (and the NATO settlement is nothing more than Kosovo's independence on the installment plan), the United States and its allies would be strengthening the very faction most likely to stir up additional trouble in the southern Balkans.

War against Serbia is unwarranted on strategic, legal and moral grounds. Serbia is the fourth country Clinton has bombed in the past seven months. That record is one of a trigger-happy administration creating an image of America as the planetary bully. Decent Americans need to make a stand when it has reached the point of a full-scale war of aggression against a country that has done us no harm.

Reprinted from *USA Today,* March 26, 1999. © 1999 by Ted Galen Carpenter. By permission of the author.

Against Internal Aggression
William Safire

Never will so many nations inflict so much destruction with so little relish.

Because outrage is absent and the public's war spirit is lacking; because few in NATO want to see the collateral damage sure to be inflicted as bombs go astray; and because foreign policy is so foreign to our economy-fixated discourse, Americans are asking as we go in: What national interest impels us to intervene to stop an independence movement from losing?

Four categories of answers, the first three of them unhappy:

1. *The simplifiers.* President Clinton painfully gives the reason designed to stir emotion and rally popular support: "President Milosevic . . . has again chosen aggression over peace." Serbian forces are "burning down Kosovar Albanian villages and murdering civilians."

2. *The thoughtful internationalists.* Senators like Richard Lugar and John McCain are reluctant to see us lurch into combat commitment with no end in sight. They find themselves forced to support the bombing of the Serbs because to do otherwise after all our threatening would be to reveal the alliance of Western nations as a pitiful, helpless giant.

3. *The anti-Wilsonians.* Henry Kissinger exhibits "great unease" at NATO's decision to intervene; his conceptual framework holds Woodrow Wilson's principle of self-determination to be unduly idealistic and destabilizing. He stops short of saying we should not join the bombing because he does not want to disestablish the foreign policy Establishment.

4. *The America Firsters and the quagmire-avoiders.* Now that the McGovernite left has fallen silent about taking sides in a civil war, anti-war voices are mainly from the Republican right, and they alone are unconflicted. They condemn the multilateral intervention, arguing: If Serbia refuses to allow a province coveted by neighboring Albania to secede, outsiders have no right to label such defense of its national borders "aggression" and to support the rebels. Russia agrees: If NATO can help the Kosovars break away from Serbia, then it can help the Chechens break away from Russia. That's why Yevgeny Primakov had to turn around and go home.

I'm in a separate school with President Wilson, who was three generations ahead of his time. Wilson was an arrogant idealist, a trouble-making rearranger of national borders who summed up his vision thus: "Every people has a right to choose the sovereignty under which they shall live." (Great principle; bad sentence structure.)

We now live in a world of satellite-televised brutality and computer-samizdat suffering; repression is hard to hide. If a large ethnic group dominating the demography of a province wants to be independent, it can assert its desire for self-determination in a dramatic way that earns a decent respect of the Opinion of Mankind.

Sometimes this desire is misplaced, overlooking the strengths of national diversity and the blessings of the melting pot. Quebecers think about separation; unrepressed by Canada, they decide democratically to stay in. Puerto Ricans, able easily to dissolve ties to the U.S., wisely choose not to. East Timor, bloodily annexed by Indonesia, can now opt in or out.

But what happens when a people—bonded by linguistic, cultural, racial or religious ties—is denied the expression of its culture, and then demands sovereignty from despots? If those oppressees are ready to shed their own blood and that of their territorial hosts, their some-times self-induced agony, projected on the world's attention screen, becomes a persuasive argument for "humanitarian intercession."

If the repressing country is powerful, the sovereignty does not change; too bad for now, Tibet.

If its leadership is savagely dictatorial but vulnerable, as in Iraq, repression is restricted from outside: We'll enforce your autonomy, you Kurds, but no independent Kurdistan lest your compatriots in Turkey and Iran get ideas.

If the villainous sovereign is relatively weak and the potential bloodshed is horrendous, then in we go (with bombs, not troops) to save the Kosovars.

Consistent and principled? Not quite. But the trend at century's end is toward self-determination, propelled by a world audience humanely averse to seeing casualties up close.

students

CHAT ROOM

Aussie
a liberal
Jewish Palestinian

Gino
a moderate
Democrat

Jesse
a conservative
Libertarian

John
a liberal
Democrat

Shane
an African American,
liberal Democrat

When and Where Should We Intervene?
★ ★ ★

Dr. Bauer: Ted Galen Carpenter, vice president for defense and foreign policy studies for the conservative-libertarian Cato Institute, says in his article, "U.S. Doesn't Belong in Kosovo," that the Kosovo war is "unwarranted." What are his reasons? Notice that he wrote his article at the start of the NATO bombing. Where did he say it would lead us?

Jesse: Into setting the precedent that countries are allowed to intervene in other countries' internal affairs within their borders. For example, would France and Britain have been justified in invading the United States during our Civil War—either to stop Union aggression against the Confederacy, or the Confederacy's aggression against the slaves? I think all Americans would say absolutely not. What's the difference between then and now? I personally don't see one. I think it is reprehensible what is happening there, but nations are supposed to stay out of each other's internal affairs. The Kosovo conflict is none of our business.

Shane: I disagree. I don't agree with bombing, but I also don't agree that the oppression of a minority is no business of ours. We have a moral responsibility to respond to genocide.

Jesse: Does that mean that we can bomb Ceylon, Sri Lanka, because of the treatment of their minorities? They have repressed their people who were trying to secede just as much as the Serbs have the Kosovars. So, are we not justified in bombing them, too?

Shane: I would say that there are different ways to stop oppression short of bombing. But I don't think that the wrongs being done in any country should be ignored by the world community. It should not turn its head away and say that's their problem. No. If there are wrongs being done they should be acknowledged and dealt with in some manner.

Jesse:	Okay, then in Carpenter's article, when he says, "Could China and Pakistan argue that India's suppression of secessionists in Kashmir [is] a humanitarian tragedy and a threat to the peace of the region, justifying joint military action?" would you like to try and right all those wrongs?
Shane:	I would oppose the use of military action there and everywhere. Just because I want to pay attention to humanitarian issues and human rights offenses doesn't mean I want to use force to fix them. But this is one globe, and we have to deal with the reality that the world is a global village now.
John:	If we want a global economy, we have to have a global consciousness. I mean, we always look at Kosovo like the United States alone is doing the bombing, but it's a NATO operation. It is many, many countries bombing this one place. Sure, we are the biggest country involved, but we are not the only country. I think this is the wave of the future: nations working together to form a kind of global police force, keeping the peace, and keeping the world economy moving.
Dr. Bauer:	Let's go back to Jesse's point about national sovereignty; that a nation should be able to do whatever it wants within its own borders. Carpenter has a point. When we use "aggression" to describe what the Serbs are doing in their own country, we change the meaning of that term. What states do inside their own borders is not usually labeled *aggression*.
Shane:	Well, I would address it within the framework of injustice. It doesn't matter if the injustice is happening in our own country, within our own state, within our own neighborhood. Injustice is injustice, and it needs to be addressed. I really disagree with Mr. Carpenter when he says a country can not commit aggression in its own territory.
Aussie:	Would that mean that Hitler exterminating the Jews was not aggression against the Jews? That because the Nazis were within their own territory that they could do whatever they wanted?
Jesse:	Well, let me say this then. If we are saying that it is our responsibility as a moral nation and as the world's only remaining superpower to respond to things like this, two things have to happen: First, we have to respond to all of them or as many of them as we can put resources toward. That's why the Russians and the Chinese are so nervous, because that would include Russia's aggression against Chechnya, and that would include China's aggression against Tibet and against their own people. Don't forget the Tiananmen massacre was ten years ago this month. Second, we would need a defense budget that would allow us to field millions of troops, plus thousands of ships, planes, boats, and resources to support them.
Dr. Bauer:	That's only true if we always want to use force to deal with human rights offenses. We used force in Kosovo because they were actively engaged in an ethnic cleansing that presented an immediate threat to Albanian lives. But that leads me to another point. Here is a question that every first-year political sci-

ence student should wrestle with: Can America always get what it wants out of foreign policy through the use of force? We are the only true military superpower in the world, but does that mean that America can tell other countries what to do? The goal of foreign policy is to get what we want. Did we get what we wanted in Kosovo?

Shane: Force doesn't always get us where we want to go. We bombed the Serbs, but if our goal was to stop ethnic cleansing in Kosovo, we lost. The Serbs did exactly what they wanted, and when they had burned down every last ethnic Albanian house, they signed a peace deal.

John: There are limits to what a military action can do. One of the lessons of Vietnam was that after all our bombing, because the people in Vietnam didn't want to go where we wanted them to go, we lost.

Gino: Vietnam was a tiny Third World nation, without any of our sophisticated weapons. But they had people power.

Aussie: Look at the Middle East. Compared to the power the Israeli government has, if power can be measured in weapons and technology, the Palestinians don't have a chance. Yet, in the late 1980s, the Palestinians began something called the *intifada*. You know what weapons the little boys used against the Israeli soldiers? They threw rocks! They threw bottles! That was it! But they wouldn't give up. Every once in a while, a terrorist bomb would explode, but mostly the *intifada* was a bunch of stone-throwing teenagers. The Israelis had been trying to keep the Palestinians in line since 1967, when the Israelis invaded and kept the West Bank of the Jordan River, where most of the Palestinians lived. The Israelis couldn't get what they really wanted, which was not only land, but peace, through the use of force. The Palestinians forced them to give up land for peace, and both groups signed a peace deal based on that. In part, because of a bunch of stone throwers!

Shane: What makes the Kosovo thing so interesting is that the Albanians are the majority in Kosovo itself. Ten percent of the population was Serbian, but they ran everything. Told them they couldn't speak or teach their own language. Disbanded their own elected parliament, where the Kosovar Albanians had a huge majority.

Jesse: But in Serbia as a whole, the Albanians were a minority. And Milosevic talked about Kosovo being a part of Serbia. As long as Kosovo is genuinely part of Serbia, the Kosovar Albanians would be a minority population of the whole country. Like if California becomes majority Latino, which it will soon, it still is a part of the United States. The Latino majority in California is still a minority in the whole country, so they can't run California exactly as a Latino country.

John: But we allow the Latino minority enough power and self-expression that they don't want to take California and secede from the United States. This is what Safire's article, "Against Internal Aggression," is all about. He wrote, "But what happens when a people—bonded by linguistic, cultural, racial or religious ties—is denied the expression of its culture, and then demands sovereignty from despots?"

Dr. Bauer: Did you notice in Safire's article that he defines all the foreign policy choices, and comes out on the side of the idealists? What's interesting is that Ted Galen Carpenter, who is, like Safire, a major figure in American conservatism, comes out on the other side. Which side is that?

Gino: Carpenter would call himself a realist. Safire calls Carpenter's opinion one of the "America Firsters and the quagmire-avoiders."

Aussie: This may be the first and last time in history that Bill Safire agrees with Bill Clinton.

John: That's one of the things I find fascinating about the Kosovo war; it split the conservatives.

Dr. Bauer: Why, do you think?

Jesse: Because, during the Cold War, the conservatives set themselves up as realists. They were tough-minded, anti-Communists willing to use force and not at all interested in the idealist position, which was to negotiate and have treaties. That's why the true conservatives turned on Nixon, when he went to China and when he promoted treaties with the Russians. True conservatives loved Reagan, because he would go on and on about the "Evil Empire," while Nixon was willing to have dinner and a movie with them.

John: Okay, but who are the realists and idealists today? Do those two categories even make sense anymore?

Aussie: I think the categories still make sense. Safire is an idealist. He agrees with Woodrow Wilson. He also agrees with Jimmy Carter, but he won't write that in the newspaper! It was Carter who started the foreign policy of putting human rights ahead of any other national interest. And it was Carter who first brought the Arabs and the Israelis together. History may be kinder to Jimmy Carter than the voters were.

Gino: I don't know if the categories work. The realists who wanted to fight the Commies everywhere, no matter what the cost, have turned into the House Republicans who voted against supporting the war in Kosovo. But those same Republicans supported the Gulf War. Very confusing!

Jesse: But the Gulf War was easy; one nation invaded another nation. Still, the Democrats mostly voted against it.

Shane: I didn't get it, when the anti-war Democrats started lining up to support Clinton's bombs. That didn't make sense. The only people singing my song were the House Republicans. How often is that going to happen?

Dr. Bauer: I think it may be a mixture of idealism and realism that supported the NATO attacks against Serbia. There are idealists, like Safire, who are on the side of people who basically want their own nation, their freedom. And you have to give Safire points for consistency; he regularly lights into the Chinese for oppressing the people of Tibet. Then there are those such as Clinton and Britain's Tony Blair, who are not just upset about immorality, they are worried that a conflict like this can spread. They are realists, in the sense that they want to nip this problem in the bud, before it inflames passions all over the Balkans. It used to be that realists bombed and idealists negotiated. In that sense, I think those two labels have worn out their usefulness.

Gino: Which means that foreign policy is no longer a useful issue in American elections, at least for now. Especially since Clinton's side won in Kosovo, and the House Republicans tried to make a big political issue out of stopping him. That's going to be worth nothing in the 2000 elections; it may even hurt the Republicans, because now they look silly.

Jesse: When we still have troops in Kosovo five years from now, and it costs the taxpayers billions, they might not look that silly.

★ ★ ★

For Additional Reading

Go to InfoTrac College Edition, your online research library at

http://web1.infotrac-college.com

Enter the following search terms using the Subject Guide or Key Terms.

Cold War	isolationism	Vietnam
Gulf War	NATO	
Iraq	United Nations (UN)	

Meet the Students

Andrew Nicholas

I grew up an imaginative and muddy little boy. Shortly after moving from Wyoming in the late 1960s, my father and mother built a house on five acres just east of a tiny town called Parker, Colorado. There were countless gullies, trails, and reeds to run through. I would while away the hours with my red wagon by hauling my cargo of empty milk jugs to all the different "outposts" in our backyard. We were just a small family of four living out in the vast plains of the West.

My father, Bob, a Harley-Davidson mechanic and former United Airlines computer programmer, is a talented and extraordinary man for whom I have a great deal of love and respect. He is a conservative man with most of the social and economic views of the traditional Republican Party. My mother, Paula, a college English teacher and outspoken rebel, has a passion for people and jumps into life full force. Politically, my parents were on either end of the seesaw. Thank God, my older brother Michael and I were wise enough not to bring up any hot political issues at the dinner table. Honestly, it's a wonder they got along as well as they did until their divorce in 1987, shortly after I turned nine years old.

The years to follow were shocking to a young Andrew Nicholas. Michael chose to live with my father and stepmother in Huntsville, Alabama, while Mother and I moved into low-income housing near downtown Denver. From a rural farm boy to an urban "city slicker" was not an easy transition, to say the least. As the years progressed, I began to enjoy what the city had to offer: more people and stronger neighborhoods. The community just seemed altogether more connected. By the time I was a teenager, I was calling the city home.

At eighteen, college was the place to realize my dream of becoming a pilot. As though it were placed there by providence, the college that was rated second in the nation for aeronautics was literally blocks from the center of Denver. It was certainly the college for me and was the only college I applied to. As a graduation present, my folks put some money together to purchase my first round of private flight lessons. Shortly after I registered for my classes and declared my major, I took my first flight. It was awful. At that moment my future was truly blank.

Most recent college grads will tell you that the major you choose when you enter into college will change at least once before you graduate. It seemed I was getting that out of the way early. With no real plan of action, I checked out what the Metropolitan State College of Denver had to offer in other departments. I took a few classes in philosophy, geography, Russian, political science, and even weight training. After the first few semesters, I found myself drawn toward the philosophy of law and politics. So, I ended up helping out on a few political campaigns, doing an internship for my local congresswoman, Diana DeGette, and even working on the Oklahoma bombing trial at the United States District Courthouse. Learning about politics allowed me to find a side of myself that was exciting and stirred up a natural passion deep within me, a passion that I could certainly follow for the rest of my life.

Today, I feel fortunate in several ways as I look back on my development as a political person. First, that my upbringing afforded me an emotional exposure to the entire length of the political spectrum. Second, that my study of politics and law is driven by a passion to learn more about what I love and is not just the expression of partisanship. Those fortunate circumstances have allowed me to understand the emotional and intellectual side of politics without placing myself in any one particular camp or political ideology. Even though I am gay, that does not necessarily shape my political thinking in any significant way. Ultimately, I believe that I can overcome biting partisanship and narrow political ideologies by simply sticking to reason and maintaining a strong sense of objectivity—the things that will truly serve a community and make me a stronger leader.

Sarah EchoHawk Vermillion

My full name is Sarah Susan EchoHawk Vermillion. I am an enrolled member of the Pawnee Tribe of Oklahoma. As an American Indian woman, much of my life has been and continues to be influenced by my cultural background. I take great pride in my American Indian heritage and plan to pursue a career as an American Indian attorney.

As a child, I was often the only Indian student in school. To fit in, I tried to hide my background by avoiding any public expression of tribal values and culture. It was not until I reached the age of twenty-one and gave birth to my son that I realized the overwhelming value of my cultural heritage and how much it meant to me. For the first time, I understood that it was not something to hide, but a source of great pride.

I attended college right out of high school, but still possessed the self-doubt that had plagued me throughout childhood. Not sure of where I was going or what I wanted to do, I elected to take some time off from college. I married the following year and gave birth to a son in July 1992. My son died when he was two days old from complications stemming from his birth. The loss was completely unexpected and totally devastating. The grieving process was long and difficult, but eventually I began facilitating a support group for parents who had suffered the loss of a baby and cofounded an organization offering one-on-one support. I came to realize that helping others was the only truly worthwhile work for me, and it was this insight that brought me back to school—to pursue a degree in political science and go on to law school.

I come honestly by my drive for law school. My father is John Echohawk, the American Indian attorney, and I am very proud of him. Through his work at the Native American Rights Fund (NARF), he has given a voice to the native people of this country. Prior to the founding of NARF, few native peoples had legal representation—their rights were seldom recognized or honored. Now, a quarter of a century later, many tribes have legal representation and have won recognition as sovereign governments with the right to self-determination. The battles, however, are not nearly over, and there remains a need for more native people to become attorneys and continue to represent the best interests of our people.

Politically, I am a registered Democrat and extremely liberal. I credit my liberal politics to growing up with parents from the sixties generation. When I was born, Richard Nixon was president, and I can still remember my father's voice telling me that Nixon was a crook. Last summer during a family reunion, I saw slides of my father wearing a peace sign on his law school graduation cap in protest against the Vietnam War. My mother is a feminist. She attended college when I was in elementary school, and I can remember her wearing her "ERA" (Equal Rights Amendment) T-shirt.

As I near graduation, I am hopeful for the future. It is my hope that this book will inspire students to become active participants in our political system. I believe our country and our government are in a period of enormous transition. But those of us who step up to the political challenges can, and will, create a valuable and lasting impact on the future of our nation.

Laura Barfield

What has brought me to this point in life? My history is not easy for me to discuss but may be typical of today's redefined family. I was born in Chicago in 1969, the younger sister of twin boys just thirteen months older. My mother is a nurse and my father, well, I don't really know, I suppose you could say he was a "jack of all trades." When I was four, our family moved to Florida, where I spent my youth.

My parents divorced when I was six, and I have not seen my father since. He was not the family type. In my early years, my mother was away at work all the time, and when she was home, my father abused her. After my father left and my parents divorced, my brothers and I were alone a great deal. I was a latchkey kid. I began to resent my mother, who, as I realized later, was doing everything she could to keep her small family's head above water. Money was tight, and I longed for more—more love, more physical comforts. As an unhappy child, I learned to fight early and became increasingly argumentative and challenging. My mother would say I should be a lawyer because I love a good fight!

From high school I went to a local college, dated a young Republican, and began to learn about politics. At eighteen I registered to vote as a Republican, although I had little understanding at the time what "Republican" meant. But I began then to explore the power and fascination of politics.

I moved around, even traveled to France, and discovered that I wanted to know more about international politics—how the countries of the world interact with each other. Comparative politics still interests me more than local politics, and when I moved to Colorado and decided to go back to college, I knew I would major in political science.

The Republican Party is still my party of choice—not just out of habit. The older I got, the more I realized I had made the right choice. I consider myself a moderate Republican, although I'm conservative on fiscal and family issues, because, in my own life, I have seen the breakdown of the family and decay in social values.

For me, comparative politics is a gateway to the world, which I hope to explore. We Americans take for granted so much that doesn't exist in some societies. The wars of my generation were in Iraq and Kosovo, where we saw the absolute need to intervene on behalf of those who could not defend themselves. The United States is the political leader of the world, the only remaining superpower, and if we are to keep that role, I want to be part of it, to assist in whatever way I can. I want to work to improve international relations.

I graduate this May and am moving to Washington, D.C., immediately after graduation to pursue a career in international politics.

Steve Hites

My areas of study are political science and criminal justice, and my goal is to go on to graduate school. Maybe I will become a teacher or work in corrections. But whatever happens to me in terms of my career, I know what my politics will always be. My attitude toward politics was shaped long before I ever became a college student.

I hate being told what to do. I never liked my parents deciding things for "my own good" and, as an adult, I hate it when either my government through legislation, or my fellow citizens through the democratic process, decide issues of morality on my behalf. I like having the freedom to make decisions that might be bad for me without others forcing my hand. I'm willing to take responsibility for my own mistakes, but I also demand to have that initial freedom to decide for myself how best to lead my own life.

I'm what you call a Libertarian. Basically, that means I'm pro-choice on almost everything. I'm in favor of legalizing drugs, prostitution, gambling. I'm in favor of eliminating strict gun control laws. I'm in favor of gay marriages. I'm extremely pro-choice on abortion, and I've never found a form of speech yet that I consider obscene or offensive. I also believe strongly in civil rights and the necessity for search warrants and safeguards against the excessive power of police. I'm for small government and individual choice, and I worship our Constitution and view it as broad, sweeping, and unbendable—our political Bible: absolute and the ultimate authority.

Growing up, I was always kind of a loner. I had my friends, but I was a quiet kid. I didn't play well with others and I think that translated into how I see politics as an adult. In high school I never felt any obligation to try and have "school spirit" simply because that was the particular school I went to when, most likely, any of the other schools in the area were just as good. In short, I'm not, nor have I ever been, a social type of guy. I've never felt a sense of community, nor a social obligation to my fellow citizens other than to mind my own business, and I've always expected the same in return.

I became attracted to Libertarianism because, in my view, it was the least intrusive ideology. For such a pluralistic society, one that contains so many different people and ideas and movements, the most conducive form of politics to such a country as ours, in my opinion, would be one most open to allowing everyone their own interpretations and expressions. Libertarianism limits government involvement in individual life, both economically and socially, and at the root of its foundation is the idea that each individual should be free to pursue his or her own truth.

I guess I've always been angered by the constant need of every political party and interest group in America to force their particular beliefs onto everyone else. Whether it be the Christian Coalition trying to legislate their religious beliefs or liberal socialists trying to give more of my paycheck to somebody else, I've always feared those who would try to control my behavior because of what they think is best.

I'd like to end my essay with a quote from a writer every political science student should study. Although he lived and wrote in the nineteenth century, his words are still important as we enter the twenty-first century.

"What then, is the rightful limit to the sovereignty of the individual over himself? Where does the authority of society begin? How much of human life should be assigned to individuality, and how much to society? Each will receive its proper share, if each has that which more particular concerns it. To individuality should belong the part of life in which it is chiefly the individual that is interested; to society, the part which chiefly interests society."

—John Stuart Mill, *On Liberty*

Jesse Wilkins

I was brought up to believe that I had the freedom to make my own choices, provided I took the consequences for my own actions. That has guided me in all my political choices, including my choice to enter the military.

After graduation from high school in 1988, I enlisted in the Marine Corps. I was assigned to Panama, where I saw firsthand the lingering corruption from the Noriega government and the inability of the U.S.-installed replacement to address even the most basic reforms. Like many service members, I was often pulled over by Panamanian police and threatened with jail if I didn't pay the "fine" on the spot. Panama was also a primary focus of the "War on Drugs." We spent billions on crop destruction and interdiction, and the prices for most hard drugs are cheaper today than they were before I got to Panama.

In 1992, I was transferred to Guantanamo Bay, Cuba. I saw the effects of centralized planning on the Cuban economy. During my tour, I met Cubans who were so dissatisfied with life under Castro that they would cross two minefields for a chance at freedom. This also had an effect on my political ideology.

In 1993 I was assigned to drill instructor duty in San Diego. After Panama and Cuba, I felt politically homeless. I registered as Independent because I felt that neither major party was in tune with what I thought. Democrats argued that society has an undue influence on individuals, which can cause some to engage in inappropriate behavior, and that society has a duty to provide for all. Republicans, in turn, said that society has an undue influence on individuals, which can cause some to become "moral degenerates" and engage in inappropriate behavior. Democrats argued that I was not responsible enough to own a gun, even though I was apparently responsible enough to train other young men in marksmanship. At the same time, Republicans thought that I was responsible enough to own a gun, but not mature enough to make my own moral choices. Neither party seemed to believe that individuals were capable of making their own informed decisions, and both parties sought to protect me from myself by restricting or outlawing behavior they considered inappropriate.

In 1995 I heard about a third party that seemed to agree with my philosophy. The group espoused personal responsibility, miniscule government, and individual rights. In 1996 I joined the Libertarian Party.

Libertarianism is the idea that, as P. J. O'Rourke says, "We only have one duty, the duty to do as we damn well please. With that comes only one responsibility, to take the consequences." Libertarians see Democrats and Republicans as two sides of the same coin, who both stand for bigger, more-intrusive government. The only difference is in what the particular agenda is on a given day. Government programs are akin to giving yourself a blood transfusion, but spilling half the blood in the process.

I don't know what's best for you. I know, however, that you don't know what's best for me. That sounds simple until we talk about saving people from the consequences of their own behavior. Both mainstream parties want to save us from ourselves by regulating our behavior. I want to be free to live my life without asking permission. The simple fact that the majority decides that certain behavior is questionable or praiseworthy does not give the majority the right to regulate behavior or impose it. Majority rule is like the idea that three wolves and a sheep should take a democratic vote on what's for dinner!

To paraphrase, "if you vote how you've always voted, you'll get what you've always gotten." I chose to fight for my freedom and my rights by joining the Libertarian Party. I will defend my inalienable rights at the soapbox, the ballot box, and the jury box.

Shane Jackson

I'm a twenty-eight-year-old Afro-American born and raised in Denver, Colorado. My mother is a counselor and my father is a college professor at Metro State College. I have two sisters, one sixteen years old who attends East High, and the other, who is thirty years old, works at a satellite TV company in Englewood. I was raised in a middle- to upper-middle-class family in Park Hill.

Park Hill is a diverse neighborhood both racially and economically and has a relatively long history of being an "integrated" neighborhood. My neighborhood gave me a broader perspective of people, myself, and society, and it gave me a firm foundation on the cultural differences and similarities that exist. This environment made me see others and myself as equals rather than opposites, and it demolished many stereotypes.

Like most inner-city neighborhoods in America there was a "white flight" episode in Park Hill. Many whites left Park Hill in the late sixties and early seventies as blacks began to move into the neighborhood. But many also decided to stay and create a relatively interracial community and an organization called Park Hill Inc. Some of the white families who stayed included those of the future governor Roy Romer and the governor at the time, Dick Lamm, among other whites with power. In the eighties a debate broke out over the bussing of predominately black students in Park Hill to other communities for integration.

I attended a public school and had no idea what was going on. One year I was at one school, the next I was bussed to another. My friends were black, brown, and white; we didn't know about the depth of racism. My only memories of the bussing controversy are of two of my white friends going to private schools the following year. I'm not saying that my neighborhood was or is perfect, but in many ways it helped me to see myself as a young man, not simply as a black young man, because I never viewed white culture or people as better than other cultures or people.

I left home at sixteen to play hockey in Canada and the United States and didn't return until I was twenty-four. It was during that time that I discovered that most of white society saw me as black, and therefore as threatening, poor, uneducated, and second class. It didn't matter that I had lived in three different countries, attended college, or traveled throughout the United States; what mattered was that I was a black male. This eventually led me to view most white American people as ignorant, semiracist, biased, and self-defensive concerning anything racial.

During those years I was called a "nigga," followed by and pulled over by police twenty to thirty times for nothing and generally treated unfairly—treated like a "nigga." That unfair treatment made me identify with the problems of male Afro-Americans throughout the United States. The unjust treatment made me read, research, and debate the problems and solutions of Afro-Americans. It made me take more pride in my African and Cherokee heritage and get involved in helping minorities that weren't given as many opportunities as me.

My political views are a product of the people, situations, and environments that I have had the opportunity to be exposed to. It is very hard for me to say which political party I belong to. In my opinion, the Democratic and Republican parties are two heads of the same monster, serving the few and feeding upon the many. In my opinion, our political system does not address the real issues and problems that affect our country and the world. These neglected issues include the contrast between what we spend on social welfare (AFDC, school lunches, and housing assistance amounts to $50 billion per year) and corporate welfare (which amounts to $170 billion per year). Here's just one example: We spent $11 million to promote the Pillsbury Doughboy in foreign countries! Another neglected issue is racism in lending practices, where certain neighborhoods are targeted, and people in those communities can't get mortgages. The more knowledge I gain, the more I question my country, the world, and myself.

I no longer view America through rose-colored glasses, nor do I see all white people as being the same. Living in Europe and Canada has taught me that white Americans are different than whites in other countries. I look at the problems and solutions in the United States and throughout the world with a broad view. And I realize that the only person that can define me is myself.

Asaliyeh "Aussie" Rabih

I am a senior with a double major in history and philosophy and a minor in psychology. I am going to attend law school and become an expert in international law. My dream is to someday follow in the footsteps of Golda Meir, who also once lived in Denver and become a leader in Israel.

Honestly, I believe in politics, and I believe in the state of Israel and also the state of Palestine. How is that possible? This is how: I was born in Jerusalem to an Arab father and a Jewish mother. My father is hard-core Muslim Arab and believes in the nation of Palestine. On the other hand, my mother sees Israel as the homeland of the Jews, given to them by God. Growing up in Israel, I was torn between these two ideologies. I spent the majority of my childhood surrounded by the Palestinian view toward the Israeli government. Due to changes in family circumstances, I was later able to experience the Jewish belief. I have experienced both worlds, I have experienced both communities, and I am able to see both sides clearly, without taking sides. In order to take a side, I would need to disregard my experiences with the world I grew up in.

My experiences have taught me a lot about the importance of politics. As for my ideology today, I must say I am proud to be associated with the Democrats.

Politics is a lot more extreme in Israel. In 1981, my parents got divorced and my mother got involved with the Jewish Defense League, which is the most controversial of all Jewish organizations. They train themselves for the defense of Jewish lives and Jewish rights. They learn how to fight physically, for it is better to know how and not have to, than to have to and not know how. The JDL motto is "Never Again," and it refers to the Holocaust slaughter of the Jewish people during World War II.

I didn't learn much from the JDL as a young child. I saw and understood the concept of war. The Intifada, the Palestinian uprising against the Israeli government, took place while I was growing up. As for the Palestinians, their Palestinian Liberation Organization told me that all Jews hated the Palestinians and wanted to kill them.

My past didn't teach me about peace, love, and acceptance. It taught me to fight for what is mine and what was taken from me, on both sides. Both sides had valid reasons to hate. To this day, I still love Israel–Palestine, and one day I shall see peace.

Change is not easy. The political system has changed, and so have attitudes. We are witnessing a country in the painful process of defining its future rather than living in its past. I am an example of what Israel can be in the future: both Arab and Jew trying to understand each other.

Gino Stone

The path that has led me to my current political beliefs began during my freshman year of college, just last year. I was seventeen years old, and I had some knowledge about the government, but for the most part you could smell the political ignorance on me. I thought that Communism was impossible because no two people were alike, that people on welfare should get up and get jobs, that the government shouldn't interfere with any business no matter what, and that Democrats were all bleeding-heart liberals. I am amazed when I sit back and look at this short list of ideals that I believed were right on mere blind faith. I had never truly educated myself on any of the topics that I have mentioned; I merely took all that my relatives, teachers, and newscasters had to say as gospel.

After I started college, I realized that I was so wrong and that I actually believed in the opposite of most of my previous political beliefs. I read Karl Marx's Communist Manifesto and it made more sense to me than capitalism and the economics of Adam Smith! I realized that welfare was not a handout and that no civil society should sit back and allow citizens to starve in the streets. I learned that the government had tried to stay out of the business markets up until the early twentieth century, and all that we got from it was tainted meat, disabled workers, and children working in factories. Finally I am a registered Democrat who attends as many Democratic functions as he possibly can. All of those factors combined make up a large part of the ideology that I will use in any political argument.

The fact that I am a Democratic Socialist only means that I believe in a democratic system of government, with a majority will of the people making the majority of the decisions. It also means that I think the government should control a majority of the aspects in the society. For example, I believe that the government should regulate pay rates, provide more welfare for those who are less fortunate, provide a free education to anybody who wants it—including *any* college education that you would like—and protection for all of the inalienable rights that men are born with, namely life, liberty, and the pursuit of happiness.

Some of the other aspects in my ideology are a belief that the notion of property is wrong and that the practice should be abolished, and that the conservative Christian view of human nature as bellicose and selfish is not human nature at all, but rather a factor of the economic system that we are raised in, namely capitalism. After all, is it inconceivable that humans are selfish and greedy because they are raised in a society that supports greed and selfishness with success?

Thus my ideologies have changed, however they are now my ideologies. I am no longer trapped behind the ideals of my parents or teachers. I very rarely listen to any opinion that a newscaster decides to inject in "objective" interpretations of the news. It is important to keep your eyes open and remain open to the ideas of others. Sometimes that which we see as gospel is not even close to gossip. If you close your mind and set your beliefs in stone you become a fundamentalist, and conflict is sure to follow. However, if your mind remains open and you are open to the ideas of others, compromise is possible, and the government under which you live prospers.

John Mahaney

I grew up in St. Louis, Missouri, in a middle-class family that was far from being political. My parents never seemed to care much about politics. My father would get pissed when the president of the United States would interrupt one of his television programs to deliver a speech! My parents don't belong to any political party, but they do vote in the presidential elections.

The first time I ever voted was back in the presidential election of 1992. I voted for Clinton because he looked good and had a lot of charisma. Those were two presidential qualities that were at the top of my list back then. I had no idea what his political views were. I didn't even know what Democrat and Republican meant. I flunked American Government in my first attempt at college, because I only showed up for class three times.

In the past five years, a few things happened that changed my views on politics. First, I met my wife, who is very vocal on political issues because she grew up in a family that talked about politics around the dinner table. This caused some tension early on in our relationship, because I had no real opinions on the subject. That was until I started reading the daily newspaper, not because I wanted to, but because it was the only thing that kept me awake at my 5 A.M. job at the YMCA. I read it from cover to cover every day and became addicted to current events. Call me crazy, but the stories that interested me most were those about the government. I read about the conflicts that went on in Washington between the two political parties and started to discover that I strongly disagreed with the conservative, right-wing view.

The third deciding factor in my political history was my career. For three years after college, I jumped from job to job because nothing challenged me and, more important, I didn't feel like I was doing anything of importance. So I decided to quit my advertising job and go back to school to become a high-school history teacher. I feel that I can make a difference in young people's lives. In short, I have become a liberal, '"I can save the world"' Democrat. I feel very passionate about my political views. In the future, I see myself becoming more involved in political activism and maybe running for political office someday, as long as I don't have to wear a tie.

Krystal Bigley

My parents had never attended college, and the issue of college was never discussed in my household. Still, influenced by friends and teachers, I came to believe that college was a necessary first step in life. Many factors influenced my political philosophy, but I believe community, family, and school are the main players in the political socialization process. No doubt those institutions influence everyone, but how individuals respond to institutions varies greatly.

For example, I attended a Catholic elementary school in Colorado for the first three grades but stopped because of my father's disappointment with the Church; my mother had been raised Lutheran, and the Catholic Church never accepted their marriage. So I was sent to public school. The first day, reciting the Pledge of Allegiance with my class, I was the only student to say "Amen" at the end. I had always assumed that was part of the pledge! I think that was the last time I said "Amen" out loud, and perhaps the first time I started to see the differences in the cultures around me and began to question institutions.

Every summer in high school, I went to Europe, particularly Norway, where my mother's relatives lived. Travel gave me insights into the United States—a country that the media and citizens of other countries see quite differently from the way Americans do. In those years I started to articulate my political beliefs, which now include various elements of democratic, representative, and socialist systems. Democratic, because I believe people should be able to make their own decisions. Representative, because those decisions should be reflected in their government. And socialist, because of the support that I saw the socialist government in Norway give *all* its citizens. Obviously, capitalism has worked to benefit most people in the United States, but I am concerned about the negative impact, the suffering even, that a capitalist system can inflict on workers in our interconnected world.

Like many other people inclined toward socialism, I am against military actions. It seems to me that, historically, the longest-lasting changes have been made through peaceful means. I oppose the death penalty and am pro-choice on abortion. Who am I to judge what other women should do with their bodies?

In short, in American politics I am a liberal. Of course, I am always learning new things about myself and my surroundings. I live in Littleton, Colorado, a place much in the news lately, where two teenagers at Columbine High School killed twelve students and a teacher and then turned their guns on themselves. I had thought never to see such violence and tragedy in a staid, suburban community, where the fences run for miles and the houses sit quietly next to one another. Now I know that frustration at being on the bottom of any hierarchy, be it economic, political, or the popularity scales of high school, exists and hurts just as much in homogeneous communities. At the age of twenty-two, I have graduated and joined the ranks of people with a bachelor's degree. I have learned the need for each of us to recognize every individual—and be recognized ourselves—as a valued member of the community. I hope I can help to spread that lesson.

Suzanne Bowen

I grew up during the fifties and sixties, spending part of my childhood in Germany because Dad was in the military. I remember Berlin before the wall was built and how scared I was when Dad went to the small island that was West Berlin that he would stray into Communist hands. My early politics were shaped by the Cold War with its clear definitions of Good Guys (us!) and Bad Guys (them!). My parents never discussed American politics, even though both were well read and my mother was college educated. But they did raise us to believe that being an American was the greatest thing in the world.

One thing set me apart from other children. I was born with an orthopedic birth defect and spent most of my childhood in a wheelchair. I couldn't go to school because the federal law guaranteeing all children an education was not passed until the seventies. Schools didn't even have entrance ramps. So a tutor came to my home twice a week. This worked until the tenth grade, when the tutor told my parents that she could not assist me with high school courses. I could keep the books, however, and was welcome to come to school when I was able to walk and no longer a safety hazard in the hallways. After years of surgery and physical therapy, I am able to walk. But I'm slow and don't do stairs or rough ground very well. The experience influenced my politics and left me with a life-long interest in those with disabilities.

I came of political age in the late sixties. I had married a military man and watched as our brothers and friends went to fight a war I couldn't justify. For the first time in my life, I realized that just because our government did something, it didn't mean it was right. I associated the war and excess spending with the Democrats. I wanted government to be run "lean and mean" like a business. As a junior college student in my twenties, I worked hard for the Republican Party. I cried and cursed the Democrats when Nixon resigned; I campaigned long and hard in a strongly Democratic district for Gerald Ford when he ran against Jimmy Carter.

In 1980, I joined the civilian world when my second husband left the military. It's not so easy out here. For the first time, I felt the insecurity of being without guaranteed health care or employment. People I knew, who were responsible and worked hard for their families, were fired, got eviction notices, and had their utilities cut off. I put my education on hold, because just living was tough.

I grew disillusioned, not only with the Republicans, but with the whole political process. I began to look at individual people and issues. Living in a part of New England where local government was conducted in town meetings and people could have a say, I learned that most people will get involved only when an issue interests them personally. If a high-school sports item was on the agenda, people would attend who hadn't been seen in years; then they'd disappear again.

By 1993, my children grown, I was bored. Really bored. Bone-numbing bored. My husband had the solution: I should go back to school. In May I will graduate with a B.S. in political science and criminal justice. Two weeks ago, I received an acceptance letter from the University of Denver College of Law.

So today I'm a grandmother looking forward to law school and whatever lies ahead. I'm still a registered Republican, but find that I often vote for Democratic candidates. I am not as sure as I once was that I know what the country needs or how we can get there. But I'm an American, and that's still the best thing to be.

Turi Gustafson

I am a twenty-eight-year-old white female and have recently returned to school after a seven-year absence in the performing arts. I pursued an acting career in Los Angeles, struggling to make ends meet as a waitress. I was successful enough, I suppose—small parts in television shows like *Cheers, Melrose Place,* and *In Living Color,* and I played one of Ellie Mae's bridesmaids in the film *The Beverly Hillbillies*—but I missed singing, my first love. I moved to Nashville and within three months got a record deal with a small, independent record label. After recording and singing background vocals, however, I realized that I didn't want to spend my life touring—something was still missing. I decided to move back home and finish college.

Perhaps it was inevitable. I am the daughter of two educators. My mother is a full-blooded Spaniard raised in a poor family in the Bronx, New York. She is now the well-respected principal of a trilingual (English, Spanish, and sign language) elementary school—and a liberal. My father teaches fifth grade and classifies himself as a moderate Republican, mostly because of his views on gun control and limited government.

My parents have always voted, always been politically informed. I have always been vocal, opinionated, and liberal, but, although I voted in every presidential election since I turned eighteen, I never participated in local politics. It was not until I took an American government class that I realized I could make a difference in society. That class really challenged me to think about government, to pay closer attention to current events and political issues. I had never liked watching the news, but to my surprise—and my family's—I soon found myself watching the morning news for current national and local events, being drawn especially to the political segments on the *Today* show and CNN. The class took place during the Clinton impeachment hearings, a significant factor, I suspect, in triggering my new attention to the political world. Suddenly I felt engaged in a political issue. I recall going to the Republican Party headquarters to give our opinions on the impeachment hearings; we carried signs, pro and con, for all to see (and honk at!)

I consider myself a firm liberal whose main concerns are education, civil rights, the environment, animal rights, and nuclear proliferation. I especially want to see the environment become a priority for the American public. With my newfound interest in political issues, I look forward to discovering and educating myself about new items on the political agenda.

A political newcomer, I am proud, as well as grateful, to live in a country where I can think and act according to my beliefs. I can seek any information and knowledge without the control of the government and use that knowledge to make informed decisions about my life. I plan to become more politically aware and active and work for my beliefs and those that will benefit society as a whole. I continue to be grateful to that one American Government class for opening my eyes and opening the doors for a chance to make a difference. Now my goal is to become an active participant in my community and nation.

Will Schneider

My family had a relatively small impact on my political development. My grandmother was the only member of the family with a strong political identification. She was as conservative as they come. She was very interested in both local and national politics, and she cherished her right to vote. My parents, on the other hand, had no desire to be a part of a government that they felt was dirty and corrupt.

Not only did my mother lack any sort of concrete political identification, but she also shunned the idea that politics was worthy of anything more than a passing thought. She did not participate in politics in any way. My father echoed similar sentiments, further concluding that the significance of politics paled in comparison to spiritual and philosophical revelation. His interest in Eastern philosophical thought, particularly Taoism and Buddhism, led him to desire spiritual as opposed to political participation. When it came time to vote, he voted for the candidate that would do the least amount of damage. Because of the fact that my family played a minor role in actually encouraging my political development, I was forced to look and search on my own.

One might be inclined to think that such a background of negativity with respect to politics would invariably lead me to political apathy. Yet, an opposite effect occurred in my life. Influenced strongly through my college education, I began instead to formulate a definitive political ideology. The introductory political science courses had a profound impact on my political development. The most significant impact a teacher has ever had on me came my freshman year when I enrolled in a political ideology class. Throughout the course, the teacher discussed the various political thoughts and their origin. I became so interested that I took additional courses in the subject, eventually adding political science as one of my minors. The accumulation of knowledge only furthered my interest in politics.

Along with this formulation of a definitive political ideology came an inherent belief that politics was a very vital and essential component of existence. The framework was set for me to explore the world of Democrats and Republicans.

My problem was that party lines are no longer so clear. Though I realize the difficulty in deciding which side of the fence to sit on, I strongly believe that this is a necessary step in the development of one's political ideology. It is extremely difficult to take a stand on a controversial issue. However, I believe that the nation's tendencies toward the middle represent its lack of strength in character and in mind. It is in this spirit that I declare myself to be firmly pro-working class, pro-choice, pro-gay rights, and anti-death penalty. Additionally, I disagree with the direct combining of religion and government that is predominant in the Republican extreme right. Though I am a white male, my experiences with people of other races and gender have been plentiful and have contributed to my belief in equality in all aspects of life.

The main problem that I have with American politics involves the compatibility of democracy and capitalism. In my opinion, a government for "the people" clashes quite overtly with the inherently egotistical nature of capitalism. Combining the Eastern philosophical and spiritual lessons from my father with that which I have learned in an academic framework, I have concluded that a balance between the self and the community must be obtained. Consequently, my political ideology is based upon the premise that a priority must be placed upon the community good at the expense of big business and capitalism. This belief in selflessness leads me to support strong welfare policies and the idea of helping those in need.

As is quite evident, I believe that there exists a powerful correlation and relationship between politics and real life. Though my family had a minimal positive contribution to this conclusion, a number of my life experiences and a quality education have allowed me to develop a very strong political ideology. My first political science courses in college introduced me to the world of politics—a world I wish to be an active participant in, now and in the future.

Clint Hess

I don't know why my interest in politics is so strong. At home, the subject never even came up. My parents never cared about politics. But my grandfather served as president of the Chamber of Commerce for Caliente, Nevada, before running for mayor, and my uncle has served two terms as city councilman there. My mother, the youngest in a family of twelve, grew up in this little town of about one thousand people. She is a Democrat, open-minded, and somewhat liberal.

My father grew up in a much less stable family. He dropped out of school when he was seventeen, joined the army, and spent time in Vietnam, providing chopper support and rescue. He couldn't be categorized as a Democrat because he is far from liberal, but he could never consider himself a Republican.

I went to a tough high school. There were fights between different races; people just didn't get along. I watched some of my friends get caught up in drugs, others in gangs. I even had a friend go to prison for killing a man. It became harder and harder to stay honest, but somehow I managed. Then I was struck by a car. I spent a week in the hospital and six months on crutches. I had nothing to do but homework, so I studied and studied. A terrific teacher enrolled me in my first political science class—a college-level class—and I breezed through it. I enjoyed politics. I participated in the student legislature at the state capitol, and I engaged in a national mock trial. That accident changed my life. It opened my eyes to the importance of a quality education.

Although I've lived in a big city for the last sixteen years, I consider myself a small-town person with the sensibilities of a country boy. My parents were never political or religious, but they have a strong sense of ethics. My mother is a Mormon, and my father is Christian; they let me choose my religion, and I'm an atheist. I have a hard time agreeing with religious ideologues, but I've never had a hard time getting along with them.

I would consider myself a moderate-to-conservative Democrat. When I vote, I vote almost entirely straight ticket. The Democrats always seemed to be there for the working class. I am pro-choice because I have seen too many of my close friends ruin their dreams by having a child before they were ready. I am a strong advocate for the separation between church and state. I support the military, a more punishing prison system, and I distrust welfare.

I am now advancing toward a double major in political science and criminal justice. I want to serve in the Federal Bureau of Investigation—a tough but not unattainable goal.

Mike Nuñez

I was born to a poor Hispanic family in 1977. I lived in the projects for a good majority of my life, and to this day, I live with my mother in subsidized housing. Needless to say that those who are registered voters in my family are Democrats. So by design I first considered myself a natural-born Democrat.

My family never cared much about politics. They voted only in key elections and only for Democrats. Being raised in an apathetic family, I too became politically apathetic. That was until I found a personal interest: taxes! At age seventeen, with really hard work and persistence, I got a good job working at a local network affiliate television station. I started to make more money than anyone in my family. With that, my attitude changed. Keep in mind, I was young and naive, I started to get into the mind frame of Republican ideals. I got embittered that a lot of my tax dollars were going to help people who wouldn't get off their asses, work hard, and make a good living. I grew up in poverty, and I pulled myself up. Why couldn't they? So I was against the very institution that kept my family going. Now that I look back on it, that attitude is very counterproductive. But nevertheless, I changed my political identity and became a Republican.

In June 1997, I came to terms with myself in an important and life-changing way. I discovered that I was a homosexual. That realization changed my political thought, interest, and action forever. I watched television and listened to those self-righteous Republicans (who at one time I admired) tell me how evil and awful a person I must be. I was just astonished. And on the other side, I watched Democrats defending me and who I am. That meant more to me than any conservative belief about taxes. So now I guess I could be called an activist and a Democrat.

As for my media experience, I've been working in television news since I graduated from high school in 1995, that really is all I know how to do. I personally find it interesting to listen to people imply that the media has a liberal bias when they cover politics. At the station I work, we had a meeting to discuss our tactics for our coverage for the 1996 presidential election. A reporter raised his hand, and in jest he said, "Are we going to cover the election with a liberal slant this year?" The whole newsroom roared with laughter. I know that in particular instances reporters can and sometimes do put their own slant to a story, but as for any news organization as a whole, I don't think that is what they aim to do. The bottom line for a news company, and for any company, is to make money. Hype attracts viewers, and viewers attract advertisers, and more advertisers bring more money.

Being the only out-of-the-closet gay male in the television station, I have become a "gay reference" for the writers and reporters there. Now during these days of gay bashing and public defamation of gays, the newsroom doesn't know where to go to get sources, so they come to me. I see that as giving me some small power to push my agenda.

Many news stations are run and operated by white, straight, male businessmen. Many minority communities, such as the black community, Hispanic community, and Jewish community, would not have a voice if there were not members of those communities working as professionals in the media, pushing the producers to do stories that affect each individual community. Knowing that I represent the homosexual community in my workplace can be hard at times, but I realize that it is needed.

My career, journalism, is the only nongovernmental occupation protected by the Constitution. That protection not only protects my career but my beliefs, my opinions, my civil rights, and my right to tell all who will listen all what is wrong with government. As a student of political science, I have become more aware of what the Constitution means for me, as a media professional, as a gay man, as a Hispanic, but most of all as a person with rights.

Robert Cohen

It took sixteen years, much urging by my wife, and the birth of a son for me to return to college and finish my degree. (If I can give some academic advice, finish school when you're young—it pays great dividends.) My first college experience was in 1980 at Colorado State University. I lasted one year—long enough to take the famous Introduction to American Government course. Later, I went to Denver University for two years, majored in hotel and restaurant management, and took more political science classes: State and Local Government, International Politics. I worked full-time—sometimes more—in the restaurant business, where I got to know some of the big-time sports figures in Denver. That was fun, but I needed a college education. I graduate in May with a major in behavioral science (a combination of anthropology, psychology, history, economics, and political science).

My life has always been filled with politics. My mother is a staunch Democrat who graduated with a degree in political science when JFK was coming up. My father is a weak Republican, and I began my political life as a Republican. I didn't know why, I just knew that I was. I remember in 1968 my friends and I used to sing "Humphrey, Humphrey, kick him in the can: Nixon, Nixon he's our man." When I was thirteen, I fell into my mother's party and worked with her on the Democratic candidate's campaign for Colorado governor. My job was to clip newspaper articles and file them; why, I still don't know. When I first started working, the headquarters was filled with lots of enthusiastic volunteers. When our candidate started losing ground, the volunteers stopped showing up. By the end, well before the election, the headquarters closed with little fanfare: It was over. That was my introduction to practical politics.

The last major political change in my life came with Reagan. I knew the country needed to stop the expensive, over-optimistic plans of the Democratic Party. Ronald Reagan was the answer. How could I support a party that nominated ultra-liberal George McGovern and elected Jimmy Carter as president? The conservative slant still appeals to me. I belong to the party that supports fiscal responsibility.

I do not vote straight party lines, and I don't like career politicians. I vote for the candidates that support the same ideals I do. I would never vote for someone just because he or she was a Republican. I'm a cynical citizen, always asking, "What can my vote really do?"

Political science classes taught me to read between the lines. Our news, be it on television or in print, tells us one thing, but rarely the whole story. Dig deep for the truth. Good luck with your studies in American government. We need more voters who have a clue and more people to participate in running our government.

Sonya Marquez

I am currently a double major in speech communication with a broadcasting emphasis, and political science with an American politics area of study. As a result of the close involvement between those two areas, I spend the majority of my time either explaining the media to my poli-sci classmates, or defending political scientists to my broadcasting classmates. I frequently struggle to find some kind of balance between the two disciplines.

I grew up in Arvada, a suburb of Denver. I'm the only female child of a Mexican American, Catholic, middle-class couple. I can remember how much I wanted the same privileges and range of freedoms that my two brothers had. Eventually I seized that goal (within my family). It was a hard-fought battle and resulted in my strong support for women's rights.

My parents are not politically active but do vote every general election. Although they've never mentioned being registered Democrats, I know they usually do vote Democrat. Their habitual voting has lead to my participation in every general election as well. However, our political similarities end there. My parents are socially conservative because of their faith and very traditional childhood. In contradiction to those ideas, they are financially liberal. I'd have to place myself under quite different political belief systems: financially conservative and socially moderate. I don't think my opinions were developed as any kind of rebellion toward my mom and dad (with the exception of women's rights).

I have a lot of trouble balancing my political belief systems (a predicament similar to the situation with my two majors). Recently a lot of moderate Republicans have had the same conflict. It's a shame that groups like the Christian Coalition are ruining the Republican name. That's one of the main reasons I am a registered Independent and never vote for only one party.

It's a rare occasion that I even mention any harmony with Republican views in a city as Democratic as Denver. Actually, it's hard for me to bring up current politics at all because I usually feel like someone who tuned into a football game after halftime, constantly trying to catch up with what's already happened. Other than my customary voting, I've had no experience in real-world politics. Until I began studying political systems and theories in college, I rarely thought about politics at all. I never noticed the political culture of the Denver metro area until college either. One aspiration I have after college is to land a job in another state in television, and finally experience living somewhere other than Denver. Perhaps then I will be better able to judge my home town's political culture.

Tony A. Young

Born on July 4, 1974, I have always felt destined to be involved in the American political process. I am a Colorado native, born in Denver, and I spent my childhood on the front range of Colorado. At an early age, my parents encouraged me to pay attention to politics and who was in power. My parents, African Americans who grew up during the Jim Crow era, know how important it is to be involved in all the decisions affecting your life.

My personal interest in politics began in 1984. It seemed that virtually every person in Colorado was absolutely mesmerized with Senator Gary Hart and his attempt to become the first Coloradoan elected president of the United States. Of course, Senator Hart lost, and former Vice President Walter Mondale became the nominee. Mondale also inspired me to become personally involved in politics. Mondale stared America in the face and told us the cold, hard truth, a quality I thought Americans would appreciate in a candidate. To bring us out of the mounting debt brought about by Reaganomics and Cold War spending, he was going to raise taxes. I admired Mondale for telling the American public the truth rather than making empty promises like we hear from so many other politicians, even though he lost and Reagan was reelected. It was then that I knew I must be involved in the process to allow others who spoke the truth a chance for victory.

I registered to vote shortly after my eighteenth birthday and declared the Democratic Party as my own. My freshman American Government professor, Bob Hagedorn, was running for the state house of representatives. He won the election, and I thought how amazing it was to be learning from someone actually involved in the political process, not just lecturing about it. The next year, he invited me to intern for him at the state legislature, and I took him up on the offer.

I was absolutely inspired by my time in the state house with Representative Hagedorn. The state house shattered all of my stereotypes about politicians. The vast majority of the people were there because they wanted to make a difference, they were concerned about the community in which they lived, and believed the most positive way to make change was from inside the system. These were people who were giving of themselves. They were willing to eliminate having a personal life to come to Denver for five months a year. They took time away from their families, their careers, and their homes in exchange for a salary that barely measured five figures. Their passion for the job rubbed off on me, and I believed myself to be destined for a career in politics.

I was invited by a family friend to a meeting of the Elbert County Democratic Executive Committee. I went and eagerly listened to the conversation about county politics and who might run for office. I left the meeting with an overwhelming desire to fill one of those gaps on the ballot. In 1994, at the age of nineteen, I filed to run for Elbert county commissioner. The incumbent commissioner, also a Democrat, filed a month after I did, and soon two Republicans threw their hats into the race. I was involved in my first election as a candidate, and it was a dog fight. The registration in Elbert County favors Republican over Democrats by a margin of more than two to one. The African American population in the county does not even register a full percentage point. But none of that discouraged me. Numbers meant nothing to me because I was running on ideals. I was convinced the strength of my ideals, philosophy, youthful energy, and character would carry me through.

I participated in several debates all over the county, and I held my own in each of them. Republicans came up to me after each debate and told me how well I did. I thanked them and asked for their support, but was constantly met with "Sorry, I can't help you. I vote the straight Republican ticket every time."

The primary election came, and I surprised everyone by defeating the incumbent by a landslide (ten votes!). After winning my first election by that slender margin, I am now more convinced than ever that every vote counts, and I will firmly believe that until my dying day. The media attention began to pour in. Newspapers, radio, and television started paying attention to this twenty year old who had proved his candidacy to be real. I ran for county commissioner to control the rampant growth in my county, often ranked as the second fastest growing county in the state and the sixth-fastest in the nation.

I lost the general election by twelve points. I performed better in the county than fellow Democrat Roy Romer, the incumbent governor, but in the end, my youth and party affiliation had hurt me. That was 1994, a good year for Republicans, the same year Newt Gingrich became Speaker of the House. My political involvement did not end there. I went on to the internal workings of the party, working to promote the party and elect other candidates.

Since that election, I have held many offices for the Democratic Party, including leading the Young Democrats in Region 7, covering several Western states. Through all of that activity, I earned the Colorado Democratic Party Democrat of the Year Award in 1996. I also went to the 1996 Democratic National Convention in Chicago as an elected delegate from my congressional district. I was even interviewed by Jewel on MTV about what it meant to be a young delegate at a party convention, as well as what issues were important to me—truly one of the highlights of my life.

I have also been paid staff for the Denver Democratic Party, the 1996 Colorado Coordinated Campaign, and the Colorado Student Association. Most recently I served as field staff for the Wellington E. Webb for Mayor Campaign. Politics for me is a way of life and an absolute necessity. There must always be someone involved in the political process, and if I don't like what I see, I must make the effort to change it. Simply complaining about anything has never brought about positive change. Someone always has to, as Ross Perot said, "get under the hood and tinker" with the system. To create real change, I have chosen to work inside the system, and I hope that you will choose to do the same.

By reading this book, you may not be as inspired as I was to run out and do everything you possibly can, but I would encourage all of you, particularly those who are not political science majors, to read through this book carefully. Don't take the book as biblical truth, investigate politics on your own. Volunteer with a campaign. Give them four hours a week and see if you do not feel you made a difference. If you find a good candidate or issue, I guarantee the emotional highs and lows you feel will be better and more stimulating than any other experience you could ever have. Trust me, I have done skydiving, four-wheel driving, and all sorts of activities, but nothing is more exhilarating than a good campaign!